Keep v 2019

BEARING WITNESS

Also by Celia Morris

Storming the Statehouse:
Running for Governor with Ann Richards and Dianne Feinstein

Fanny Wright: Rebel in America

Celia Morris

BEARING WITNESS

Sexual Harassment and Beyond—
Everywoman's Story

Little, Brown and Company
Boston   New York   Toronto   London

First Edition

Although this book is the result of extensive research, some of the individuals involved have asked that their anonymity and that of those involved in some of the incidents described be respected. For this reason, many of the names, locations, and identifying characteristics of the people and incidences described in the book have been changed.

Excerpt from *All the King's Men* by Robert Penn Warren. Copyright © 1946 by Robert Penn Warren; copyright renewed 1974 by Robert Penn Warren. By permission of Harcourt, Brace and Company.

Excerpt from "On the Pulse of Morning" from *On the Pulse of Morning* by Maya Angelou. Copyright © 1993 by Maya Angelou. By permission of Random House, Inc.

Library of Congress Cataloging-in-Publication Data

Morris, Celia.
  Bearing witness: sexual harassment and beyond — everywoman's story /
  Celia Morris. — 1st ed.
      p.   cm.
  Includes bibliographical references and index.
  ISBN 0-316-58422-3
  1. Sexual harassment of women — United States. I. Title.
HQ1237.5.U6M67 1994
305.42—dc20   93-29383

10 9 8 7 6 5 4 3 2 1

MV-NY

Published simultaneously in Canada by Little, Brown & Company (Canada) Limited

Printed in the United States of America

For

my grandmother, Emelia Reinke Buchan
who endured

my aunt, Leo Bernice Fix
who created

my second mother, Thelma Valentine Hamrick
who loved

and for
Anita Faye Hill
who showed us the way

CONTENTS

ACKNOWLEDGMENTS

Even more than my earlier work, *Bearing Witness* springs from my friendships, and to such an extent that I find it impossible even to name all those to whom I am indebted. Scores of people across the country shared in the spirited conversations that inform this book, and so many put together book lists, made suggestions, and polled their friends and colleagues that ultimately I had to let many chances for interviews pass.

My primary debt is to Marianne Walters, who gave abundantly from her experience and insight as a psychotherapist, and, along with her daughter Susanna, read my analyses with a keen professional eye and a deep commitment to justice. Mildred Wurf not only contributed a challenging mind and a sustaining heart, but a beach with wondrous creative powers and a willingness to read the manuscript time after time as it evolved. C. Vann Woodward suggested that I get in touch with Elisabeth Muhlenfeld and Carol Blesser, both of whom responded generously. My reporter friends Kay Mills, Julia Kagan, Sue Kaufman, and Peggy Simpson gave me lists of people to see and offered homes that turned into sanctuaries. Many women in organizations, but especially members of the National Women's Political Caucus and its affiliates throughout the country, called on their networks. Bob and Pat Spearman, Nancy and Harry Ransom, Chandler Davidson and Sharon Plummer, Holly Stocking and Bill Timberlake, Steven Redfield and Patricia Pippert, Josephine, John, and Claudia Elliott, Barbara Bode, Phyllis Klotman, Sally Leach, Jane Bond, Barbara Karkabi, Jack Ratliff, Sara McClendon, Lael Stegall, Ceil Cleveland, Kathy Seddon, Jinny Barnhart,

Molly Gregory, and Linda Mitchell recommended women with stories to confide and, from time to time, helped me find places where they might feel comfortable enough to do it. With unflagging patience and generosity, Jack Milne put his computer genius to work and rescued me repeatedly.

Blanche Wiesen Cook, Roger Wilkins, Diana Kealey, Shirley Garner, John Maguire, Marie Tyler-McGraw, Van Ooms, Claire Foudraine, Les Whitten, Taunya Banks, Martha and Speed Carroll, Joanne Omang, Mary Paul Taylor, and Tanya Melich all brought their unique perspectives, their learning, their wit, and at times their tears and laughter to bear on successive drafts of the manuscript.

Four people at Little, Brown and Company — Eve Yohalem, Mark Del Franco, Betty Power, and Mih-Ho Cha — did their jobs so ably, and with such good humor and dispatch, that the process of producing a book was almost a pleasure.

My abiding thanks go to my agent, Ellen Levine, whose superb professionalism has never precluded her holding my hand through the hard places, and to my editor, Fredrica Friedman, whose thrilling enthusiasm for my project was matched by the judgment and care she brought to each stage in its evolution.

Most of all, I am indebted to the women who summoned their courage and told me their stories. Less than a third of those stories found their way into this book. But each deepened my understanding of the way sexual harassment and abuse damage women and left me all the more determined to do something about it.

BEARING WITNESS

1

ANITA HILL SPARKS A REVOLUTION

Telling the world is the most difficult experience of my life, but it is very close to having to live through the experience that occasioned this meeting.

—Anita Hill

Revolutions often begin quietly, and this one was no exception. For me, it all started somewhere around nine o'clock on Sunday morning, October 6, 1991, when Nina Totenberg of National Public Radio told the listening world that United States Supreme Court nominee Clarence Thomas had been charged with sexual harassment. I heard the news while propped up in bed, drinking coffee and working my way through the pile of Sunday papers, and I was much too absorbed in this weekly ritual to be more than mildly interested. Organizations I supported had fought Thomas's nomination, friends had testified against him, and a Senate committee had recommended him to the parent body with a decided lack of enthusiasm (the vote was tied seven to seven). Nonetheless, his elevation to the Court seemed ensured, and I had already reluctantly pegged this as one of the many battles my side had lost over the last three decades. I had no idea that the morning's announcement would mark a watershed in American political history and change many people's lives, including my own.

Thirty minutes later, a good friend called from Baltimore with news and insights that would jump-start that whole astonishing transformation. Her name is Taunya Banks; she is a professor of law at the University of Maryland, where she came after spending five years at the University of Tulsa in Oklahoma; and she is an African-American I met in 1983 when she taught at Texas Southern University in Houston and I moved back to my native state to organize a voter registration project we called Texas Women for the '80s. Over that next year, as I learned the pitfalls of organizing — even in a good cause I passionately believed in — Taunya came to my rescue more than once, and there are few people I trust more.

Thomas's accuser, Anita Hill, turned out to be an Oklahoma law professor who had worked for him at the Department of Education and the Equal Employment Opportunity Commission a decade earlier. And Taunya began by saying, "I know Anita Hill — she's conservative, religious, and intensely protective of her privacy — and if she makes this charge, I believe her. Partly because it would explain something I've never understood: why a woman with a degree from Yale, a good job in Washington, and a terrific future would move back to Oklahoma to teach at Oral Roberts University."

Taunya trusted Anita Hill; I trusted Taunya; and so that Sunday's challenge was converted to something quite different. The papers slid to the floor as this new chance to take on the right wing resurrected my Texas organizing skills, and I spent the day telephoning women who could galvanize large organizations. Others in Washington and all over the country were having the same or similar experiences, and by late that evening, we had a network of political women mobilized to carry the fight against Thomas to a new level.

Over the next ten days, people wandered in and out of my home a few blocks from the Russell Office Building, where the Senate Judiciary Committee presides. On the first day of the hearings, Taunya brought in Kimberle Crenshaw, a young African-American law professor from the University of Southern California, and Louise Stevenson, a white sociologist from the University of Illinois — both of them authorities on sexual harassment. Kathy Bonk, who codirects the Communications Consortium, a nonprofit advocacy and media group, was joined by her colleague Emily Tynes, an African-American woman gifted at persuading people to listen. Taunya tends to be manic, Emily to be calm. And all of us rocketed between those extremes, often several times a day, until Thomas was confirmed on Tuesday, October 15, by the narrowest margin of approval for a Supreme Court justice in this century.

So our side lost that particular fight. But over the course of the next year, I grew convinced that the hearings had been a key skirmish in an ancient struggle, and that because of them, women in the United States of America may finally have the chance to win — albeit not in my lifetime — the struggle for full equality with men.

The hearings were that important because Americans had sat before their television sets transfixed by a spectacle unprecedented in our history — yet at the same time, by a scene that felt painfully familiar: an obscure woman publicly accusing a powerful man of verbal sexual abuse and intimidation, and in response, a jury of even more powerful men abusing her once again. The Republicans on the committee treated Anita Hill as though she were deluded and very possibly psychotic, while the Democrats sat inertly and ineptly by.

The hearings had everything — sex, race, and power — and so they aggravated psychic wounds and nerves left tender by the uncompleted work of the great American experiment in democracy. Both accuser and accused were African-Americans, while the jury was made up of white men. For more than three hundred years, black people had been enslaved in a country that committed itself rhetorically in 1776 to equality but denied women the vote until 1920. White men had written its rules, and then interpreted and enforced them, and though by 1991, most laws that mandated inequality had been stricken from the books, the sight of the fourteen-member Senate Judiciary Committee made it inescapably clear that white men still ran the show.

Furthermore, the dynamic of power in the hearings revealed how insistently the male point of view still dominates our culture. As psychologist Lenor Rosenman says, this remains "a society that protects men, and one way we do it is by not exposing them." Explaining Hollywood's reluctance to show men nude when naked women are a commonplace in movies, Rosenman was speaking literally, but what she said is true socially and psychologically as well.[1]

Men can do very terrible things to women — they often do — and then count on a blanket of silence to shield them. Edmund Burke, the eighteenth-century Irish defender of the American Revolution, called it "the decent drapery of life." The dense texture of this silence is woven of economic facts, social realities, cultural prohibitions, and psychic shame so tightly bound that women have colluded in it. But by breaking the silence, Anita Hill had ripped so big a hole in the drapery that many of us looked through and saw large chunks of our own reality far more clearly. The anger that erupted in the wake of the Hill/Thomas hearings signaled the fact that the bills were falling due.

Women now make up a majority of the American population and over 52 percent of those registered to vote, and it is not surprising that a new stage in our struggle for justice should be sparked by an African-American woman. That is the way we've always done it; both our nineteenth- and twentieth-century women's movements grew out of movements that protested the way we treat black people. In 1848, a determined group of abolitionist women who had discovered painful similarities between their lot and the lot of slaves came together at Seneca Falls, New York, and for the first time demanded the vote for women. (This most controversial of their claims would not be granted for seventy-two years.) In the 1960s, young women involved in the civil rights movement found themselves stuck with menial chores while the guys decided strategy — though Stokeley Carmichael gave the game away when he said the place of women in the movement was prone. These angry young women soon became the shock troops of the women's movement that exploded with great force in the early 1970s. (The other major impetus came from Betty Friedan's *The Feminine Mystique,* which galvanized women who were already married and bored witless while raising children in the suburbs.)

Now American women as a whole had yet another chance to look at their own experiences through a lens shaped by what had happened to a black woman. And both the hearings and their dramatic aftermath convinced me that if enough women followed Hill's lead and shared their own stories, we could come closer to ending male sexual abuse of women — for our sakes, for theirs, and for posterity's. The time had finally come to break silence big-time.

Women for whom the Hill/Thomas hearings had been a transforming experience responded according to their own bent. Dorene Ludwig, for instance, a Los Angeles actress, had recently published a performance manual, *But It Was Just a Joke . . .! Theater Scenes and Monologues for Eliminating Sexual Harassment.* Six months after the hearings, the *Los Angeles Times* called it part of a booming "cottage industry," as Ludwig staged workshops for increasing numbers of companies and unions ready to address the problem.

In a monologue that takes the form of "a day in the life of . . .," she runs across men — at a shoe-repair shop, a gas station, a grocery store, the post office — all of whom make sexual cracks that knot her stomach. With each remark, she asks herself, derisively, "Dorene, in the future of the universe, how important *is* this?" But finally she realizes that it *is* important and stands up for herself: "This *is* my universe. *My* space. *My* body, *my* mind, *my* spirit, *my* emotions, this is where I *live,* this is where I am a being. . . . The irony [is] you don't just hurt me. You don't just hurt women. You hurt yourselves. When you go home, and you don't understand the coldness, and the distance — don't look at what the woman in your life is doing. *Look at what you do, Buster. Just take a good long look at what YOU do!*"[2]

Some put out guides for organizations in which men and women share a workplace, and with their help we discovered that "50 percent to 85 percent of American women will experience some form of sexual harassment during their academic or working life" and "90 percent of sexual harassment victims are unwilling to come forward for two primary reasons: fear of retaliation and fear of loss of privacy." Suggesting the breadth and depth of the problem, psychologist Stephanie Riger made it clear that "sexual harassment . . . is the most recent form of victimization of women to be redefined as a social rather than a personal problem, following rape and wife abuse."[3]

My own response was to crisscross the country listening to women's stories. In *Writing a Woman's Life,* Carolyn Heilbrun had shrewdly observed that "power consists to a large extent in deciding what stories will be told, [and] male power has made certain stories unthinkable." The Hill/Thomas hearings had forced one of those "unthinkable" stories into the open — a story that many women knew to be rather ordinary. Along with Heilbrun, I believed that "we must begin to tell the truth, in groups, to one another. Modern feminism began that way, and we have lost, through shame or fear of ridicule, that important collective phenomenon."[4]

I was convinced that if we resurrected that will to truth-telling, the weight of evidence could then help us shift the focus from the women who are abused to the men who do the abusing. In a decisive turn away from blaming the victims, we could begin changing the questions from What did she do to deserve it? and Why did she stay? to Why did *he* do it? and Why did the people around him stand there and *watch* him, and in some instances *help* him do it? Finally, we could ask what we could do to *stop* the abuse.

For me, then, the first step in this exhilarating process meant asking scores of women a simple sequence of questions: "Who were you — how did you feel about yourself — when the story you're about to tell began? Exactly what happened? What did it feel like? How did it affect you? How did you react to the Hill/Thomas hearings? What light did it shed on your own experience?"

The stories I heard were the stories of women whose mothers' voices, for untold generations back, had been muffled. Some had been frightened, coerced, or bribed into silence. Others had been shouted down or driven mad. Most had simply accepted their fate and done the work the Lord, it seemed, had set them. As Heilbrun put it, the white, middle-class, male tone that for centuries had passed for universal had for the most part shut their stories out. Since no one had wanted to know the hard things about women's lot, or to be shocked or even tantalized, women themselves had fallen in with the idea that they should tend their own gardens and keep their counsel.

And so, because these stories are relatively new on the world's stage, they can help us understand more clearly how men use women's sexuality to stunt and frighten them — and thereby keep them in "their place." Ultimately, these stories, and others like them, can give us the tools and energy to reshape our world.

For the ferocious struggle during and after the Hill/Thomas hearings about what it all meant highlighted a revolutionary fact: the cultural hegemony of white men has begun to disintegrate. As commentators wondered incessantly whether Hill was a Jezebel or a Joan of Arc, one thing at least became clear: that men and women, whites and African-Americans, and each combination of those categories, have particular ways of interpreting reality based on their own special experiences. And for the first time in history, large numbers of women, along with people of color, were no longer willing to accept an explanation that let white men off the hook.

Ofra Bikel, for instance, an accomplished Israeli who directed a film for the Public Broadcasting System on the African-American com-

munity's response to the hearings, assumed initially that they had nothing to do with race. But she could make such an assumption only
because white Americans have buried so many stories connected with
race and sex in this country that *they have no idea* how we got where
we are today. And the stories have been buried in part because they
reflect so badly on white men.

In fact, we can't fully understand even the hearings themselves,
much less our complicated responses to them, without recovering certain key stories from the history of slavery over a period of three
centuries. For as James Baldwin understood, "The great force of history
comes from the fact that we carry it within us, are unconsciously
controlled by it in many ways, and history is literally *present* in all that
we do." Or as William Faulkner put it, the past isn't over: it isn't even
past.[5]

In order to understand what happened in that Senate Judiciary
chamber, then, we have to take on the Fathers, who've denied or trivialized a fact at the heart of American culture: that white men systematically abused black women all through slavery. While we have offered
modest reparations to the Nisei interned unjustly during the Second
World War, and while the Japanese have set the example of apologizing
to the Korean "comfort women" they forced into prostitution, the
fraction of Americans who even *know* what happened to slave women
is probably quite small — and limited, for the most part, to the African-American community, historians, feminists, and Southern writers.*[6]

The truth itself is plain. White Southerners owned black slaves,
who constituted property with no legal rights whatever. Their protection, such as it was, lay in their market value as workers, but a slave-
owner or overseer who enjoyed indulging his power over the weak more
than he relished the increased production of his fields — even if he were
a man with a sadistic bent — rarely suffered legal penalties.

Slave women were valuable as breeders and were commonly so
advertised. Here a white man's economic interests were by no means at
odds with a psychic need to dominate — quite the contrary — and lust

---

*When Toni Morrison won the Nobel Prize for Literature in the fall of 1993,
however, the subject was virtually guaranteed a larger audience. Her *Beloved*, one
of the truly great American novels, tells the story of slavery from a black woman's
point of view. The courage of Morrison's truth-telling, along with her breadth of
vision and the magnificence of her prose, had finally won their just reward.

has played a gigantic if insufficiently recorded, role in history. In ante-bellum America, rape was defined by law as an act of sexual violence against a white woman, which means that legally a black woman could not be raped — even if she were free! According to historian Adele Logan Alexander, "The only legal impropriety involved if an adult female slave was forced into an unwelcome sexual encounter — by any man, black or white — could be a charge of trespass or injury against the property of her master."[7]

We have no way of knowing what percentage of slave women were forced to have sexual intercourse with the white men who owned them, with those who directed the plantations on which they worked, or with white men simply passing through. On rare occasions, tender and even loving relationships may have developed between these women and men: black nannies often nursed white children, and bonds established in infancy between a white male child and his black mother may have enhanced the likelihood of his wanting a black lover when he came of age sexually. At the same time, white men who could make their lives easier must have been attractive to many slave women. But if these liaisons were not invariably hideous for the black women caught up in them, one key fact remains: their alternatives to resisting a white man who wanted them sexually were often torture and even death.

Slave narratives, along with eyewitness accounts by whites, tell of women stripped naked and beaten unconscious in front of their children; of nursing women lashed so cruelly that blood mixed with their milk as it ran down their bodies; of trenches dug to hold a pregnant woman's belly so that she could be tied face down to stakes and whipped until her tormentor dropped with exhaustion; of women hung by their thumbs from rafters and beaten until their blood pooled beneath their feet. Many died; most did not. For all practical purposes, slave women had no choice, and these sexual relations were tolerated by polite society.

By the 1920s, more than 75 percent of the African-Americans in the United States were of mixed race. For a variety of reasons, the number of mulattoes produced by intercourse between a white woman and a black man was statistically insignificant, so the burden of responsibility for this legally sanctioned abuse of power lies almost wholly with white men.[8]

To get an idea what all this felt like, we can look at it initially through the eyes of a white writer, Robert Penn Warren. In his Pulitzer Prize–winning novel *All the King's Men,* Warren brilliantly recreates a scene in a slave-trading barracoon, or barracks, that would have been repeated throughout the South for almost three centuries. In Lexington, Kentucky, a French speculator is buying "fancies" for Louisiana:

The Frenchman was staring at . . . a very young woman, some twenty years old perhaps, rather slender, with skin slightly darker than ivory, probably an octoroon, and hair crisp rather than kinky, and deep dark liquid eyes, slightly bloodshot, which stared at a spot above and beyond the Frenchman. She did not wear the ordinary plaid Osnaburg and kerchief of the female slave up for sale, but a white, loosely cut dress, with elbow-length sleeves, and skirts to the floor and no kerchief, only a band to her hair. . . .

[The slavetrader] grasped the girl by the shoulder to swing her slowly around for a complete view. Then he seized one of her wrists and lifted the arm to shoulder level and worked it back and forth a couple of times to show the supple articulation, saying, "Yeah." That done, he drew the arm forward, holding it toward the Frenchman, the hand hanging limply from the wrist which he held. . . .

The men standing around titter, and one of them calls, "Ain't she got nuthen else round and soft?" The trader lifts her skirt above her waist, wads it up, and walks around her, "forcing her to turn (she turned 'without resistance and as though in a trance') with his motion until her small buttocks were toward the door."

"Round and soft, boys," Mr. Simms said, and gave her a good whack on the near buttock to make the flesh tremble. "Ever git yore hand on anything rounder ner softer, boys? . . . Hit's a cushion, I declare. And shake like sweet jelly."

The Frenchman then moves forward to examine the wares more carefully:

[He] reached out to lay the tip of his riding crop at the little depression just above the beginning of the swell of the buttocks. He held the tip delicately there for a moment, then flattened the crop across the back and moved it down slowly, evenly across each buttock, to trace the fullness of the curve. "Turn her," he said in his foreign voice.

Mr. Simms obediently carried the wad [of skirt] around, and the body followed in the half revolution. One of the men at the door whistled. The Frenchman laid his crop across the woman's belly as though he were a "carpenter measuring something or as to demonstrate its flatness," and moved it down as before, tracing the structure, until it came to rest across the thighs, below the triangle. . . .[9]

Apologists for the antebellum South would pile all the blame here at the feet of social riffraff. But those who indulged in the practice of buying, selling, and copulating with black women who had so little control over their own lives were not all the dregs of southern society. James Henry Hammond, for instance, sometime governor of South Carolina, took as his mistress an eighteen-year-old slave with a year-old daughter, and when the child turned twelve, he made *her* his mistress as well. The latter liaison apparently provoked his wife into leaving him for several years but had no effect on his political career or the esteem in which he was held. (His incestuous relations with four nieces, however, managed to send him into a thirteen-year political exile, although he was subsequently appointed to fill an unexpired term in the United States Senate.) Good men in the North who deplored slavery, like good men in the South who loathed the sexual abuse of slave women, for the most part stood idly by since the rights of property were held to be inviolable.

Thomas Jefferson himself may have had a thirty-five-year-long sexual relationship with his slave Sally Hemings, as Fawn Brodie argues in her biography of the man who incorporated the great idea of human equality into our Declaration of Independence. Sally's mother, Betty Hemings, was an octoroon who bore six children to her master, John Wayles, Jefferson's father-in-law. So Sally was therefore not only very nearly white, but a half-sister to Jefferson's wife, Martha. At least three of her own children, in turn, were so light-skinned they apparently "passed" into white society — according to her son Madison, two married whites — and tangled relationships like these were common in the South. In this way, down through the generations, the complexion of slaves gradually lightened and the tension within the African-American community between pale and dark-skinned people inexorably mounted.

Perhaps our most powerful record of what all this felt like to a black woman is Harriet Jacobs's *Incidents in the Life of a Slave Girl: Written by Herself.* Telling the truth about slavery meant confessing that she had been forced to violate "sexual standards in which she believed," and in her humiliation, Jacobs frankly envied male slaves like Frederick Douglass who could tell their stories and emerge as heroes. Females, she discovered, had to abuse their own dignity in order to tell theirs.

To describe "the all-pervading corruption produced by slavery," Jacobs writes:

The slave girl is reared in an atmosphere of licentiousness and fear. The lash and the foul talk of her master and his sons are her teachers. When she is fourteen or fifteen, her owner, or his sons, or the overseer, or perhaps all of them, begin to bribe her with presents. If these fail to accomplish their purpose, she is whipped or starved into submission to their will. . . . The profligate men who have power over her may be exceedingly odious to her. But resistance is hopeless.

Beauty, she says mournfully, is a black girl's greatest curse. As for Jacobs herself, when she became fifteen, she entered "a sad epoch in the life of a slave girl."

My master began to whisper foul words in my ear. . . . I turned from him with disgust and hatred. But he was my master. I was compelled to live under the same roof with him. . . . He told me I was his property; that I must be subject to his will in all things. My soul revolted against the mean tyranny. But where could I turn for protection?[10]

Jacobs's master refused to allow her to marry a free black man she loved and said he'd "shoot him as soon as I would a dog" if he came on the premises. He then put unremitting pressure on her to submit to him sexually until finally, to escape a tie that filled her with loathing, she made an alliance with a white man in town who fathered her two children. (He was later elected to Congress.) While the children were small, she hid for *seven* years in the crawl space of an attic before she managed to escape to the North.

So white men systematically abused black women and forced black men and white women to stand by helplessly. (Their power over their wives was nearly as absolute as their power over their slaves.) Many wives took refuge in fantasy, as Mary Chesnut, the wife of one of Jefferson Davis's most trusted aides, noted: "The mulattoes one sees in every family exactly resemble the white children — and every lady tells you who is the father of all the mulatto children in everybody's household, but those in her own she seems to think drop from the clouds, or pretends so to think." Some slave mistresses became just as brutal as their husbands, jealousy and outraged impotence having their predictable impact on character. The profound distortions of soul and spirit that are the natural offspring of abuse were then left to make their way relentlessly down through the generations like a hereditary taint in the blood from which it would seem that only death might release us.[11]

*   *   *

Until recently, white male cultural hegemony was so powerful that the standard histories were quite innocent of sympathy or outrage for slave women. Nor did the South's defeat in the Civil War do much to tarnish the appeal of the patriarchal image. If anything, in fact, the glamour that attached to the boys in gray who fought "the lost cause" burgeoned into a sentimental cult that glorified that stately old gentleman with side-whiskers, sitting on his wide porch in a white suit, sipping bourbon and reading Cicero.

But while the South's "peculiar institution" became a thing of history, its consequences, especially as they concern the relations between men and women, and blacks and whites, live on to afflict our personal lives as well as our attempts at democracy. Enmeshed in an intricate web of dependence and exploitation, terror and fascination, time and again we have faltered while working toward a multiracial society. And so slavery and its consequences form an inescapable backdrop for understanding Anita Hill's confrontation with Clarence Thomas, as well as the range of our responses to that galvanizing encounter.[12]

The locus of the problem centered on the family, and apart from its momentous entanglement with race, the southern version of the patriarchal family simply exaggerated the characteristics of middle-class families in other parts of the country, with the notable exception of the frontier. The husband was to be head of the household and emissary to the world of business and public affairs, and the wife was expected to make their home a sanctuary for tender feelings. The man was to develop his brain and the woman her heart, and together they were to create a whole upon which the health of the society at large would rest. As the home of elegant manners, the South could therefore not only have a marked appeal in Great Britain, as well as in parts of Europe, but a decided influence throughout this country.

In this way, a society grounded in sexual coercion, secrets, and lies became a model to emulate — with a courtly gentleman whose word was law at its very center. To hide the most fundamental violations of trust and decency, silence therefore reigned on subjects like sex, race, and money; literature that addressed such topics was hidden under floorboards, if read at all, and polished conversation was prized in proportion to its vacuousness. An engaging African-American woman admitted to me mischievously: "I'm good at the repartee that says absolutely nothing but doesn't offend. Southern women start learning how to do that early."

The odds were therefore decidedly against mutually respectful and trusting relations between white men and women, assuming that such relations are ordinarily grounded in common experience and understanding. Outspoken, dissenting women left when they could. Those who remained tended to dissemble when their husbands and their society expected it and thought little further on the matter. It was not mere defensiveness on the score of its slave history, but the tyranny of patriarchal rule that turned the South so nearly into the "closed society" one writer called it in the 1950s.

The power of patriarchy in the South has had momentous political consequences for women, for it has been the region most unalterably opposed to nation-wide efforts to extend their legal rights. Nine of the ten states that did not ratify the suffrage amendment were southern, and eight of those nine also refused to ratify the Equal Rights Amendment. (Those voting against suffrage included Virginia, Maryland, North Carolina, South Carolina, Georgia, Alabama, Louisiana, Mississippi, and Florida. Maryland subsequently did ratify the ERA.)

The cultural and psychological consequences have been weighty; white men held on to their cultural hegemony by keeping their dependents poor, ill-informed, and at war amongst each other, while black men emulated them within their own families. Because they had been humiliated during slavery by the white man's sexual appropriation of "their" women, it became all the more important for black men both to *protect* their wives, sisters, and daughters, and to *dominate* them in order to regain what they took to be their masculine prerogatives. Suspicious that black women had colluded with the white enemy, with whom, after all, many had been intimate, the black man also resented the fact that as the decades passed, the black woman was more likely to find steady work.

Therefore, the model of the white patriarch and his presumably devoted wife exercised a powerful influence over the African-American community, and an even more exaggerated form of patriarchy developed within it. To rebuild the black man's ego, to restore her own good name, and to "elevate the race," the black woman was expected to put race before sex, and complaints were taboo — expecially when white people could overhear them.

Largely because of the sexual abuse of black women, then, the country came out of slavery with two potent Victorian images firmly attached to race: the white lady on the pedestal and the black whore. This hyperbolic splitting of eros from respectability has had devastating consequences for American women, both black and white, who have been denied the ordinary range of human needs and feelings that inform a healthy sexuality.

Because black women had been sexually attractive to their husbands, white women projected onto them the very lustfulness to which they had fallen prey; that is to say, they blamed the victim. The African-American writer bell hooks cites an instance in which a white mistress discovered her husband raping a thirteen-year-old slave girl and "responded by beating the girl and locking her in a smokehouse. The girl was whipped daily for several weeks. When older slaves pleaded on the child's behalf and dared to suggest that the white master was to blame, the mistress simply replied, 'She'll know better in future.'" White women, then, commonly thought black women low and promiscuous.[13]

Black women, in turn, distrusted white women, who had failed to protect them from their masters; who had often used them harshly out of jealousy or plain mean-spiritedness; who had gobbled up their lives and worked them overtime as servants; and who had seemed to lead idle, frivolous lives at their expense.

More than in most parts of the Western world, sex in the South was considered lower-class and raunchy — nice girls simply didn't engage in it. As historian Adele Logan Alexander has said, "The prevalent image of the black woman as less than a 'lady,' sexually available, even promiscuous, untrustworthy, her word always questioned and often held invalid, has prevailed through most of American history." To counter this stereotype, middle-class African-American families were even more repressive to their daughters than white families. Until the sexual revolution of the 1960s and the development of a pill that would reliably prevent pregnancy, an exaggerated sexual restraint governed the lives of middle-class women.[14]

Within the slave communities, the house servants had ranked above those who worked in the fields, and those who served in the Big House, who were more likely to be mulattoes, inevitably began to resemble the people who lived there. Studies of prisoners of war have demonstrated that they commonly identify with their captors, so even many blacks came to consider whites superior. And because so much blood from the master race had been mixed with the blood of slaves, a crippling color prejudice developed within the African-American community: the lighter the skin, the more prized the person. The 1960s civil rights movement, and the resounding cry Black is beautiful! mitigated that prejudice but did not obliterate it.

White men began to project onto black men the desire to do to "their" women what they had done to black women. During the antebellum period, few black men had been convicted of raping white women, and there were even instances in which prominent whites took a black man's side when a white woman accused him of rape. Nonetheless, after the Civil War, a phobia against sex between white women and black men flourished in the white community. The white man's need to keep black men "in their place" became the subtext that justified decades of lynching all through the southern and southwestern states, and any excuse might serve as a pretext. After President Theodore Roosevelt had Booker T. Washington to lunch at the White House, Senator "Pitchfork" Ben Tillman of South Carolina said: "Now that Roosevelt has eaten with that nigger Washington, we'll have to kill a thousand niggers to get 'em back to their place."[15]

As Catherine Clinton writes, "Pollution of the symbol of cultural purity — a white woman's body — threatened white supremacy. This created a bond among white men and a form of social bondage for white women." (Clinton adds caustically, "This protection racket was a deeply embedded tenet of Southern honor.") Whether from a lust for revenge or because once a forbidden desire is named it acquires an unholy power, some black men *did* come to covet white women. In *Soul on Ice,* Eldridge Cleaver boasted that he raped black women as practice for raping white women, and LeRoi Jones advised young black men, "Rape the white girls. Rape their fathers." During the civil rights movement of the 1960s, black men often blackmailed white women into proving their commitment to equality by sleeping with them — and vice versa — and Alice Walker's novel *Meridian* testifies to how deeply black women resented that.[16]

Long after slavery had ended, then, the potential for distrust and bitterness between American men and women of different colors was boundless, and between men and women of the same color, it was by no means inconsiderable. All this would become vividly clear by way of a kind of national teach-in.

More than a century and a quarter intervened between the end of slavery and the Hill/Thomas hearings, and by that fateful October day in 1991, when two African-Americans presented the Senate Judiciary Committee with mutually exclusive versions of reality, we had lived, according to historian Gerda Lerner's estimate, for some thirty-five hundred years under patriarchal rule. And the possibility that the patriarchy's hold might be loosening was by no means evident in the pictures beamed from the Russell Office Building to bars, corporate headquarters, clubs, beauty parlors, and homes around the world.[17]

Fourteen upper-middle-class white men — the youngest of them pushing fifty — sat behind the long mahogany dais in a baroque committee room, while aides who were primarily white and male slipped in and out behind them. Inside the Beltway, we knew that when the gavel banged, these men were there under duress, and a widely distributed photograph suggested why: seven congresswomen had charged up the Senate steps to insist that their colleagues delay Clarence Thomas's confirmation to the United States Supreme Court until they heard Professor Anita Hill's charges against him.

For by accretions so small as to be very nearly invisible to the untutored or cynical eye, women had finally achieved a measure of real political power. To be sure, there were only two women in the United States Senate and twenty-eight in the House of Representatives. There were only three female governors, and women made up no more than 18 percent of the state legislatures. However, women constituted not only a majority of the population, but 52 percent of those registered to vote. And for more than twenty years, polls and surveys had indicated a significant gender gap, demonstrating that women often voted differently from men. Since most politicians want to be reelected, they couldn't afford to dismiss a complaint that had the force of organized women behind it.

Not that they didn't try. The members of the Senate Judiciary Committee had known about Hill's charges for months but had ignored them, and when the congresswomen banged irately on the closed door of a Senate chamber, they initially replied that strangers were unwelcome.

So women rallied together to pound on every door they could find. Over a period of three and a half days, more than 750 women scholars signed a petition to members of the Senate Judiciary Committee explaining that "public perceptions reflect widespread misunderstanding and stereotyping of individual responses to victimization in general, and of women's responses to sexual harassment in particular." Katharine T. Bartlett of Duke University got together a group of 118 women law professors to petition the senators to postpone the vote: "Failing to examine these charges would send a message that sexual harassment is not a serious offense and that alleged acts of sexual harassment have no bearing on a nominee's judicial qualifications."

The word in Washington was that the Democratic Senate leader-ship was furious at being forced to change their plans for an early confirmation vote, and for months afterward, they seemed obsessed with the question of who had leaked the story to the press and taken control of the matter out of their hands. But there they sat on an October Friday — men who had discovered that the opportunity to go on exercising their power as United States senators might well depend on the women's vote.

To many women watching the hearings, the crucial fact about Anita Hill was that she was a "nice," proper woman who had played by the rules. Loyal to her family and faithful to her church, she was modest, soft-spoken, and respectful — a witness who had not rushed forward in self-righteous disgust but instead had come reluctantly, upon request. In fact, she had done everything patriarchal society had re-quired of women, except to marry, and women all over the country shuddered to remember things in their own past that might be used to discredit them by a committee like the one before which Hill sat so demurely. But as Anna Quindlen later put it in the *New York Times,* Anita Hill was about to demonstrate that "no matter how impressive your person, how detailed your story, how unblemished your past, if you stand up and say, 'He did this to me,' someone will find a way to discredit you."[18]

The hearings themselves were unprecedented, and perhaps most important, they were televised. People with cable television could even watch the coverage gavel to gavel, and many did. A member of the journalism faculty at Indiana University told me that in her decade there, the lounge with the television set had been jammed only twice: once for the Challenger disaster and now for the Hill/Thomas hearings. "Without fail," she said of the latter occasion, "the women were saying, 'Yeah! This has happened to me! I can identify with this!' And the men were absolutely numb."

For what happened during those three days had the weight and resonance of a morality play, with the actors bearing far more sig-nificance than their mere roles as individual players could have carried. The networks dropped their scheduled programming, and reporters labeled it a war between men and women. PBS producer Ofra Bikel called it a national soap opera: "Everyone I knew was watching, many of us in anger — anger at the fourteen men sitting there looking down on one woman; anger at the men we knew who just didn't get it." "Getting it" became the buzzword for an era.

Subjects that had seldom been even hinted at, much less explored in polite company, dominated the screen. TV commentator Jim Lehrer warned, "Please be advised that [these scenes] include graphic descriptions that some people might find offensive." For three days, the nation sat transfixed, and men and women, blacks and whites tended to read the script differently.

In his wrenching opening statement, Thomas "categorically denied" Anita Hill's allegations and then turned the focus on the process itself. "My family and I have been done a grave and irreparable injustice. . . . I am not here to be further humiliated by this committee or anyone else, or to put my private life on display for prurient interests or other reasons. . . . I am a victim of this process. . . . There is nothing this committee, this body, or this country can do to give me my good name back. Nothing." He refused to answer any further questions about his private life.

Following Thomas, Anita Hill was cool and contained, the authentic voice of generations of black middle-class female propriety. As R. W. Apple wrote in the *New York Times,* she testified "with a prim earnestness that seemed to bespeak reserve and reluctance to discuss such subjects," leaving the senators with only two options: "either she was telling the truth or she is a sociopath."

As she sat before the committee with her large family ranged behind her, Hill was very specific in her charges. Thomas had told her "about acts that he had seen in pornographic films involving such matters as women having sex with animals, and films showing group sex or rape scenes. He talked about pornographic materials depicting individuals with large penises or large breasts involving various sex acts. . . . [He] told me graphically of his own sexual prowess." And so on. She assured the committee that she spoke out of a sense of duty rather than a desire to "get" Clarence Thomas. "Telling the world is the most difficult experience of my life," she said, "but it is very close to having to live through the experience that occasioned this meeting."

Asked why she had not reported these events a decade earlier, Hill explained, "I was aware that [Judge Thomas] could affect my future career and did not wish to burn all my bridges." Admitting that she might have used poor judgment, she nevertheless confessed that "the course I took seemed to me to be the better as well as the easier approach."

After the dinner recess, Thomas appeared again before the committee to call the process "a high-tech lynching for uppity blacks."

(Later he claimed he'd "have preferred an assassin's bullet" to confronting the senators.) He said disdainfully that he hadn't listened to Hill's testimony, speculated that he'd offended her by preferring lighter-skinned women, and dwelt on the infamous way Americans had caricatured black men as sexual beasts.

Saturday morning's newspapers reported that another African-American woman, Angela Wright, a former colleague at the Equal Employment Opportunity Commission, was prepared to level similar charges at Thomas — he had repeatedly asked her out, inquired about her breast size, and come to her apartment uninvited. Wright, however, had been fired from her job at the EEOC and had an erratic work history, and because she seemed more volatile and less prim than Hill, reports circulated that she would be a more vulnerable witness. Thomas's supporters began collaring reporters to attack her character.

When the committee reconvened, Anita Hill was subjected to a chilling onslaught of slander and innuendo that reminded many spectators of the late Senator Joe McCarthy. As the *New York Times* would have it, "several Republican Senators seemed to give up any pretense of digging out the truth in the two starkly opposite stories, and began aggressively attacking Professor Hill." Using his cross-examination of Thomas as a stage, Senator Orrin Hatch of Utah suggested that the idea for Hill's charges had come from the novel *The Exorcist* as well as from testimony in a sexual harassment case in Kansas. Professing to be incredulous that any man would use the alleged language to a woman he hoped to please and expected to work with, Hatch speculated that Hill had colluded with "liberal interest groups" who had hired "slick lawyers — the worst kind" to concoct the campaign against Thomas.*

Calling Hill a "torpedo below the water line," Senator Alan Simp-

---

*Hatch used his platform to quote extensively from a *Washington Post* op-ed piece by an African-American staff writer, Juan Williams, detailing the putative campaign to destroy Thomas and charging his opponents with "indiscriminate, mean-spirited, mud slinging, supported by the so-called champions of fairness: unions, liberal politicians, civil rights groups, and women's organizations." The article was not only quoted frequently by Republican senators during the hearings but was picked up by newspapers across the country. A few days later, however, the *Post* announced that at the time Williams wrote it, he himself had been charged with several counts of sexual harassment for which he was subsequently disciplined. Editorial page editor Meg Greenfield, who was responsible for publishing the article, said that she had been ignorant of both the complaints and the investigation at the time she accepted it.

son insisted that he had derogatory information about her: "I really am getting stuff over the transom about Professor Hill. I've got letters hanging out of my pocket. I've got faxes. I've got statements from Tulsa saying, Watch out for this woman. . . ." He refused to say what the charges were, however, or to reveal their sources. After tediously cross-examining Hill and exploiting apparent inconsistencies between her original statement to the committee's investigators and her testimony the day before, Senator Arlen Specter of Pennsylvania charged her with outright perjury.

The character assassination of Anita Hill came from senators who had access to Angela Wright's similar charges against Clarence Thomas, but the fact that there was corroborating testimony did not blunt their onslaught. Writer Toni Morrison would suggest that the hearings evoked "the deeper, more ancient secrets of males bonding and the demonizing of females who contradict them." At any rate, sources talking to the *New York Times* pinned the decision to go after Hill on the White House itself: the president had decided that the only way to save his nominee was to attack the accuser's character, so his top aides had worked with people from the Justice Department and the EEOC to fashion the strategy.

Although the committee was dominated by Democrats, it treated Thomas quite differently, accepting his refusal to talk about his private life and handling him gently. Even Thomas's supporters had admitted that he liked pornography and talked about it freely, but he was never asked about it when he sat before the senators. Men were talking men's language, and with so lopsided an approach, any pretense of getting at the truth ultimately foundered.

Members of Thomas's former staff subsequently testified to his probity and demeaned Professor Hill: one called her a "very hard, arrogant, opinionated" woman who "looked out for herself first" and overrated her own abilities; another speculated that she had "had a crush on the chairman." While Angela Wright was not called on to testify to her own experience with Clarence Thomas, a man who professed that Hill had fantasized his interest in her was allowed to go on for more than half an hour. The technical term for the condition of which he accused her was said to be "erotomania."

The testimony supporting Hill came from people with nothing to gain but the austere satisfactions of truth-telling. Several reported that she'd told them of Thomas's unwanted attentions years before, and Judge Susan Hoerchner, a former law school classmate, called her "one of the most level-headed people I have ever known." Although Hill passed a polygraph test, President George Bush declared that using a lie detector test to resolve the dispute was a "stupid idea" and Thomas evidently refused to take one.

But it was earlier, when Thomas accused the senators of staging a high-tech lynching, that the Democrats lost even the appearance of controlling the search for truth. With that inflammatory charge, he had managed to divert their attention from the case against him, which is to say away from the issue of what men do to women, onto what white men historically have done to black men, which was *not* the subject before them.

Now our generations of silence about race and sex took their heaviest toll. Many of us were dumbfounded when Thomas made the charge — and even more dumbfounded when it worked for him — for sex had certainly been connected with lynching, but not in the way Thomas implied. The "justification" most often given for lynching was that black men rape white women and that terror and frontier "justice" were the necessary tools to keep blacks "in their place." (African-American journalist Ida B. Wells dedicated her life to showing that the threat of economic, rather than sexual, competition was behind most lynchings, and that black women were also tortured and strung up by lynch mobs.)

Still, there Clarence Thomas sat, with his white wife behind him, while his accuser was a black woman. No black man had *ever* been lynched because he was suspected of sexually molesting a black woman. In fact, it seems unlikely that American society as a whole had ever *cared* if a black man sexually molested a black woman. In 1859, in fact, a higher Mississippi court had reversed the conviction of a slave named George charged with raping a nine-year-old black girl.

Thomas himself, on the other hand, *had* done what white men in America had repeatedly mutilated black men for doing. Behind him sat the dramatic evidence that he had violated the most potent taboo in American culture: a very dark black man, he was legally authorized to copulate with a very white woman — his wife, Virginia Lamp Thomas. And he was flaunting that fact before some of the most prestigious white men in America — among them Strom Thurmond of South Carolina, who had made his political mark by defending segregationist laws that "have proven to be essential to the racial integrity and purity of the white and Negro races alike."[19]

So when Chairman Joseph Biden assured Thomas that the presumption of innocence lay with him, this was only the latest bizarre note among many. Since such a presupposition is mandated in a criminal trial but wholly inappropriate for a confirmation hearing, I wondered what emotion could work so powerfully as to befuddle a panel composed for the most part of lawyers. Did they go easy on Thomas because they were afraid of being held to account for their own transgressions and/or losing their own sexual prerogatives? Was it their acute denial of white men's historic abuse of sexual power — or some atavistic guilt at the shameful things their ancestors had done to black men — that turned a fact-finding hearing into a mockery of justice? Or were they terrified of acknowledging, even to themselves, that deep inside they were revolted by a black man who had sex with a white woman? (A prominent Washington psychotherapist called their response counterphobic, which is a fancy way of saying they bent over backward not to react naturally.) The standard political answer — that the Republicans wanted to get their guy past the Democrats and so brought out their heavy artillery — is patently true, but it is inadequate to account for either the Republicans' vitriol or the Democrats' ineptness.

So far was Thomas from being lynched, in fact, that at enormous cost to the American taxpayer, and by virtue of the most sophisticated technology in history, we were invited to watch a group of powerful white men cosying up to a black man while they insulted and demeaned a black woman.

Patricia King, a professor at the Georgetown Law Center, had already testified against the Thomas nomination after confessing that "as a black woman, it is difficult for me to oppose the nomination of a black individual who has known great personal struggle." She had decided, nevertheless, that "Judge Thomas's extensive record and personal posture is so antithetical to the interests of women and blacks — especially black women — that I feel an obligation to testify against his nomination."

Now King's husband, Pulitzer Prize–winning journalist and historian Roger Wilkins, gave a spirited exposition on National Public Radio and PBS that disabused listeners of Thomas's claim to be the victim of a high-tech lynching. Kendall Thomas, an African-American professor at the Columbia University Law School, wrote an op-ed piece saying that Thomas's charge "does a disservice to the memory of the suffering and death inflicted on those with whose stories [he] invited comparison" — those "who rarely received the legal process the judge has been afforded." He accused Clarence Thomas of pulling "the scab off one of the ugliest wounds in the history of this nation" and inflicting another. Truth had less power now, however, than sensationalism.

Senator Edward Kennedy of Massachusetts had said little during the first two days of hearings. On Sunday, however, he reminded his colleagues that "these points of sexual harassment are made by an Afro-American against an Afro-American. The issue isn't discrimination and racism; it's about sexual harassment." So much for the lynching analogy, but when he insisted forcefully that the Republicans had treated Anita Hill shamefully, Senator Hatch taunted, "Anybody who believes that, I know a bridge up in Massachusetts that I'll be happy to sell them!" This reference to the tragedy at Chappaquiddick where Mary Jo Kopechne was killed in Kennedy's car served notice that Kennedy's reputed philandering had undermined his effectiveness as a spokesman for outraged women.

Before Hill's charges hit the wires, according to an ABC/ *Washington Post* poll, 65 percent of American men and 61 percent of the women thought Thomas should be confirmed. After she testified, 59 percent of the men and only 43 percent of the women would have voted for him. On the day after the hearings ended, 61 percent of the men and 57 percent of the women supported him. So both men and women ended up believing Thomas by a margin of almost two to one. More than one-third of African-Americans polled believed that Thomas should be confirmed *even* if the charges were true, compared to one-fifth of the whites. CBS's final poll gave Hill only a 19 percent favorable rating among women, against 40 percent opposed.

Majority Leader George Mitchell characterized the hearings as a "search and destroy mission" that warned women who might complain about sexual harassment that they would be doubly victimized. But some senators, according to the *New York Times,* found Hill "too controlled and unemotional," especially compared to Thomas. Others found her unsympathetic because "she seemed too calculating and careerist" in staying with Thomas rather than "storming out in a huff." Most women understood, of course, that if Hill had torn her hair and beaten her breast during the hearings, as Thomas had, she would have been dismissed as a hysterical woman.

Three Democrats switched from Yea to No votes, but most with substantial black constituencies voted to confirm, told as they were that sentiment in the African-American community was solidly behind

Thomas. As Mary McGrory bitingly put it in the *Washington Post*, the senators "had to choose between their black constituents and their women voters. They had only the polls to guide them." The vote to confirm Clarence Thomas to the Supreme Court was 52 to 48: no successful nominee had *ever* received so many negative votes.

By demonstrating so vividly to women — and especially to women of color — how relentlessly powerful men trivialize their claims, the Hill/Thomas hearings paradoxically undermined white male cultural hegemony, exploding the illusion of consensus on matters of grave importance. Men said things women would never forget — whether or not they forgave them — and anger that had been repressed for centuries erupted like a chain of wildcat oil strikes. Over a single weekend, the political and cultural landscape was transformed, though the future configurations of power will depend on whether women can forge new alliances across class and race lines.

African-Americans had watched the hearings through a lens shaped by centuries of being enslaved by whites and then treated as inferiors and outsiders to American democracy. If there is such a thing as ancestral memory, nothing can have evoked it more powerfully than that bank of white men looking down on two black witnesses. It conjured up the era in which they had had to second-guess men like these — whose whim could kill, maim, starve, or exile them from those they loved.

Even African-American men and women who had opposed the Thomas nomination on the grounds that he was unqualified to serve on the United States Supreme Court were loath to see him humiliated before men like these, and a high proportion of the community suspected that Hill was being used by whites as a tool to destroy a black man. In fact, they wondered if Hill and Thomas weren't *both* being used as pawns by whites who had their own agenda, and they bitterly recalled the stereotypes of oversexed black people: the men who lusted after white women and the women who were naturally promiscuous. As historian Paula Giddings put it, "Black people were defined by their being sexually different from white society, [and] anything that confirms that view makes us nervous."

Since the charges seemed almost to parody the most degrading stereotypes about black men, the spectacle was arguably hardest for African-American men to stomach. As James Baldwin had written, "To be an American Negro male is also to be a kind of walking phallic symbol: which means that one pays, in one's own personality, for the sexual insecurity of others."[20] When producer Ofra Bikel asked Roger Wilkins how he'd felt as the confrontation neared, he replied, "I thought, 'I don't want this guy on the Court, but I don't want him defeated for this reason. I don't want to see a black person go through this.'"

To many African-Americans, the idea that a black woman might act to bring a black man down was very nearly terrifying, for where, except from women, had men found the support that had sustained them over the hard, hard years? In Atlanta, the Reverend Wiley Jackson harangued his congregation in the most flamboyant black-preacher style: "The devil had done dug up a black sistuh! If the woman in my life is pullin' me down, God, where can I turn to? One thing all of us men know is that when you got a great woman behind you, encouragin' you, sayin', '*They* may not say you're a man, but *I* know you're all man, you got what it takes!' *that*'ll make you stick out your chest then and say, 'I can take it!' So if the devil can divide us, he knows he can divide and conquer."

African-American women, on the other hand, watched one of their own who testified in circumstances that could hardly be more intimidating, but who conducted herself with exemplary grace and dignity. Like many blacks, Anita Hill had come from humble beginnings, and by dint of hard work and determination, she'd succeeded far beyond the hopes of most people, black or white. She had made the American Dream work for her, and this had to be a source of pride.

At the same time, Hill was violating a nearly sacred taboo: she was undermining a black man in the eyes of the white world. Patricia King pointed out that "it's been drummed in us since birth that you don't betray black men." As African-Americans, they'd been taught to put the race first. As women, they'd been taught to put men first, and to identify their own interests with those of the strongest they could find. "So many people saw [Hill] as a traitor to him and to the community because she washed all that dirty linen in public," said King before adding, "I'm glad she did."

It was on the rock of that choice — sex versus race — that the African-American community splintered during the Hill/Thomas hearings. By most accounts, a majority believed Hill's charges but — at least during the hearings — didn't believe that she should have made them.

Ancient imperatives to silence still held power, and in light of the tortures and troubles black women had suffered in this country, Hill's problems seemed positively trifling. (By her own account, he hadn't even touched her!)

From the most modest ranks of society to the most exalted, African-American men lashed out at Hill and insisted that different standards of sexual propriety prevailed in their community. Taxi driver Leroy Thomas of Macon, Georgia, spoke for many when he said: "I'm against what she did for harmony's sake, for racial peace and pride. . . . I don't think I could assassinate a brother or sister just because of some disagreement we had years ago. Womanizing has never been as important in the black community as it is in other communities." In an op-ed piece for the *New York Times,* Harvard sociologist Orlando Patterson referred to Thomas's "down-home style of courting" and wrote, "I am convinced that Professor Hill perfectly understood the psycho-cultural context in which Judge Thomas allegedly regaled her with his Rabelaisian humor (possibly as a way of affirming their common origins), which is precisely why she never filed a complaint against him. Raising the issue 10 years later was unfair and disingenuous." He declared Thomas justified in lying to preserve his chance for a seat on the Court and blamed "neo-Puritan feminism with its reactionary sacralization of women's bodies" as the villain that had so exaggerated the importance of the issue at the heart of the hearings.[21]

As they listened to men trivialize the pain that sexual harassment inflicted on women, African-American women began to sort out their priorities and marshal their troops. My friend the Washington media consultant Emily Tynes explained the conflicting pressures on them: "When do I speak up for me? And when do I subjugate my desires for the good of the race? What do we tell our daughters? [Do we say:] 'No matter what your ambitions are, no matter what you want to do with your life, you should sacrifice your mental health and your physical well-being to advance the race'?"

Some African-American women split along generational and class lines. Since most older women had themselves put up with far worse treatment than Anita Hill alleged, many thought she should have felled Thomas with a knee to the groin, verbal or literal as the spirit moved her. "Anita should have just left everything alone," one woman told Ofra Bikel. "Let the dirt stay behind closed doors." For young women like those at historically black Spelman College in Atlanta, however, Hill was a heroine. And in newspapers across the country, a group of more than sixteen hundred women, most of them professionals, took out a full-page ad with the heading "African-American Women in Defense of Ourselves," praising Hill and insisting on their right to define their problems in their own way.

Tynes put their dilemma precisely: "Where am I going to go with all the anger I've suppressed because I didn't think it was safe to stand up for myself? I think black women are very angry about the many, many roles we are called upon to play: we are nurturers, we have careers, we are activists, we are race people, we are the supporters of black manhood. We are the workhorses; we work harder and we get paid less. White women want us to embrace their issues. We're called upon always, always to support black men. *You know, there is no superwoman!* What happens when you have to internalize all the frustrations — to be so many different things to so many different people — and at the same time cannot express or work through some of the trauma that we as black women experience?"

As for the white men watching the hearings, they had grown up, after all, with the idea that people who looked like them ruled the world, and they were dismayed to realize that their hold on it might be slipping. It was unsettling that a woman — especially a woman who was black — should present a compelling case that her humanity ought to be considered, even as a matter of public policy. On one occasion or another, most had made teasing comments to women that they began to think might be misconstrued — mirabile dictu, they might even have been inappropriate — and the idea that they themselves might not be able to determine where the line of propriety is drawn and what constitutes crossing it was quite stunning. They were dumbfounded at the idea that the old maxim "Boys will be boys!" might soon be pronounced out of date.

And then there were the white women like me, who'd been called the chosen ones. To celebrate our beauty and virtue, poems and symphonies had been written, ships launched, and buildings dedicated. As tributes to our power, great cities had gone up in flames. Down through the ages, in song and story, we'd been called the force behind every successful adventure; men did it all for our sakes, and it was our spirit that infused the world with meaning.

But the hearings demonstrated that the rhetoric has been basically a cheat. Through the lens of our personal struggles to live with joy, dignity, and justice in a man's world, many of us saw the paradigm of our own experience: the panoply of male power arrayed against one woman. And we recognized what so often happens to women entangled with men who want to do it all their own way: absent love and respect, after the deferential courtesies are passed, men belittle, degrade, dismiss, and finally betray women. When love and respect are part of the mix, men sometimes behave differently and sometimes they do not. And while the bad guys brandish their knives, the good guys stand aside and let them do their business.

Women like me, who had been taught to depend on men like those on the dais, had too often been profoundly disappointed. I listened to senators who would have us believe that otherwise respectable men would never do what Anita Hill accused Clarence Thomas of doing — men who noisily insisted that if he had, a decent woman would have left — and I knew they lived in a different world from mine. Whether or not they really believed what they were saying was wholly immaterial, because I had learned long since that people tend to believe what it is convenient for them to believe.

As the hearings progressed, then, women drew closer to one another, although the politics between and among them remained complex. If white women on occasion seemed obtuse, black women certainly knew that their common ground was mined with explosives; as a stockbroker put it to Ofra Bikel, "American feminists cannot deal with race [because] they never remember that they were liberated from their kitchens because my grandmother cleaned them." And African-American women who already felt torn about working with whites — in effect putting sex over race — were taunted by African-American men like Orlando Patterson and labeled as traitors.

In the end, however, many women like me — brown, yellow, black, and white — experienced what Edmund Wilson called "the shock of recognition" and admitted openly that men could be very dangerous to our health. And with years of experience behind us in reaching across the barriers of color, Taunya Banks and I talked to one another; Kathy Bonk and Emily Tynes talked to one another. Angry women all over the country began talking to other angry women — many of us telling stories we had never told before. Madeline Lee, a foundation executive in New York, put our feelings succinctly:

I think men are the problem. I don't think they're evil, but I wish they weren't running my life, and I wish they weren't running the world, because I don't like the way they do it. Most men literally can't help it. What was horrible [about the Hill/Thomas hearings] was what *wasn't* going on, the looks of horror that *weren't* on their faces, the phoniness of the dialogue, the radical dissonance between what women were saying to each other in their homes and on the phone, and what was going on on the national screen. They were different languages, [and] the gulf was breathtakingly painful to watch, because suddenly you realized that nothing you cared about mattered to the people who were going to make the decision. . . .

For women like investment banker Jewelle Bickford the hearings were decisive:

Anita Hill changed my life forever. I realized that the sexual harassment I've experienced had *nothing* to do with my behavior. I'd always assumed that if I tried harder, if I were perhaps a little bit less aggressive, or a little bit funnier. . . . There was always the "if." But after Anita Hill, I knew that it had absolutely nothing to do with my behavior. That's what changed forever in the minds of many American women, and that's why there's no going back. As we began to insist that men be responsible adults, they gradually realized that the privileges and excuses they had taken as a birthright — their very grounds for believing in their superiority — might well be heading for extinction.

More than sixty years earlier, Virginia Woolf had speculated on men's reasons for anxiety at feeling a modicum of power slip away:

Women have served all these centuries as looking-glasses possessing the magic and delicious power of reflecting the figure of man at twice its natural size. Without that power probably the earth would still be swamp and jungle. . . . If she begins to tell the truth, the figure in the looking-glass shrinks; his fitness for life is diminished. How is he to go on giving judgement, civilising natives, making laws, writing books, dressing up and speechifying at banquets, unless he can see himself at breakfast and at dinner at least twice the size he really is?[22]

Perhaps he would have to learn, for Anita Hill had played a key role in what would become a burgeoning revolution: she had shattered a culturally imposed silence and freed untold thousands of women to follow her lead.

*   *   *

Now what we needed most, it seemed to me, was corroborating testimony: stories that might demonstrate how common — how even tame — Hill's initial experiences with Clarence Thomas had been. And so I set out to listen to a representative sample of American women — all ages, classes, shapes, colors, and sizes — talk about their own experiences of sexual harassment and abuse. My strategy was somewhat less than scientific, since I was doing neither a survey nor a poll, but looking instead for authentic voices. So when I went to Tennessee or Indiana to speak on my book about women in politics, I'd mention my new obsession and someone in the audience would invariably volunteer her story. I sent hundreds of letters to people and organizations and ran up a phone bill that seemed to increase geometrically as the months went by. Friends recommended friends and acquaintances. Women I interviewed told me about others, and people mailed newspaper and magazine clippings from all over the country. I borrowed cars, living rooms, computers, and kitchens. Word would spread that I was interested and could be found at such-and-such a place on, say, a Wednesday afternoon. My interviews became, as it were, a family project, and happily, my family grew as the year passed.

As I listened to women across the country — white, Asian, Latina, African-American — I gradually began to make the necessary connections between sexual harassment and other forms of male violence against women. Victims of child abuse, for instance, and particularly incest, were often victimized again at work, since abuse can so damage their protective mechanisms that, as adults, they are likely to walk unsuspectingly into abusive relationships with antennae too crippled to sense the danger. (In the same way, abusers are commonly found to have been abused as children.) Furthermore, it made no sense to separate women's experiences in factories and offices from their experiences at home; wives worked at home, whether or not they held paying jobs, and their ties to their husbands or partners were far more binding than those to the men they worked with, especially when they had children. Nor did class privilege seem to make things easier; an executive's or a preacher's wife was as likely to be battered, coerced, or humiliated as a field worker's. A corporate lawyer was as likely as a plumber to blurt out indignantly: *"What gave him the right? Where did he get his sense of entitlement?"* Since a 1980 United Nations Report had announced that "Women constitute *half* the world's population, perform nearly *two-thirds* of its work hours, receive *one-tenth* of the world's income and own less than *one-hundredth* of the world's property," these became the crucial questions.

A majority of the women who confided in me chose not to be identified, a fact that speaks loudly to their fear that a male-dominated society still has the power and the will to damage them. These are among the first, but by no means the last words on this profoundly important story. Some of the personal narratives that follow are vignettes, like snapshots taken from a passing train. Some are short stories that illuminate a woman's whole life. In their scope and depth, and in their compelling detail, these stories teach us that male violence against women is endemic, that it cripples us all profoundly, and that we can do something about it.

2

VERBAL SEXUAL HARASSMENT

. . . but words will never hurt me.

— Author unknown

Whoever said "Sticks and stones may break my bones, but words will never hurt me" was probably not a woman. He was also not very astute, though my generation nevertheless grew up with this maxim promising social and personal disgrace if we murmured faintly of pain. I would never underestimate the destructive power of guns, knives, whiskey, cocaine, heroin, or any other of the fashionable weapons people use to do themselves and/or their comrades in. Words, however, are at least as effective, though death may come more slowly. They maim the spirit and drain the soul.

Verbal harassment is the use of words, labels, quips, catcalls, letters, and innuendos to intimidate or coerce. In *The Sexual Harassment of Working Women,* legal scholar Catharine MacKinnon defines harassment broadly as "the unwanted imposition of sexual requirements in the context of a relationship of unequal power." From the 1984 EEOC guidelines, we can understand verbal harassment to be "unwelcome sexual advances, requests for sexual favors, and other verbal . . . conduct of a sexual nature" that a woman must put up with if she wants to keep her job or advance in it but that interferes by "creating an intimidating, hostile, or offensive . . . environment."[1]

As Dorene Ludwig puts it in her teaching monologue, an accumulation of sexual cracks can make a woman feel that she's being diminished, piece by piece, by a man who needs "to break someone else and glue their pieces onto him to make himself feel bigger." It shrinks her to her sexual parts. When a student whose mentor had failed repeatedly to seduce her was taunted with the charge that she had slept her way to a place at a distinguished university, she recognized his ploy as psychic terrorism. "Men have these ways of pulling women's chains," she told me. "Verbal harassment is motivated by that need to slap you down, to force you to acknowledge that the most important thing about you is sexual."[2]

On the first day Deborah Hyde showed up for work at the veterans hospital in Atlanta, Georgia, for instance, her supervisor greeted her by exclaiming, "Oh good! We've got another member of the itty bitty titty club." Hyde is a Ph.D. candidate at the Georgia Institute of Technology, and she was shocked, for she was clearly being told that she would not be taken seriously, either as a worker or a woman.[3]

For more than a decade, the women at this hospital had been subjected to a barrage of sexual comments, and one who'd left after seventeen years charged that the women had been merely toys for the men to play with. A male professor of civil engineering who worked there part-time had tried to warn the director four years before the story hit the newsstands, and the harassment was common knowledge, needless to say, among women employees. Still, it took a congressman's intercession with the Veterans Administration secretary to jump-start an investigation.

The classic put-down for women who complain about verbal harassment is "Boys will be boys!" — a quip designed to make them feel that their resentment is not only frivolous but runs counter to the nature of things. The sap of life, it would seem, runs thinly in their veins. Furthermore, women who are adept at sparring verbally with men are invariably thrown up to those who aren't — or who object to the exercise — as somehow stronger and more womanly.

Women who want to ingratiate themselves with men in power — either to advance in their jobs or to hold them more securely — have often winked at their antics and even joined in the harassment. In this way, women are played off against each other, and their chances of changing the environment in which they live and work diminish accordingly. So long as they remain isolated from one another, and out of sympathy, nothing can be fundamentally different.

The stories that follow are from personal interviews that I conducted over a period of a year and a half. In the interests of readability, I removed most ellipses that indicated words or whole sections that had been omitted, along with the square brackets that signaled words I added for the purposes of clarity and grammatical coherence. This "cleaning-up" of the text may give a misleading illusion of succinctness. My storytellers were no more precise or infallibly to the point than the rest of us in conversation, but these marks were distracting to the reader and we could not afford the space necessary to suggest the larger context. For the most part, emphases indicated in the text reflect the speaker's voice.

Abigail McDowell's story illustrates the dilemma of a single woman up against men with real power over her life. Though for one brief moment she was tossed on a couch, her real trouble came from words and attitudes. Abigail now serves as president of her own company, which she started seventeen years ago and built so skillfully that today it grosses several million dollars annually. It is part of the fashion and celebrity business, and Abigail has the presence to maneuver in an atmosphere flush with clamorous egos. I met her in her sleek New York offices, where she ruefully recalled how powerful men treated women when she was starting out.

I've worked from the time I got out of college — I was a journalist and then in magazine publishing — and for those of us who've worked all our lives, the notion that Anita Hill might not be telling the truth was ludicrous. Anybody who doesn't look like an absolute witch, in my opinion, has been harassed in the workplace.

I was an original women's libber. When I got a divorce from my first husband, I didn't want alimony. I had two children, and I must have been more stupid than brave; I didn't even ask for child support and got very little. So I had to work every minute to pay for next week's groceries. In that situation, I couldn't afford to lose a job. I had too much responsibility.

I had a job on a magazine, and I was very good at what I did. I had a publisher I liked very much, who was very good at what he did and who was notorious for playing around. (He made no bones about that.) I was on a trip, and suddenly I found myself in the same city with him and staying at the same hotel. He called and asked what I was doing. I reported on that, and then he said, "Why don't you have breakfast with me tomorrow before you go to your appointment?" I said "Fine," and he said, "Why don't you just knock on the door?" I really didn't give it too much thought.

He answered the door in his pajamas and said, "Come in! Look at the lovely suite I have!" And I knew I was in trouble. I kept my eyes averted and sat very properly as far away from him as I could and reported what I was doing while looking at the ceiling and the walls. He came over and put an arm around me, and I said I was late for my appointment and thought I'd better report another time. I acted like I didn't know what was happening.

If I got angry, he might fire me. If I laughed, he might not be able to live with that — he had *such* an ego. So I talked very fast and said, "Oops, I'm late!" and went scooting out. I felt terrible — dirty and besmirched! I wondered if I'd given him any encouragement. And I was *very* concerned about whether this was going to be a pattern. We worked together very closely, and so I tried hard to stay away as much as I could and to be very cool when I was with him.

About six months after that, we were on a plane going to a business meeting, and he alluded to finding me very attractive. "Wouldn't we be absolutely wonderful together? Think if we were married!" I knew his ego, and out of desperation I said, "You're absolutely wonderful, and if I were not working for you, I'd probably jump into bed. But my job is very important to me, and I think my being here is important to you. We're much better as friends." And it worked! I'd flattered him by implying that was the only reason he was being rejected.

When I was in journalism, I had editors who were constantly making passes. One man was the top executive for a very large magazine group. He was married but interested in me. He was always calling me for lunch, and I was always finding reasons not to go. But you can only say no so many times; he was an important executive, and I was a lowly editor. So I made a date for lunch and he said, "Come pick me up at my office."

He was in very large, posh corporate offices. I went through three secretaries. And he said, "Come on in, you've never seen my office." So I went into an absolutely spectacular room, probably thirty feet square, with windows all around overlooking the city. And he closed the door. The next thing I knew, he was pushing me down on the couch. This was at twelve-thirty in the afternoon! I could *not* believe what was happening. It was like everything you've ever heard — casting couches in Hollywood, that sort of thing. I scrambled to my feet and probably laughed. He started telling me what a wonderful affair we could be having. I thought men could bear it if you left their egos intact, so I said, "I can't. I'm very involved with somebody." Which I was not. He pulled himself together and straightened his tie. We walked past his secretary and went out to lunch, and I wondered how many days a week she watched that happen.

I got away with it, although he never took no for an answer. I never saw him at a company function when he didn't come over and put an arm around me and try to paw me. He seemed to think I'd eventually give in. I felt demeaned and angry that somebody would think I was a pushover. Why didn't people respect me for what I contributed? Why did I have to put up with that?

I found Nissia Delgado at her tiny apartment in a town in the Central Valley about an hour from Los Angeles. She had left the door standing open while she raced to the store for a spice she thought crucial for dinner, and so I met her first through the tangy smells of a stew on the stove. Her trust was breathtaking.

A Latina about to turn thirty, Nissia's ethics derive from the Gospels, and her politics from the experience of her people. She is small and gestures expressively. We sat at a round table before an open window, and the early fall wind billowed the curtains as she told me her story. When she spoke of the insult she'd received at the hands of community leaders she'd admired unreservedly, her voice grew still and she wept. But the thought of the nuns she works with now restored her spirits. "Men need to learn to respect women," she said firmly, "respect them as friends and equals."

I'm originally from a very, very small town — like two thousand population — in the San Joaquin Valley of northern California. My parents are laborers, and I worked with them in the tomato fields from the time I was nine years old. I have three sisters and two brothers, and I was the first to go to college and graduate. It was a hard thing to do because I wasn't prepared for college. I struggled through, but it was really difficult. A lot of times the funding doesn't go into those rural schools, so the curriculum's very limited; they might have one algebra class and one Spanish class, but no other foreign language.

When I was growing up, a lot of my women friends were older than I. In the sixth grade, one of my best friends was a sophomore in high school, and she wanted to go to college — that was her dream. And she influenced me a whole lot. She told me, "You have to get out of this little town!"

I went to Fresno State University and graduated with a bachelor's degree in journalism. Then I went to work on a newspaper in Delano for a while. Caesar Chavez comes from there, and the Farm Workers Union was focused there for a long time. He was definitely a hero, and we'd see him in the fields. So because of Chavez, I thought Delano was a very conscientious city, but I was *real* disillusioned. I saw a lot of racism there — not so much against Latinos but against African-Americans. And a lot of my stories were gutted. The city's very close-knit, and they really controlled the politics and the media there.

I needed to go somewhere and do something worthwhile with my life. I didn't want to be somebody who just sits in an office and does something to make money. I need to love my job. So I came to Los Angeles to see what the big city was like. I got temporary jobs and lived with friends who were going to UCLA, and then I got involved with an organization called HELP. A lot of the people who worked there were very active and political. (I grew up political but didn't know it: my parents picketed stores, boycotted grapes, and talked about racism. But to me, that was just life.) So I met these students who shared my values and had an intense desire to do something for the community, and that motivated me to read more and get on top of what was going on.

The executive director of HELP was named Pedro, but the program director, Jesús, was actually the brains behind the whole organization; Pedro just did what he said. Jesús is in his late fifties, and Pedro's about thirty-eight. I went in real idealistic; we were going to conquer the world! There were about eight of us who taught English as a second language, which is an important course because it helps the Latino community understand the system and the language both. That's necessary to create motivation. And those classes attract recent immigrants because they want to learn English. Since you have a lot of people listening, you can throw in political plugs and be teaching at the same time.

We had big classes — thirty to fifty students. The program was centered on Whittier Boulevard in East Los Angeles, the main Latino capital. The teachers were just college students or recent graduates like me, and all of us were real dedicated. We'd become very close to our students, and our students would be committed to us because they knew we cared and wanted them to learn. It became like a family.

Then they promoted Pepe Dall to the administrative staff and hired me to be testing coordinator. They had a grant that required comprehensive testing for ESL students; everybody had to be given a "pre-" test, and then, after six months or so, they had to be given a "post-" test. We had thousands of students, so they had to have somebody full-time. So I tested students. The state would compare the signatures on the daily attendance sheets with the "pre-" tests and the "post-" tests to make sure they jibed. Then they'd reimburse us. If the tests weren't there, we wouldn't get funded for that person. So it was really important.

But after about a year, we started to see double standards in what Pedro and Jesús were doing and in how the money was being used, and we were starting to get very disillusioned. Pedro and Jesús are very involved in heavy-duty politics in Mexico and in East Los Angeles, and they got threatened when they noticed that people were starting to pay attention to us. They'd thought, They're intelligent kids; let's make 'em believe they're doing something for the community so they won't ask questions. And sure enough, it had worked.

But now the teachers began to be very dissatisfied, and a division was created between the administrators and the teachers. So Pedro and Jesús began to call special meetings to try to figure out what was going on. They'd say they wanted to talk to us and wanted to be good directors. During one of those meetings, on a Saturday evening in December, I walked out because I had to leave early.

That night, my boyfriend left about ten-thirty, and about two o'clock in the morning, I hear these screams: "Nissia, open the door!" I lived in Echo Park on Glendale Avenue. It's a heavy-duty street, and people are walking around all the time, so I thought it was probably somebody in the park. But they were so loud and so close! There's maybe a six-foot fence around my building, so it's very difficult to get in, and my apartment was way on top. If I knew you were coming, I could go downstairs and open the gate. But usually it's locked.

So I wake out of a deep sleep because somebody's screaming "Nissia!" Then I hear banging on my door. An old man lived right in front of me, an elderly lady lived on my left, and an elderly man lived upstairs. The apartments are really close, and so if somebody's yelling, the whole world's gonna hear. And I thought, they're gonna be waking everybody up. So I went to the door and said, "Who is it?" "It's me, Pedro"—the executive director of the organization! "Can I come in?" I said, "What?" Then I asked, "Who's with you?" I started to crack the door, and they put all their weight on the door and pushed me back. Jesús, the program director, just fell on my floor. So they both came in, and they were both under the influence of alcohol. They said they'd jumped the fence. I was in my robe and pajamas, and they could see my bedroom. I felt naked and didn't know how to act. It was two in the morning!

Pedro is very articulate and manipulative; he's a salesman and very good at convincing people to do what he wants. So I'm saying, "What are you guys doing here?" and he's saying, "Come on, Nissia. Why are you acting that way? We're your friends, we love you." Pouring it on. Jesús is on the floor. And they say they just want to find out why I left the meeting early. I say, "Why couldn't you just ask me on Monday or something?" "Well, we were taking a walk around the block and we thought we'd just come and say hello."

They're the kind of men who are real macho. If you show any fear or look like you might be losing control, they'll feed on that. I was getting upset, and they were starting to notice. Pedro would say, "Are we intimidating you?" I'd say, "No, but I'd like you to leave." I remember feeling that I wanted to cry —but thinking, You can't cry because they'll just laugh and stay longer.

Jesús could see my bedroom through the glass doors, so then he says, "Oh your bedroom looks so nice! I'd really like to go into your bedroom. I really want to make love to you." I'm grossing out because I'm not in any way attracted to Jesús. He was like a father figure to me. I went into that organization really admiring him and Pedro because I'd heard they were great community leaders who were doing so much. God, I'd really admired them.

Then Jesús says again, "I want to make love to you," and Pedro says, "Do you know that he has the power to raise your salary? He can double it. He can triple it." So he says, "Why don't you make love with him." And I say, "Never. You guys just gross me out."

They knew I was afraid. The thought of them in a sexual way was really terrible to me, and I didn't want to do anything to encourage that. So basically I tried to stay calm. I'd say, "I'd really appreciate it if you guys would leave!" Pedro's like, "Come on, Nissia, we're your friends." They were there about half an hour, and the whole time I was asking them to leave.

Finally, both of them stood up and went to the door. Pedro was going to kiss me, and I ducked under his arm and opened the door and then kinda pushed 'em out. They were still saying things like "Come on, Nissia, why are you so upset? We wouldn't do anything to hurt you." Then Jesús says, "I'm not leaving until you kiss me." It's so late and we're outside. But he's adamant, and he's starting to get louder. So I give him a kiss on the forehead and say, "Okay. Get outta here!"

When I walked into the apartment, I felt completely drained and started crying. Right away, I called the cops and asked if they'd come by. Then the phone rang, and it was Jesús. He was saying, "Why didn't you let us stay the night? You know we wanted to make love to you. You know you wanted to do it." I hung up on him and then the phone rang again. It was Jesús, and I hung up again.

The third time it was the police, and they said they were outside the apartment building and would I come down? I was so scared I didn't go. My apartment was way on top, and you had to go down this flight of creepy stairs. They're real dark, so I didn't go make out a report. I told the lady on the phone that it was too dark and I was afraid. I cried the whole night.

On Monday I had to go pick up my check and I was apprehensive, but I needed to pay my rent. I remember walking into Jesús's office. He said, "Boy, you look beautiful!" I said, "Jesús, I'm here to pick up my check." He said, "I'm not giving you your check. You didn't make love with me last night." I said, "You have to give me my check!" And he said, "I don't have to do anything."

I turned around and left, and on the way back to the office, I started crying. I didn't know what to do. I didn't think anyone would believe me. Or if they did, they couldn't do anything about it. I was really humiliated. I went into my office and called Pepe and asked him to come. When he saw my face and said, "What's wrong?" I told him, and he said, "File a complaint." I said, "Are you serious?" He said, "Yes," and I went and filed it then. At last, I got the check. Jesús sent somebody over to give it to me.

A week or so later, a lot of us teachers submitted our resignations to the board, and in mine, I mentioned the sexual harassment. Because it was the last one I mentioned, one of them said it must not be important. I said I was emphasizing it.

The hardest thing has been to hear them denying and justifying everything, like it was kid stuff. Another woman who had some of that stuff happen to her won't testify because she says, "They're just messing around." All the other teachers are willing to testify. Ultimately it's made me stronger because it really makes me believe that women need to stand up for their rights. It's not just games. Men need to learn to respect women as friends and equals. I felt like I was supported by Anita Hill. And I felt like I was supporting her, too. It was terrific. She said and did things that made me feel like I had done the right thing.

Sometimes it's hard for my attorney, who's a male, to understand what I want. He says, "You probably won't get any money." What I want is in-house training on sexual harassment. I want men and women to get literature on the subject. And I want Jesús and Pedro to resign from the organization. They say they're never going to resign; they founded it and they're the leaders. So my attorney says, "You know what you're asking is very unrealistic." And I tell him, "No, it's not. Our community doesn't need people who are going to be abusing women. I'm one woman who could defend herself. But they work with a population of women who will *never* be able to defend themselves. Maybe in a few years, but not yet." These women come from Mexico, not knowing any English, afraid of the system, afraid of any man who has some form of influence or power. Guys like that could manipulate them and get them to do anything they want. And the women won't be able to defend themselves.

I tell my lawyer that if I let this go now, and Pedro runs for senator or governor, and I hear later on that a woman got raped or killed by him, that's going to ruin my life because it will be my fault for not stopping him. There are times I've wanted to change my attorney. I don't feel he understands. He says, "Why do you want to ruin these men's lives for an hour of bullshit?" But I work for a nonprofit organization, and I barely get paid enough to survive. So I've stuck it out with him, and I'm grateful to him for sticking it out with me.

Now I work with a woman-run organization. The camaraderie you develop with the women is a force that drives you to know and to do what is right. Every day I see women who could be victims of Jesús or Pedro, and a lot of them have become very close friends. A lot of them are like my mom. I could never imagine my mother going through something like what I went through. It would just kill me if that happened to her, and that's what's empowered me to continue.

In the story that follows, the actual exchange between the man and woman is more fleeting than anything in Abigail's or Nissia's experience. Katherine McNamara's adviser did nothing gross, and what he said might have been brushed aside as trivial. In fact, she tried to do just that. Ultimately she discovered, however, that her rebuff had pricked his ego, and he took it out on her indirectly.

I met Katherine, a writer in her middle forties, at her Upper East Side apartment in New York City. Books lined the rooms and stood in piles on tables and alongside chairs, while that grainy big-city light that filters through windows far too high to be easily cleaned played across the parquet floors. We sank into deep cushions and drank strong black tea while she told me her story.

As she spoke, I was struck by her stunning beauty, her artlessness, and the intensity she brings to ideas, and I could see how this combination might be unsettling to men; they couldn't peg her as mere beauty or mere brains. A woman with a spirit so free that she can say, "I made sure I had beautiful underwear and a good haircut, and for the rest — I was finding out about the world," can be both a joy and a conundrum. Married happily to her second husband, whom she met in Alaska and who negotiates the practical world for which she feels so little affinity, she has no children.

In the late 1960s, I was a young graduate student in my middle twenties married to my high school sweetheart. I'd gone to undergraduate school at a Catholic women's college and on to an Ivy League university, and my husband and I ended up in the same history department where he'd been an undergraduate. I was wide-eyed and naive — and *thrilled* at the idea of the life of the mind. Having learned from the nuns a kind of hierarchical discipline, and the subordination of scholarship to something else, I was excited at the prospect of studying the history of ideas.

My university had a system I still like in theory: by the end of the first year, you chose a major adviser, who chose you back, and then you worked together to design an academic program that satisfied the needs of the department as well as your own. It was a kind of apprenticeship system, so of course everything depended on the relationship you established with your adviser.

I knew nothing about people and must have thought they were basically nice. I was reclusive, terribly studious, and very, very shy of boys. As the oldest in a big family, I'm internally confident, but I was used to being different from everybody else.

My husband's major adviser, who was the departmental chairman and eminent in his field, had proclaimed that no woman would teach there as long as he was chair. But I couldn't take seriously such a statement. It didn't seem to touch me. I didn't know I was a woman, you see; I didn't know there was a split in the gender of the mind. So I just brushed it off.

My second year, they hired this bright young man just out of Harvard who would have been only five or six years older than I. He came on in a rather stellar way — it was 1969, an interesting time — and there was a whiff of change in the air. And what really surprised me was that he was young.

He was going to be my adviser, and when he came on to my committee, I was excited because this was for me! He had just come back from France, where he'd done his work. What he had to teach seemed to be pretty interesting. And he arrived with a very beautiful, very intelligent, honey-blonde-haired woman, and they lived together. Within the first month, phone calls started coming in to the department from his ex-wife, who would call up to say he was a womanizer and to ask implicitly why they were hiring him. It was part of the common gossip because she called the secretaries.

I was intelligent in a way that made sense in university life — and I wanted something that wasn't *about* everyday life — so I didn't understand that universities are composed of people who run on their strong inclinations. I thought the life of the mind was more dissociated.

During my third year, we lived in a small apartment house with a landlady who drank gin. I was studying for my orals and liked my seminars. And I was very curious about this man. I didn't know much about him, but he'd moved in upstairs, the blonde had disappeared, and he was living alone. One day he knocked at the door rather insistently at a time when I was worried about something. He asked if I didn't want to come upstairs and talk about it. It was the end of the afternoon and my husband wasn't home. I said sure, but I didn't feel like doing it then and politely asked if we could do it tomorrow.

I half noticed that he said, "Why don't you come up now?" Some part of me — my nice-Catholic-girl side — said, You don't go to a man's apartment alone. Then the other part said, That's the nun in you speaking. That's not what life's about. . . . Also, you're curious when you're young: you have these rules of behavior, and you don't know if they apply in every situation. And without knowing it, you just trust your teacher; you think, He knows something I don't know about this situation. So I went upstairs.

When I'm in a private space with a stranger — especially with a man I don't know — I'm kind of tense and rigid, and I sit with my arms crossed. I vaguely remember doing this. And at some point, he said, "Well, Katherine, would you like to get involved?" I said, "Well, no, I don't think so," and when I moved to the door, I think he kissed me. I was deeply embarrassed because I didn't know how to behave *without* being embarrassed. I didn't know how to rebuff him smoothly. I wasn't worrying about his ego or anything. I just had no savoir faire; I'd been completely taken by surprise. I was so innocent I didn't know what a womanizer was.

Whatever curiosity I had was a writer's curiosity, a girl's curiosity. The only man I'd ever slept with was my husband, and even then, it had taken him two years to persuade me. I was a nice Catholic girl, but the voice inside was the writer's voice, clicking and noting. It said, Don't lose face. . . .

I had no desire for my adviser. I was only curious about him as a kind of literary character. When my husband came home, I told him, and he thought it was a power move against him. He got frantic. I had to calm him down. I told one or two other graduate students but had no idea whom to go to or what to do. Also, you think it's just a little blip on the screen; it will have no consequences. The next day I had his seminar, and I sat right across from him and kept my countenance.

In the next few years, we moved a couple of times, and eventually the marriage broke up. I realized I wanted to go to Paris to work on my dissertation in history, and the lucky carpet rolled out and I got the French equivalent of a Fulbright. I wanted to read the work of Marcel Mauss, who founded French ethnology and was a nephew of Durkheim, whom my adviser had written about. After about fifteen months, I began to understand that I'd gone there to be a writer. Then, on an impulse, I went to the west coast of America, and from there to Alaska, where I stayed for four years. I ended up as an itinerant poet who lived in the bush.

Everything was unfolding: I was free; I could think for myself; it was splendid. I made sure I had beautiful underwear and a good haircut, and for the rest — I was finding out about the world. The world is a pretty awful place, but wonderful things happen. I was learning rich new things that academia hadn't had a clue about — especially my secular and agnostic university — among native people who have an essentially religious and highly ceremonial life in a way that's not at all obvious to the visitor.

In 1980, I was ready to leave Alaska and write the dissertation. I was excited about living, and I thought I finally knew what Mauss was talking about. When I'd read him in Paris, I'd talked to his students who were by now old and eminent, and I thought I understood what they were saying about what he'd talked and written about. So I called my adviser and said, "I want to come back."

When I arrived, he sort of welcomed me, but a moment came when he looked at me and said, "Something happened the year after you left." He had apparently become rather notorious for dating undergraduates, and a guy who'd been his student had written a long letter to the tenure committee calling him a womanizer and telling what had happened to me. (I don't know how he described it, but he clearly said the professor had made a move on me.) My adviser said the tone of the letter was very strong, like that of a rejected lover. He was very cold and analytic about it.

There was a kind of sexual hum in the air, but I knew our exchange was really about power; he was telling me that he was going to be in charge. I didn't want to be close to him: he gave me the creeps. Once again, I had to engage in a mind/body split. He was my adviser and I wanted to write the dissertation, so I dealt with the matter by not dealing with it.

I went off to write the first draft, and eventually I sent him four hundred or five hundred pages. He sent back an angry letter that made me cry, saying it read like a field report and he wasn't going to read it until I edited it. It was a cruel response, which was not unusual, but it *was* galvanizing.

I sat down and did it, and *it was so good, it was so exciting.* Everything clicked! I had this great beginning: "We will begin with mind." It was complex; I had had to go into a lot of disciplines, even quantum mechanics. I had met some of the major anthropologists in the world, one of whom had been Mauss's pupil and another an editor of the posthumously collected papers of Mauss. I was thinking through and about a whole lot of things and tying them up with what I'd learned in Alaska.

As I was writing, I'd felt myself getting braver, though I could hear this little internal voice saying, He's not going to go for this. (Don't compromise yourself, actually, was my watchword.) I had bound copies made and sent them off to the members of my committee. The anthropologist sent it back with checks in the margins. My way of thinking seemed to interest him.

But my adviser kept raising questions, and they irked the hell out of me. I called him up — I hadn't seen him in about two years — and asked to schedule a meeting. And he said two things. One was, "I have twenty-five dissertations to review; you've introduced so many different things, and I don't have time to learn anything new." At that point, I truly did *not* have anything at stake. The Ph.D. was *not* my goal, and I suspect it had *never* been my goal. But I wanted to do the work, I wanted to think, I wanted to write those sentences. I was very excited about the dissertation — or, as I called it, the piece of work. So when this man said he didn't have time to learn anything new, when I had just spent two years, and before that four years, learning this whole new stuff — whatever I felt, pity was surely part of it.

The second thing he said was, "You're not a student any more. Why don't you just publish this book?" I think he also suggested that I show it to a professor who had just come on. I didn't know the man and it didn't make sense to me. So I said, "I guess we agree to disagree," and rang off. That was that. I didn't even get to defend my dissertation.

This had been a power struggle, and I hadn't compromised. I'd used the writing of the dissertation not only to think for myself, but to do battle with my adviser in an arena where I was his equal. *I didn't openly challenge him, but when you say no to a man in authority, he is furious! He'll take revenge in some way, and the revenge is never about the substance of the issue. I was an upstart woman, and he wanted to prevail. In my mind he did not.*

But I thought I had something to offer — not the small "I," the ego, but the gift that I was given. The intelligence, whatever facility with a sentence I had, the insights into the human heart that I had accumulated over time. I wanted what I had to say to be taken seriously, and it wasn't; it was ignored and then pushed aside.

What I learned about myself from that experience is that any woman who stands up and speaks — whoever can be named as the outsider — will be driven off. I saw it in the faces of those men on the Judiciary Committee; I saw it in Alaska; I saw it in my adviser, who would not be crossed.

I knew that my conflict with my adviser was a fight between a man and a woman. The man expected to dominate and the woman would not accept that. I wrote the dissertation, on one level, to stand up for myself. I learned to think for myself. That turns out to be very disturbing. . . .

Harriett Whitman is a cheerful professional in her mid-forties who works at a large state university in the Midwest. I met her when I was in the state of mild derangement that comes from driving into a city for the first time and getting lost twice in less than a quarter of an hour. She assuaged my confusion by leading me to a pleasant restaurant flooded with light and filled with exotic smells, where we could spend a leisurely hour learning something about one another. With my balance restored, we went back to her office for the formal interview.

Harriett's story shocks her still. Her voice tenses up and her eyebrows rise in indignation as she tells it. The incident she describes happened at a seminary, so we have to recognize that no calling or profession is so lofty as to be free from mashers.

My husband is an ordained minister, and a decade ago, all our friends were in the ministry. At that time, he held an administrative position in our church, and I was working at a Protestant seminary as the assistant to the director of continuing education. I was doing things like writing copy for brochures and helping to run events for people in the ministry. Being a mother was my number one role; my children were ten and thirteen. And when I talked to the director about the job, I said I'd take it if I could be home when they got on the bus in the morning and again when they got off in the afternoon. He agreed to that.

One of the professors at the seminary was attracted to me, though he never touched me. He was married and had five children, and he knew my husband very well—they'd worked together on committees. At that time, he was the director of the graduate program. My office was in an open area, and the faculty offices were off a hall. And this man began to make comments to me that at first were very slight, suggesting that he wanted to go to bed with me. Then they got much more direct. But he was very, very discreet. I'd see him looking up and down the hall to make sure no one else was around before he said anything.

This had gone on for a couple of months when, one day, I was down on my hands and knees adjusting the heating ducts because the pipes were pounding. So I had my back to him when he came in and asked, "What are you doing?" I said, "I'm trying to adjust these pipes." And he said, "I'd sure like to adjust your pipes." I turned and glared at him, and I knew then that I had to put a stop to this.

I talked with my boss and said, "I want you to know this person is making inappropriate comments to me and I'm very uncomfortable." So he said, "What's he saying?" And I told him about the pipes. He said, "Well, he doesn't mean anything by it," and I said, "I don't think he does either, but I want you to know I'm uncomfortable with it." He said, "It's very inappropriate for him to do this. How can I help you?" And I said, "If you could catch him at it, you could put a stop to it." So we kinda collaborated.

Right outside my office was a large marble stairway. (This seminary is all glass and marble.) About a week later, my boss was in his office with the door open when this man came up the stairs. He couldn't tell my boss was there, and in fact he was supposed to have been somewhere else. So this man made another suggestive comment, and my boss heard it. He picked up a large stack of papers at the corner of his desk, including a clipboard, and came out of his door like a bull. And he literally roared! He made this guttural, roaring sound. At this point, the man went down the stairs as fast as he could go, and my boss took the pile of papers and the clipboard, and he threw them as hard as he could down a flight of stairs. He yelled the man's name and said, "You sonuvabitch, don't you *ever* do that to her again!" The whole faculty had to have heard it, it was so loud.

For years, my mother was a secretary in an office, and she was sexually harassed by a man who'd literally pat her in inappropriate places. She'd come home and tell us, and I'd say, "Why don't you report that?" And she'd say, "Oh, he's just being fresh." I always thought it was pretty awful that she'd pass it off — even though she said, "He never does it in front of anybody else, so how could I prove it?" So when it happened to me, although in a slightly different form, I was mad.

But I never told my husband — even though every Thursday night we got a sitter and went out with my boss and his wife. Since my boss and I were very professional at work, a lot of people may not have known we were also good friends. But it was never brought up. I didn't make a conscious decision not to tell my husband; I kept my home life at home, and my work life at work. And I didn't realize I was so angry until the Anita Hill hearings.

But when I told my husband, "I believe every word this woman says!" he was startled and said, "Why?" And I said, "I have something to tell you. . . ." Of course, he asked the question: "Why didn't you tell me then?" And I'm not sure I could answer it right, except to say that I hadn't been able to put a name to it. I didn't know it as sexual harassment.

Rachel Jackson is a corporate lawyer in southern California who grew up in New York City, and we met in a noisy, bustling restaurant on Wilshire Boulevard in Beverly Hills. In this sort of place, where you expect to be jostled by Batman and Robin, Rachel holds her own by way of the New Yorker's instinctive view that the world takes brass and brains to negotiate.

Now in her mid-fifties, she was married and had children when she went to law school but subsequently got a divorce. Despite the repeated harassment she spelled out over lunch, Rachel is quite successful in her field. Nonetheless, she bristles at what she's had to put up with, and the vigor of her storytelling so enthralled me that I forgot the time and got a parking ticket.

I became an attorney at thirty-eight and got my first job in 1977. After going to a Grade B law school, I was hired at a firm that wanted a woman to work with the bereaved and elderly. But I wanted to be a litigator. I was the only female, and I knew I'd never be a litigator there — I'd be in a back room shuffling papers and dealing with old people — so I left after five months. I wanted a job in entertainment law and had an opportunity at a major television network. That's always a difficult first job to get; they want somebody with experience, but you have trouble getting the job to get the experience. Mine consisted of being married to an actor.

What I didn't know was that the man who hired me only hired women he wanted to sleep with. He was based in New York, and most of his staff were women. Normally his second-in-command in California would do the hiring, but he happened to be in Los Angeles at the time I showed up, and I think it was because he pressed the issue that I got hired. He came back and took me to a lunch that lasted three hours. It wasn't a business lunch at all — it was much too friendly — but I was happy he was friendly; I was thirty-eight and yet very naive. On the way back, he said, "I wish this could last until evening, or that we could meet again."

I knew he was making overtures, and I found it rather alarming. It was my first job for a company, and I didn't know what it meant if your boss was making overtures and you weren't interested. Did it mean that you'd get fired eventually? Or that you'd get the worst work to do? Or that you'd never get promoted? I was already in over my head because I was given a job to do for which I had nobody to teach me.

So here I was—faced with a situation that made things worse. Fortunately he was in New York. He was married, but I found out subsequently that he made a play for everybody and was sleeping with various people. When I'd visit the New York offices, one of the women attorneys would be draped over his arm. He'd take us to lunch and she'd lean forward, cleavage showing, and it was pretty clear that something was going on between them. I don't personally care, but you wonder; is she getting promotions because of it? Is this the way business is done?

Then I went out to lunch with an agent—I thought I should get to know these people—and he hit on me at lunch. I was really overwhelmed because now I didn't know whether he'd give me a hard time on closing the deal, or whether it would come back to my boss that I wasn't doing a good job because I wasn't playing along. And the agent was *lots* of fun until he started hitting on me. He was a type I recognized from New York—same kind of background and experience. Then he said something like "Do you ever fool around?" He didn't leave a lot to the imagination.

When I'd been there maybe six months, a new person was brought into the business affairs division. I was walking by his office and saw him sitting there. He was a mature man, in his late thirties, maybe early forties. He'd been with a good law firm and I knew I'd be working with him, so I walked in and introduced myself. And he said, "Sit down, let's talk. What do you do?" Blah, blah, and then he said, "Are you married?" I said yes. I thought it was just a query. Less than a minute later, he looked at me and said, "Do you fool around?" I didn't get how people could talk that way: *I didn't know where his sense of entitlement came from.* Why would a man want to appear to be so crass and gross? What was his protection? After all, he'd just got this job. My eyes bugged out, and once again I felt very threatened. He was a new person on the scene, with more power than I had and with something to say over my fortunes. He was like somebody going into a market and squeezing the cantaloupe and saying, "I'll take that one!" It had no real emotional meaning to him—which is also frightening.

I was a little more savvy now, so I said, "No, I'm married and have two children, but I'd certainly like to have a good working relationship with you." I was trying to strike some kind of balance so he wouldn't feel so alienated that he'd have a hard time working with me. Had I been the person I am today, I'd have walked out and gone into Personnel, and that would've been the end of him. But that was 1977 and he's still there. It's a man's world and he knew they'd support him; he had the pulse of the company.

I was married and my husband was paranoid. I couldn't discuss any of these experiences with him. (I guess it was a compliment that he thought every man in the world wanted me.) And I didn't have any professional friends to talk it over with. I decided to watch and learn and scope it out.

I got a job at another studio, where I worked on a regular basis with the head of the theatrical division. I had meetings with him every week because I was doing a special project that he was overseeing. He had a suite of offices and was very charming. He could also cut you dead. He was somebody you had to be on the right side of—and I was, because I was honest and hard-working and always well prepared.

I'd have to meet with him in his office every Wednesday at eleven o'clock. I'd sit where the secretary was until he was off the phone, and then she'd send me in. He had this big desk, and behind that was a bathroom. On several occasions, I went in and he'd get up to go to the bathroom and pee. Well, you could hear right through the door. So I'd turn around to go back to the outer waiting room, and he'd say, "No, no, no! Just sit there." I knew it was intended to be sexually provocative. He could've peed before I walked into the office. I didn't think he was going to leap on me, but he was using me for his titillation, and I didn't like it. All that separated him and me when he pulled his cock out was a door. And I had to sit there and listen because he told me to. I didn't have the balls to say, "I prefer to wait outside."

What I see where I'm presently employed is a rampantly sexually charged atmosphere. There are affairs going on between secretaries and bosses that are known to everybody, so that when a secretary has a three-hour lunch, all the other secretaries are enraged. When you see the boss of your division hanging around like a fool, hoping to catch a glimpse of her, it *does* have an effect on the level of morale. It also has an effect when you hear remarks like, "Oh, don't fire her, I like looking at her legs!" Or, "If you have to fire her, hire somebody else with nice legs and a nice ass." This is 1992! And it's not being said behind closed doors.

I was talking to one guy on the phone just after I'd come back from Europe. (When I go to Paris, I don't go to relax. I run around like crazy—which is relaxing.) So I said, "It was great! I did so much, I'm exhausted!" And he made it totally sexual, turned it into my having had a lotta men. And he was going on and on, so I said, "I understood what you said the first time. I want you to stop!" For six months, the relationship was very strained. It was no longer,

"Hi, how're you doing?" I think it diminished my opportunities there. In order to have opportunities, you have to have access, which comes from support.

I had the opportunity to work with a woman who's very powerful in Hollywood, and one time she said, "I think I'll just sleep my way to the top, like women used to do. Why should we be giving it away for nothing?" And the fact of the matter is, many women now *are* giving it away for nothing. There are others who *do* know how to use it—and do! I don't know that that's colluding to a greater degree than the man who learns how to play tennis and invites his boss to a private tennis club, assuming the cost of the membership so that he can have a good personal relationship with him.

I heard one woman say to her boss, "You'll get in trouble some day!" like she was wagging her finger. And I said, "Why do you talk to him like it's a joke? It's not a joke. It's not cute. And none of us should talk to him like it's cute. Not one of us." But she wants to keep on his good side. Everybody wants to keep on someone's good side.

Penny Cameron is a prominent psychotherapist and a consultant on organizational development whom I have known for more than a decade. Now in her late forties, she holds both the master's and Ph.D. degrees and has received many awards, though she has the innocent good looks of someone who might sell patio furniture or kitchen equipment on consignment. Until I chanced to ask her, I had no idea she had ever been sexually harassed, nor did our closest mutual friends.

A small, fine-boned woman with a big, lopsided grin, Penny greeted me in her airy office on the outskirts of a major southwestern city. She has the upbeat spirit for which her region is noted, but when the tape was running, she sometimes found it hard to speak. "The pattern," she said slowly, "was always the same: first a threat and then a sexual invitation." The story below is only one of several she told — each of them with serious consequences. The first incident, in fact, had forced her to change her graduate major. By the time we parted, the grin was gone.

When I was thirty-seven, I was the director of a project working with the city. I'm from a large urban area, and by then, I'd been married for thirteen years. I'd been professionally involved all my adult life, which means I'd dealt primarily with men in workplace situations. In my first job, only the secretaries were women and I was ten years younger than the youngest man. There were lots of sexual innuendos and outright comments. Once, when a guy made some tacky remark, I said, "You're just projecting onto me what's happening with you." And he said, "Oh, am I projecting?" and put his hands over his genitals. That sort of thing was fairly common. He was verbally abusive, but it was no big deal.

I'd developed a program serving neighborhoods that had become quite successful. It started out as a small program, and then each year it had increased by somewhere between 100 percent and 500 percent in terms of the number of people and the budget involved. The man I encountered worked for the city and had a program he thought was competitive, and he was concerned that mine could potentially supersede his. So when I'd go to meetings, he would do a variety of threatening things. One was that he'd sit next to me, or approach me as I was leaving, to tell me how he was going to wipe out my program. He'd say I could expect to be doing something else the next year. At first he said it as though it were a joke — it was supposed to be funny — but it wasn't. Second, he'd ask me to go out with him.

As I said, the pattern was always the same: first a threat and then a sexual invitation. This went on for at least a year — once a week or once every two weeks. Enough so that every time I was going to see him I felt sick to my stomach. Our work put us together quite a bit, and he kept asking me to go for a drink and even to go to bed with him. I'd try to act like it was a joke. Once, he told me that people who'd crossed him in the past had had their tires slashed. I said, "Are you threatening me?" And he said, "I'm just telling you what happens." So it was always this same kind of power play, with sex as one of the elements.

When it got to the point where I didn't want to come to work, I decided I'd have to do something. I'd never considered filing a grievance because anybody who filed one was a marked woman, a troublemaker, and you were out as far as future jobs were concerned. And I didn't trust the system because the office through which you filed a complaint would have been under him organizationally. Whatever I did, I was going to be the loser, and I felt torn because I sure wasn't gonna quit my job. But when I got the threat about the tire-slashing, I went to my boss's boss and told him. He seemed angry, but he said he'd take care of it. And he changed the reporting relationship so that I wasn't reporting to this man any more. He was also told not to have any further contact with me. And that stopped the harassment.

I believe I lost a lot of credibility in my organization because I'd raised the issue, although this would be hard to prove legally. But the implication was that I'd asked for a favor, and now I owed them something because they'd granted it. I hadn't been able to handle it without asking for their help, so I lost face and ultimately lost contracts as well.

Verbal harassment is commonly less gross than at the veterans hospital in Atlanta, although subtlety in such matters can be even deadlier. A woman knows she's been hit when a guy remarks on her "itty bitty titties." She may think she's been complimented when he asks if she "fools around," but she's most likely mistaken.

None of the women above did anything to "ask for" the attentions they got. Quite the contrary: they were going about the ordinary business of their lives and work when they were harassed or assaulted — either term will do — by men for whom they felt no affection. For ever so long, we've been asked to imagine that women somehow give out signals that they are available, like the proverbial spider weaving her silken, sticky web, and that hapless guys simply fly or fall into it. This is misleading.

Of course women sometimes entice men, since women are sexual creatures just as men are; since they've been taught that their business in life is to be pleasing to men; and since they've been for the most part denied the means of making their way in the world on their own. But we are dealing here with something else entirely. These men were predators: they had positions of authority and used the leverage that gave them to prey on women over whom they had power.

Twenty years ago, women like Abigail McDowell handled the harassment all alone. "I never talked about it," she said. "I wouldn't have dared: it could have gotten back to them. Always there were fewer women in my profession than men, and we didn't network. There was a very different feeling then than now."

The standard answer the others were given if they complained or asked for help was: Leave it alone! That's life! You can't do anything about it. And the feeling behind the words was that *they* were causing the trouble. Like Nissia Delgado's lawyer, people wanted to believe that it was all a bunch of foolishness for which men should not be held accountable.

Commonly, other women tried to dissuade my confidantes from taking the put-downs seriously. Nissia's colleague who'd also been harassed refused to testify at her trial on the grounds that "They're just messing around." The words of Harriett's mother rang loudly in her ears: "Oh, he's only being fresh! You *can* put up with it and you *can't* do anything about it."

These are the excuses that women have traditionally made for men, and the accommodations they've been expected to make. The Hill/Thomas hearings called those excuses and accommodations finally into question. As Abigail put it, "The Hill/Thomas hearings were a milestone in our history. Women talked together for the first time. We sat there and realized, I wasn't alone in this; it's happening to everybody else. She did us the most enormous favor." For women had learned to treat men like children, and everyone was paying for it.

So long as men have had controlling power over women's lives and the lives of their children, many women have believed they had to stay on their good side. But in doing what they felt they had to do, they've also been crippled; tenderness and sympathy have curdled into sentimentality, as women have made excuses for men who could certainly behave decently if held to higher standards. At best, women's readiness to forgive has undercut their own sense of decency and therefore the ease and confidence with which they negotiate the world. At worst, they've played on men's vanity and weaknesses to manipulate them. And the women who've been willing to play along with men have betrayed the women who haven't.

I don't want to be misunderstood: I am *not* blaming the victim. The responsibility lies with the men who abused their power. But to change this crippling dynamic, women *have* to stop playing the game. Meanwhile, we are in a period of transition, and quite apart from the pain and confusion, refusing to go along can still prove costly: Katherine did not get her Ph.D.; Penny suspects that she lost contracts; Nissia had to leave the work she loved. Most of them were wounded in their souls and spirits.

Verbal harassment in its "playful" form can be met with humor. Retired brigadier general Pat Foote once instituted the "crotch mentality award of the week" for the soldier who had most recently outdone himself in being gross. Her underlings came to dread this presentation so much that they actually cleaned up their act, if only relatively speaking. But women who use ridicule as a weapon have to be *very* smart and *very* clever because ridicule, like all two-edged swords, can be dangerous. Coming from a woman, it can terrify men — and many women as well.

Governor Ann Richards of Texas is high priestess of the art of cutting people down to size with words, and her current popularity makes it plain that it can be used effectively. Still, no one should forget that Richards's 1990 victory was as precarious as they come: she won with 49.97 percent of the vote, and for the last six months of the campaign her admirers complained that her advisers refused to "let Ann be Ann." In fact, they'd muffled her because her tongue kept getting her into trouble.

My own favorite Richards crack is her definition of the cowboy as "the guy who kisses the horse instead of the girl before he rides off into the sunset." To ridicule a Texas icon is the political equivalent of doing the high-wire act at Ringling Brothers without the net: it is thrilling to watch because she's taking big risks. To pull it off, she has to be extraordinarily intelligent, but also, as Alison Cook put it in the *New York Times*, "tough as boiled owl." And the plain fact is that many women don't want to be tough as boiled owl.

For a rapier wit can not only shield, but seal off the sensitive parts of oneself. Women forced to use their verbal skills defensively are always on guard, concentrating their mental and spiritual energies on strategies of defense and attack — a posture that leaves these energies unavailable for more celebratory and life-enhancing ends. But you do what you have to do. Women who are temperamentally suited to the slash-and-burn style will find it easier to get along in many American workplaces than those like Gelsomina in Fellini's *La Strada*, whose gentle, lilting spirit broke before it hardened.

For most women, there is fortunately a middle ground — a space that is easier to occupy if other women share it. When all the women in an office turn their backs, figuratively speaking, on men who make "itty bitty titty" cracks, they have a better chance of making them stop. A woman alone is a different matter altogether, for if one woman perceives another as a competitor rather than an ally, the men who control the workplace can easily play them off against each other and usually do.

3

THE LAYING ON OF HANDS

We're all dangerous, I guess, when our egos are damaged, but because men have a disproportionate hold on the reins of power, they can do disproportionate damage to us. And we understand that intuitively.
— Sybil Masters

As often as not, sexual harassment goes beyond words. Men reach out for a breast or thigh. They grab and grope and kiss, and as they do, they tend to take women by surprise. In due time this feeling modulates into confusion, revulsion, panic, and/or dread. And not infrequently, a kind of existential terror follows: women find themselves in a menacing world where not only strangers but men held in some esteem treat them like objects. Physical pain has nothing to do with it, for the terror comes from a sudden withering of their faith that others will grant them the fundamental respect they grant themselves. And until quite recently, the powers that govern their world have for the most part refused to notice, much less come to their aid.

For many women, of course, this experience begins in adolescence. In June of 1993, the American Association of University Women issued a report based on a survey they commissioned pollster Louis Harris to make on sexual harassment in our high schools and junior high schools.

With a base of 1,632 students in grades eight through eleven in seventy-nine schools throughout the country, Harris discovered that 76 percent of young women had been subjected to unwanted sexual comments and looks, while 65 percent had been "touched, grabbed or pinched in a sexual way." At least a third of those had been so upset they didn't want to go to school or talk in class, and almost as many found it hard to pay attention. Four-fifths of the damage was inflicted by other students, and the remainder by teachers, custodians, coaches, and other adults.

As executive director Anne L. Bryant carefully put it, the AAUW report suggests "that schools are not what they were ten or twenty years ago. The climate in our schools is more hostile to all kids." Young men, if in smaller numbers, were also subject to harassment, and so it was clear that since sexual behavior is now far more overt than in earlier generations, the psychic hardening necessarily begins sooner.

Still, fellow students are roughly equals. As a male sixteen-year-old Washington, D.C., sophomore put it, "When you're a teenager and your hormones are kicking in, you don't quite know what's wrong and you don't quite know what's right. You may think it's no big deal. But once you're an adult, you should have absorbed what sexual harassment is. There are boundaries that make common sense."

Large numbers of men cannot claim this boy's wisdom. The five stories below represent forms of male sexual aggression in the workplace that stop far short of rape but involve physical contact. By the time they have jobs, men are likely to have gotten that disproportionate hold on the reins of power that Sybil Masters notes above, and therefore the damage they can do is more considerable.

Dr. Toby Myers and I grew up in the same part of Houston, Texas, and we met after many years at her office a few blocks from the neighborhood theater where, as teenagers, we'd all been scared witless. At midnight movies, mummies would rise inexorably from a bog or wildly painted Indians would brandish bloody hatchets and dangle a fistful of scalps, and we'd loved every minute. (The theater — wouldn't you know? — is now a porno palace.)

Toby works with modern perils that are less melodramatic and a good deal more real, concentrating on men who batter their wives. And with nothing of the ideologue about her, she has a chance to win the trust of men who need to change. Now in her mid-fifties, she was about thirty and working at the Texas Research Institute of Mental Sciences, the research and training arm of the Texas Department of Mental Health and Mental Retardation, when the following incident happened.

I was in my office talking on the telephone to a suicidal patient, when one of our physicians came in and started kissing me in the ear—*licking my ear.* I was absolutely horrified! I was the lead rehabilitation counselor there, which was a professional job but one that certainly didn't carry the status of physician. And I'm quite sure he did it because he saw how vulnerable I was and how involved in this other crisis. Of course, I couldn't react angrily to him because I had a suicidal patient on the line. I just sat there and kept moving away.

I think women always tend to blame themselves. But this was so blatantly something I had nothing to do with that I could give full vent to my outrage. I went to the chief of the service, who was a young, witty doctor we all really liked, and reported this behavior, looking for him to do something about it. And he said, "Congratulations!" So that was the last reporting I ever did.

Sara Moreno came to the United States from Mexico on a visitor's permit, and since she doesn't have a green card, she works illegally as a cleaning woman. I met her in the heart of the East Los Angeles barrio, where she lives in a kind of group house with children running all about and the sizzle of frying tortillas and the smell of salsa coming from the kitchen. She has a solemn face and a still, proud manner that made me think of the ancient Mayans. In the midst of the bustle, she seemed very much alone.

Anne Kamsvaag, my translator, sat on the big sofa between us and explained that Justice for Janitors, the organization through which I found Sara, is part of the Service Employees International Union (SEIU). "Most employers know if their workers have papers," Kamsvaag said. "If the women don't, their options are limited. In Los Angeles, there's a whole subculture of places where they pay way below the minimum wage, they don't pay overtime, there's a lot of sexual harassment, and employers aren't at all shy about saying, 'If you don't like it, there are twelve other workers out there who want the job.' So Justice for Janitors has had to come up with a lot of creative tactics." Though Sara carries herself with dignity, women like her are easy prey for men with a little power but no joy or beauty in their lives.

I've tried to live according to the rules that were shown to me, since the most important thing is to feel good about yourself. I came here with the idea of studying and learning about this country and making a better life. I've been here for one year, but the experience has been very hard. I don't understand how people can behave so badly.

In Mexico, I worked in places like the Fine Arts Institute, where I was part of a team that did presentations for children and sometimes adults. I knew that when I came to this country without knowing the language, I'd have to do things like the maintenance work I'm doing in buildings to pay for my expenses. I'm studying English, which is what is most important to me now. But I'd like to study directing and maybe go back to Mexico and do theater-directing on a professional level.

I have no family here. I got across the border and called a friend in Los Angeles, who gave me my first place to stay. She put me in touch with the union to get the janitorial work, and that's when I first started feeling the harshness, the lack of humanity, that people live through here.

They started sending me out to jobs, one day here, another there, usually replacing people. I struggled to get one regular job, especially since I don't have a car and they often send you very far away. So the union tried to find a place for me here downtown, where I ended up having the bad experience. I still can't get everything straight in my own mind, even though I lived through it.

I got to this building, and the man who worked for the cleaning company explained the work in front of everybody. But when everyone else had gone to their work places, I was confused. When you're in a building for the first time and don't know the layout, it's easy for you to be misled about where you are. I didn't understand why he started explaining things to me again. But he went around the twelfth floor with me ten or fifteen times. I'd start working in one place, and then he'd say, "No, no, go over there. It's easier if you start over there." The building's like a whole block, and if I was working on the side that overlooks Flower Street, he'd send me over to the side where Figueroa Street is. He'd leave me alone awhile, and then he'd come back. If he found me cleaning on one side, he'd say, "No, the kitchen on the Wilshire side is more important." So he'd send me from north to south, or east to west, in this rectangular building. I was trying to be polite and obey.

I don't try to be on guard while I'm working or pay much attention to hierarchy. At break-time, he came up with two cans of soda. By now, we'd gone from about five-thirty to ten at night. Very happily, I took the soda. From what I can remember, he started dominating me and I started feeling very bad — kind of dizzy and sleepy. I suffer from low blood pressure, and I wonder if it could have been that. I leaned back against a desk, and he grabbed me and told me to sit on his legs. As bad as I felt, I said no. Fortunately, his beeper went off, and he went to answer the call. I left the office and went out to the hallway to sit down in a chair. When he came back, he touched me on the leg. That's when I shouted and told him to leave me alone. He left and didn't come back. The next day he called and asked how I was doing. I have to wonder whether he cared about my health. But at that point, I didn't believe he was a bad person.

Later, when I was working on another floor, he tried to do the same thing. He seemed to think it was okay with me, and that's when I started to feel a change in me. I challenged him in front of another person. I told him I wasn't interested in having an affair, or an involvement with anyone, and I didn't want him to be taking time away from my work. I said I wasn't going to cure the psychosexual problems of anybody. He looked at me in a really bad way but didn't say anything. So I kept on working.

It seemed like if you complained, he'd back off, but then he'd come back and do the same thing. He'd come when I was working on a floor, and start turning off the lights. Then he'd come to me in the dark and touch me on the breast or somewhere else. So it got to where, if he'd come to the floor, I'd try to leave. I'd say, "At least leave the lights on where I'm working," and he'd say, "No, the owners get mad if you leave the lights on." Once again, I complained and tried to talk to him like an adult, but he was like a rock. He calmed down for awhile, but then, later, I ended up riding in the elevator with him. Nobody else was in there, so he grabbed my blouse. I hit him — or shoved him.

That's when the retaliation started, and it's still going on. He said that one of the prerequisites of that job was to accept those attentions, and I realized that two other people working there were dealing with the same thing. He asked one woman to go out with him on a weekend. I don't know what she said, but he fired her.

Now he's started trying to get rid of me. He'll spread garbage on an area I've just cleaned and then call a shop steward and say, "Look how dirty she is!" Once, there was a suite that hadn't been cleaned yet, and he sent somebody in to clean it and then wrote me up for not having done it. I know the union has trouble dealing with this, but finally I went to them and said this guy was abusing what power he had.

Then the maneuvering started. Some man I think was his supervisor came and said, "If you're not happy here, we can find you another place." And I said, yes, I wanted to leave, but first I wanted to speak up. I wouldn't accept blame for things that were not my problem. I was very angry. So for ten or fifteen minutes, I told him everything this guy had done. So he said he was going to talk to his own supervisor, and when I got there the next time, they told me I was suspended. They said they had no work for me, and somebody else was doing my job. They hadn't talked to the union.

Roxanne Behring works in a state legislature in the Southwest, and on a weekend when the capitol building was very nearly deserted, except by its ghosts, we settled into a corner of one of its lofty rooms. Quickly I realized that I was in the presence of a survivor — a woman whom life had continually battered. Roxanne hopes to return to journalism, and her story suggests why it means so much to her.

I was older than most cub reporters because I didn't finish college until I was thirty-six. Everybody'd said, "Why's a fat woman going back to college at thirty-two to be a journalist? That's a young person's profession." And I'd say, "That's what I want to do!" I had to try. By that time, I was divorced and had a ten-year-old child. I'd convinced a medium-sized city newspaper to start a capital bureau and let me cover the legislature because I'd always dreamed of being a political reporter. So here I was with a little desk up in the press room in the capitol.

I was a liberal, and one of my heroes was a state senator I'll call Jake Barnes. He was funny and played the guitar. He was overweight, but hey! To me there was a certain charisma about him. He was from a city close to mine, so I talked to him a lot. And after about a year, I went into his office to interview him about worker's compensation or something, and he just grabbed me. He fondled me and kissed me. Just all of a sudden! I'd worked with him before, but I didn't know what to do. Do I tell other people? I can't slap him. I can't tell him to get his grubby hands off me. So I just left.

It was so awful because I had a history! I was a molested child — not by my father, but by my uncle — and my anger really did affect me in a negative way: I got fat because men were always coming on to me. I'd matured real young and had a fantastic figure, and so my uncle and my father's best friend all victimized me. My uncle fondled me and finally had intercourse with me. My father's best friend fondled me.

I was the classic victim. I thought it was my fault, and so I didn't tell anybody. I don't think my mother knew, but my grandmother knew and didn't do anything. *It taught me never to trust weak women. Whenever I see a weak woman, I run the other way.* So I handled my anger by getting fat. I hid, and I learned that you just didn't talk about it. (Especially in my father's family; they were Cajuns.) So I ended up with low self-esteem, which is characteristic of a sexually abused child. You don't think you're worth making a fuss over.

I'd had a bad marriage and gone back to college at thirty-two. I weighed 290 pounds. I'd tried to commit suicide, and when it didn't work, I thought, Why don't I try living? And I did well at a city university, where I was part of a ragtag, guerrilla, urban bunch. All of a sudden I became part of the "in" crowd, and we had a wonderful time! There were Vietnam vets and other battered women and older women. It was a "real folks" place and that helped.

When this happened with Jake, I didn't say anything. It bothered me that I was the victim again because I didn't know what to do. Do I make a scene and lose that contact, so all the senators and the other guys in the legislature will look at me as a screaming she-bitch who tells? Will they say, "You dressed like that?" Or, "You threw yourself at him?"

He just kinda laughed and said, "I thought you were a hot momma," or something like that. He didn't say, "Don't tell anybody." He wasn't gonna have any problems: I was just a new reporter in town. I had trouble from then on doing my job and interviewing him. I was also worried. What would he tell the other state reps? Would he tell 'em I'd given in? He did the same thing to a television reporter, who got it on film and showed it, and that empowered me! I love her for that, because he was so used to getting his way he was impervious.

Marjorie Carroll is one of the most influential women in the country. Now in her early fifties, she came from a prominent family in the Midwest and went to a prestigious undergraduate institution in the East. She has been the first woman to hold a string of enviable jobs at the same time she has raised a remarkably attractive family. We met for morning coffee at the Willard Hotel in downtown Washington before she went off to do one last read-through for a lunchtime speech. It was a week or so before the presidential election, and the Willard, along with the capital itself, was nearly deserted because the votes are on the other side of the Beltway. We took our time.

It was difficult in the early sixties for young college-age women to figure out how to deal both with early sexual experiences and with a kind of attention from older men that we weren't used to. In high school, the oldest guy you looked at might be a freshman in college. Then suddenly you got to college, and your faculty members start seeing you as a potential sexual object. And that's a very tough transition.

My whole feeling about surviving in a large university was to get to know my faculty members, so that when they were grading the papers, they were dealing with a person. So I'd always try to meet the people who were teaching my courses. When I went about doing that, one of my professors made an appointment for me to come to his office in the evening. I didn't think anything was weird about it. It wasn't convenient, but everybody had busy schedules. But when I got down there, it was quite clear that he had something else in mind. And it was very hard to figure out how to react. He kissed me, and I didn't know what to do at first. I got slightly involved, and then I thought, Wait a minute: this is really weird. And I found a way to get out of the office and back to my dormitory. Clearly, if I'd been willing, we'd have had sex right then on the floor of his office.

When you're in a relationship where there's a significant disparity of power, the weaker person is drawn by the attention. In a university situation, of course, the excitement that comes from an intellectual relationship combines with the excitement of a potential sexual relationship. For me it was enormously confusing, and I didn't know what to do with it. I'd probably be overstating it to say I was scared, in part because I was fairly self-confident, but it was hard to get out of his office.

One night, we were all sitting around and talking about the course, when it became clear that a number of women in the class were having exactly the same experience with the same person. (There are probably some people for whom needing to engage in inappropriate sexual behavior with young women is part of an illness, and I suspect that's what we were dealing with.) So in the end, four of us went to see the head resident, who was a graduate student living in the dormitory, and explained what was happening. And he told us not to say anything because this faculty member was up for tenure and we could get him into trouble! This was an area in which I'd intended to major, and I ended up shifting the field of my study because I knew I couldn't deal with this and didn't want to have to. So as a result, I changed what I was concentrating on as an undergraduate. And he got tenure.

After I graduated, I went to work for the United Nations for the summer and was offered a continuing job there. But the person I was working for, it turned out, was also someone who couldn't leave young women alone. In your early twenties, you don't immediately say, "Don't touch me!"—particularly if you haven't had any social experience and if sexual harassment hasn't been discussed. So I didn't know quite what to do. You end up getting a little involved and then saying, "Wait a minute. I don't want to be here! What's happening?" You get confused about whether this is flattering, whether it's real, whether it's appropriate. At the time, it hadn't been defined as inappropriate, but I knew it wasn't the kind of work environment I wanted. So I basically turned down the job at the United Nations and went to work someplace else.

What bothers me most about these stories as I look back on them is that *I was put in a position where I had to change what I wanted to do in order to avoid those encounters. In the end, that's where the wrong was.* In my first job, I encountered this sort of thing a couple of times. But by then, I was married and it was a little easier to deal with. One could just say, "I'm not interested: I'm married," rather than getting into this whole awkward mess by saying, in effect, "You're my boss and I'm rejecting you. . . ." The label "wife" was a protection.

Much more open discussion about questions of sexual harassment began in the late seventies, certainly in academic institutions. I don't suspect one is going to wipe sexuality off the books, but what's become easier for women is an ability to say yes or no or "I'll have lunch but not dinner." To define the terms on which they want to relate to other people.

Sybil Masters is a highly respected professor and administrator at the most prestigious university in her part of the country. Now in her early forties, she was inspired by the Hill/Thomas hearings to tell her own story publicly for the first time, appearing at a campus rally where a friend heard her and arranged subsequently for us to meet. We had afternoon tea in a spacious faculty lounge where male professors with trademark leather elbow patches and slightly bent spectacles wandered desultorily in and out of the arched doorway across the room. Although the experience took place almost twenty years ago, Sybil was nervous about talking to me. She fidgeted as she mulled over whether it was safe to use her own name, and her anxiety was infectious: I spilled my Earl Grey all down my sweater.

I was a twenty-three-year-old graduate student, and like many people in my generation, I wasn't terribly aware — and I certainly wasn't very sophisticated. I had a strong self-image that was at the same time fragile. I'm in a very male-dominated, macho discipline where women have traditionally held positions as laboratory workers and helpmates, while the men go out and do the heroic escapades in the field. As a woman contemplating field work, I needed support and encouragement from my mentors and all but one were male. The great women in the field rose to prominence during world wars, when the men were occupied elsewhere.

This happened in England, where I was doing graduate work at one of the great universities, and it began when my professor and I went to a pub to discuss a paper I'd written. When we got back into the car, he just leapt on me and started kissing me. There was no prologue; he hadn't tried to touch me in any way, though he hadn't been particularly willing to talk about my paper. I'd kept trying to reroute the conversation while he tried what we now recognize as all the classic maneuvers to remove our conversation from a professional, work-oriented context by asking about my relationships and my past. This had been in the pub, where I got more and more unsettled.

I have some difficulty reconstructing my frame of mind then because it's been so important for me, in looking back, to focus on the fact that I rejected him. That's been so important for my self-respect. But I do know that I went through what I call the "lightning calculus": I instantly tried to assess the degree of risk this posed. I felt vulnerable, though I also felt that this was all slightly ridiculous because he was maladroit. But I focused on the risk. This was a powerful person, and I wanted to figure out before I handled the situation — as women feel they must handle the situation somehow — what he could do to me. And I decided I wouldn't need him. We worked in geographically different areas — our interests were on opposite sides of the world — and even though he was very powerful in the hierarchy at this British university, I'd be coming back to the United States to finish my graduate career, and he wasn't in the networks of those with whom I needed to be connected.

So I made the assessment that I could blow him off. (This took about four seconds.) In retrospect, I see that I was naive in understanding the extremely constricted world of my profession. He left the British university shortly thereafter, came to the States and started teaching, and now he sits on many grant boards to which I apply, and on the boards of professional journals, some of which are extremely high-powered. And he has an inordinate amount of power within them.

The British specialize in not taking things gracelessly; it's part of their public face. And I was able to put a naive girl's moral code on this: "Why goodness, you're married, and I'm involved with somebody else, and this wouldn't be right. . . ." Of course, the morality was the last thing that was concerning me. But the morality pose would allow him to save face. I wasn't rejecting him sexually, I was rejecting a situation that was questionable. So he put the best possible face on it. And we ended up sort of laughing about it in that hearty British way.

Then he started calling — hoping, I guess, to pierce the protective shield I'd erected by putting it in a less threatening context: "Well, come with me to dinner at the High Table. . . ." Now, this is a very prestigious invitation. But because I understood that it had nothing to do with me professionally, I didn't want to have anything to do with it. So I kept trying to say no nicely. At first, I said I was busy. Next, it was, "Honestly, I don't think it's a very good idea, after all, you *are* married. . . ."

I was feeling anxious, trying to keep these partitions up between a world that was guided by professional and work-related interests, and the world driven by sexuality that he was trying to make overlap and even replace it. We as women don't want our rejection of a person to connect with his sexuality because it then becomes a question of ego. We're all dangerous, I guess, when our egos are damaged, but because men have a disproportionate hold on the reins of power, they can do disproportionate damage to us.

So I kept trying, and I remember feeling how desperate this enterprise was becoming — maintaining these partitions — because I was running out of prevarications. And when I didn't have much left, he socked it to me. *He damaged me quite singularly when he got impatient and said, "Really, you needn't take the moral high ground with me because we all know how you came to be at this great university."* He then mentioned the name of one of my undergraduate mentors and his proclivity for indulging in sexual relationships with his female graduate students. He was saying I'd slept my way to this prestigious place! My mentor's dalliances had been well known: he'd just cycle through several in the course of a year, and since it was a big graduate department, he had a lot of choice. So for me, this snide remark was a crushing blow. My accomplishments as an undergraduate had been substantial; if I wasn't first in my class, I was pretty close because I had a perfect 4.0 average. I graduated summa cum laude and Phi Beta Kappa. But this pervasive ideology — that women are willing to provide sexual services to men (and there are some who are) — just trivializes women's accomplishments. It's there indefinably in the ether, potentially affecting anyone to whom I speak.

I don't even remember how that conversation ended. Everything was frozen for me in that horrible moment. I can see everything that was in the room at that time, I can hear it, I can feel the heat from the radiator. It was the moment when everything I'd worked for was taken away. When he said, "We all know . . .," I was sure they all believed somehow that I was not there on merit. And the aftereffects continue to this day!

The pattern that I've continued was set that second year, when I was due to take my exams. For five days, morning and afternoon, you sit and write. It was the only time I was going to be able to demonstrate that I merited being there and the only way I had of clearing my name. So I became obsessed by these exams. I did very well, but it took a terrible toll. In the two months preceding, I ceased to eat normally. For the whole week of the exams my stomach muscles were in such a state of tension that it was physically painful to swallow. I couldn't laugh. I hardly slept for the ten days preceding the exams. I was a basket case by the time they were over.

I'd never done anything but fine in my whole life. If that hadn't happened, I'd have felt nervous about the exams, but they weren't life and death to me. My grant-getting possibilities weren't dependent on them. So I see this extraordinarily obsessive behavior on my part as stemming from the realization that this was the only way I could prove myself beyond any doubt. Years afterwards, this experience continues to demean me by undercutting my achievements. I continue to feel like I have to keep proving myself and move on to the next achievement.

No more than in our earlier stories did the women here invite their punishment, and the only one who was not instantly revolted was Marjorie Carroll, who was young, briefly confused, and mildly flattered. None were sexually aroused by being pounced on or licked in the ear, and the way the men behaved suggests that they simply wanted to *score*.

Perhaps men do these things, oddly enough, to enjoy themselves; sexual overtures may cut the boredom or rev up their engines. Perhaps they want to make their lives racier, and obviously an audience of other men ups the ante. Perhaps they're doing a cock-of-the-walk routine. I don't pretend to understand male sexuality, but one is reminded of peacocks spreading their tails.

Whatever their immediate or conscious motives, the men in these stories used their sexual claims to show off and exert their power over women. Their assaults were ways of saying, "I can do this to you, but there's nothing you can do back. You can play along or not, but you certainly can't hurt me." For there's no sign that any of them expected to be held to account, much less to suffer for what they did, and there's no sign that any was mistaken.

The men had higher status and more money. For the most part, they had something specific the women needed: a supervisor can promise a job; a professor gives a grade or at the very least influences a student's academic standing; a legislator offers a reporter tips or an inside story. But the women here had nothing the men couldn't get from another woman. So the men were the aggressors, but the women paid, and they most likely paid in ways beyond the obvious.

For eros plays as important a role in a woman's life as in a man's: it is a fundamental source of energy and motivation. And the difference between the way women and men experience sex, at least hetero-sexually, is suggestive, for a woman opens her body to a man, as the mind and spirit open to new ideas and feelings — in short, to adventure. When she is sexually imperiled, she will almost instinctively fold in upon herself, throwing up barricades against whatever threatens her. Behind these walls, erotic energy is turned inward, protecting her vital space.

So a woman who has to defend herself against sexual assault is shut down, turned off, locked in, and sealed away — with obvious consequences to her ability to do her work. In such an atmosphere, she no longer has full access to her resourcefulness and creativity. And when women who are sexually bombarded retreat, they concede the game to the aggressor.

4

PUTTING UP WITH IT

At first it hurt. And then I said, Maybe this is the type of life I have to get used to. I was afraid to make remarks back because these were my customers, and maybe I'd lose them. And then where would I be?
— Dolly Wleklinski

Women often put up with harassment because they need the jobs and their chances of finding a workplace free of risk are minus three and counting. Setting those plain facts aside, they put up with harassment because they've been raised to believe that good women are forgiving and resourceful; it's part of their job description.

But Americans find the notion of being trapped so nearly toxic that when we hear a painful story about a woman being sexually abused by a superior at work, we instinctively say, "Get out!" And it is here that our native optimism, so mocked and envied by Europeans, plays us false. *So long as we persist in believing that a woman on her own can beat the system, we run the risk of being not only unkind but misguided. For the alternative to naïveté is not cynicism and despair, but organizing in a common cause.*

The five stories that follow illustrate what women put up with in a wide spectrum of workplaces — from taverns in the Midwest to the toniest restaurants in New York City, from skating rinks to state universities. This is the real world, where women have to work if they are to work at all. And for most, there *is* no alternative.

Claudette Haynes is a beautiful, forty-year-old New Yorker with masses of wavy black hair that falls just below her shoulders and an air of whimsical reserve that makes her an enigma. She might as easily pass for a Spanish countess as for an undercover agent, and Velázquez would have loved to paint her. I met her one Christmas Eve at her apartment in lower Manhattan, where she'd laid out a holiday spread of such delicacy and distinction that I knew there must be a story behind it.

Claudette, in fact, turned out to be a prize-winning chef, and several months later I climbed the stairs to her apartment as eagerly as a kid on a lark. The dominant note in her rooms is white, which forms a dramatic backdrop to her own dark coloring, and the sensuous textures of wood and fabric invite the touch. We slowly ate our way through a platter of pears served with thin shavings of Parmigiano Reggiano as she told me how she became who she is today.

In 1974, I was twenty-two and a half-assed photographer — which is to say I was a very good photographer, but not a professional. I grew up in New York and came back here after college. And in order to make the most money possible so I could study with the great photography teacher I had, I started working as a waitress in restaurants. I could make a lot more money doing that than working in an office.

So I bought myself a new skirt and went into every place I found between Fifty-ninth and Eighty-sixth Streets looking for a job. I figured I'd make more money on the East Side. And one of the places I walked into was a very famous French restaurant; let's call it Chez Nous. It's a great restaurant with a terrific chef, and I didn't even know what it was. I walked in and said, "Do you hire women?" All I saw were these old-fashioned waiters. (I wasn't a conscious or active feminist; I just wanted to know.)

They said, "Yes, yes, yes, go fill out an application." Two days later, they called and said, "We want to hire you." They and about four other restaurants had been taken to court by the American Civil Liberties Union on the grounds that they had no women in the restaurant, and the ACLU won. We're talking 1975, and I didn't even know this.

So I go, and I'm given this uniform they sorta pull together for me. This was a very old-fashioned, absolutely beautiful restaurant with greenhouses and flowers — and a wonderful wine list. It had very fancy French service; you boned Dover soles by the table and flamed ducks. But the kitchen was downstairs. Upstairs you'd see this very refined restaurant, and you'd sit and think, How lovely! And then you'd go through the kitchen door into another world — a world of men, working in a very hot environment, who'd never seen a woman down there. All the waiters were from Europe, and they'd *never* worked with a woman. I was totally unsuspecting; I just wanted to have a waitress job to make enough cash to support photography lessons and dark-rooms.

I was sophisticated largely because I grew up in Greenwich Village in a very affluent, highly educated, and artistic family. I knew how to handle street stuff and social situations very well. I'd just gotten out of college, I had a degree in liberal arts, I considered myself an artist. And I guess I had a lotta stars in my eyes, because I didn't really consider what I was walking into, I had no idea. But I figured I'd try it.

Well, what I was getting into was a union job, which meant working fourteen-hour shifts. You'd go down to the kitchen and put the food on a tray. It would be plated and covered. Or it would be on big copper platters full of food that would then be heated by the table. So I was lifting these trays that would sometimes hold twelve people's dinners. They were absolutely enormous, and we'd put out three hundred dinners a night. It was incredible, and I didn't really consider what I was doing to myself.

The waiters and most of the kitchen staff thought: Oh, girls! We're gonna have to do most of the work for 'em. I was *constantly* being grabbed. When I went down to the kitchen, I'd often have to elbow people who were grabbing me. I got lots of sexual comments; the mildest ones were jokes like, "If she walks by the hollandaise, it's gonna break if she has her period." They made endless gestures with phallic-looking foods and repeatedly asked questions about whether I was a lesbian. Wouldn't I go for one of the men? A waiter spent an entire lunch asking me to go out with him, and he kept telling me he had a big cake. (He meant cock: his English was not very good.)

One chef was French and very handsome — probably in his thirties. He'd expose himself to the women in the kitchen. You'd walk by, and he'd whip out his prick and laugh — and incite the other men. They'd all laugh! At one point he'd gotten an Easter lamb, and I left the kitchen when he was making gestures of buggering the lamb with these three guys around.

I learned to deal with it by proving, in two ways, that I was their pal so they'd do it to other women, and not to me. One way was by doing everything beautifully and lifting all this terrible stuff. I learned to do all the things captains did until finally I was promoted to captain. The other way — which was very detrimental to me — was that I got as foul and sharp and funny a tongue as any of them. They'd say something to me, and then I'd just outdo 'em.

I was defending my emotions and the soft parts in myself by cutting them off, and I realized that later. (While I was at Chez Nous, a teacher looked at my photographs and said, "Claudette, I think you need some therapy.") It protected me, but it also cut me off from pieces of myself because it was too dangerous to be that vulnerable. So I went to a really amazing woman therapist who has since become a friend. And I realized I was acting chronically and constantly in defense; it got so bad that when there was a man I liked who was perfectly civil, I'd even do it to him.

One night I woke up from a dream with this perfect knowing: Of course, I should cook! I quit my job a week later, I was so sure. So I was aware enough to get out eventually and move on to other things that I really wanted to be doing. Some people didn't.

Susan Stegall is a student in her mid-twenties at the University of Texas Law School, and when we sank into a lounge sofa in a corner room flooded with light, she told me how she got there. While growing up in the state that sets the national standard for machismo, she worked in places where pretty young girls are easy targets, and she'd been no exception. That morning she came as close as anyone can to clenching her teeth and talking at the same time, and her disgust reminded her why she was studying the law.

When I was fifteen, I worked at a skating rink. I was the person who did the concession stand; I sold popcorn and pizza, or whatever, and it was a great job because all my friends would come and skate there. So I could see 'em and hang out and get paid for it. My boss's wife was directly over me, and he ran the business part. And this disgusting man used to come into my little concession stand and put his hands all over me. I'd say, "Stop! Get away from me!" But he'd act like it was a joke and do it again. He'd make little comments about why I'd push him away. I felt like I couldn't tell his wife, who was my real boss, about it. She wouldn't believe me, or she'd blame me. So I didn't tell anybody.

This was Texas, where you always hear dirty jokes, so I felt like if I ever laughed at one of his, I was implicitly accepting any kind of behavior. If I wore tight pants, then if this guy touched me on the butt or put his hands on me, then I was inviting it. I felt like that even though I have a mother and an aunt who are very strong feminists. I felt, I'm trying to make myself look pretty when I come here, so I'm asking for it.

He was about three hundred pounds — huge, but shorter than me. And when there was a whole group of people, he'd tell really dirty jokes or make comments specifically about me. When I'd turn away to walk off, he'd make comments about my rear end. His wife was around when he'd make those comments, and she put up with it.

It was just terrible, and I hated it. But it was my job, and I wanted the money. I had fun there otherwise. One day I just didn't go to work. I didn't tell 'em I was quitting, I just didn't show up. Maybe I felt sorry for my boss: her husband was so gross.

From the ninth grade until I graduated from college, I worked as either an aerobics instructor or a waitress. And in those jobs, you almost always experience sexual harassment. In the aerobics place you wear leotards and tights. My boss would make comments all day long. He'd say, "Are you cold?" or "Are you turned on?" or "I just love it that you all have to wear leotards and tights!" You always had to put up with that kinda stuff from your boss.

Men who were managers were so bad! That's probably the only power they ever experienced over pretty young women, and they sure were gonna take advantage of it. At the Steak and Ale Restaurant, you had to wear a wench-type skirt and a very low-cut shirt, and put up with all this crap from businessmen coming in for lunch, asking you out, giving you tips because "your boobs look so nice." I wanted to work because I wanted to have my independence. But it seems like in every job, I ran into men being really gross.

The first time I had a paying job working in a family violence unit doing some legal work, I felt so much better about myself because I wasn't being sexually harassed. I was being empowered by all these strong women getting protective orders against their batterers. I was helping them get out of abusive relationships, so I felt vindicated by doing that.

In the latter half of my college career, I started getting involved with feminist organizations and reading books. My aunt is not only a domestic violence counselor, but an incest counselor. We talked all the time, and somehow it clicked. My class on women in politics came up to Austin and interviewed Ann Richards, and I felt empowered by that experience.

After starting the women's law journal with ten other women, I feel so much better about myself. I feel like I have an *identity* now. I wouldn't take the slightest kind of crap from a guy now. I know I don't have to, and I'm strong enough now. I'm empowered by getting a law degree and being in a professional school. I'm going to California after I graduate because I'm tired of the "good ole boy" attitude in Texas—that country-and-western stereotype. It's worse here than in California . . . I hope!

Laura Amendola is a college professor whose most recent book chronicles the changing roles of women in the United States. A woman with crinkly eyes, a gentle smile, and dark hair streaked with gray, she took me to a remarkable restaurant that sprinkled nasturtiums in its salad and squash flowers in its soups. Over a dessert called "Death by Chocolate," she told me her story.

In 1978, when she was about to turn forty, Laura went as an assistant professor to a large midwestern university. Married at nineteen, she is now divorced, and her youngest child had just started college. As the only woman in a department of nineteen, she became a "lightning rod" for sexual comments and innuendos.

I'm from California and had been living in the Bay Area, so it was culture shock. A California divorcée seemed an exotic species in this small midwestern town. When I went for my job interview, the acting chair said, "Is it true what they say about California girls?" I said, "I don't know about California girls in general, but about this California girl, absolutely not." I was very apprehensive, but I needed a job.

For years, I was the only woman in my department at a research-oriented university, so I was a lightning rod: I had a good degree, and I was good copy. The pattern was set early. When I went for my interview, there was a party for me, and a woman whose husband was very attractive and who was either drunk or a chronic alcoholic said, "I had to check out the competition. My husband raved about you." And then, through the years, she'd come up and say, "He's still faithful to me!"

So people were projecting their anxieties and fantasies on me from the beginning. The first year, one of my colleagues said, "Laura, you and I are going to get to be very close, but we have to be extremely careful not to fall in love." I thought to myself, Well, it might be a problem for you . . .

I was clearly an affirmative-action hire, even though I had better credentials than most of the men. (I had a couple of articles that had already been published.) But I'd married young and then been a suburban wife, and I hadn't done anything to challenge the status quo and attract this kind of attention. Being a lightning rod was a brand-new experience for me. I have a gregarious personality, and I'm used to having people act like they *like* me. So finding out that I was *loathed* by some of these guys who had their degrees from local universities — that was a shock! They resented the fact that I clearly aspired to a national reputation and people in the administration saw me as a fair-haired girl because I was hard-working and ambitious, and because I was going to national conferences and taking initiatives they weren't.

After I'd been there for two months, I went to a conference, and the first night I was hanging out at a bar. A colleague was sitting with several men at a table, and I went over to join them. We chatted for a while, and I should have left when I realized they were getting loaded. But I didn't, and they invited me to go to a topless bar. When I said no thank you, one of them said, "Dennison wants tits." He was the colleague: he'd been married several times and was the department Bluebeard.

There were two chief perpetrators who showed a real aggression and hostility and ugliness. Somebody wrote "Laura is a whore" on my office door, and Dennison, I think, was the one with the resentment who was erratic enough to do that. I'm reasonably convinced that it wasn't a student, because students don't think of you by your first name.

Another guy, Hurt Thomas, said all kinds of things to me without so much as a by your leave. He kept up a constant patter of sexual innuendo of a very ugly nature. One of the worst was a piece of paper someone put on my desk that said, "What are six things a man has that a woman doesn't? Two balls that don't bounce. A cock that doesn't crow. . . ." And the punch line was, "What are you smiling about? Your pussy won't catch mice." So I picked that up and went out into the hall and said loudly, "I don't have to take this!" Hurt had a nearby office, and he popped his head out and said, "Oh, I thought you'd think it was funny." I showed this to my department chair, and I showed him the "Laura is a whore" flyer. He was horrified.

Everybody knew there was a problem. But it was like these guys were rogue elephants. We voted Dennison tenure, in part because people were sure that if he was denied it, he'd have sued. And he was one of those people who has something *on* all kinds of people. At one point, I said, "Why doesn't someone go after this man? He's so crazy." But I was told that everybody was afraid that in any court case, he'd bring out the goods on everybody and go down in flames, so nobody wanted to fight this particular fight.

Hurt Thomas did things that were only directed at me. Once I'd made some self-deprecating comment about being clumsy, and he said, "You're lame where they can't put a cast." When I was getting ready to leave, I said I was eager to get home to California, and he said, "Let's face it, Laura, you've been on short rations the whole time you've been here." I'd have had to file a suit or a complaint, but I felt so isolated I didn't want to be the focus of a huge campus brouhaha.

The whole eight years, you never knew. As a friend put it later, my personal life was available for prurient speculation. And I found it totally intolerable. All the women were supportive, and my colleagues of goodwill were also upset about it. But none of us knew quite what to do. I didn't usually say anything back to these guys because I was always so staggered — and appalled. I also found out there were constant rumors, when anything good happened to me, that the dean was looking out for me for "special" reasons. A colleague told me on one occasion that he agreed I'd been treated unfairly on an evaluation, but he said that if he'd tried to defend me, it would have been said that he'd done it because he had a "special" interest in me.

One colleague went to the dean and said that after the way Thomas had treated me, he should never be department chair. The dean said he agreed, but I'd have to confirm the rumors about the way he'd behaved. So I did; I didn't initiate it, but I did confirm it. And I found out recently that he said I'd ruined his career.

At one point, I testified to the faculty council, which is like an academic senate, on behalf of a more stringent sex harassment policy at the university. The academic vice-president gave me a lot of credit for that. And the whole theme of my new book is how sexual innuendo is used to keep women in their place.

I stayed long enough to get tenure, and then a much younger man who was very attractive came into the department. He was very flirty, and everything about him was bad news. Getting involved with him would have meant parting company with every bit of decent judgment I'd tried to cultivate in myself, yet he flirted with me constantly. And in such a barren environment, it was hard *not* to feel attracted to him. One night we went out, and when I got back home, I said to myself, "By God, I'm only attracted to this character because of this bleak environment." The next morning at nine, I called the associate dean and said, "I'm leaving." I was sick and tired of being humiliated.

Sally Sharpless works at a nonprofit agency in Chapel Hill, North Carolina. She heard about my project through the women's center there, and when I saw her walking up a friend's drive in Raleigh, I'd have pegged her at eighteen. She has long, straight blonde hair and a face as open as Judy Garland's in *The Wizard of Oz*. She turned out to be in her middle thirties; she recruits and trains volunteers to provide peer counseling for women; and she is working now on a master's degree. We sat before a huge window absentmindedly watching chipmunks and squirrels scramble up and around the pine trees and a woodpecker making a nuisance of himself on a neighbor's roof. The distraction was welcome because Sally's story was hard to tell and hard to take.

When I was twenty-three, I began working at a fifteen-person insurance company as a receptionist and administrative assistant. The bosses were men, but all the underlings were women. I remember being told that one reason I was hired was that they liked the way I looked and the way I'd dressed for the interview. That seemed like a natural thing to me, and I was just grateful that I met the grade. Several men were more flirtatious than I'd experienced in the past, but again, I chalked that up to a friendly environment. I wasn't particularly straight-and-narrow anyway; I liked to go out dancing, and I was a party animal at the time.

An older man named Joe, who had a filthy mouth, used to make sardonic remarks when women were around — not so much telling blatantly dirty jokes as using innuendos and making puns about women's anatomy. Using words that were not in the dictionary at the time. He got great delight out of embarrassing the younger women in the office. I got the feeling he knew we felt unable to defend ourselves. He laughed a lot and thought he was just funny as could be. And of course the other men laughed, which just egged him on. Although he was married and had two children, he tried to date, but no one wanted to date him: he was certainly not physically attractive or intelligent or charming.

The first week I worked there, he grabbed me and hugged me and wouldn't let go. It was at a Christmas party in the office — and everybody gathered around and laughed. I felt uncomfortable, but I also felt it would be unwise to ask him to stop. If I didn't go along, I'd be labeled — not just as a prude, but not one of the team. And I felt that somehow I was to blame; maybe if I hadn't dressed as attractively, maybe I was too friendly. I started feeling dirty.

When he and I had to work late, he'd ask me to come home with him. He'd say his wife was out of town and invite me to dinner, and he tried to get me to drink liquor with him at the office. (He drank heavily after hours.) I remember feeling frightened. He was a very large man and could have overtaken me physically had he wanted to, but he chose instead to try to persuade me. As the weeks went on, he began suggesting that it would be in my best interests to go along. Frankly, I was repulsed by him — so repulsed that I found it difficult even to put him off in a congenial and appropriate way.

The older women liked him very much. He'd repair their cars and do things for them. He was an errand boy, if you will. One of the secretaries was his niece, so she was no help to me, and the others thought it was all very funny. He'd make the same remarks around other women, but most of them were married and felt less threatened. We were all in one big open area — there were no cubicles — and everybody could see what was going on. No one intervened or expressed disapproval; quite the contrary, they were egging him on. So I felt very uncomfortable.

I'd have to go back to the stockroom from time to time to get supplies. And every time I walked back there, Joe would come back, too, and he'd get very close and start mumbling things in my ear. I think he was trying to sound incoherent so I'd ask, "What did you say?" I kept moving farther and farther away. And then he started putting his hands on my shoulders and saying, "Come here, I want some." Later he started putting his hands around my breasts.

It got to the point that every time I'd go to the supply room, he'd do that. I'd push him away and say, "Just stop it, Joe!" and walk out and feel humiliated because he'd think it was funny. The other men thought it was funny, too, and after a few weeks, I'd finally had enough. I'd try to go get supplies when Joe had gone out to lunch, but that wasn't always possible.

So one time, when Joe and I were in the supply room and he put his hands around my breasts again and started fondling me, I screamed as loud as I could. I'd decided I'd do that as if I were startled, though by then I was pretty desensitized. People ran back to the supply room and Joe's face was as red as a beet and he kinda shuffled out. Everyone knew why I'd screamed, and no one said a word. But he never did it again.

One night my roommate and I were out at a club, and my manager and a friend of his happened to be there, too. They came to our table and asked if they could join us. I didn't want them to, but I didn't know how to tell him no: he was my boss. So they sat down and joined us. And then Terry said, "My friend wants to take you to a hotel tonight, and I suggest that you go with him. It's okay, I won't tell anybody. Why don't you just go back with him and have a drink? It'll just be our secret."

I didn't particularly care for the friend, but I was afraid that if I didn't, I wouldn't have a job. So I said, "Well, Terry, I'm really not interested in spending the night with your friend or anyone else. But if he wants to go for a drink at the bar, I'll do that." So I did, and the friend of course asked me to spend the night. I said no, and he said, "I won't tell Terry." But I refused, fearing all along that I'd lose my job.

The next day Terry said, "What happened?" I told him, "Nothing," and he didn't believe me. He said, "You can tell me! I won't tell anyone." Again, I said, "Nothing happened!" He gave me the feeling that if he ever wanted to set me up with a friend again, I'd better comply. I remember feeling pressured to be almost a concubine.

When I began, I was incredibly naive — I've always looked very young for my age — and I think they enjoyed taking advantage of that. It was part of the fun. Because it was very difficult for me to behave as if I was unaffected, they liked pushing the limits, and I think they felt free to do it because they were supporting each other. There was no retribution. In retrospect, I'd almost rather they'd lined up and gang-raped me, because the stress of going to work each day was just mounting.

Part of what kept me there was the potential for a good career, because there was free training and the benefits were quite good. Also, these men were rather well known in the community, and I was quite honestly fearful that they'd try to keep me from getting another job or moving up. And my goal was making this my last secretarial job. I still have nightmares about the four years I worked there.

This experience has strongly affected my relationships with men because now I tend to avoid commitment. I get very, very angry about jokes and comments directed against women, and I got furious about the way they were trying to trap Anita Hill. Watching the hearings brought up all the old feelings again. The men were in power in that courtroom, and they were going to protect one another. She didn't stand a chance because they were treating what happened to her as a joke. I wanted to jump through that television screen when they kept asking why she remained silent. It could've ruined her whole career to speak. She had to choose, but what choice did she have?

I met Dolly Wleklinski at her daughter's home in Bloomington, Indiana, where she now lives. She'd recently moved from Hammond, a steel-workers' town where she ran a tavern for more than a quarter of a century, and she felt a little disoriented. The tavern was a kind of neighborhood institution, but Dolly, who is close to seventy and struck me as a very sweet Polish lady, was insulted from time to time in ways that still make her cry.

In 1968, when I was about forty-five, I was in a state of remorse because my husband had just passed away. We'd had this tavern since 1953 because he'd always wanted one, and we ran it together, except that I was always home taking care of our children. His death was sudden, and I had three children to raise who were seventeen, fifteen, and thirteen. So the only thing I knew was to take over the tavern. I promised my children that I'd give it a year and if it didn't go, I'd give it up. I said, "We're gonna have to stick together and you're gonna have to help me."

My husband's customers were friendly, neighborhood people, and they treated me with respect. They were real good to me. But maybe 25 percent came to harass me when I was behind the bar. When new people came, little innuendoes about sexual stuff started.

I wasn't exactly a holy person. I was attractive, I think, and I had a nice figure. I dressed because I wanted to look nice, and I always had my hair well done. They'd notice if there was one little mistake. "Oh, your hair isn't quite right!" Or "Who rumpled you up last night?" Or "Your husband's been dead a while now. Don't you need some?" I didn't know how to answer. I was afraid to make remarks back because these were my customers and maybe I'd lose them. And then where would I be?

So I did grin and bear it. The days wore on, and the weeks wore on. And the good people kinda made up for the bad people. I didn't like any swearing, and if anyone said something, I'd cut 'em right off and say, "That's not allowed in here. I'm sorry, but I'm a woman and I can't take that kinda thing." They respected me for that. I won that kind of argument, but they kept making those sexual remarks as easily as falling off a log.

Some of those remarks you always remember. One guy got pretty friendly by comin' in a lot, and then he said, "You know, if they're bigger than a grapefruit, just put 'em back." And I knew what he was referring to. Later he said, "If it's more than a mouthful, that's not good, either." I could feel myself blushing and getting embarrassed, and not knowing what to say. The men sitting around thought it was all funny. To me it wasn't funny. But I told myself I had to stick it out.

I mostly talked to my daughters about this, and a good friend across the street who worked in Youngstown. She said it happened at their workplace, too. She'd say, "But what can we do?" And I'd say, "I guess we just have to take it."

I survived ten years of it, but the harassment didn't stop. They seemed to think I was there as a specimen for them to do that to. And I wasn't supposed to act like I was annoyed because they were macho. I can't say I developed a hatred of men, but every time I approach one now, I've got a shield in front to protect myself. I learned how to fight for myself! I've gotten very tough and I don't think I'm sorry.

There was a guy named Jack who'd come in a lot and got to be a good customer. One night I had to close up at two o'clock, and after I got into the garage, a car pulled up and it was Jack. He'd had several beers, so I knew he wasn't completely clear-minded. He said, "Dolly, I left my wallet at the tavern and I need it for work tomorrow." I said, "Jack, is it that important?" He said, "Yeah, I need it." So I said, "Okay, follow me."

We got inside the tavern, and he grabbed me by the arm. He said, "I'm gonna rape you." I thought it was a joke. I said, "Jack, you're not talking sensibly." He said, "I'm gonna rape you." And I thought, Wow, what am I gonna do now? Instead of getting mad or showing that I was afraid, I thought maybe I'd better just talk to him. I told him that if the other customers heard about it, they'd really get on his case. Finally he released me, and I said, "Now Jack, don't you think you've just had too many beers? You don't know what you're talking about." I was just trying to get out of there. I ran as fast as I could, I was so scared. I never did that again, and I never saw Jack after that.

When I heard about that gang rape in Boston, I thought, My God, when a whole bunch were here and I was tending bar alone, anything could've happened. But it was probably too early; my husband passed away in 1968, and things like that weren't happening then.

For the most part, these women stayed in jobs where men treated them shabbily — not because the women were perverse, weak, or wanting in spirit, but because these seemed the best or the right jobs for them. Dolly was widowed and had three children to raise, and she inherited the tavern from her husband. Laura was an older Ph.D. graduate in a tight job market. Claudette needed the money to finance her true work as an artist.

Sally stayed too long in a bruising office situation, but Susan put in roughly the same time in a series of restaurants, gyms, and clubs. Both had the kinds of jobs the young are likely to get, and both tell of the spiritual pounding they took in places where men felt called upon to compliment their "tits" or feel them up.

When the women were in jobs where women are traditionally expected to be, men were boorish and cruel. As they worked their way into territory that is traditionally male, men were boorish and cruel. And the men behaved the same way whether the women were stubborn, self-critical, or submissive. So to analyze what the women did as a way of looking for answers is to misdirect one's time and spirit.

To be sure, fortitude is an excellent thing, but these stories suggest that the virtues of putting up with a bad situation are likely to be overrated. Women who were brought up to look always on the bright side have too often taken on psychic burdens that merely drained them and that they'd eventually have to analyze and shake. For it is one thing to endure the slings and arrows of outrageous fortune, but quite another to suffer adolescent behavior from grown men. Fate and fatuousness don't weigh equally in the scheme of things.

Claudette looked on her new job as a challenge. "I'm the kind of person," she observed wryly, "who'd say, 'I'll show them!'" Years later she realized that she'd been emotionally crippled. Despite being raised by feminists, Susan blamed herself, as women have been programmed to do. Years later she discovered that instead of putting up with it, she could join with other women to change it.

More often than not, in fact, putting up with it turns out to have meant squandering precious energies that could never be recovered. For most of these women, the shock has never wholly passed, and the scars have proved lasting. The experience of being treated like an object left Laura permanently incredulous: "Sexual harassment was so *alien* to me. I didn't *not* believe it, but I didn't fully believe it, either." Putting up with it meant increasing the chasm of misunderstanding between the sexes, and some of these women grew frankly hostile to men.

5

FALLING INTO THE TRAP

I wanted to be part of a social network where people helped each other out, and I needed links with the people I worked with. But it was very clear that he wanted a sexual relationship. And whatever my moralizing, whatever I was feeling, at some point he got what he was looking for.

— Tessa Vendler

The trap many women fall into is the belief that giving themselves sexually makes them safer. Behind the romantic folderol attached to sex lies the conviction that it is finally what a man wants and needs from a woman, and that when she has allowed herself to be the most vulnerable, he will protect her. In this way, sex becomes the most precious thing a woman has and her ultimate weapon in a precarious world. And if she gives her best treasure, no woman is likely to believe she has thereby put her neck on the block. Quite the contrary: she thinks she's made a pact with the king, the hangman, and the priest to spare her.

Sometimes she *is* safer. In such matters, we have no way to measure how many women who have kept their jobs or managed to advance might have lost them or stagnated if they hadn't slept with a boss. But when the other side fails to keep its part of the unspoken bargain, and a woman is unceremoniously dumped, many will find themselves awash in bitterness, and those who've been entirely willing participants may want to forget that they got themselves into it. In the midst of one woman's story, I thought, This isn't sexual harassment. This is an affair she hoped would get her out of a bad marriage. But the fact is that no matter who flirts first, it is women who ordinarily pay the heavier price.

Office romances are common, and now and again, women start them. The thrill of sex aside, they've been bred to *feel* better when they're connected to a man. And so when men and women are thrown together at work — when the men as usual are running the show and life is dull or unpromising otherwise — the women sometimes go after them. Abigail McDowell, who told a story of fighting off her bosses, recalled having lunch with a well-known woman who burst suddenly into tears. "She started telling me about this young woman who was the new mistress of a movie director. This girl had a huge diamond, and my friend said, 'I've worked so hard all my life to get where I am. All she did was sleep with him, and now she's driving around town in a chauffeured limousine. It's not fair.'"

The dream of being rescued by a sensationally rich guy who'll throw jewels at their feet has inspired multitudes of women, whether or not they're poor, in the same way the dream of being a basketball superstar inspires kids in the ghetto. But when the romance sours, as it almost always does, and the pathos of her Prince Charming fantasy is plain, a young woman who is left with no skills, no job, and no income is in big trouble.

More often than not, it is the men in an office who go after the women. The most self-respecting woman takes it for granted that the attention is offered because she is a good and interesting person — not merely because a man wants sex. Others often feel bewildered by the notice and then pressured. They believe that their job depends on their boss's goodwill, and they need the work and the money. When they give in and sleep with their boss — or some other, relatively powerful male colleague — the women are usually the losers. The stories that follow belong to women who learned that lesson the hard way, and the common note was anguish.

Janet Turner is a soft-spoken African-American woman with hazel eyes and long chestnut hair, and halfway through her story, she dropped her head into her hands and wept. We were sitting on my sofa, and the part of me that still insists that people should get what they deserve was clamorous with indignation. Janet is beautiful, gifted, and kind. Her friends are devoted. She does important work that is highly valued. How, then, do we come to terms with so many years of pain?

After Tony and I were separated, I was hired by a congressman and his administrative assistant. The AA was sort of attractive, though I wasn't attracted to him, and both of them obviously had power over me. After I'd been on the job maybe six months, the AA suggested that we have dinner, and I said, "Fine." After dinner, he suggested that I go to his apartment, and I went. I knew what I was doing, but I went and we had sex. This happened about five other times, and it was so cold; it was fornicating. I never had sex like that before or since, but I felt like I had to do it. He hadn't ever said, "If you don't do this, I'm going to fire you," or "You won't get your salary increase." He didn't threaten, but something in me said, "I've got to do what this man says." I had no respect for myself for doing that.

One day the congressman and I were walking down a hallway. We came to the cracked door of a broom closet, and he grabbed me and pulled me into the closet and pressed me against the wall and started kissing me. I got out of there and walked quickly away, and I never said anything about it to anyone, including him. I pretended it hadn't happened. I didn't talk about it for years.

At the time I felt much worse about what was going on with his staff person. But I was taking care of three people — my two children and myself — and my job was really important; I couldn't afford to go without a week's pay. I didn't have anybody to turn to for money. My ex-husband was not helpful; my father was dead. So I had the whole burden of our economic situation.

I had such low self-esteem! I felt men had a right, and there must be something I was lacking that justified the treatment I got. It took me so long to realize that I was a good woman! I was always so surprised when anyone thought well of me. And then I'd think they must see things that aren't there.

So I went around with this baggage that led me to be a victim, in some ways, of men. Elements of that lasted until very recently. So many of the men I got involved with made me think I just had to accept the realities of life: I had to accept the lower status of women, and of black women, and of me. In that order.

At fifty-one, Meredith Curry has had two highly successful careers — one in television production and the other in government service. She is now the president of her organization and on the verge of taking on an even more prestigious job. Everything about her underscores the professional woman. As we sat in her Chicago offices, Meredith was so immaculately groomed and tailored that I knew exactly what the lining and seams of her soft gray wool suit would look like. But as she told me stories she had never told before, she cried over humiliations she still felt decades later.

I knew *instantly* that Anita Hill was telling the truth. It took me back to a time and place when I thought it was maybe just me. I thought it was my fault, or maybe I was just stupid or naive. I wouldn't have *dreamed* of telling somebody. We didn't have a name for it, and besides, I'm by nature a discreet person, so I wouldn't have told even my roommate or a girlfriend. For decades, this was entirely in the back of my experience and my mind.

I came to Chicago at twenty-one as what I thought was a worldly young woman. I'm a graduate of one of the Seven Sisters colleges. I'd traveled and lived for a year overseas. I came here full of energy and hope and aspiration with what I thought was a pretty sophisticated approach to the world and people.

I'd arrived as a virgin, though I'd had lots of boyfriends. It was the middle-to-late sixties, and things were changing. I was single, I was on my own, I was new to Chicago. I had a college degree and an independent spirit. Even before the women's movement, I knew I wanted to find my work and make my place. I had lots of dreams and hopes, and it was all very exciting.

I worked my way up, learning as I went. I shared an apartment with another girl for a while, and then I had my own. I went out probably four or five nights a week with men from different fields. And at that time, sexual harassment was the way of the world; for men it was normal. I don't know if they talked about it, but I was a target. I was no great beauty, but I was lively and intelligent and eager, and I suppose that did it. During those first five or six years, I was easy prey, though I only know that in retrospect.

These situations always took the form of a kind of seduction over dinner: "You're a bright young woman! Let's talk about your work. Where are you going? What would you like to do?" The fact that they could affect my progress or promotion was never mentioned; it was never so gross as that. The flirtations were so frequent I have to assume that at least in the production and entertainment industry, that was the norm.

It always started with "Let's have lunch," and then "We should continue this conversation. Let's talk at dinner on Friday. . . ." At some point it became

"When can I see you?" It's humiliating to remember, even though it was always couched in work terms. I was probably flattered by the attention, and I actually believed they were interested in my potential for learning and growing and doing good work. In one job I cared about, where I thought I had a good future, the seduction ran its course—and then ended. I was dropped like a hot potato! Suddenly there was no additional interest in my mind or my future. I still didn't have the language, but something was beginning to dawn on me.

My younger sister, whom I loved very much, had a breakdown and was hospitalized, and I decided to get some therapy. I thought it would help me keep my balance, understand what was happening to her, and at the same time get a grip on my own life. A therapist was recommended through a friend of a friend, and I went to talk all this through once or twice a week for about six months. During this time, my sister committed suicide, and this was a profound blow to me. Then one night the therapist invited me to stay after one of the sessions to have a drink, *and he seduced me.* We ended up having sex probably five or six times, and I continued to pay for my sessions for another six or seven weeks. But finally I started saying to myself, I don't think this is the way it's supposed to work. I cut it off, and it was entirely unresolved—both the therapy and that situation. I bounced back and life went on. (I'm rather strong and I've come to terms with it.) But it's left some unresolved things in the back of my mind. This goes back twenty-five years, but I remember it as if it were yesterday.

Until this moment, I've never spoken of these things because I am still ashamed of them. I am bearing witness now: this did happen—and not just to young women who were utterly stupid and without resources. It happened to thousands, maybe millions of us. I'm not extraordinary. I'm not incredibly rich or beautiful. On the other hand, I'm not powerless or uneducated. I was somewhere in the middle of that; *I was a regular person.* The fact that it happened to me indicates that it must have been happening to a lot of people.

Now I'm protected by rank and power, so that sort of thing doesn't happen to me anymore. When it happens to my daughter, I hope she's empowered with an understanding of what's going on and by having the language with which to respond. Whether she says yes or no would be a matter of conscious choice, but at twenty-two and twenty-six, I didn't have that choice.

Dr. Pamela Cutrer has M.D. and Ph.D. degrees from two of the most distinguished universities in the country and works in the top administration of a federal agency. We met by chance at a reception in a downtown hotel near the tray piled with cheese and fruit, and as we

stood there nibbling, I told her about my book. (If you are truly obsessed, you approach strangers on the street, and I've done that, too.)
When I spotted the giveaway click in her eyes, I asked if she'd like to
tell me her story. Two weeks later we were facing each other across my
coffee table.

She is a sassy woman: at a spectacle of the human comedy where
the egos are more than usually inflated, her needle would deftly prick
all the balloons. Though she looks much younger and actually bounces
as she speaks, she had just turned fifty-five, and the story she told is
apparently the only one in her past that still has the power to upset and
shame her — and to make her angry.

I liked to flirt a lot. I had three younger brothers, and I raised my family because
my mother was quite ill. So I grew up in an all-male world with more male
than female friends. I was very late in developing: I was over fifteen when I
went through puberty and twenty-one when I had sex for the first time. So
for me, sex was a sport. It had no emotional weight, for the most part. I could
love a man and not have sex with him, or have sex with a guy and have no
emotional attachment.

It started in 1973, when I was thirty-five. I was an assistant professor at
a posh medical school when this happened. I'd just graduated from my residency
— I'm extraordinarily credentialed — but I'm on the fringes of my community
in that I test the limits. I was the only woman in my profession as a resident
and on the faculty.

At the time, I was in my second marriage, and my husband and I had
agreed to stay married in order to have children. Although we'd been married
long enough that there was no overwhelming intensity of affection, there was
an intensity of consideration. We had what might be called a sixties marriage,
in that it was open. Basically the agreement was that if either of us found sexual
satisfaction somewhere else, it was probably acceptable but we didn't bring it
home. And that had worked.

I'd been married once before and fallen in love with another student. I'd
broken up my marriage, but by 1973, I thought it was probably stupid to break
up marriages over that. So when I contracted for the second marriage, that
was part of the bargain; I was allowed to be on my own. In fact, at that point
I had a very good lover who had helped train me. He was a mentor/lover who
was one of the few people who had faith in me. He took an interest long
before we became lovers — he was lousy as a sex partner, actually — but the

excitement of being with him and his training me was very important in those days. I had no trouble leaving him when I finished my education. I'd say I loved him, but I wasn't bound by him. He knew I'd go on to be actually better than he. (I still have sex with him once in a while, and he's still a lousy lover.) But he's a nice man, and if I could ever do anything to help him, I would.

In 1973, I was with him at a convention in Barbados, and we were having a good time. (I was frisky in those days. I still am, actually.) And a man was there who'd been at the university with me — I'd thought he was an asshole. But at that conference we were flirting, and he somehow propositioned me on the dance floor. So I accepted, which was pretty standard for me at that point, and I had sex with him there. He was well-known in our field, and my medical school had just started to look for a new chairman. He seemed quite a bright, aggressive person. And I knew he'd get the chairmanship. So whether my motivation for developing an affair with him was based on just my sexual friskiness or on the fact that I thought I'd have an advantage in a very cutthroat system, I can't really tell. I'm ambitious enough that if I'd thought that sex would get me anywhere, I'd probably have done it.

Sex can be enjoyable, but you can't share it with people unless you have something in common. And he and I certainly had a lot in common. He provided me with some stimulation, and I did the same for him. He then *did* come to my university; the affair continued; and people couldn't figure out what was going on. (Some must have assumed we were having an affair.) I think our affair continued on a consensual basis until I was about six months pregnant. That's when it became clear that I was not going to get my raise unless I continued to have sex with him. I was pregnant and showing, and I remember sitting in his office and crying. That was the turning point between the sex being consensual and forced. We were negotiating the raise, and I don't remember the words — only the emotion.

I could quit, but how can a woman who's six months pregnant get another job? There's no way to do that if you want to be a professor, and I was not willing to give it up at that point. We had sex and I got the raise.

After that, I would never have intercourse with him unless it was literally in the darkroom — the photographic room, where it was pitch dark. And I'm a person who likes sex in the light. I don't like sex from the back, and I would never allow him to have sex with me again except from the back. I'd allow him to have intercourse and then stop. And since fortunately he's a premature ejaculator it didn't take long.

That continued for two and a half or three years — until the birth of my second child. At which point, I was able to schedule my life so that I never interacted with him again. Even though he was my chairman, I was able to avoid him. I changed my schedule; I parked in a different parking lot; I'm not sure what all the mechanisms were, but I stopped seeing him. There are so few things from those three years I can concretely remember. I remember crying in his office. I remember leaning over a stool in the darkroom and avoiding him after the birth of my second child — and then fighting with him a year or so after that.

A lot of my feeling went out of those three years. I could probably be hypnotized to remember, but I'm not sure there's much point. I know I was having intercourse with him probably once a week, or every other week. That's maybe a hundred and fifty times, give or take fifty. Hopefully, take fifty.

The year I backed off, he started an affair with his next-door neighbor. Eventually his wife found out and dumped him, and he married the other woman. It got back to him that I'd been at a conference and confirmed the rumor of his affair, and he came into my office and said he was going to destroy my career because I'd been tattling on him.

He'd already started to be very mean. Meetings that I should have been attending, he let men attend. He tried to give my work to people who hadn't done their own. But I was too wiped out to pay attention. Finally I had three small children, I was working very hard, and I was exhausted all the time.

Our affair had stayed fairly quiet for several reasons. Number one, I didn't want anyone to know because I was ashamed of it. I wasn't in love with the man, I couldn't stand him, it was as near as I could get to not having sex. Then he promoted the guy who'd started the rumor at the conference and told me he'd ruin my career. That's when I decided I was out of there. I was so angry I decided that if he denied me tenure, I'd take the sexual harassment to court, even if it destroyed me. So I consulted a lawyer, who gave me some advice. I got a voice-activated tape recorder and worked it into my clothes. And I went in to see him. I hadn't had sex with him in a number of years, and he told me I wasn't good enough for tenure.

I think he underestimated me a phenomenal amount. He told the faculty that I'd agreed to go on the clinical track and not get tenure. On the tape it's very clear that I didn't agree to it, that it was under duress, and that I was leaving as a result.

I didn't know God was about to give me a spectacular job, but the day after he told me I wasn't good enough for tenure, I got a job that controls all his patents! I took it, and I've been very careful. If he calls me, I make sure somebody else is on the line. He now tells everybody how wonderful I am and licks my ass. If I want something, I write the letter and he signs it. He's the only guy I absolutely hate. I'll stab him in the back whenever I can.

The whole thing forced me to move my family from one coast to the other. And some days when I think about what I gave up, I want to kill him. It was only after Anita Hill that I could tell my husband that it was because of sexual pressure that I left. Anita Hill did us all a favor. She made it legitimate to say, "Seven years ago this happened to me . . ."

I don't like this part of my life. It's a part that I feel was disgusting, when I was not in control. When you talk about things like that, you're not a happy camper and you're likely to take it out on people. Telling your shrink isn't enough, but you can't tell other people because it makes you look like a scumbag.

I'm a person who thinks sex is a bodily function like everything else. Even though I'm having hot flashes, I can still get myself propositioned. Now I proposition men. So to me sex is still an ongoing thing, and now the fun has come back into it. It's only for that three-year period that sex was a burden..

Since I can't get involved with men in my field in this decade of ethics, I'm learning a lot about all kinds of things I never learned before. If it's good sex, you probably want to do it again. So you gotta talk to 'em. Christ, men want to be talked to, not just fucked. It's really awful. Now I can get along with men who run the gamut from ex-cops to the most radical social activists. I don't care as long as they screw well. I don't lie to myself about what I'm really after.

Tessa Vendler is a thirty-year-old political scientist who was teaching at a fine university on a one-year contract when we met. A group of women had gathered at a brown bag lunch to hear me talk about the Hill/Thomas hearings and the book that was emerging from it, and I issued a general invitation for people to come to the women's center that afternoon and tell me their stories. Tessa came.

Nevertheless, she seemed painfully reticent. Her large, gray-lavender eyes spoke as tellingly as her soft voice while she explained that her father is a physician, her background is privileged, and she considered herself sheltered. Originally from Missouri, she had gone first to an all-girls private school and then to a small progressive college in the Northeast. After a year, she'd transferred to a midwestern university, where she is getting a Ph.D. Two-thirds of the way through her story, she began sobbing uncontrollably.

When I was eighteen, I was extremely naive. I'd had no sexual encounters, and so I was probably unprepared to handle anything sexual. I was having trouble at my college because I saw more experimentation than I'd ever seen before. But the student/teacher ratio was so good you got to talk to your teachers and have wine and cheese with them, and so it excited me.

Near the end of one course, my professor asked two of us students to go out to dinner, and the other woman ended up not being able to go. I remember not being thrilled that it would just be him and me, but I don't know if it occurred to me to back out. I must have thought, What an opportunity! This sort of thing was one of the reasons you went there. I know I thought, Do you want to be paranoid? So I ended up going.

The dinner was good. There was this discussion of ideas and I was getting more comfortable. And then I remember this comment: "Tell me, Tessa, do you enjoy making love?" I was immobilized; the conversation had gone from light to dark. I don't think I'd have been able to handle that from a peer, much less an older faculty member. I felt such shock and dismay that I didn't know how to respond, but I remember saying, "I never have . . ." His reaction was sort of, Isn't she cute! And I remember thinking, I don't want to be cute. I wanted to be sophisticated, I wanted to be able to talk intelligently.

I don't remember whether I was graceful in getting out of it. I had my own car, so there was no transportation problem. But I was afraid to tell anyone, thinking I'd get this belittling reaction. I felt this tremendous blame, like I didn't quite fit in with these open-minded, cerebral people who were going to experiment. I was shy, and I didn't want more responses like "Isn't she cute!" or "Don't you think it's time to grow up and move on? . . ."

It was a double bind. I felt this guilt for being there, for having stupidly put myself in this situation. But on the other hand, *I was so shocked.* I don't think I told people for a long, long time afterwards, and I didn't go back to his class. There were two or three weeks left, and so I handed in whatever I had to, and I passed. But I didn't want to go back to find out if I could have done better.

I transferred from this small college to a big university. And for the rest of my undergraduate career, I didn't maintain any relationship with my professors. I walked into class, I walked out of class. The only thing a professor would have known about me was my work, and the only thing he could've based a recommendation on was a grade. For the most part, I put blinders on; I didn't want to know! So I maintained a sheltered life.

I graduated with my master's degree and, when I was twenty-four, took a semester off to work on a political campaign. I was the youngest campaign manager in the city who was running a significant race, and I was dealing with people a lot older than me. Some social events involve drinking, some involve eating, you're working from eight in the morning until eleven at night. *And I was not going to pay the price of **not** knowing people. I had to be prepared for any situation. I told myself, You can't hide through life,* and rationalized that my college experience was isolated — it wasn't the kind of thing I'd have to deal with.

My guy won. I took a job with the administration, and I wanted to maintain contacts with all those campaign people. I knew they socialized, and I'd felt left out both because I was younger and because I was a woman. My whole undergraduate education had handicapped me because I wouldn't get involved. Then I did something with my coworkers over a weekend, and the only sense of impropriety came from a couple of compliments like "How pretty your eyes are!" And since nothing unpleasant happened, I started thinking, This is safe, this is better.

My colleagues would go to Chamber of Commerce lunches, and afterwards, they'd go out drinking. So what was I supposed to do? Go home? Something kept telling me, Just do everything to forget your vulnerabilities. Then I made a casual bet with a cabinet-level person that involved something vaguely sexual in nature. I lost that bet, and in the car I said, "Oh, you were just kidding," and he said he wasn't! *Suddenly, somewhere, the terms of discourse had just changed. I don't know what happened. Somehow he implied that I wasn't competent: he was impugning my work and my life, as though I was a little girl.* I thought, Wait a minute! I happen to be a woman who's accomplished quite a bit. . . .

He obviously expected me to go to bed with him. He took me to his house even though I said, "I don't really want to go." He said, "I won't do anything." I said, "I just don't want to go. . . ." I was feeling *way* in over my head, and the sense that I couldn't handle it made me feel worse and worse. There was more at stake here than just saying no, but that night I was able to go home. Still, he'd convinced me that *he* was the norm, and *I* was strange.

All kinds of things were going through my mind: Wasn't I smart? What have I done? I still wanted to be part of a social network where people helped each other out, and I needed links with the people I worked with. But his whole tone changed; there was no more conversation, and it was very clear that he wanted a sexual relationship. And whatever my moralizing, whatever I was feeling, at some point he got what he was looking for. . . .

I don't know how it happened! I kept saying that it was wrong, and I told him how distraught I was — *I said it!* But maybe I was sick of being this naive little girl and maybe I felt it would make me deal much better. But I knew the second I did it that it was wrong. I needed out. And getting out of it was even harder.

I went on vacation afterwards with my family, and I couldn't eat. I couldn't sleep. It was that act that I couldn't explain. I'd never done anything like that. I'd had one sexual relationship in my life, a three-year relationship. If you'd told anyone who knew me, they wouldn't have believed it.

I knew I'd let my sense that I had to overcome this handicap betray me! I couldn't tell anyone because I didn't want to admit it had happened. But I couldn't live with myself.

Now I've reverted to the old mode. I'm spending a great deal of time *not* letting myself get into those situations. I'm in a male environment — teaching — and I do *not* ask anyone to go to lunch. If there's a group I may go along, but I do *not* put myself in a situation where there's a sole person. I will avoid — at the expense of losing out on community life — any chance of repeating that mistake. I'll make *any* professional sacrifices I have to. I still talk myself into believing that it didn't happen. And my biggest fear in talking to you was of not being able to say it didn't happen any more. I don't see the torture ending. . . .

All these women were coerced, though Pamela's affair began as a consensual arrangement and Meredith's seduction was exquisitely subtle. Both Tessa, whose imagination was essentially virginal, and Pamela, who is sexually sophisticated and game, were overpowered. In most instances, work was at stake, as well as money to live on.

The men were predators, fundamentally indifferent to the feelings or even the personhood of the women they coerced. Such indifference may well be a function of pure narcissism, and they may have taken it for granted that the women would be grateful. On the other hand, perhaps the only way they could *feel* their power was to impose it on a woman. Like Zampano in *La Strada*, bullying a woman made them feel like a man.

But a definition of "manliness" for which someone else must pay so dearly has outlived its evolutionary purpose. To be used like an object in the most intimate and intensely personal experience that human beings can engage in is to suffer emotional damage that is bound to linger. (A mother nursing her child is the nearest approximation in intimacy that I know, and the tenderness of that exchange stands in stark contrast to the feelings the women describe above.)

In these women, erotic energy was contaminated; their sexuality was used to betray them in some fundamental way, and in their hurt and anguish, they sealed off their feelings and turned that energy against themselves. All of them spoke of emotional deadness at the core and they became inaccessible even to themselves.

Meredith hopes that her daughter will be better equipped than she was to deal with sexual invitations from men at work, since the term "sexual harassment" gives a focus and clarity that wasn't available to her twenty-five years ago. The term itself, in effect, says, This is aggression, and since the players don't have equal power, it isn't fair. With this understanding, women today can see that what earlier generations took to be caring is more likely to be mere self-indulgence, and they can talk more openly with each other in ways that may help them keep their balance.

Pamela's experience with her first mentor/lover shows that sexual relations between women and men with grossly disparate power need not be exploitive; hers was tender, exciting, and productive. But I venture to imagine that it is the exception rather than the rule. For no matter how many naked people we see now on the screen — and no matter how exhaustively people talk and write about sex — it remains a stunningly powerful, often mysterious force. And it is intertwined so fundamentally with each person's sense of self that trifling with it can be profoundly dangerous.

Sexual relations by themselves are fraught enough without adding the complications of office politics, and the commonsensical approach would be to avoid sexual entanglements with coworkers altogether. The sense of exquisitely heightened life may linger but won't last, and when it goes, there is the proverbial devil to pay. Colleagues will be suspicious and often angry, so lines of communication may be tangled; time will have been dissipated in cover-ups; inordinate amounts of energy will have gone for naught; and the woman's sense of self-esteem may well be mangled.

For the self-hatred of the woman who has given recklessly of herself, merely to be used and abandoned, can be poisonous. Tessa was very nearly crippled by shame; Meredith and Janet were humbled; and even Pamela, who is as feisty and self-confident as they come, was afflicted.

Better, I would think, to take "man" in the following lines to apply even more truly to "woman," and resolve, with A. E. Housman:

Therefore, since the world has still
Much good, but much less good than ill,
And while the sun and moon endure
Luck's a chance, but trouble's sure,
I'd face it as a wise man would,
And train for ill and not for good.
                    (A Shropshire Lad)

6

EXTORTION

He told me I had to have sex with him willingly, and I said that was not in our contract. My job was to clean his house in return for room and board. But he told me he had paid for my trip, and I couldn't oppose anything he would ask me to do.

— Maria

As you move down the class scale and see people living more nearly at the economic edge, you're likely to find women in vastly increasing numbers whom predatory men spot as handy targets and easy lays. Though psychological vulnerability cuts across class lines, its concrete effects vary among the classes, with poor women, for instance, more likely to resort to prostitution. (In fact, some think that putting out for money is a lot easier than waiting tables for ten hours at a stretch or working on assembly lines or construction projects with guys who hate their guts for invading their territory.)

Abusive men feast on women who have no money, little education, few institutional supports, and a bleak future, and those who don't speak English are perhaps the most at risk. The Church helps sometimes. A tightly knit family with protective brothers or uncles can provide something of a shield. A handful of neighborhood institutions may offer shelter or solace and, on occasion, some clothing and a little cash. But the veneer protecting these women is very thin indeed.

The first story that follows chronicles the traumas of the truly defenseless, a Spanish-speaking illegal alien, and the second, of a woman from the lower middle class who ultimately pulled herself up and out. Those who don't find two stories enough can turn to the metro sections of their daily papers, to television series with cops in gritty, urban settings, to maybe one out of four Sunday-night made-for-TV movies, and to fiction, whether pulp or fine.

In Sonoma County, California, you can not only see some of the country's blue-ribbon vineyards but also hear stories of the systematic sexual abuse of immigrant women. Marie De Santis, who has worked for almost five years as a counselor at a family-planning clinic in Petaluma, told me as we walked through the fields: "I've heard so many stories from women trapped in the wineries. At almost every stage of their lives, they're forced into one form of sexual slavery or another. If they get caught crossing the border, they can choose to have sex with an immigration officer or go to prison. When they're working in a household, it's very common for the employer to demand sex. Spousal violence increases for immigrant women because their isolation is so extreme. And if their husbands find out they've been raped, they often abandon them because they feel shamed."

It was through Marie that I learned about a twenty-two-year-old woman named Maria who had left her three children, her husband, her parents, and her small town in southern Mexico in February 1991, to come to Petaluma on the promise of work in the home of chiropractor David Noles. Her youngest child was desperately ill and needed an operation, and Maria had decided that her only hope of finding the money lay in the United States. Marie gave me the tape of the story Maria had told her.[1]

I came to San Diego because my baby needed an operation. I've been here two years. My husband is seven years older than me. I was fifteen when we got married. Now I'm twenty-two, and I have three children. My husband drank and hit me, so I separated from him. When my daughter was born, she was ill and needed the operation. I didn't have money, and every day she got worse. I had to provide for her. My parents couldn't help me, and neither could my friends. I looked for work in my country as a housekeeper, but it paid far too little.

I found out that I could come to clean a house in Petaluma. A couple from the United States owned a house near my parents. They would come every year to Mexico, and we became friends. In December of 1990, I saw the man [David Noles], and started telling him about my problems. He told me he could help me. I was to come to the United States and clean his house in exchange for room and board. And then I could also find a second job and send money back to my family. I left my town with three outfits and no money at all. The only other time I'd traveled was to go to a beach nearby. I was very scared to come, but the sadness of not being able to help my daughter kept me going.

I left my children with my mother, since my husband and I were separated. The trip was okay up until Tijuana. Then after we crossed the border, immigration caught the coyote [the man who was smuggling her across]. I managed to run, but I got lost in San Diego. Other people found me and took me into their home and helped me. I didn't have a phone number for the doctor, but the lady who found me was somehow able to contact him.

This lady sent me to San Francisco by plane, where another coyote was waiting. Then he took me all the way to the house where I was to work. I was scared because the coyote didn't wait. He simply dropped me off and left me in the house. Everything was very hard because nothing of what the doctor had told me was true.

The first thing he did was take advantage of me sexually. Afterwards, he left me there and went upstairs to eat. I didn't know what to do. When he came down, he told me I had to have sex with him willingly, and I said that was not in our contract. My job was to clean his house in return for room and board. I told him my job was not to come sleep with him. But he told me he had paid a coyote, and he had paid for my trip, and I couldn't oppose anything he would ask me to do. I was very scared, I was so far away from my family. I didn't know anybody except the coyote.

We talked and talked and talked about the contract. But at the end, he told me that if I didn't accept what he was telling me, he was going to send me to Tijuana as a prostitute. He was going to sell me to other men. My world was closed. I didn't know anybody, I didn't know what to do. In the meantime, my daughter's life was constantly on my mind. But I knew my life was in danger as long as I stayed there. He used me sexually for five days.

A few days after I got to the doctor's house, a man called to tell me that he knew what was going on. All of a sudden, I got hopes that I could get out.

But when the man came over to help me leave, he told me that in exchange, I had to have sex with him. In other words, it would be the same as the conditions I was living under then. Since I arrived, everything had gone so bad for me, and I didn't know what to do. All I wanted was to leave. . . .

The doctor never hit me, but he kept threatening me. He used words that made me feel very bad and very scared. He kept telling me I had to do everything he told me to and please him every way he asked. And if I didn't do it by my own will, he would force me since he'd paid for everything and nobody knew I was there.

I didn't know anything about the police. I didn't even know how to use a telephone. In Mexico, when a woman calls the police under the same circumstances, they'll ignore her. If a maid or housekeeper calls the police, the employer will simply pay the police off, and that will be the end of the case.

The doctor would leave to go to work, and he knew that I couldn't leave because I didn't know anybody and I was scared. But there was a woman living in the same building. I have no idea who she was, and she did not speak Spanish. I tried being very nice to her, and we communicated through a dictionary. She'd write the words in English for me. Finally, I showed her the bedroom. I was crying, and I think that's the way she was able to understand what was happening. I showed her the bloodstains on the bed and on the floor. I was menstruating, and he still did whatever he wanted to. His way of having sex with me was very brutal and disgusting. I don't know how we did it, but she understood me and called a women's center and the police.

Once your life is in danger, there's no need to be ashamed or embarrassed. What counts then is to save yourself. It's embarrassing to go in front of the judge or the doctor and be asked all those questions, but compare that to losing your life! He could have killed me and thrown my body somewhere, and nobody would have known. I was so far away from my town.

Somebody at the women's center spoke Spanish. She asked why I hadn't called the police, and I said because I didn't know I could do that. So they called the police and kept me on the phone until the police got there. I was trembling all over. I didn't know if I should leave or stay. I thought the police would do the same things to me. I was scared of everything. I didn't know where I was going. I didn't know what was going to happen to me. But one of the police officers spoke a little Spanish. He tried to calm me down and tell me I was going to be okay. He said they were going to take me to a safe place. I didn't know if they were going to send me back to Mexico. I just kept crying. I didn't know what a women's center was. I didn't know anything.

The police kept me a long time since I didn't want to talk to them. I was scared and I didn't want to press charges. But then an investigator asked if I wanted to let the doctor get away with what he'd done to me. He had hurt me a lot, and they needed me to testify. Without me, they wouldn't be able to do anything. He said many men like him did those things, and the victims were too afraid to talk. He told me that if I testified, everything would change for me because it would be a big load off my chest. That's what changed my mind. He asked me then if I was willing to press charges against the doctor and I said yes.

As soon as I decided to press charges, they took me to a doctor. He examined me, and then they took me to the women's center. After I got there, I was fine. They gave me everything I needed. Two people there spoke Spanish. They treated me very nicely. All they wanted to do was help me because they knew I was alone. They told me about my rights as a woman and found a lawyer for me. They gave me advice. I was sick, so they took me to the doctor. They bought me glasses because I use them but I didn't have them any longer. They told me not to be afraid of the court.

It was very, very hard to talk about the case because I didn't really understand the translator. It was so confusing. The questioning went on about two months. He'd tell me he wasn't trying to make me feel bad but he had to know everything. There were fifteen tapes. Immigration interviewed me as well. All that went on almost a whole year — doing those interviews and going to court.

After I reported [David Noles] to the police, he said I was crazy and I'd provoked him. He said many bad things about me to the press. He said I was a typical hot Latin woman, and the best-known newspaper in town printed that. If he's in jail now, it's not because of what he did to me. [Eight months after the original charges were brought, the district attorney dropped the case against Noles on the grounds that another man claimed to have had sex with Maria in Noles's house. This claim, if sustained, presumably made her, as Noles had said, a "hot Latina" who didn't deserve the law's protection.]

I never imagined they would dismiss my case. I went to court and did the best I could, but nothing happened. A friend of his made a tape saying I'd agreed to have sex with him, but that wasn't true. He also said I was expecting his baby, but of course that wasn't true either. I can't have any more children.

I found a job in a hotel, and I was fine there. But all the female workers were Mexican, and they didn't want to talk to me because they thought I'd asked for it. They blamed me for what had happened. It made me feel bad, so I left my job. The only people I had were a family I stayed with when I left the women's center. They gave me room and board without my having to pay them anything until I found a job. They gave me hope. They told me not to get desperate. All I wanted was justice.

I never imagined all the bad things that were outside my town. I felt it was my fault because I didn't know his intentions toward me. I felt I should have known, and if I hadn't come here, it wouldn't have happened to me. But now I understand it wasn't my fault. [In February 1992, three months after the charges in Maria's case were dropped, Noles was arrested again on eight new counts of sexual assault, this time of a seventeen-year-old local girl who worked in his office. Three months later, he was arrested again *in jail* for trying to prevent her from testifying. In November 1992, he was convicted on ten felony counts and the following March was given thirty-five years in prison. In sentencing him, the judge said he would not be eligible for probation because "he was a danger to the community due to his lack of remorse."]

Cleo Justus grew up in what she calls a dysfunctional family in a town near Chicago, with a father who was an alcoholic and withdrawn and a mother who was "always trying to fix him." She struck me immediately as the actress she is: she uses her hands *con brio* as she speaks, and she's given to the grand gesture. If I'd asked her to choose which actress she'd most like to have been, I suspect she'd pick "the divine Sarah" Bernhardt.

She is blonde and vital, and so sunny that her story jolted me like a sudden cacophony of bells on a still morning, and I can't remember how I hid my astonishment. Perhaps I didn't. She works now as a storyteller at coffeehouses, bookstores, and an assortment of gatherings, and she is either an extraordinarily good fake or she really has come to terms with the burden of her past.

We weren't really allowed to have our own thoughts and feelings; we were only allowed to have my mother's. If I tried to describe *my* day, the focus of the attention became *her* response, *her* feelings about my day. She was center stage all the time. And she cast me as her best friend, so I just thought I had a mother who loved me more than other girls' mothers loved them.

When I was sixteen, I lost my virginity. It was a normal, innocent losing-your-virginity story. Now I know it's a beautiful story. But my mother was into eavesdropping and reading my journals. And when she overheard this phone conversation, her and Dad took me downstairs. My dad said, "Are you a virgin?" and I lied, because I knew there was no room for the truth. But my mother ran out of the room screaming, "My daughter's not a lady, my daughter's not a lady. . . ." My dad came over and held me, and said, "No man will ever respect you. It's because we love you that we're telling you this." It was a pretty significant trauma. I started to cry, but I choked back my tears because Mom's were so big. There really wasn't room for my response. Somehow I'd killed my mother. I'd destroyed her fantasy. We argued from then on.

Shortly after that, I got my first job as a hostess at a Polish restaurant called Sawa's Old Warsaw. Everybody got in on the game called "Let's get the hostess." The waitresses were much older — in their thirties, maybe. Most of them were Polish immigrants, and something was at stake for them. They started teaching me to drink, and at sixteen I had a pretty normal curiosity about that.

My father was a quiet, get-drunk-and-pass-out alcoholic. Everybody in the family pretended nothing was wrong, but I knew there was. It made me frightened of drinking, but it was my first job. The waitresses had interesting accents — it was very dramatic — and they seemed cosmopolitan. I wanted to be anything but a suburban Chicago girl. I was prone to fantasy because I'm an actress, and even then I was tied to my imagination. I wanted to be a heroine in some novel rather than Cleo Justus living in my parents' dysfunctional household, which was eating me alive.

One night, Yola was challenging me to drink shots of vodka. They gave me a Polish name, and she was calling it and saying, "Do it, do it, do it. . . ." And I got more upset and scared, but I was pretending I was cool. The bartender — Larry — intervened: "Yola, leave her alone. She's just a kid. Don't hassle her. Cleo, you're fine. Yola's just that way." So he set himself up to be the hero. He said, "I'll take you home." And in the car, he said, "Look, you're not ready to go home; you're too drunk. We'll just go somewhere and sober you up." There was a place called Some Other Place Pub, which was clearly a pick-up joint, and I knew that. But at that point, I was still pulled in by the idea that this man was taking care of me. So he brought me into the pub, and we had a drink. And then I was, like, "I gotta go home. I really do!"

So on the way home, he said he had to stop by his trailer to get something and I should come in instead of just sitting in the car. I had a sense of "Don't make this man mad — whatever you do." And I felt a certain allegiance to him for what he'd done for me earlier. As soon as we got into the trailer, he grabbed me and sat me down on the couch, pulled my underwear down, and was inside me. It was very quick. He just did his thing, and then he was done. I felt shocked, powerless, dirty! I was saying to myself, What do I do? What do I do? . . . Oh shit, now what?

Then he reached under a pillow on the couch and pulled out a gun and put it to my temple. He looked straight at me and said, "You're not gonna tell anybody about this, are you?"

"No, I'm not gonna tell anybody. . . ."

I don't know which was more violent, the rape or the gun. I didn't say anything, he didn't say anything. His tone was that I was this piece of low shit — a little sixteen-year-old piece of nothingness. Then he did it again before he took me home. He fell asleep on me for forty-five or fifty seconds, and I remember how horrible that was — lying there under him not being able to move and not knowing what to do.

I didn't tell anybody. I just went home and lay on my bed. I felt like I needed to pretend everything was okay; it was just a yucky night, and he was a jerk, but hey, I'm a woman and shit happens. And I remember putting my makeup on the next morning and how important the makeup was to cover up, and make me look like I was okay. That feeling stayed with me a long time. Sometimes, even today, I can't wear it because of its connection to masking pain.

The next day I went to my job, and the boss said, "Larry told me you slept with him. I can't believe you did that. You're supposed to sleep with me!" He acted very betrayed! I was much more frightened of Bill than I was of Larry, and now I was very sober. It was my night to stay late and take the food bar down. Yola pretended she was sick, so Bill sent her home and said, "I'll take you home." We walked down the hall to go out the back door to the car, and he said, "I have to stop in my office to get something." He didn't come out, and I waited. Then I said to myself, "I wonder what's happening," and walked into the office. He slammed the door and said, "You're gonna sleep with me tonight, and you're not gonna tell anybody about this. 'Cause you were supposed to sleep with me and not Larry, and you're gonna pay for it. We're not gonna do it here. I'm gonna take you to my house and we'll do it in my bed." He said otherwise I'd lose my job and he'd tell my parents. I said yes. . . .

He drove me to his place and took me on the bed. And then he drove me home. By then it was like punishment: I was being punished for being a whore. There was a sense of inevitableness to it. I know now that to survive, you go inward with your anger and rage. When he drove me home, he said, "Sixteen'll get you twenty" [referring to the possible jail sentence for sexually abusing a minor]. He'd not only raped me, but he was gonna bypass the law too, since I wasn't gonna tell anybody. They were both so sure of their power that they gambled I wouldn't tell.

The rest of the summer, I kept trying to please them! They shamed me for what I'd done, for what a whore I was. And I wanted 'em to like me again.

It was very, very confusing, but there wasn't anybody I could talk to about it. Until about a year ago, my memory was that I'd slept with those men because I was promiscuous. I was crying, and my therapist said, "Were you ever raped?" And I said, "Well, one time this guy put a gun to my head." And then I slowly retrieved the whole memory of the coercion and pain. *For a long time, my sense was that they'd cut my tongue out. That was the real rape. What they did to my body was nothing compared to the loss of my sense of my right to cry out!*

I had this victim sense — I had a big V written on my forehead — so I was open and available to predators. And then, when the predators did bad things to me, it would confirm my sense that it was all true. So it just played itself over and over and over with different men for years and years. I got very split off within myself. Intercourse was one thing and sexual play was another. I was unable to maintain a relationship and would get myself caught between two men. I was unable to have satisfying intercourse with my nice boyfriends, and that would undo our relationship ultimately. I'd somehow engage with a sexually addicted male while I was breaking off, and then that wouldn't work. But I'd be able to have sexual feelings with the wild, slightly abusive men.

The beginning of the change was about seven years ago, when I started going to Adult Children of Alcoholics. That's when my denial began to break down. I started to look at how my father's alcoholism had affected my behavior, and I went into therapy with a woman. I read a lot and got an intellectual understanding of my experience. And eventually I learned how to feel the feelings and tell those guys, in my imagination, to "Get the fuck away from me!" before they could even get close. I became my own guardian warrior, and now nobody can come near unless I want them to.

I don't have the V on my forehead any more. Sometimes I see the predatory males now, and you know what? They don't even look at me. I'm not in the same world they are any more. . . .

If a society is to be judged by the way it treats its weakest members, ours must throw itself on the mercy of the court. A poor woman has problems enough, but a woman who is sexually tainted finds few champions. Religions that equate women's virtue with virginity and chastity have prompted us to look down on women who aren't "pure," though purity is a category properly assigned to minerals rather than to flesh-and-blood people. So we need to remind ourselves of the biblical injunction: Let him or her who is blameless throw the first stone.

Aside from insisting that she should call the police, offering counsel to women in straits like those described above would be presumptuous, for what can we say? Don't be young? Don't be poor? Don't work in restaurants or clean people's homes? Don't be pretty? (If you are, other women may spitefully collude with men in your humiliation.) For if it touches the heart of the matter, all our advice is inane because it can be reduced to "Don't live!" Although Cleo managed at last to find a measure of economic independence through luck, education, and hard work, women like Maria are less likely to have her options.

But the rest of us need to know that ideas matter, and the idea that "Boys will be boys" has not only far outlived its usefulness but grown dangerous. We must *stop* making excuses for shabby and unscrupulous men. We need to see that the maxim "Life's unfair" has made us callous to human suffering we can alleviate.

We need to know, further, that institutions we support with whatever money and influence we can muster really *do* help. Women's centers and battered-women's shelters provide an often necessary and certainly useful first stage for women trying to pull themselves out of abusive situations. Journalists need to know that focusing the spotlight of public attention on abuses of power like Dr. David Noles's may well not only put one dreadful man out of commission but discourage others. Women's organizations need to know that there are multitudes of women they can help and many ways to help them if they choose.

Noles was certifiably criminal and, mirabile dictu, finally got his due — though not for raping and abusing Maria, so clearly, one avenue we must never abandon is the legal system, biased and pitiful as it often turns out to be. But laws need to be sharpened and police enforcement strengthened before poor women can count on something more nearly like decency to prevail.

7

BLOWING THE WHISTLE

How is it that if a woman's attacked, it doesn't mean anything to a man? They think, You're a woman: you should expect it. I don't expect it! I don't think it's right!

— Theresa McDonald

Women who blow the whistle have usually put up with harassment for a long time before they go public. They keep doing their jobs by finding ways to get along with men who are making their lives exceedingly unpleasant, and at the very least, they learn to work around them. Often they make excuses for their tormentors and/or for those who stand by and let the abuse continue, and many act only after the stress has made them sick. Invariably they discover that the personal cost of speaking out is very high, and so the notion that hordes of women are making irresponsible charges against hapless innocents is pure fantasy.

The process of objecting is stressful, tedious, and time-consuming. It can become extremely expensive. Often it undermines a woman's ability to do her job, and typically it keeps her from advancing as far or as fast as her talents and gumption warrant. Not infrequently, it means that she will lose the position on which she's depended and the work she's loved. *Always* her protest takes her places, both literal and psychological, where she never expected to be.

While we as witnesses may find ourselves wondering, from time to time, why a given woman did not do thus-and-so differently, plumbing the depths of another's soul or exploring her psyche is beyond our scope here. I am far less interested in imagining what might have been than in discovering what was.

Each of the stories that follow reveals the woman's inner world — the evolution of feelings that erupted finally into protest, and the complex system of beliefs that made protest not only possible, but necessary. At the same time, each sketches the practical issues and complications every woman has to confront and in some way resolve. These are stories about what you do and how you do it — about what works and what doesn't — and so all are about the country we live in, the systems that govern us, and the men who run them.

I'm sorry that three of the six emerge from academia, for that may make the selection seem unbalanced. There are reasons, however, why academic women are more likely to bring suit than their counterparts in business, for instance. First, since institutions of higher learning presume to act on pristine motives and uphold high standards, when they fall short, the betrayal inherent in their excuses can be exposed more readily. Second, since ideas are at the core of the academy, it is the natural place to challenge those that experience and reflection have found wanting. Finally, it is the business of academic women to think, and as Socrates knew, thinking is subversive. So it is only logical that these women would be among the first to connect the dots that spell discrimination and abuse and then find colleagues who'll form a supportive environment while they try to force their institutions to live up to their claims. The ideas refined on campuses often spread through the society at large, and what happens there eventually influences the way all of us live and the beliefs we cherish. Therefore, we need to pay special attention to what academic women face and how they fare.

Next to the Hill/Thomas hearings themselves, the most highly publicized recent case of sexual harassment involved Dr. Frances Conley, a neurosurgeon at the Stanford Medical School. In 1991, the fifty-one-year-old Conley made headlines throughout the country when she resigned her tenured position to protest Dean David Korn's decision to appoint Dr. Gerald Silverberg chairman of the neurosurgery department. Silverberg was notorious for harassing women, and for years, Conley had endured her colleague's sexist comments and behavior. But she had made her position plain to the dean: she believed that giving him the chairmanship sent the wrong message to the young. Her resignation sparked a national protest. Korn eventually withdrew Silverberg's appointment, and Conley withdrew her resignation.

I met Fran Conley almost two years later when she came to a conference in Washington, and we talked in her hotel suite while she nursed an ankle she'd twisted on her morning run. She is a trim, vigorous woman who throws the javelin on weekends with her husband, who represented the United States in the 1956 Olympic Games, and her air of command is evident even when she is in jogging clothes and has one foot propped on a chair.

The daughter of a Stanford University professor of geochemistry, Fran has spent her life on or near the Stanford campus, and every summer of their childhood, she and her siblings went on field trips with their father. There they watched women working alongside men, and it seemed to her that the women were treated as equals. From these days came her decided convictions about what's right and what's wrong in an academic environment. She is a graduate not only of the university itself but of the Stanford Medical School, and so it was her institution in the fullest sense that she saw tarnished by irresponsible behavior.

The type of harassment that occurs in my work environment is not the touchy, brash type of harassment about which everybody can say, "Yes, that's inappropriate behavior for a work environment." What women in the medical field put up with is more subtle. But it can be just as devastating because it happens far more frequently, it's pervasive, and it's a cultural thing. It's like a ton of feathers. We all get hit daily by a feather of verbal abuse dropping on us. The individual feather doesn't hurt you at all. It hurts only when they add up to a ton: it's cumulative. Mary Rowe of MIT calls these microinequities. They're verbal barbs directed at the person who's different within a workplace environment, and because of that difference, be it on the basis of gender or race, you're never going to be a member of the club. If you didn't hear these barbs every single day, you'd pass 'em off, saying, "He's insensitive!" or "He's a boor." But when it happens daily, all of a sudden, one day you say, "Hey, I'm not going to put up with this any more!" You can't really give concrete examples that will make people gasp for breath and say, "Gee, how awful!" Every woman understands exactly what I'm talking about. Men don't at all. And that's part of the problem.

The environment for women in medicine is not pretty. But when you're young, you take it in stride, so I don't remember bad episodes happening when I was in medical school. It's tough — and people tell you it's going to be tough — so you work hard. It was when I decided to go into surgery that I got the message that I was being given a unique invitation. The prevailing attitude was, "Fran, we think you're capable of doing it, and we're going to give you this invitation, but you'd jolly well better be grateful as hell from now on. That means you abide by our rules." Of course the rules aren't stated for you.

During residency training, when I was being taught how to be a surgeon, most of the general surgeons treated me as if I were a cute little piece of fluff. I don't think any of them believed I'd have a career in surgery; that was unfathomable. I was tested far more than my male colleagues, and among other things, they tested me in terms of what I was willing to put up with in the way of dirty jokes. If I had it to do over, I'd probably draw the line of decency a little bit more stringently. When I joined the faculty, I was no longer a piece of fluff. I was going to be in the hierarchical structure. And suddenly I was a threat. I think that's when the trouble really starts for women.

Dr. Gerald Silverberg, whose leadership I challenged, had gotten away with outrageous behavior over the years. I'd frequently ask other men what I could do about him. (My world is men; there were no women to ask.) And they'd invariably answer, "There's no way you're ever going to change him! Just put up with it." Had I wanted to make a one-on-one statement about this guy, I'd have made it years earlier. I can work with him because, although his behavior is egregious, he's not the only one. There are lots of 'em out there — men who fully believe that women were put on the earth to serve them. That group of men you're probably never going to change, though I'm going to keep trying.

My challenge to Silverberg was about a leadership decision. I was distressed when he was put in as permanent chair because then his residents and mine would look at him and say, "He has achieved what I want to be ten years from now, or twenty years from now. And if his behavior got him there, that's the behavior I'll adopt." That's what I wanted to stop.

I'd been watching Silverberg for years treating nurses like playthings, like the dirt under his feet, and I'd find it embarrassing as hell to watch. They've suffered a lot more than I have, in terms of being touched and propositioned. For me, it was a regular reminder that because I was a woman, I was never going to be as good as he was. That sort of thing is always done before an audience, and I just happened to be a female bystander. He was also showing what he was getting away with to other men, like a little boy lifting a girl's dress in front of other little boys.

His remarks to me sound totally trivial. He'd always call me "honey." Well, I'm not his honey. His wife's his honey. I'm married, he's married. I probably never objected forcefully enough. But when you think about what it does to you as a professional, its importance hits you with stunning clarity. Once I was in the room with a patient and Silverberg opened the door and said, "Hey, hon, can you come into my office for a minute?" Well, in that situation, I'm not a neurosurgeon, I'm a honey.

Another time I was in the operating room where I was expected to be leading a team. (I was doing a craniotomy.) And he walked in and said, "Hi, honey, how's it going?" He also called the nurses "honey." Nurses are true professionals, and we work as a team, but suddenly we're a bunch of honeys trying to operate on a patient. It took five minutes to reestablish my authority. I said to the nurses, "I don't think it's appropriate for him to call me honey. How do you feel?" A couple said it didn't matter to them, but several others said it did.

In our earlier days, Silverberg would frequently ask me in front of a crowd to go to bed with him. With other women, he was not merely verbal. He's a good neurosurgeon, but it's not appropriate to put that kind of person into a position of executive leadership.

So my challenge was about *leadership*: do you put somebody into a position of power and control, where their behavior is seen as the zenith of academic achievement and they are therefore copied? If a boss is racist and sexist, your environment will be racist and sexist. It's guaranteed. So my challenge was to a much higher level than Silverberg. It was to the dean and the administration.

Almost four years ago, the chairman retired — the man who'd brought me onto the staff and was very supportive and proud of my achievement. Gerry was named acting chair, and I told the search committee that if Gerry were chosen permanent chair, I'd resign. Everybody knew I'd leave. Then the dean called me one evening and said, "Fran, I've just appointed Gerry as your permanent chair." I said, "Thank you for letting me know. You'll have my letter of resignation on your desk tomorrow morning." He said, "Think about it." And I said, "I've already thought about it."

I think the dean was calling my bluff. He knew I'd looked at other jobs, since I'd been very unhappy since Gerry had come in as acting chair, and he probably thought I'd realize I was stuck there and would stay. He was wrong. *There were a lot of people interested in my career and in the fact that I was the only tenured full professor of neurosurgery who was female in the world.* I'd done what no other person before me had done, and a lot of people took pride in that. So I wrote an op-ed piece.

I showed it first to a good friend in the communications department, and she didn't say a word about how volatile it might be. She recommended that I send it to the editors of five different papers, and so I did. The editor of the editorial page at the *San Francisco Chronicle* gave it to his news desk, and they started calling Stanford and talking to medical students who'd had problems with sexual harassment. They wrote the story the next day — "Sexual harassment is rampant at the Stanford Medical School!" — and put it on the front page. And of course it went out over the wires and the story blew into a big atom bomb.

When you get thrust into the limelight, it's so disruptive. I lost ten pounds in about three weeks. I was skin and bones. I couldn't eat and had zero appetite. It was a very interesting experience — and not one I'd want to go through again. The editor apologized later and said he hadn't intended to cause me discomfort. But the most important weapon I've had in this whole crusade, as my husband labels it, has been the media, which has forced the school to do things they didn't want to do. Even today, I think it's the only weapon available to academic women. The academic community abhors anything negative.

Once the story broke, I recognized rapidly that I was going to need some legal help. I have a very good attorney who's been with me for years, and he was ready and waiting in case I wanted to file a lawsuit. He's reluctant to take on Stanford University, though he's there as a threat and occasionally sends letters to the administration. But the important thing is that they know he's there and that I have legally actionable material.

I also have a very good friend in the Harvard School of Education who's a labor-negotiation lawyer. Soon after this broke, he called, and I said, "I'm going to need your help." From three thousand miles away, he could prepare me for sessions with the dean, with whom I had four discussions over the summer. This fellow was able to role-play with me, so I could go into those sessions very well prepared.

After each session with the dean, I'd go back and write up our meeting and send the dean a copy and say, "Please comment on this." I wanted a written document of what had happened. After about four sessions, he said, "Next time, if you want things transcribed, I'll have somebody there." And certainly if I'd had another meeting with him, I'd have said, "I'd like the meeting transcribed." You have to have a paper trail, and he recognized that I was playing my cards very well.

When the media blitz hit the dean, he put the appointment on hold and waited till the medical students left for the summer—they'd been very supportive of me. Then in mid-August, he tried to get the appointment through his executive committee. (The dean can't make an appointment without its concurrence.) I'd been the faculty senate chair for the previous two years, and I'd sat with that executive committee and knew a lot of people. They said, "No way!" I think they saw me as an honest, good person. They knew I wasn't crazy. And some of them had seen Silverberg's behavior.

I'd made my resignation effective September first, since that was when my role as faculty senate chair was up, but the executive committee's refusal to confirm Silverberg's appointment meant the dean had to do some very proactive stuff. He had the media sitting on his doorstep every day saying, "What the hell are you going to do?" So he set up an office for women in the medical sciences and funded it, and that office has been very valuable. It's the first time the women faculty in the medical school have had a chance to meet each other and, together as a group, exchange information about our pleasures as well as our problems about the jobs we do.

Second, he set up an investigative panel to look into the allegations I'd made. They took a long time and interviewed anybody who wanted to come forward, and some twenty-odd women felt strongly enough about the negative impact Silverberg had on the environment to go before that panel. Their report was made final in the spring of '92, and based on its content, the dean elected to remove Dr. Silverberg from the active chairmanship and he is now undergoing "sensitivity training."

It's still hard. Here's a school I gave my life to, and it turned around and bit me. I still feel badly about bringing down another negative on the university, yet I feel I had no recourse. At the same time, I feel vindicated: people now recognize that the appointment was inappropriate, though in the year before the report came out, a lot of people thought I'd truly lost my marbles.

I still think that what I did will ultimately be a career-ending move. I will *not* advance further; I will *not* be an attractive candidate for positions at other academic institutions—ever. I regret that because I feel like I have a tremendous amount to offer in terms of the medical environment and how we teach medical students. I'm primarily a teacher—not a neurosurgeon. My joy is to teach the next generation, and I'd have liked to have the decision-making capability over that environment. That will be denied me. I'll have taught by example, rather than by being an administrator making those decisions.

I met Jean Underwood in Oakland, California, and as we talked in a friend's upstairs study, I struggled to connect the woman sitting before me with the sketch of her life she'd given me by telephone. But I simply couldn't do it. I had to listen to her and see her struggle to tell her story with dignity before I could fully accept the fact that all this had really happened to her.

At thirty-five, Jean looks like the sort of woman you might see presiding over a Girl Scout bake sale. Married at eighteen, a mother at nineteen, she has three children. In 1985, with her youngest in kindergarten, she went to work part-time for the city of Concord in California. Three years later, she began working full-time for the mayor and the city council. As we sat in a chilly, darkening room, I felt as if I were caught up in a Greek drama, with one discovery or revelation leading inexorably to the next. No other story in this book illustrates so powerfully both the personal cost of blowing the whistle and, at the same time, the potential gain.

The entire time my kids were growing up, I worked part-time so I could still be a mother and volunteer at school, and it worked out very well. In 1988, I wasn't sure I was ready to work full-time, but the opportunity arose to have a job that was the ultimate for a secretary who didn't finish college — being secretary to the city manager and city council. So I applied and got it. At the time, my husband's job wasn't as stressful as it is now, and we did a role switch. He took on more responsibility at home and I took time off for weekends with my family, so we still had family time.

In January of '89, our city council passed a controversial AIDS anti-discrimination ordinance that made history. The media put a lot of pressure on my office to get to the city manager and the city council, and while all this hullabaloo was going on, it created a lot of stress. Then three new members were elected to the city council. The top vote-getter was Byron Campbell, who wanted to come in and virtually run the city. Our vice-mayor, who was slated to become mayor, lost her seat because she'd voted for the anti-discrimination ordinance. The mayor is elected by the council, and Byron Campbell was chosen mayor. It was very unusual for a new city council person to become mayor.

Byron demanded a lot of staff time; he'd pull people in and try to get them to help him do whatever he wanted to do. He'd have me in his office for two or three hours at a time. He'd say, "Come in, I want your opinion about something," and then he'd tap on the table and say, "This is just between you and I!" Or he'd say, "I want to make this [unprecedented] change in the city. How do I go about doing it?" If I'd say, "You can't do that, it's something the staff has authority to do," he'd say, "Who do I need to ask?" And then it would become, "How do I do this without asking?" If I'd say, "You could do it that way, but it's not the way you really should do it," he'd say, "That's not what I'm asking."

I always told my boss, the deputy city manager, about these crazy ideas, and Byron would get furious. "Don't tell!" That was continual, day in, day out. He wanted me to tell lies for him; he'd fabricate a story about why he couldn't come to a meeting or something and expect me to tell it. After a while, it got real difficult for me.

He was in his fifties, the same age as my father, and once he put his arm around my waist to escort me out of his office, and when we were walking down the hall, I thought, Gosh, I hope nobody thinks I want his arm around me. I felt this fear and this burning. We came to the counter where I worked, and he was standing beside me with his arm around me and his hand close to my breast with his fingertips on it. The door was closed to the city manager's office, and I thought, I certainly hope nobody comes out, because they'll think I want this man's hand here.

Yet I couldn't muster the courage to say, "Please take your hand off me." I thought, He doesn't realize where his hand is. He's just a middle-aged man who doesn't know how to behave in an office. There were complaints, and I'd say, "I don't feel his touching is right — but that's the way Byron is." Everybody seemed to have the same attitude.

He told me I was the best executive secretary he'd ever worked with. He bought a case of wine to give me and then collected the money from the city council. He sent a huge bouquet of flowers and a bottle of wine for my birthday. (That was also officially from the city council.) I decided he was being very generous, and maybe he was. But he'd touch you on the leg or the hand; he called women cutesy names — I was Jean-Jean, there was Blondie — and it made women very uncomfortable. We had a twenty-year-old student intern, and he'd feel her clothing and ask her what kind of material it was. Once he said to me, "You've changed your hair. I don't like it that way. I want you to change it back." We thought, This man is absolutely nuts! but we laughed at him. And of course, we were supposed to cater to the elected officials; whatever they wanted, we were supposed to carry out. I thought he was just like my dad, and so I dismissed his behavior. I thought I was just a little girl who shouldn't tell anybody because it's no big deal. Finally, the city manager had so many complaints that she and the personnel manager went to him and said, "Stop." He said, "I'm just being friendly. That's the way I am."

Then I got to the point where I got nauseated every time I had to go into his office. Once, when he wanted me to lie for him again, I told the city manager I couldn't work with him anymore and be a part of his conspiracies. I was very upset and I was crying. So we hired another secretary; as he upset me more and more, she took over more of my responsibilities. She could laugh it off for a while, just like I'd been able to do. Six months later, I left to have a hysterectomy and was gone for six and a half weeks. I'd had episodes of bleeding for forty-five days at a time and been in extreme pain constantly, but I'd learned to live with it and didn't realize how much pain I'd been in until after the surgery.

One day after I went back to work, I was standing at the counter, and when he came over to ask me a question, he touched my back—and then his entire hand rubbed across my bottom. He jerked his hand back and said, "Oh, I'm sorry." Again I thought it was an accident. But whenever he said something nice, I'd feel sick to my stomach and think, "Why does he think I'm going to come back and work for him?" By then, the sexual harassment allegations had mounted. More and more women were talking about it, and then we began to see a pattern. As individuals, we'd dismissed his behavior. He knew how to pick his targets, and he knew what he could get away with. But the more stories you'd hear, the more you'd realize you weren't the only one. We got a new city attorney who's very protective of women's rights. He began to press the city manager to do something and the whole thing started ballooning.

The press got wind of it, and they started contacting the women so they could put a story together. But I wouldn't participate. I'd been told by the city manager that I didn't have to fear losing my job, but I was scared to death. *It was okay for everybody else, but I didn't want to be part of it.* Now I understand that it was because I'd kept a secret from the time I was nine years old. If I admitted that I had a problem with the mayor, maybe I'd have to admit that I had a problem from way back. And if it went to court and I had to testify under oath, I'd have to say what had happened to me. They'd ask questions about your sex life and your history. And I didn't want to share those things with anybody. *Nobody* knew those things but me. So I was scared that somebody would get me.

I'd told my mother some of the sex harassment stuff, and she turned up her nose. I said, "The press is pressuring me," and she said, "Well, you just better not say anything! Let somebody else do it. You don't need to be part of any of it." But in January of 1992, they hired a private investigator, and Byron told her, "These are just nameless, faceless people." And I became so angry I talked to the press. I said, "I have a name, and I have a face, and those things *did* happen." And when other women found that I'd given my name, they came forward with their names, so six of us came out with our stories and it was on the front page of the paper.

I told my parents what I'd done. My dad didn't say much, and my mother didn't want to hear about it. Maybe they thought that if I was doing it to this man, I wouldn't go back into my past. But it was really important for me to come forward and to ask for Byron to resign. Four council members and some community people asked him to resign, but he's still on the council. [A three-month investigation produced a report critical of Campbell, and by a 4 to 0 vote, with Campbell abstaining, the Concord City Council directed him to seek counseling and stop behaving in the manner that had been criticized. The local newspaper called for his resignation, as did the president of the Concord Association of Professional Employees. Nevertheless Campbell stayed on the council until November 1993, when he was defeated for reelection.]

I was crying all the time, and I myself didn't know what it was. But I saw the city attorney as a kind of protector, and finally he said, "Jean, you really need to get some counseling." It's available to city employees, but I was scared to death. Nobody in my family, except my little sister, had gone to counseling, and everybody thought she was crazy. My uncle is a social worker and into psychology, and he and I are very close. But my family had always thought he lived in another world.

So even though I knew I needed to do it, I was scared to death. Would I be admitting I was really crazy? I was absolutely terrified. The first time I went, I shook so much I could hardly talk and cried the entire time. The therapist said, "I think part of what's happening to you stems from the sexual harassment, so can we talk about that?" And I said, "I've already dealt with it." She said, "I don't know if that triggered something. I have no way of knowing if you were molested as a child." I sat there with a straight face as if it absolutely had *not* happened to me.

I went four times and cried every time. After the third session, my mother called and said, "Were you ever going to call me again?" And I said, "Well, yes, but we've been busy." She said, "I understand you're going to counseling." I have *no idea* how she found out. Then she said, "*Why* are you going?" I said, "I don't think that's anything that concerns you. But I've been very emotional, and I have some issues I need to learn how to deal with. It has nothing to do with you." She said: "Tell me *right now* why you're going. You need to *stop* going! Were we such terrible parents? Are you going to write a book about us?" She drinks some and likes to be controlling, but this was extreme even for her. I said, "No, I'm not writing a book. I'm not going to have anybody put in jail. I'm not going to accuse anybody. I'm going for myself, and you just have to accept that." She said, *"I'm not going to accept it, and you need to stop going right now!"*

I was so upset and angry that I called my uncle and said, "She just went totally crazy." It turned out that my mother had called him; she thought he'd put me up to going into counseling, but I hadn't spoken to him in months. She'd said to me, "Your uncle made you go!" and she'd said to him, "Why are you telling her to go? Are you telling her that we're just terrible?" He'd been flippant with her, and that had driven her off the deep end. But it was so absurd to him that she was calling and accusing him, when it shouldn't have been any big deal that I was seeing a therapist.

Two nights later, my little sister Deanna called. She was just frantic, and she said, "What's going on? Mother's called here all night long, Debby (our other sister) has called, and they're threatening me. They're saying, 'Are you and Jeanie writing a book? Are you out to get us? Are you out to sue us?'"

Now I have to go back sixteen years. When I was nineteen and Deanna was sixteen, she told me she couldn't take the abuse in the house any more. My father had a terrible temper, and he'd hit us at times, and my mother drank at night. So I got a phone call at my mother-in-law's one afternoon; my mother said the sheriffs had come into the high school and taken my little sister into protective custody. They'd taken her to the children's receiving home, and when they'd asked if her father beat her, she said, "Yes." Then they'd asked if her father had molested her, and she'd said she didn't know what that was. So they'd said, "Does your father ever touch you or fondle you?" and she'd said, "Yes, he does." My mother said, "They've taken her on these false charges because we've forbidden her to see her boyfriend." I said, "Mother, I believe her," and hung up.

I don't remember this day. I recently told my mother-in-law the whole story, and she said, "Jeanie, you told me that day your mother called, and you were absolutely hysterical. I held you for hours. You said, 'I know she's not lying; she's telling the truth! And I have to help her.'" Now, at that time, I wasn't sure I wanted to be married. My husband put me on a pedestal; he loved me with all his heart, and I had a fifteen-month-old baby. But I'd been in love with somebody before, and I wasn't mature enough to sort all those feelings out. I thought, This will just devastate my entire life if I tell what's happened to me. But I believed my sister and wanted to help her.

A day or two later, my mother called and said, "Your father has tried to commit suicide. If you don't come here, he'll die." He drank and took a lot of Valium, and she couldn't wake him up. But she wouldn't call anybody for help, and I had so much guilt for not being there that I went into denial. I went to the house, and he looked pitiful. My mother said, "How could she have done this to us?" My father put his hand on mine and said, "Jeanie, I didn't do it. I did things to you that I regret. But believe me, I never, never touched Deanna." In my mind, he needed me. And I believed that he never touched her because I thought it had only happened to me and nobody else would have to know.

So in the end, I didn't believe my sister's story. I believed that she wanted out of the house so she made it up. She kept saying to me, "Jeanie, I *know* it happened to you!" The district attorney called my house around the clock. I had a sheriff tell me, "You need to tell the truth! If you ever have a daughter, it's gonna happen to her." And I wouldn't let their words penetrate. I'd say to myself, It won't happen to my daughter because it didn't happen to my sister, and it didn't happen to me.

My sister had looked to me as a mother, and I abandoned her; I had to believe my father. The case was dismissed, but they removed my sister to foster care on grounds of irreconcilable differences. When she was eighteen, she married the man my parents didn't want her to see. And for about eight years, she didn't want to have anything to do with me. I knew I was lying about myself, but I didn't believe I was lying about my sister. I remember, when he was molesting me, thinking to myself, I can handle it, but he better not ever touch one of my sisters.

These weren't repressed memories. I always knew it had happened, but I didn't tell the counselor. I never said "No, it didn't happen!" I said to myself, You'll never know, and changed the subject. Because I knew that this time, I couldn't lie. So the night my mother got so angry at me, I told my sister Deanna that I was going to counseling and said, "It isn't fair that she's drawn you into this." But she became very angry with me and said, "Have you ever told them what your father did to you? I think I'll call the press and tell them." I was sick and scared to death! And I had to keep her quiet! So I admitted it to her, and then she told me her story, and I believed her. I wrote a very simple letter to my mother, telling her to leave my sister and my uncle out of it. I said the bad-parent police were not coming to get her and no lawsuits were going to be filed. I still hadn't admitted to myself that I was going to do what I was going to do.

But the next week, the counselor said, "Were you ever molested?" And I said, "Yes." I felt this shock within myself. Then she said, "And who molested you?" And I said, "My father." I still don't know for a fact that my mother knew, but her behavior makes me think she had to. That makes her as culpable as my dad. She didn't protect us; she always put my father first. I'm angry at my father, but without my mother in the way, I think he probably would have sought help. He knows he's a very sick man who needs help, but my mother's denial is protecting him.

Two months ago, I mailed her a ten-page letter and sent copies to my two sisters, my brother, and my uncle. I haven't heard from my mother. My uncle just sat and cried with me. He said, "The signs were there; I should've seen them." My sister and I have been a support for each other, although she still has a lot of anger. My mother hasn't spoken to me, and neither has the sister who lives near them. [Six months after Jean told me her story, this sister admitted that their father had also molested her.] I called my brother, who wouldn't speak to me, so I talked to his wife, who said he was very angry at me. I asked, "Do you think I'm making it up?" and she said, "How could anybody make that story up?"

My husband has been very supportive, but a month ago he got very angry. I'd gotten to a point where I couldn't handle it anymore. When I mailed the letter, I'd given up my parents, and I needed someone else to be powerful for me. But my husband had changed jobs, he was working twelve to fourteen hours a day, and he needed me to support him. I couldn't do all that. And he got very angry — probably the angriest I've ever seen him. We've worked it out, but I spent a whole day not knowing if my marriage was going to last.

I not only have a good therapist but a strong network of friends. I told people one at a time because it's very scary and I didn't want anybody to reject me. Nobody did, and that surprised me. I have days when I feel like I've gone to death and backwards, and I think, "If I hadn't said anything, I wouldn't be suffering like this." But when I come out of it, I feel that much more ahead.

Theresa McDonald has had trouble adjusting to her celebrity. A total stranger even put a congratulatory wreath on her door. At the same time, she has also been ridiculed in the press; her lawyer's tires have been slashed; and she's come close to having a nervous breakdown. All of this happened because she spearheaded a lawsuit against a probation officer that charges him with abusing a number of young women, and the clippings on the case so intrigued me that I drove two hundred miles to hear her story.

With an air of being tough and fragile all at once, Terry has two children and was divorced ten years ago. Now in her late twenties, she looks older, for reasons her story makes plain. I found her in a frame bungalow in an old neighborhood of Terre Haute, Indiana, where she was born. As we talked, a big yellow alley cat pounced on and off my lap without taking my neglect personally. Terry's daughter Peggy was another matter altogether, and so we bribed her with money for a Coke into going to the store.

Terry's arrest for driving without a license led to the harassment that led in turn to her lawsuit. But you cannot appreciate what it took for her to stand up to some of the most powerful men in the world she lives in without knowing her story up to that moment.

I worked two jobs for a long time. I wasn't able to get welfare assistance because my daughter had a certificate of deposit in her name that my grandfather put in trust for her till she was of age. She was only two at the time, and the bank wouldn't let me touch it. My ex-husband paid no support. So I worked two jobs; I was bartending, waitressing, and working in factories.

I'd married Mick when I was sixteen and had two kids before I was twenty. My mother had me when she was twenty-five, and I was the youngest child who moved out at the youngest age. I was very naive and married an alcoholic. My husband was eight years older, and I'd lived with him a while before we got married. But I didn't even realize what an alcoholic was until after the first few months of our marriage. I'd go to Alcoholics Anonymous meetings at the age of seventeen to figure out what I was married to. I was really worried. But they didn't give me any input on how to deal with my marriage. His friends and family blamed me, but when I first met Mick, he was drinking. And he always drank. I've never been into alcohol, probably because of what it did to him, because I loved him a lot.

He got drunk one time when we went fishin'. We was with another couple. I was just bendin' over backwards to get along with him because I'd just found out I was pregnant the second time. (I'd filed for divorce three days before I found out I was pregnant; it caught me really off guard.) But there was no gettin' along with Mickey. He pulled out his gun, and he was shootin' other people's fishin' bobbers in the lake. People started clearing out left and right. I got in the truck and told him to get in. He fell down, and I was afraid to go get him up because I thought he was gonna beat me up. He shot at me a coupla times, and I took off down the road in the truck. Larry, his best friend, kept tellin' me if I didn't go back, Mick was gonna take it out on me worse.

So I went back, and he came right up to the truck and pulled the gun on me and said he was gonna shoot me. I threw open the door and knocked him down, and I went out the other side. Then he shot between a friend and me. (There was two feet of space at the most between us.) I took off runnin' up a hill, and he dragged me down into a ditch. He beat me about the head and knocked me unconscious, and I woke up in an ambulance.

I didn't stay with him too much durin' my pregnancy and divorced him after the baby came. I was really afraid he'd kill me or hurt one of my children. He hit Peggy in the head with his fist when she was eleven months old and he was tryin' to hit me. He tried runnin' me and Peggy down. A posse from a tavern down the road seen him do it and took out after him. I had to jump and fall on the other side of a ditch.

I was attacked one night when I was eighteen. I was in a convertible, and I reported it. I wasn't sexually assaulted, but he attacked me; my knee came up and I was able to get him outta the car. Mick pretty much blamed me, so he beat the crap outta me. The cops showed me these pictures, but I said I didn't believe the guy was in 'em. They kept on sayin', "Look at it, look at it. . . ." One of 'em looked similar, and I said, "Well, that could be the guy." (I was eighteen, and they kept pushing.) A few days later, they put him in a lineup, and I said, "To tell you the truth, I don't know." Mick come down on me really hard. And finally, I didn't want nothin' to do with it. I wasn't raped, I'd got him out.

Then I was sexually assaulted about five years ago by two guys. I was hurt and embarrassed and angry. I was raped mostly by one — the other guy was in on it, but he kept sayin', "Come on, let's go." I wanted somethin' done, but I was told I wasn't a credible enough witness: I was pregnant at a young age and I'd reported assault before. I was really torn up about that. I tried to bring charges, but the prosecutor wouldn't let me. The police said it was two men's words against mine. They said I'd reported assault before and backed down. I told 'em I'd take a polygraph, but they wouldn't let me and I burst into tears.

So here I was, workin' two jobs, and the only way I could get to work was in the car. Then I got several tickets for drivin' while my license was suspended. A car ran a light and hit me. It was right after my divorce, and I didn't have any car insurance. This one cop would just see me and arrest me. I'd say, "What do you want me to do? I don't get no welfare; I don't get child support." I was workin' two jobs and barely able to open my eyes. I got my license taken away for life, even though I've never been arrested for intoxication. My ex-husband has been arrested five times for DWI, and he has a license. *Where's the justice? What I did was against the law, but I was put in a predicament: either I do this, or I can just forget about my bills and my house and my kids. You're leavin' me with no options.*

The first accident wasn't my fault, but the second was. I hadn't been arrested for years for drivin' while suspended. So I went to court, and I was told I had to do eighty hours of community service. That's when I first met Tom McQueary. It was July 9, 1991. I had to go into the community service office and sign up.

I didn't start my community service then. I didn't have no license, so I had no way back and forth. And my kids were outta school because it was summer. I tried tellin' 'em that at the time. So they took me back to court for not doin' my community service and gave me an extension for sixty days. That's the period when there were four deaths in my family in one month. My mother had a stroke, and they didn't know if she was gonna make it through. At a very low point, I was in a stress center for a coupla weeks; everything came down on me pretty hard all at once, and I checked myself in. It was really bad.

Then I showed up to do my community service, and the second day, I went into McQueary's office, and he asked me if I'd go to the west side of town. I said, "I don't have a car and don't drive," and he said, "I'll take you," so I said okay. Then he sent everybody else somewhere different, so it would be just me and him.

He lives in West Terre Haute, and on the way to the Water Works, where I was to do my community service, he said he had to pick up some bank deposits at his house. When we pulled up, he said, "It'll take a few minutes. Come on in." At first I said I'd just wait. (I shoulda been more skeptical. There was something shady about this man.)

When we got in, he did grab a bank book, and next thing, he was talkin' about how I was goin' to jail! I was goin', "What do you mean?" He said, "Judge McClain put a girl in jail not too long ago for a year, and she had less hours than you. So he ain't gonna mess with you." McQueary's best buddies with Judge McClain, and if you get sentenced to community service and don't do it, you go back to court and get in trouble.

Then he asked me if I'd be interested in cleanin' his house, and I said no. It was just filthy. Then he's talkin' about how he's gonna remodel his house, he's lightenin' up on the stuff about McClain and actin' like he was helpin' me out by tellin' me these things. And he starts bringin' me through the house: "See this carpet I'm gonna replace," and "See this. . . ." So he wants me to walk with him, and I am, and that's when I saw that he was gettin' real close. I turned around and seen this door partly open, and I could see the bathroom. So I said, "Do you mind if I use the restroom?" I was gettin' nervous.

You have to go through the bedroom to get to the bathroom. I went in, and I told myself, Surely you didn't set yourself up for this again, Terry, surely you didn't. But when I opened the bathroom door, there he was — undressed except for his pants and an undershirt. His belt was unbuckled. I froze. He's a big man, and I was, like, "What are you gettin' undressed for?" Then he's takin' me by my shoulders and tryin' to get me to sit down on his bed. It was a waterbed, and he was backin' me up. He pushed me down so I was sittin' on the rail of the bed. He had his TV on, and I wouldn't go back on the bed, and he said, "Let's watch TV in here." I said, "I don't wanna watch TV," and I forced myself back up and I'm tellin' him no. He's puttin' his hands on my shirt and tellin' me he's gonna help me out, he's gonna be my friend. He won't let Judge McClain throw me in jail, he'll talk to him for me about gettin' those hours wiped right off.

By this time I'm shaking, and I just wanta go. He sees it and doesn't care. He unbuttons a coupla buttons on my shirt, and I hurry up and get 'em back on. I've got his hands in my hands, fightin' him. Then he kinda pushed me back with one arm and undid my belt buckle, and I did it right back up. After that, he used his weight to push me back on the bed. He lifted up my shirt and my bra came with it, and he licked my nipple.

I jumped up, and it was, like, we were gonna fight it out; he was either gonna rape me or he was gonna let me go. I think when he realized it was gonna be one or the other, he started sayin' I was settin' him up, I coulda had a bug on me. I said, "I'm just tryin' to do my community service." I'm tryin' to calm him down then because I was afraid of what he'd do. I was sayin', "I don't have anything against you, I just don't go to bed with just anybody, you know. If I knew you or something, but I don't even know you. . . ." He still had that pissed-off attitude.

We got in the van and went to the bank. I could tell that bank lady knew there was somethin' wrong from the way she looked over at me, and I just looked down. Then he took me to the water works, and I was shaking and upset, I couldn't hide it. He came in and told the lady there, "I'll be back to pick her up at three." He was cold and rude, and then he left. I started doin' my work. And about twenty minutes later, a woman named Florabelle came in and said somethin' about McQueary pickin' me up at three, and I said, "I'm not goin' anywhere with that man." She said, "What's the matter?" And I told her what happened. Florabelle called the prosecutor, and we reported it to the police. I got the impression from the chief of police that I was wasting his time, and I do believe he's the one who tipped off McQueary.

I called my therapist right after the attack, and I have a girlfriend who came over. I don't smoke, I don't like people to smoke in my house, but that day I was beggin' her for a cigarette. Florabelle and Vicky arranged my ride for the next day, and they came and picked me up and took me back. My mother's a CPA and I work in her office durin' tax season, and when they found out that

I could do bookkeeping and use computers and things, they told McQueary they had enough work to get me through.

They'd told me, "Don't worry. He never comes back out after he drops somebody off in the mornin'," but around eleven o'clock that day, Florabelle runs back and says, "McQueary's here!" First I'm hidin' in the toilet, and then they take me outta the building. He kept askin' where I was at, and they said I musta took a lunch. He was tellin' 'em there was a report that I had a bad attitude, and he said, "Does she have a bad attitude with you?" And Florabelle says, "No, she does everything we ask her to do."

The next day he comes back again, and they're really freakin' out. He more or less told 'em he wasn't leavin' 'til he talks to me. I was in the back room doin' bookkeeping, and they told me just hang in there, they were gonna watch me through the door and in a coupla minutes they'd come in. And Florabelle did. McQueary was askin' how I was gettin' to the water works and where I lived. He was tryin' to find out how to get to me. The state police were investigatin' him, and he was tipped that I'd went to 'em.

The prosecutor's investigator came out and had me draw a diagram of the house to prove I was in it. He told me about a girl who come in with her father and made a statement against McQueary, so I knew there was another one. The state police asked me to make a formal statement, and I went down there and did — on tape. I thought somethin' would be done. They asked me about three other girls who had apparently complained against McQueary, but I didn't know any of 'em. My probation officer asked if I'd be willin' to take a polygraph, and I said yes. I did, and I passed. Another girl did, and she passed. I didn't hear anything after that for months.

Then I found out the prosecutor wasn't gonna move on it. I asked why, and a drug prosecutor who wanted me to help 'em in a sting operation said the case was too political to push. He said, "If it had been my call, I'd have done something. But the district attorney chose not to." That really upset me, so I left a message for this guy to call me, and he did. I put him on the speakerphone so my boyfriend could hear what he was saying. He told me no criminal charges were gonna be filed and McQueary probably wouldn't be fired. He said the commissioners had decided not to act on it.

I got really motivated and said, "How do you know that he ain't takin' girls to his house and actually raping 'em? And they'll be too afraid to say anything about it because they'll go to jail." He said, "He possibly could be." My mouth just dropped to the floor, and I said, "And you don't care? Are you just gonna piss this off?" He said, "I'm not pissin' this off." I said, "I know there's other complaints besides mine. If you're worried about my credibility, how is it that other girls can report the same thing and they don't know each other?" He said, "Well, it just takes time." "How much time do you need?" He wouldn't respond.

I was really upset. I said to my girlfriend, "How is it that if a woman's attacked, it doesn't mean anything to a man?" They think, You're a woman; you should expect it. But I don't expect it! I don't think it's right! First I wrote to the National Organization for Women, and they couldn't help me. I knew I couldn't get a lawyer in Terre Haute because of McQueary's and McClain's political ties. So I went to the library and got phone numbers and started callin' several law firms in Indianapolis and explained my story and asked who'd be best. The name Michael Sutherlin kept comin' up. I paid him a $150 retainer, and he took the case on contingency.

I filed a complaint with the state civil rights commission against the district attorney for not filing charges. And at first it was real scary. Mike Sutherlin and several others have got their tires slashed and windows have been shot out. After we did a press conference, the media just chewed me up. They brought up my sexual assault before. Judge McClain got on the news and said, "You need to look at these people. . . ." He blasted me big-time—judged my character without even knowin' me. I felt the world had come down on me, because now I had the *whole system* against me.

I cried for two or three days. My mother had to go shoppin' for me, I wouldn't go out of the house. My boyfriend had said, "You better know what you're gettin' into when you're filin' this suit." And I said, "You never know what you're gonna do until you're put in that position. Either I do something about it or let him be in office and keep doin' things like this. What's right?" But I don't feel like it shoulda been left to me!

[McQueary pleaded guilty. The charges against him were dropped from seven class-C felonies to one class-A misdemeanor with seven subparts, and he was asked to admit to each and every act of bribery as stated in the original charge. He received a thirty-day sentence, of which he served only fifteen days. A civil suit was settled out of court.]

Dr. Jean Y. Jew is a Chinese-American doctor in her mid-forties who grew up in Greenwood, Mississippi, and I first heard fragments of her dramatic story from a dean at Indiana University. Among academic women, particularly in the sciences, Dr. Jew is honored as a trailblazer. She lives in Iowa, where she provoked an uproar by taking on the state university, and as I have never been there, Jean and I have still not met. We spent more than four hours on the telephone, however, and I read the judge's lengthy decision in her case. Since she had impressed me as a capable, diligent, cautious, and — yes — honorable woman, I actually wept when I heard that she won.

Jean is the eldest of five children born to hard-working immigrant parents who counted on the transforming power of education for their children. She first encountered sexual harassment when she was twenty-five, after following Dr. Terence Williams, a mentor from Tulane, to the University of Iowa Medical School. There she became a scapegoat in the crazed tangle of departmental politics, and after spending ten years beseiged by a humiliating onslaught of false charges and insults, she decided to sue the university. Her story not only illustrates the slow evolution of a sexual harassment suit, but comments ironically on the American Dream.

I was born in this country, but my parents were born in China. My father had come over as a thirteen-year-old boy to work with an uncle who had a grocery store in Mississippi, but at that time, anyone who was nonwhite had to go to a black school. His uncle told him that to get a good education he had to go to a white school, so he sent him to another relative in Arkansas, where Asians could go to school with whites. Later, he was drafted into the army and worked at the Oregon shipyards during the war. When he was twenty-six or twenty-seven, he went back to China to look for a bride. His meeting with my mother was arranged by mutual friends. (In China, relatives find out which families have daughters of marriageable age.) My mother was seventeen, and she'd met him only once before they got married. Within a few days, they were flying to the United States.

They came to Greenwood, Mississippi, and opened a grocery store in the black section of town, and then I was born. My siblings and I attended elementary school in the fifties and high school in the sixties. At that time the schools were still segregated, but by then the Asians were allowed to go to the white school. Everyone knew their place according to the color of their skin. So I was used to a society in which my family didn't really belong anywhere; we weren't a part of black society, but we weren't a part of white society either. Without my siblings, I wouldn't have had anyone to interact with socially. The other Chinese families in town all had grocery stores and everybody was very busy, so there wasn't a lot of time for playing with other children. Certainly we weren't invited home by our schoolmates or non-Chinese families.

We lived in the back of the store, and our social environment *was* the store. As children, we were very aware of the hierarchy, but my parents would always tell us that education was the key to everything — that it didn't matter if whites thought they were better, because education would make the difference and blacks who were educated could make good. We had customers who were schoolteachers and whose sons and daughters went off to college. It was rare, but it did happen.

Like many immigrant families, the children were always urged to achieve and A's were the only grades acceptable. My parents were very proud when we did well in school, and they dreamed of us going into professions like law or medicine, where we'd have a better life and wouldn't have to work the long hours they did. They were very frugal and sent all of us to private colleges. Many of my parents' Chinese friends would tell them it was a waste to spend money to educate a daughter because you wanted her to get married and have children. They'd say that if girls got too educated, it would be harder for them to find husbands. My parents didn't buy into that for their daughters, and they'd talk to me about being a doctor. Doctors were very well-respected and earned a comfortable living — so this was what they aspired to for me.

As it turned out, I liked the sciences and did well. And I had teachers in high school who encouraged me. Our school district produced a number of National Merit Scholars each year, and a large number of my graduating class went on to excellent colleges and universities like Wellesley and Vanderbilt. I went to Sophie Newcomb College and graduated in three years, and after that, Tulane University. I wanted to do things as fast as possible and get into medical school. And nothing happened in all those years to contradict what I'd been taught by my teachers and parents. My experience confirmed the Puritan ethic: if you work hard enough, anything is possible.

Medical school was tough, but I'd been warned. It was the first place where I heard overt comments and saw overt behaviors indicating that being a woman could be a problem. There were only seven or eight of us out of a class of a hundred and thirty-five, and more than one professor told us outright that a woman didn't belong in medicine. Only two women were on the faculty, and they were very unusual. Both were nonconformists; they weren't married, they'd been the pioneers and had graduated at the top of their class. Sexist jokes were rampant, but the women just took it. We understood that since we were in a man's world, we had to learn to put up with all this, and we didn't talk about it amongst ourselves. We were bound more by common interests than by the fact that we were women.

I had male lab partners, and men I met over the cadaver table remain friends to this day. I'd go out for a quick dinner with these men, together or individually, and I was friends with their wives, too. I don't come off as sexy, and I acted just like a buddy. There were men who were sexists, but at the same time there were men who were very supportive and treated you as their equals. And there were men who enjoyed flirting but who didn't mean it in a sexual way. It was pure camaraderie.

It was at this time that I got interested in doing research and met Dr. Terence Williams, a professor at Tulane, and his wife, Dr. Glenys Williams, who worked part-time in the laboratory. He's twenty years older than I, and it was common for a professor to treat a student like a daughter. Along with others, I was invited to their home for journal club meetings or occasional social events. Dr. Williams worked late, and it was not unusual for several of us to take breaks in our experiments to go out to dinner. Sometimes there were six of us, sometimes a couple, sometimes just Dr. Williams and myself. We'd always go to a well-lighted place and come right back to work. During all my years there, I never heard anything implying that I was doing something inappropriate.

I graduated in '73, when Dr. Williams was offered the chairmanship at Iowa and invited three of us to go with him for a year. Two of us went, and within months, I started hearing these allegations about Dr. Williams and myself. Another post-doc student told me that he and his wife had met a faculty member named Crassley who told him Dr. Williams was immoral and was screwing Dr. Jew. [All the names of Jean Jew's antagonists have been changed.] I can't remember responding. I was terribly embarrassed. *We're talking about sex here,* and I'd been raised in a traditional Chinese family — very straitlaced and conservative — where we didn't talk about those things. Moreover, in the South, we'd been taught that nice people didn't talk about such things. I couldn't imagine why on earth anyone would make up something like this, and I thought that once they realized it simply wasn't true, that it was all a big mistake, the problem would take care of itself.

Dr. Crassley continued to be friendly in the hall and acted as though nothing had happened, and I didn't say anything to anybody about it. The post-doc indicated that he'd told Dr. Williams, who was the last person I wanted to talk to about it. We didn't have that kind of relationship. We weren't even *friends* at that point: I was a post-doc and he was my professor.

Within another couple of months, I saw these cartoons taped on a wall in the hallway. They were line drawings of buxom women from some publication like *Playboy* — and someone had written comments at the bottom in green ink. One had a naked woman with an older man, and the inked-in comments referred to the woman as a neuroanatomist, which I was. Another referred to my work as a microscopist. I was *really* embarrassed. The green ink just stood out from the rest of the page, and as soon as I saw that the cartoons referred to me, I rushed on by. They were outside the lab of a former acting departmental chairman—I felt sure he'd put them there—so I wouldn't have felt I could take them down, and they stayed up for days. They were in a hallway I had to pass to get to my lab, and I just kept my head down. Dr. Williams didn't talk to me about them at that time, though he testified later that he'd told the faculty member that these were very childish.

How could you go up to somebody and say, "I didn't do these things, I'm not that sort of a person"? I didn't really have any friends here then, and I'd grown up in a culture where you keep a stiff upper lip and go on about your business. That was my normal way of handling things. I'd heard about remarks that are made to women, and my experience simply seemed to confirm that no matter how unfounded such allegations might be, people are going to say things. I still felt confident that once I showed everyone that I was competent and that I wasn't that sort of person, then things would be fine. Once people got to know me, they would be decent and fair.

I realized that I really liked research and decided to stay at Iowa, but as the years went on, these incidents continued. I'd hear from virtually every faculty member that Dr. Crassley continued saying these things. He asked a new faculty member from New Orleans, "You knew Jean and Terry back at Tulane. Were they having an affair down there, too?" This man's mouth fell open, and he said, "What in the world can have given you that idea?"

Finally, I started speaking to Dr. Williams about the rumors, and he admitted that he'd heard them. He said, "Dr. Crassley has a problem, but I think if you show that you don't hold anything against him, everything will be all right." I didn't realize how pervasive the rumors were. And I thought people would see that they didn't have anything to do with my work performance.

But then in 1978, Dr. Williams came back from a meeting with the dean and told me that a faculty member who was filing a grievance had threatened to produce an *eyewitness* who would testify that Dr. Williams and I had engaged in sexual intercourse in his office! *I was totally shocked.* This was the first time I'd been openly confronted with these accusations, and I was flabbergasted. Dr. Logan, who was filing the grievance, had been denied tenure, and his strategy was to damage the credibility of the chair. Dr. Williams said the dean told him it was going to be nasty. Still, I was innocent, they weren't going to be able to produce a witness, and I thought, This is not something that affects me, I'll just keep out of it.

Then in January of 1979, I was walking down the hall, and as I passed an open doorway, I heard a faculty member named Dr. Mickle yell, "There goes that slut now!" *I thought, What is going on here?* I took a different route back to my office, but later I called the faculty member whose office I'd passed, and he told me Dr. Mickle had been drunk and had called me a whore. He'd said to him, "Jack, I wish you'd let me take you to AA [Alcoholics Anonymous]," but Dr. Mickle just left to go back to his office. Several faculty members wrote the dean expressing concern for Dr. Mickle's condition and the fact that he was disrupting the department. But none objected to what he was saying about me.

This was the first time I just broke down and cried. I decided I'd have to do something about it, and I went to see the vice-president for academic affairs, Dr. Harriet Clear. Her credentials were in philosophy and physics, and she'd worked on the Manhattan Project. So I felt she'd be sympathetic. But she told me that somebody bringing a grievance was given rather unlimited rights. I said, "What about *my* rights?" She implied that things had gotten out of hand, and it was unfortunate that I'd gotten caught up in it, but there wasn't much I could do. It was her honest opinion that I'd be hurt even more if I tried to proceed with a grievance. Then she advised me to retain my own counsel because things could get very nasty. *I said, "Why? What does all this have to do with me?" And she said, "It has nothing to do with you."*

The dean pretty much told me the same thing. He said, "This is a small town, it's a goldfish bowl, this is the sort of thing a single woman has to put up with." *What had happened to me, he insisted, was not unusual for single women who aspire to careers in male-dominated professions.* If you can't take the heat, get out of the kitchen — it was that sort of attitude — and he, too, advised me to retain counsel.

The grievance procedure *was* very nasty. They never produced a witness, but there were many innuendoes. And the faculty committee found for Dr. Logan: he was given tenure! In my defamation trial in 1990, he was asked about his claim that an eyewitness had seen Dr. Williams and me having intercourse in his office. Dr. Logan said he'd *inferred* the story from what the janitor had said and then told maybe forty people. (The janitor denied seeing it and denied saying anything that could be so interpreted.) He never apologized to me.

In 1982, graffiti referring to my sexual orientation appeared on the men's room wall. And in 1983, my performance evaluation for the first time included negative comments and my promotion to full professor was voted down five to three. The recommendation was made that I change collaborators and my research topic. No one I knew had *ever* been asked to do *any* of this before.

Professors were said to comment that women and blacks had it made and to complain that I'd had far more advantages than some of them. Then I learned that on the same day I was being evaluated, an obscene limerick about me was written on the men's restroom wall. Dr. Williams had it photographed.

I said, "Oh, please don't cause a fuss," but he ignored me and said, "In light of the evaluations, I think you ought to have these photographs in case you ever decide to do something about it."

There were no other women faculty in the department, and how do you talk to a man about this sort of thing? Still, I finally decided to go to the affirmative action office. They sent me to the academic vice-president, a man named Leffler, who saw that whenever anybody in the medical school had had a grievance, the strategy had been to attack Dr. Williams's character — and then stories about me would turn up. Anonymous letters had been sent to the dean that referred to me as "Chinese pussy." Vice-president Leffler looked at my curriculum vitae and said there was no question that I'd deserved promotion. He said, "You've done a good job and you have a good record. They're going to make your life hell, but you'll continue to progress." Crazily enough, I felt reassured by that.

But once I got back to my office, I started thinking, *Why should they make my life hell?* I'd put up with this for *ten years* believing that I would not be hurt and my career would not be damaged. But now I was sitting there with an evaluation of my performance that was setting up criteria for me that hadn't been set up for anybody else. I was being given standards to meet that were going to be very arduous, and my career *was* being affected. So the stuff the administrators had been telling me all these years was *not* true. I *wasn't* going to be all right. My career *was* going to suffer. And the stress and rumors had damaged my psyche and my ability to function.

At this time, something had just appeared in the *Chronicle of Higher Education* about the Regender decision at the University of Minnesota giving women faculty members the right to sue the university on grounds of sex discrimination. So I called several faculty women mentioned in the article to ask them who their lawyers were and whether they would recommend them. That's how I came to get in touch with Carolyn Chalmers in Minneapolis.

In December of 1983, Carolyn agreed to take my case, and the first thing she did was send a letter to Vice-president Leffler asking for some resolution of the problem. In 1984, he appointed a faculty panel to investigate and make recommendations, and the panel found in my favor: I *had* been harassed, and I *had* been discriminated against on the basis of my sex. They recommended to the university that they set up a procedure by which I could be evaluated fairly and that they call in the faculty members who'd been identified as principals in harassing me and tell them to stop. They also recommended that the university issue one statement taking a stand against sexual harassment and another exonerating me. *The university didn't do anything!* In fact, up until two weeks before the trial, the university's representatives were still saying that this was not a sexual harassment case.

In October of '85, Carolyn filed suit in order to preserve our rights under the statute of limitations and took the case on a partial contingency basis. (I'd be responsible for expenses.) We filed both a federal and a state civil rights suit — at that time, federal law didn't entitle you to damages — and we named Dr. Crassley in the state suit in order to get him to stop harassing me. The university hired private counsel for Dr. Crassley, and his counsel requested that the two cases — the university's and Dr. Crassley's — be severed. So we had *three* lawsuits going at once.

The years between '85 and '89 were filled with legal gymnastics and attempts by the university to delay and wear me down. We didn't go to trial until September of '89, and we had to keep filing motions to get access to documents. It's emotionally as well as financially draining. In early '86, the attorney general's assistant told my attorney, "There is no jury in Iowa that's going to find sexual harassment in this case. There's no jury that will believe that a man and woman who work together like Dr. Jew and Dr. Williams wouldn't expect there to be talk like this." Carolyn and I didn't know that this wasn't true. All we had to go on was our belief that if it was true, it wasn't *fair* and it wasn't *legal*.

I never knew what was going to happen next, so I had to be vigilant all the time. If I hadn't been held to a higher level of scrutiny before, I *certainly* was now. I knew very well that the university would use any chinks in my armor to bring me down. They'd argue that this was just another case of a woman crying "discrimination" when she simply wasn't good enough. So on top of the strain of fighting your institution, you were on display all the time.

Even when we got to the federal trial, the university's position was that I should have changed my behavior. The associate dean said, "In her position, I'd have taken care never to be seen with Dr. Williams outside the department and I'd never have worked at night in the lab. Then there would never have been even the appearance of impropriety." The attorney general's office represented the university and contacted former faculty members and graduate students, calling witnesses from all over this country and Canada to testify to my "special relationship" with Dr. Williams, based on the fact that we'd worked together, and car-pooled, and been seen shopping together. When my attorney protested that the conduct of the university and the attorney general's office was causing me further damage, they argued that when I decided to fight the university, I should have expected all this to happen.

The first case was tried in federal court in Des Moines, and the outrageous ways the university chose to defend itself were designed to embarrass me. I was asked about my use of birth control pills. Why had I taken them and for how long? They tried to enter into evidence the fact that my sister had worked as a Playboy bunny and to imply from that that I was morally suspect. I was asked whom I dated. Their witnesses said *awful* things to convince the judge that I was immoral and incompetent. All these questions were irrelevant to whether or not I'd been sexually harassed, but they were designed to impugn my character. (This is why I empathized with Anita Hill when they tried to make people think that she was crazy — that she was imagining things.) Their whole strategy centered on trying to prove that these allegations had been true — or that if they were not true, my behavior would have led any reasonable person to believe that they were. Protesting this added tremendously to my legal costs.

While we waited for the decision in the federal case, the university insisted on pressing ahead with the state defamation suit involving just Dr. Crassley. They were claiming that what he'd done was all a part of academic freedom and therefore protected. It was a free-speech issue! In order to find him guilty of defamation, the jury had to find that his insulting remarks were not related to his job.

I suffered from depression and eczema as a result of the ordeal. And the magistrate ruled that since I was claiming emotional damage, she would grant the university's motion that I undergo a psychiatric and psychological examination. (It's a catch-22. If you haven't lost your job and aren't a total physical and emotional wreck, then where's the damage? The fact that you're strong enough to fight something like this is used by the other side to prove you haven't been hurt!) The university chose the psychiatrist, who interpreted the results of my psychological tests and contended that I was genetically predisposed to depression. He'd asked me if anybody in my family could be described as a perfectionist, and I'd told him that my mother was fussy about having a clean house. On the basis of that, he said that there was a family history of perfectionist/compulsive behavior and that individuals with this behavior were prone to depression, independent of any stressful events! The jury heard this, and you could tell from their faces that they weren't buying the nonsense.

Their psychologist argued that I was in the high range of normal for paranoid tendencies (just short of full-fledged paranoia). My attorney then asked whether the tests on which he based his diagnosis asked questions like "Do you sometimes feel that people are following you?" "Do you think people are trying to do you harm?" "Do you think people are looking at you?" He said yes, those were the kinds of questions they asked. So she said, "Are you aware that for a week we've heard testimony about people following Dr. Jew? Saying things about her? Writing anonymous letters? Trying to look into her windows? Is it possible that the answers to these questions are yes because that's *exactly* what people *are* doing?" He had to admit that those facts would skew the tests.

One of Dr. Crassley's witnesses talked about seeing me having sex on the departmental library table. She said she'd happened on this couple engaged in sexual activity there and identified the man as Dr. Williams and presumed the woman to be me because of the color of her legs. She told the story three different times, and *her version of the facts varied significantly every single time.* When she was asked in the state defamation trial whether she was aware that her facts differed from her earlier accounts, she said yes, and there was no guarantee that if she had to say it again they wouldn't differ again. Lurid headlines about such stories appeared in the newspapers *every day* during the latter part of the state trial. The papers didn't begin covering the story until the defense came on; they showed up for all these salacious stories. And to have all this on the front pages was just sickening.

In his closing statement, the deputy assistant attorney general said, "Your Honor, this isn't sexual harassment. This is the way of the world." Dr. Crassley's attorney, in his closing statement, said, "Ladies and gentlemen, use your common sense. Here's a young woman and a man who work together, who carpool together. . . ." I think they really believed they could convince a jury something had been going on, or that I was making a big deal out of nothing.

The jury found against Dr. Crassley seven to one. It made me feel badly that there was one person who hadn't believed me. But the woman who voted against me called to tell me why. She said, "The things that happened to you were terrible, and all of us believed you. I voted against the verdict because I felt the amount of money being awarded you was insulting. It wouldn't have even begun to pay your attorney's fees." (They weren't allowed to consider legal fees, and so they'd awarded me $5,000 in compensatory damages and $30,000 in punitive.)

Then the university supplemented their motion to the federal court by saying that the jury had decided that Dr. Crassley had *not* been speaking within the scope of his employment — that his insults had nothing to do with his job — so *the university had no responsibility or liability!*

The judge didn't buy their argument. His decision finally came down on August 28, 1990. I got a call from Carolyn's secretary that morning, and she said, "Jean, we have a decision." I just got quiet, and then I said, "Tell me. Is it good or bad?" She said, "It's good." Carolyn got on the phone and said, "Jean, it's so good: he's given us everything!" After we got through laughing and crying on the phone, I went to the three men in the department who'd been such staunch supporters all those years, and we were jumping in the hallways. The stakes had become so high because the university had done *everything* to discredit us. (The first sentence of the university's last amended response before trial had read, "Dr. Jew is a plaintiff without a conscience.")

After the federal judge's order was handed down, the university waited till the last day of the deadline for filing an appeal and then filed a request for extension, saying they needed time to try to negotiate a settlement. (They hadn't even *tried* to contact us.) They said that such a ruling would set a dangerous precedent because the judge had not considered the chilling effect his decision would have on academic freedom and free speech!

Privately, we were told that the university didn't want to pay my attorney's fees, so they were trying to drive a wedge between Carolyn and me. They said it wasn't in my best interests to have this appeal, because however small the chances of their winning, there *was* still that chance and I could lose everything. So the university argued that if my attorney were really looking out for my best interests, she would lower her fees.

But Carolyn and I had become strong friends — we'd been through the wars together — and I'd also become more aware how few women can wage this sort of battle. Most women simply don't have the resources. A lot of attorneys don't take cases like this because they're so chancy. So it was *very* important to me that she and her firm be reimbursed so that she could continue to take on these cases and other firms would be encouraged by her example. With a lesser lawyer, I wouldn't have won, and so we stuck together. [The fees and expenses in Jean's case totaled $895,000.]

A core group of supporters was so incensed by this move on the university's part that they got a copy of the judge's order and raised money to make copies and distribute them to every faculty member in the university. Then letters started coming in to the administrators and to the newspapers expressing community and faculty outrage. The university withdrew its appeal. As a matter of law, the state and civil rights suit was bound by the findings of the federal court, and so the state case was settled.

I never considered leaving the University of Iowa after being vindicated — for two reasons. Academia is very small, very competitive, and very conservative. Universities don't want to buy trouble, and news travels fast. When someone's personal and professional reputation has been besmirched, there are very few institutions that would take a risk. One of our expert witnesses said that if all the press stopped now, and the university embraced me, it would be at least another *ten years* before the damage would be repaired. Since he'd had an opportunity to see my credentials and know in detail what had happened, he said he'd have no hesitation about hiring me. But it would be difficult to convince the rest of the faculty to go along. When there are other faculty applicants available — younger people who don't have tenure and are cheaper because they're assistant professors — why take a chance?

But there's a more important reason why I didn't want to leave Iowa. Time after time, when women experience sexual harassment, they question whether they should fight, and they're told, "Even when you win, you lose." I'd talked to an older woman who'd gone through something similar, and she advised me not to fight, for this same reason. But when you leave a place, you're saying they succeeded in driving you out. And I didn't do anything wrong! Why should I have to leave and start all over again?

If Huck Finn had been a girl, he'd have been Tammy Miller. She is small, wiry, and fiercely independent, and the phrase that recurs in her story is "That ain't right!" After suffering the most grotesque incident of harassment I found, she took on Hoosier Energy, one of the two largest electric power plants in the state of Indiana.

Now in her early thirties, Tammy is divorced and has a teenage son, and she's been working hard all her life. I met her at the home of her friend Sandie Vaughn, a union representative, who says of her, "She was a good old girl. She cut up with the guys and had a good time to get through the work day."

I sat for three hours in Sandie's living room listening raptly. Tammy was wound as tight as an old-fashioned corset, and she finds her story no easier to tell as the months pass.

I'd worked with men practically all my life. I grew up in a small town and trusted everybody. I never thought anybody would hurt me as long as I was fair and honest with 'em. So I got along with everybody. I'd seen what dishonest people could do, and I'd say to myself, "Well, I'm not gonna be like that." So I treated everybody fair.

I started working for chemical fertilizer companies when my son was two. In '81, my husband's company was needin' help in the summertime, when the farmers was in the fields. I went in there and started drivin' those fork-lift trucks and front-end loaders and mixin' all the fertilizer and workin' with anhydrous ammonia tanks. Off and on for five or six years, I was doin' manual labor. I also did carpentry work part-time with my dad.

Then a friend got on at Hoosier Energy, and he said, "Whoa, you need to get in down there. . . ." They hired a bunch of local people every year for temporary work. Just put your name in and they'll call you in if there's an opening. It's about seventeen miles away from where I live. So I got on, and I couldn't believe I was makin' that kinda money. They'd tell me what to do, and I'd give 'em eight hours solid work—cleaning, mopping floors, taking snuff mounds off the walls. The place was really nasty, and I kept gettin' called back. Finally I got hired full-time. The supervisor hauled me down to the front office, sayin' to the head honchos: "Look at her hands. She's a worker. *This is who she is.* . . ."

In December of '87 I was workin' in the material handling building. A supervisor I didn't know very well come up and said did I know the definition of a lesbian? I kinda stopped and looked at him, and I said, "No, and I don't think I really want to know." He says, "Well, I'll tell you. It's another fuckin' woman tryin' to do a man's job." The more I thought about that, the madder I got. So I went to another supervisor and told him, and he's like, "Whoa, he's in trouble." The man ended up apologizing to me. But that's kinda where everything started.

You have to go through a six-months probationary period, and any time in that six months, they can let you go. Three months into my probation, I was in there cleanin' and they'd hung mistletoe and I didn't know it. They started hollerin' at me to come, so I just walked out there. Then Tommy grabbed hold and kissed me so hard I had a place on my lips where his whiskers dug in. I got away from him and everybody was laughin'. I said, "Don't touch me, you guys! I don't care about water-throwin' and stuff like that, but don't be touchin' me." So they knew right then and there.

When I was still a temporary, I was up on the fifth floor sweepin' underneath this tank. There was four of us up there, and one of the guys stuck his finger down into his coveralls and wagged it. They kept hollerin' at me, and at first I thought it really was his tallywacker. And I got real embarrassed and took off. They said, "Aw, it's just his finger!" So I went across to the other side of this tank and started sweepin'. This guy named Charlie tapped me on the shoulder, and I turned around. And he had his pants down and his tallywacker was just hangin' there. Oh my God! I dropped the broom. Face went blood red. My head hurt, I was embarrassed so bad. They seen my face, and they said, "He did it! He did it!" and kept teasin' me about it.

Before the day was over, everybody knew. That's just the way this guy was. He had a nice tallywacker, and he showed it to everybody. He was a friendly young pup. You always wanted to work with him because it was never boring. I'd be drivin' the truck and he'd be sittin' with his arm across me, and he'd be jiggling with my boob. I'd haul off and deck him and tell him to keep his hands off me — and he would the rest of the time.

On May 20, 1988, we was sittin' around gettin' our orders for the day. They'd hired the first black temporary employee. I got along with him, but the guys had got up about $100 to shave this other guy's head. And the black guy said, "For a hundred dollars I'd shave her head." *Talkin' about me!* I'm like, "You and what other army?" My supervisor got a pair of scissors and gave 'em to this guy, and they chased me around the room. When he got the scissors back, my supervisor said he needed a volunteer to go to the material handling building, and I said, "I'm goin'! Get me out of here! I'm not gonna worry about you guys cuttin' my hair today."

I hadn't been over to that building for a while, and the guys was comin' in and sayin', "How you been? What's been goin' on?" I told 'em the reason I was over there was because of the scissors deal. And *they* started in, "Well, what can *we* do to you?" This guy settin' by me said, "Let's just give her a hickey — [a bite on her neck] — and let her go home and explain *that* to her husband." He went to grab me, and when he did, I got up to run and hit my side up against the table. I'm kinda limpin' and goin', "You're not touchin' me." I ended up over by the acting supervisor for the week, and he said, well, *he'd* bite me on the neck. I told him, "You can kiss my ass, you're not touchin' me." He goes, "I won't kiss your ass. I might bite your ass." I smarted off and left.

When I come back, they was still goin' on about the hickeys. So I said, "Jake, what if I'd done that to you? You'd have to explain that bruise to your wife." Things kinda settled down, but about fifteen minutes later, Arnie grabbed ahold of me and started hollerin' at Springer, the supervisor, to come over and bite my ass. I tried to get away from him, and he hollered at Tommy. *So one of 'em had ahold of my feet, they wrestled me down and turned me over, and that supervisor come over and bit me so hard I was bleedin' through my jeans. It took three men to do it.* I got up and started callin' 'em every name in the book. Told 'em they'd hurt me. Went into the restroom and dropped my pants and kinda pulled my underwear up. I was bleedin'. I hit the door, and these guys were standin' there and I said, "Look at what you did to me, you sonuvabitch." He said, "I didn't know I bit you that hard." A guy got me some medicine, and I doctored it up.

Everybody was going, "Don't say nothin', don't do nothin'. If you do, everybody'd lose their jobs." Nobody said they was sorry. At lunch, they made me set with 'em and play cards — them three and me! They were saying, "Just forget it." And then they started teasin' me. If I said anything, they'd get me down and bite the other side so I'd have matchin' teeth marks. They threatened to tell my husband. I didn't want him to know because he'd want me to quit.

I used to tell my husband everything. But they'd put wooden dildos in my lunch box, and my husband always made my lunch. I had to quit takin' my lunch because at five o'clock one morning, he's holdin' up this piece of wood that looks like a dildo, and he's like, "What's this?" (He'd lost it over the kissin' deal, so I wasn't gonna tell him about the bite.)

But I kept thinkin' about it, and I said to myself, "That's not right!" So about one o'clock, I went to my supervisor, but he said, "I'm on my way out, I gotta go to the closin' on my house." Six o'clock that night, I finally got up the nerve to tell my husband, and he called Springer, the guy who'd bit me, and Springer laughed. He said, "I apologized. I didn't mean to bite her that hard." I called the union. They laughed. The union rep said he'd never heard anything like that before.

So me and my husband decided I'd go in Monday morning and talk to the plant manager. Tell him what happened and ask him what to do. *They went too far. Somethin' had to be done.* When they found out I was goin', my supervisor and his immediate supervisor kept me in a room for about thirty minutes and wouldn't let me out until I said why I wanted to see the plant manager. They held the door, and I said, "It's between me and Harry. I need to talk to him and find out what to do." Finally I told 'em and, boom, that door was open.

Word had gotten around, and when I walked into Harry's office, there were five supervisors in there, too, and he goes, "What is all this?" He tilted back in his chair, and he goes, "You mean to tell me he bit you so hard through your blue jeans that you was bleedin'?" And I said, "Yeah, and I got pictures of it." And he goes, "Well, what do you want me to do about it?" And I go, "I don't know. That's why I'm here." The supervisor who gave the guy the scissors said, "It's just horseplay that got out of hand." I was thinkin' to myself, "That's not right." (That supervisor'd made me arm-wrestle him when I first started. I coulda whooped him. But it woulda been real bad for him to get beat by a woman, so I'd let him win. There he was all puffed up, and I'd thought, "I'll be all right since I let him win!")

Absolutely *nobody* would speak to me. They done an investigation, and the three guys lost their jobs. Supervision said I wanted them three men fired. That's an out-and-out lie. But the union business agent told me the union men had got up a verbal smear campaign and there was nothin' he could do about it. And the company wrote me up and said it was all my fault because of my takin' part in verbal horseplay.

I got me a lawyer and said, "Hey, I don't care what you do, but just keep my job. What happened shouldn't ever have happened. It wasn't my fault." I'd worked side by side with these people for a long time, and I couldn't believe they was doing this to me.

When the union's business agent found out I had a lawyer, he goes, "Would you settle right now for $500,000?" And I said, "No." He said, "Why won't you settle?" I said, "I want the truth told. You guys have took everything I've worked hard for all my life away from me. And I ain't backin' out." So a supervisor said I was an embarrassment to the company.

'Bout a year after the biting, I got a shit evaluation. I'd just been doin' my job as a utility operator, never had the first argument with my supervisor. I was so upset about it, it just throwed me. I'd thought for six months that they were givin' me a shot and everybody'd forgot about the lawsuit. So I got the plant manager and the plant personnel manager at Bloomington involved, and supervision went ape. I stirred up so much stuff they gave me a special evaluation. I proved they'd based the first one on rumors, lies, and gossip, and they admitted it. But I lost six months of on-the-job trainin'. They made me start all over again.

I asked for a shift change so I could train to advance or "step up" within the plant. A guy named Ed went to my supervisor and said, "What does she have to do to get stepped up around here?" The supervisor got a training sheet out and said, "When she knows every single thing on this paper." Ed goes, "There's not a man in this place who can tell you everything on that sheet!" So my supervisor put a three-page disciplinary reprimand letter in *my* file. I'd had two ink pens clipped on the front of my shirt. He wrote me up for that. And I'd been out of my work area to bring in some bottled water. I had bronchitis, and they'd had me in this little room cleaning big motors. I'd started coughing, so I hopped on a bike and went down to get a drink. I got wrote up for that.

Here's this three-page written reprimand: extra ink pens in my pocket, bad attitude, bringing problems from home to work, blah, blah, blah. So I asked for a shift change and filed another harassment charge. The supervisor said I had a behavior problem, and I wasn't gettin' a shift change. I finally went to the plant manager and told him, "If you don't get me off his shift, I'm goin' to every TV and newspaper that's been wantin' to talk to me for the last two and a half years, and I'm spillin' my guts." Next day I was off his shift.

Then I asked to go on this guy's crew who was a fanatic on training, because I wanted to get stepped up. But they came up with this test and said, "You're not gettin' stepped up until you pass this test — oral and written." I came out with flyin' colors on the orals. They said they didn't have the written part done yet. And I'm thinkin', "Whoa, that ain't right. Nobody else had to take a written test." That afternoon, I told the plant manager I was gonna file a grievance, and I got stepped up in four hours. Next day, they gave me a test and stepped me up again. I got stepped up twice in two days, and that was it.

Then here come Anita Hill and Clarence Thomas. Boy, if that didn't change stuff. Everybody was mad at everybody else. Everybody was givin' their opinions. "He's lyin'." "She's lyin'." "He's a nigger and he married a white woman, he's outta his race." Supervision started havin' meetings, they'd get the men off on one side and the women on the other. Automatically the men were against the women and the women were against the men. The supervisors told the men, "You stay the fuck away from the women, and you'll be all right. Don't talk to 'em, don't be seen with 'em, don't *nothin'.*" I had people come up and say, "You stay the hell away from me until your lawsuit's settled down." My supervisor said, "You don't talk about anything unless it's work-related." I said, "No problem!"

I didn't want to get stepped up then because I was afraid somebody was gonna turn a little valve this much, and an hour into my shift, it could trip the unit. And then I'd get into all kinds of trouble. So I had to write a letter sayin' I didn't want to get stepped up when all this dissension was goin' on.

I went to the doctor and gave him my gun. I was afraid I'd shoot myself or one of them and get it over with. I told him how I was feelin' and said I just couldn't get those thoughts outta my head. He gave me three different kinds of medicines, and I started takin' it exactly like he said. Then for three days I didn't know who the hell I was or where the hell I was at. Somebody had to take care of my kid. I ended up in the hospital, lost a lotta weight, wasn't eating and stopped taking care of myself. For two weeks I didn't go to work. Finally I started eatin' again and I was feelin' better. Off I go back to work.

I'd been going to a therapist, who said, "Don't get into any verbal con-frontations. Keep a low profile." My supervisor starts in on me again, and they called a surprise meeting where everybody was calling everybody else a liar. After that, my stomach was killing me, and I said I had to go home to get my medicine. My boss said, "Go home and get it, and come right back."

I still can't explain it. It was like a tape recorder goin' over and over in my head sayin' "I can't stand it no more. They want me outta here, I'm outta here." I grabbed all the medication I could find and got my radio and went up on this crane that goes across the turbines. I never should've been found. I got on the citizens band radio and asked my supervisor if he had a conscience. And I started poppin' pills. I remember askin' him, "What's the matter? Can't you find me?" And popped some more pills. That was Thursday mornin' at one A.M., and it was Saturday before I woke up in the hospital. [When she heard that Tammy had tried to kill herself,

Sandie left work, went to the hospital, and got into the intensive care unit. "They had Tammy strapped down. She was havin' convulsions: her organs had shut down. They had her on full respiration. Her lungs had quit. Her digestive system had stopped. She was in critical condition.']

Now they won't let me go back to work. Somebody paid *all* the medical bills, not just 80 percent. But everybody's passin' the buck. My lawyer says they don't want me there, I'm emotionally unstable. I'm like, "Whoa, that ain't right." I was borrowin' money right and left, 'til finally my long-term disability kicked in. Even my lawyer wants me to settle out of court, and I won't do it. She says there's no money in goin' to court, but I've told her all along I don't care about the money, *I want the truth told.* Now she's filed another lawsuit and the Equal Employment Opportunity Commission's investigatin' it right now.

The insurance said I had to see a licensed psychologist once a month, so my lawyer sent me to a guy. He was to evaluate me. I did nothin' but argue with that man. I told him I wanted to go see a female doctor, and he said, "There's no woman psychologist out there that's gonna help you. What happened to you, males did that, and the only way you're gonna get better is by talkin' to a male psychologist." He told the company I was severely depressed. I prob'ly was that day: I had no money.

Then I got a check and paid everybody off. They want me to say I won't ever seek employment with Hoosier Energy no more, and I won't do that. I coulda done that three years ago.

I cracked, but I didn't break. . . .*

Dr. Margaret Jensvold is a psychiatrist in private practice. Now in her late thirties, she planned to be an academic biological psychiatrist and sailed with great distinction over many academic hurdles to qualify. But because of what happened to her at the National Institute of Mental Health, she can never expect to realize that dream.

Consequently, she sued NIMH, claiming sex discrimination and a sexually hostile work environment, and so seriously does the mental health establishment take her that in 1992, the Department of Health and Human Services petitioned the court to ban her from the National Institutes of Health campus and to bar her from talking with its employees. Dr. Judith Herman, associate clinical professor of psychiatry at the Harvard Medical School, calls her experience the "Tailhook of the

*Forced by the EEOC, they gave Tammy's job back in May 1993. The trial was set for March 1994.

medical establishment," and many expect the Jensvold case to be a landmark in the field. Since the men she is suing are among *the* nationally recognized experts on women's mental health, her case is particularly important to women.

In another life, Margaret Jensvold might have been a Valkyrie: she is a big woman — tall, blonde, and stately. But the clarity with which she speaks betrays the scientist and teacher she studied for so many years to be. With a case she considers part of the backlash against women, she filed her first Equal Employment Opportunity (EEO) complaint on sex discrimination in November 1988, and her second, on the charge of retaliation, in July of 1989. In December of 1990, she filed a Title VII lawsuit, which will go to trial just as this book is published.

I was raised in a great family with strong, powerful, beloved women for some generations back, so I really grew up believing that women and men are equal. I was born in 1956 and grew up mainly in southern California. My father was an aerospace engineer who worked on developing satellites and later on the space shuttle, and my mother taught high school home economics until I was born.

I was the oldest of four girls. We were all in our respective Girl Scout troops; my mother was always leading two Girl Scout troops and doing community organizing, so I was always around many girls. My great-aunt was Jeannette Piccard, who was called the first woman in space in the 1930s, when she piloted the gondola in which she and her husband did high-altitude research. Then in 1974, she was one of eleven women ordained an Episcopalian priest against the canons of the church.

In that year, 1974, I started college, so I was confident that my mother's and my grandmother's generations had fought the battles that opened the doors for my generation to walk through. I've seen extraordinary changes in my lifetime, and I think my problems are part of a huge backlash.

I always wanted to go into academics and do research, and I always did really well. I graduated as valedictorian from my high school. At UCLA, I graduated summa cum laude and Phi Beta Kappa — with honors in my major, which was biochemistry. I went to medical school at Johns Hopkins and was in the top third of my class. Then I did my residency at the University of Pittsburgh, which has more funding for psychiatry research than any place in the United States other than the National Institute of Mental Health. And the Association for Academic Psychiatry named me one of the six psychiatry residents in the

United States showing the greatest promise. Even better, I was named in my third year, though usually fourth-year residents are chosen.

The week after I received that award, I interviewed at NIMH. I wanted a fellowship related to premenstrual syndrome (PMS). (I planned originally to go into gynecology.) I'd spent a year of medical school doing reading about all the conditions that vary with the menstrual cycle, so when I graduated, I had a subspecialty already. By the time I went to NIMH, I'd been working in the field for five or six years. My supervisor, Dr. David Rubinow, was the head of the menstrually related mood disorder program there, the clinical director responsible for clinical care, my residency training director, *and* my fellowship director. He's also a leading authority on premenstrual syndrome.

Biomedicine is a very centralized field; the National Institutes of Health (NIH) and NIMH fund most biomedical research in the U.S. You go there, in fact, to become part of the "good old boys" club. For most men, it functions that way. So to have a bad experience at NIMH is a very bad thing. People don't want to hire you and it basically puts you out of the field.

At NIMH, four male physicians and I were studying premenstrual syndrome. But I was repeatedly excluded from professional opportunities the male physicians had. They coauthored scholarly articles, I couldn't coauthor with them. They followed virtually all the patients, I couldn't follow the patients. They had the patients on treatment trials, I couldn't work with patients on treatment trials. They worked with the drug companies; I couldn't. They intentionally excluded me from a major international conference that I really should have been able to attend. This went on throughout my time there.

The men at NIMH did the "valued" research, and I was relegated to the nonvalued research. I was told to do a study of abuse in PMS patients and controls and ended up taking sexual, physical, and emotional abuse histories. I found an incredibly high incidence of abuse in both the patients *and* the controls. Some of the post-traumatic symptoms were expressed in interesting ways around the menstrual cycle, but they *still* don't want me to publish my research. Since the women weren't telling *them* these stories, I must be imagining the abuse, or exaggerating it.

Meanwhile, the women patients were begging me not to tell the male doctors. I'd tell them I was part of a research team and had to share my findings with the other researchers. But I assured them that what they told me would never be used against them, that their confidentiality would be absolutely honored. As time went on, however, and I saw how the other doctors were using the information against *me,* I started wondering if maybe they *would* use the information the patients gave me against *them.* At the very least, they made it impossible to complete the research. And if the men were interpreting the information, the findings would be very different from what they'd have been if I'd done it.

Dr. Rubinow characterized the way I interacted with people as "Fuck you, love me," and said my only hope of success at NIMH depended on my going into psychotherapy. He gave me the names of three psychotherapists, all of whom are male. I wanted to walk out and never come back. Unfortunately, I was still in my fourth year of residency, and if I'd walked out then, I not only would have been ending my fellowship and my whole academic career, but I wouldn't have finished my training and couldn't have practiced psychiatry.

I did start therapy with the first person on his list, since I clearly had no choice. But in my third session, the psychiatrist told me he was being paid by NIMH and worked out of my supervisor's office. And he wouldn't tell me whether I had confidentiality!

There are two kinds of sexual harassment under the law. One is quid pro quo: the expectation of sexual favors — this for that. The other is a sexually hostile work environment, which involves sexual slurs, pornography, and so on. In my case, we're arguing that in addition to sex discrimination, which there clearly was, I had to endure a sexually hostile work environment.

The things they said to me would *never* have been said to a man. One is that I'm not dependent enough upon my supervisor. Another is that I'm being excluded because I'm "competent and attractive." Then they say I'm an abused person, I'll recreate abuse wherever I go, and that explains everything that happened to me at NIMH!

They've repeatedly shown traditional forms of contempt for women. When they were interviewing people to replace me, two guys said of one candidate from a southern state that they hoped he'd be like a man who'd been there previously who'd also been southern and had told "titty-bar" jokes. (I guess that means topless-bar jokes.)

My supervisor had a Christmas card on his wall for six months or a year that shows a male physician in a jungle setting. (It's a black-and-white photograph on red construction paper of the real-life person who sent the card.) He's wearing a uniform with an ammunition sash filled with syringes instead of bullets. A nurse with a miniskirt and stockings held up by a garter belt is kneeling down with her hands raised to his chest and her face buried in his crotch. [She's apparently giving him a blow job.] And he's holding a giant syringe in a phallic position.

This was posted on the wall of the clinical director's office at NIMH. If you were sitting in my supervisor's office talking to him, you had to see that card right over his shoulder. My lawyer opened it in the discovery process of the lawsuit, and here's what it says inside: "Got to change with the times. No more of that wimpy, touchy-feely warmth and understanding stuff. We biological psychiatrists have got to be real men. And we don't take no shit from neurologists, neither."

The person who sent this card is one of the world's leading eating-disorders researchers. Almost all of his patients are young women and girls. He also does cerebrospinal fluid research, which involves doing lumbar punctures, so he's sticking long needles into the backs of women and girls all the time. He has more than $800,000 in funding from NIMH and NIAAA [the National Institute of Alcohol Abuse and Alcoholism] this year and was a fellow at NIMH for seven years previously.

The official NIMH stand about this card is that it's "trivial." It's not surprising that the lawyers for the men I'm suing consider it trivial, but it's horrifying that these guys see this as one big joke. This is a joke, I'm a joke, my career is a joke, titty-bars are a joke, it's *all* a joke to them.

I was sent to psychotherapy not because I needed it, but as part of the harassment. I saw the psychiatrist for ten sessions and then said, "Forget this! I can't continue." On May 1, 1992, he was deposed in my case and revealed, for all the world to know, my diagnosis — *according to him.* He charged me with having a personality disorder — *not otherwise specified* — along with self-defeating and paranoid personality traits.

He portrayed me as having experienced long-term abuse extending over years, and when my lawyer asked if I'd portrayed it that way, he answered by picking out most of my life experiences and labeling them as abuse! If I said my father was a bit distant as I was growing up, he labeled that as "abuse." Basically he labeled my whole life as abuse — and then said I tolerate abuse and therefore qualify for self-defeating personality disorder! That skews most women's lives.

[Dr. Judith Herman has spearheaded the effort to have "self-defeating personality disorder" removed from the psychiatric canon as a type of mental illness, which is to say, from the American Psychiatric Association's list of psychiatric diagnoses. Writing to the chair of the APA committee that decides what the profession officially considers an illness, Dr. Herman argued that "it pathologizes the normative behavior of women and other subordinate groups, (and therefore) is *conceptually* flawed and *inherently* biased." She offered the Jensvold case as evidence that the category "self-defeating personality disorder" was used "in order to further harass, pathologize and discredit the plaintiff" by defendants who "are part of the psychiatric establishment." The diagnosis, along with "forced psychiatric treatment," were weapons used "to preserve male power at NIMH and to allow "an 'old boys' network' of male psychiatrists to control and pathologize women as professional peers, as patients and as research subjects." Dr. Paula Caplan, author of *The Myth of Women's Masochism*, took a different tack: she proposed adding a complementary category of mental illness she called "delusional dominating personality disorder"— or "John Wayne syndrome." The criteria for identifying this diagnosis might include "has difficulty identifying and expressing a range of feelings" and "tends to deal with frustration through denial, avoidance, and physical violence."]

It's the ultimate blaming-the-victim diagnosis, because when they say I'm paranoid, they're saying I'm imagining the harassment. When they say it's my personality, they're saying the problem is intrinsic to me; it's not in the environment or anything being done to me. [Compare this strategy to the one used against Jean Jew.]

Anita Hill was accused of being mentally unstable; Clarence Thomas wasn't. She was accused of being possibly schizophrenic; he wasn't. She was accused of fantasizing; he wasn't. If the Senate Judiciary Committee had been her employers, you can imagine how easily they might have said, "You have to have a psychiatric assessment and then report back to us."

The American Medical Association currently has a campaign against domestic violence going on, and so far as I can tell, they're doing a really good job. But you have people at NIH and NIMH who are planning violence studies and violence initiatives who have a *perpetrator* mentality. There are two characteristics of perpetrators. One is a problem with empathy; they can't understand that if they treat other people in certain ways, any normal, reasonable person will feel pain. Second, they believe it's the victim's fault.

These people with perpetrator mentalities believe, for instance, that if you do genetic and neurotransmitter studies on children, you can determine who, twenty-five years later, would riot after Rodney King verdicts. This mind-set would devalue social injustice and poverty as being important factors in violence. They're saying that if you can identify the portion of the population you consider to be most at risk of rioting eventually — probably black males — and do whatever is our modern equivalent of lobotomies, then supposedly you will prevent these future riots. This comes from the same mind-set I was dealing with at NIMH.

In February 1992, Dr. Frederick Goodwin, as the head of the Alcohol and Drug Abuse and Mental Health Administration, announced the violence initiative, which is the number one funding priority for ADAMHA for 1993–94. In the process, he made comments that many people considered racist. Black congressmen and community leaders and scientists became very concerned. There was a conference scheduled for October on violence and genetics, but the black community rallied and got it canceled, and Dr. Goodwin was demoted from the head of ADAMHA to the head of NIMH for making these "racist" remarks. *So this is his big punishment: becoming head of NIMH!*

I was the third of three women to do menstrual-cycle research at NIMH, and all three were treated the same way. Top scientists can generally trace their mentors in a structure like a family tree: so-and-so mentored so-and-so, who then mentored so-and-so. But if you look at the ADAMHA family tree of women scientists, their branches get cut off. In nearly fifty years, *no* woman fellow or physician had ever gotten tenure at NIMH, so mine was part of a very much bigger problem.

My two years there were hell, and in my first year out, I was dealing with a lot of grief and loss, in addition to trying to start my private practice and figure out my life — since it clearly wasn't going to go as I'd always planned. In the last two years, I've been in an empowerment phase. I've been speaking up at NIH town meetings and testifying at NIH and to Congress, and I've been asked to lecture nationally.

I'm very fortunate that my experiences happened when they did. When I filed my EEO complaint, I learned about Billie Mackey and Self-Help for Equal Rights, which is a women's and employees' rights organization at NIH. Mackey told me exactly what the retaliation against me would be and how to minimize it, and she predicted everything. That was very helpful.

Several times I got a one-page description in my mail box explaining the EEO process for filing complaints. I threw the first few away, but finally I looked at it and said, "Wow, this really applies to me." There's no way such a form gets routinely put in people's boxes. So there was a good fairy.

After I filed with the EEO, of course, the retaliation set in. Coworkers wouldn't talk with me. My supervisor refused to assay samples he'd previously agreed to assay. It was all incredibly painful. But some people I expected to be most hostile turned out to be friendly.

I'm paying for the lawsuit out of pocket, and it's incredibly expensive. I was in it for ten months before the Hill/Thomas hearings, and I've been in it for about a year since, and there's a huge difference: now people recognize there *is* a problem and take sides.

I knew I was going to put my whole twenties into my education, but I didn't think I'd put my whole thirties into a lawsuit. I feel like I'm acquiring some power and fame, but it hasn't translated into love, money, or security. People keep assuring me those things will follow, but I'm still waiting. If this had happened at some Podunk place, I think I'd have walked away. But these people are so influential in women's health and in mental health in general that I had to stand and fight. It's important for all women.

No one has the right to ask another to go through what these women have. The most secure among them, Dr. Frances Conley, felt that the only way to make her point was to resign, and when she did, she had no idea that she'd ultimately be able to stay at Stanford. So far as she knew, she was giving up the institution with which her life had been entwined since childhood. And she knew she was unlikely to find a comparable job she liked as well.

Tammy Miller lost her job and wasn't reinstated for almost a year and a half. Dr. Jean Jew had to risk her career, her good name, and her financial well-being and for fifteen years see herself cruelly reduced to a grotesque caricature in the eyes of her community. Dr. Margaret Jensvold had to give up the career for which she'd trained and the dream that had nurtured her, and she may be paying court costs and legal fees for the rest of her life.

All of them fell ill, and all were heartsick. Theresa McDonald was hospitalized for stress. Jean Underwood had a hysterectomy at thirty-five. And Tammy Miller tried to kill herself. It is hard to believe that women must suffer such trauma and undergo such loss because men cannot be expected to behave like rational adults. For if its end results were less dire, one would be embarrassed to treat this behavior seriously.

And why do the men who run this world of ours punish the women who object, rather than the men who behave loutishly? Why do they label these women troublemakers instead of telling the guys to grow up? Why do men close ranks and make excuses for other men who say and do these things? Why do they attack the Anita Hills and let the Clarence Thomases set the agenda? Why do other women sometimes make excuses for the men who say and do these things? Why do we hear ad nauseam the tiresome refrain, "Can't you take a joke?" when nothing going on is funny?

Obviously these are stories about men who need to dominate women. Fran Conley became a threat when she claimed a place in a world that men had owned: "That's when the trouble really starts for women." When women join the competition — when they insist on being treated as equals — men often treat them like objects as a way of aggressive self-defense. Their behavior turns profoundly irrational and sometimes flatly dangerous.

For women who are alone, as Jean Jew was, the fight for decency and fairness is hardest, and the nature of Jean's battle changed only when she found a sympathetic woman lawyer who had already taken part in the women's fight for advancement and tenure at the University of Minnesota. Tammy Miller saved her life by joining a group of women who were rebuilding Sandie Vaughn's house and later by helping Sandie nurse her dying sister.

Women transcend their state as victims when they make common cause with other women to make sure that what happened to them won't happen to others. When she realized that Tom McQueary might be taking sexual advantage of women even more vulnerable, Theresa McDonald spearheaded a crusade. After discovering her kinship with a series of women who had been victimized over the years by the National Institute of Mental Health, Margaret Jensvold hooked into a network of women psychiatrists who are taking on the men who dominate their profession. And it was only after she joined with other women publicly to accuse Mayor Byron Campbell of sexual harassment that Jean Underwood began to face her incest, make peace and common cause with her sister, and reclaim her life and self-respect.

All these women moved into a new dimension when they put themselves on the line, and their exhilaration can be breathtaking. Jean Underwood said it finely: "I feel very good about myself, though I have days when I feel like I've gone to death and backwards and think, If I hadn't said anything, I wouldn't be suffering like this. But when I come out of it, I feel that much more ahead."

8

CONGRESS AND
THE NATION'S CAPITAL

You learn very early that celebrity doesn't have anything to do with a person's character. I hear such reverence sometimes for a real jerk.
— Eliza Edwards

As the Capitol Hill Women's Political Caucus indicates in its sexual harassment policy, the "primary characteristic of harassers is the desire to exert power and control and the belief that they can victimize with impunity — that such abuses of power will be condoned." The stories here show this belief to be pervasive. Men have been ill served by a cultural permission to control women; women, in turn, by a cultural prohibition against anger and a fear of female sexuality; and all of us by denial and silence. But if a belief that the rules of decency and fairness were written for others is not confined to men with conspicuous power as the world defines it, the men connected with the White House and the Hill are nonetheless in a special category.[1]

Those who fit the caucus's definition of harassers wear their immunity from scruples with a special arrogance, brandishing it for starstruck audiences like a bullfighter who swirls his cape to the welcome of blaring trumpets. When the president is a man like Jack Kennedy —

in an era before AIDS — the tone of a city is set. These are less flamboyant times in the nation's capital, the demise of Gary Hart flagging perhaps the end of the period when men could expect to get away with it. After his protracted silence during the Hill/Thomas hearings, Teddy Kennedy, who carried his brother's legacy in such matters, apologized publicly for his escapades, regretting the notoriety they had earned him, and retreated into what his many well-wishers hope will be the safety of marriage.

Predicting the end of surreptitious sex on the Hill, however, would demand a soul more reckless than mine. Wendy Baucus, whose husband is a senator from Montana, called many of his colleagues during the hearings to tell them how she herself had been harassed by members of The Club. She was dumbfounded to discover that they were perfectly aware that this kind of thing went on and didn't seem to mind: only one senator she contacted was surprised and disturbed enough to change his vote. "They told me about the experiences their wives and daughters had had," Baucus told a reporter, "and how much suffering they had gone through. And they were still voting for Thomas!"[2]

The men described in this chapter descend from the prior dispensation, and the behavior of which they were accused began long before anyone publicly deplored lechery in high places. The first to fall after the hearings, for instance, was Brock Adams, whom Jack Kennedy first brought into government as one of the youngest U.S. attorneys in the country, and his record of respect for professional women seemed ludicrously at odds with the charges against him. His deputy when he was secretary of transportation under President Jimmy Carter claimed, in fact, that Adams "did more to lift the glass ceiling on women in executive positions than any one person in the government of the United States." He was a leading advocate of women's causes and among the few senators with a formal policy against sexual harassment. And at the time the accusations against him ended his political career, the majority of his Senate and campaign staff were women.

But shortly after he was elected junior senator from the state of Washington, Adams was accused by a young woman named Kari Tupper, whose parents were longtime family friends, of putting something into her drink and fondling her against her will. Some four months after the fact, she filed a complaint with the District of Columbia police. As the *Washington Post* would put it, she was "alleging victimization on the grand scale of Victorian melodrama."

The authorities declined to prosecute and the story fizzled in the capital, but in Washington State, it created a sensation. "Kari Tupper was a Phi Beta Kappa in English from a close, proud family with plenty of resources," and she seemed unlikely to lie. Women began calling Seattle newspapers to claim that much the same thing had happened to them, and the papers instructed their reporters to keep listening. Then, when Adams announced for reelection, eight women agreed to sign affidavits for the *Seattle Times* that their stories were true and they would so testify if he sued for libel.

Six stories were subsequently published, two of them by women who also thought Adams had tried to drug them. The most persuasive came from a secretary who'd worked for him for more than a decade and had found his habit of pawing young women so disturbing that she'd warned prospective employees of "Brock's problem" and finally had quit. Columnist Anna Quindlen observed that "while one accusation is an accusation, eight begins to look like a trend." A billboard appeared with the legend "Brock Adams Likes Spotted Owls and Young Chicks," and the humiliations finally drove Adams from the race.

For years, Republican Senator Bob Packwood of Oregon was widely rumored to be a "fanny-patter" — a label that trivializes the problem — and reporters began working on an exposé long before the 1992 election. The *Washington Post* bombshell did not explode, however, until three weeks after Packwood won a fifth term by narrowly beating his Democratic opponent, Congressman Les AuCoin. Asked about the stories a few days before the election, Packwood had not only denied them but attacked certain women making the charges. As the *Post* put it, "Several [statements he submitted] contained descriptions, potentially embarrassing to the women, about purported aspects of their sexual histories and personal lives."

But the Packwood stories were too widespread and potent to be smothered. Months before the scandal blasted into the open, a friend had told me of finding his hand on her thigh years earlier when they were dinner partners. She'd quite forgotten the incident, but a reporter had heard it from a friend she told at the time. And when the reporter reminded her, she laughed on recognizing her style of rebuff: she'd warned him tartly, "Senator, if you don't move your hand, I'm going to spear it with a fork!"

Like Adams, Packwood had a good legislative record on women's issues, and the subhead on the *Post*'s story read "Alleged Behavior Pattern Counters Image." As a Republican moderate when his party was not only officially on record opposing freedom of choice but even called for a constitutional amendment banning abortion, Packwood had led the Senate fight for a woman's right to choose — and with such tenacity that the National Abortion Rights Action League had honored him repeatedly. Furthermore, he'd consistently hired women and promoted them, and as the story hit the wires, women held his most powerful staff positions. Like Adams, he had been one of the first senators to sign on to the Capitol Hill Women's Political Caucus's policy on sexual harassment, and he was one of two Republican senators who voted against Clarence Thomas.

Nevertheless, ten women gave specific accounts of uninvited sexual advances, and a woman who'd resigned from his staff said: "He couldn't seem to help himself. I cannot tell you how many people sat down with him and said, 'You are going to come to a bad end. All your career's work on women's issues and on progressive issues is going to turn to dust.'" Many denizens of the Hill, as well as stalwarts of the women's political community, confessed to feeling torn. As a former aide put it, "People who found his behavior objectionable also found compelling reasons to remain in his service: they respected him on other levels and found the work important." Once more, it was clear that we were moving into realms that were deeply irrational.

Packwood's stonewalling to the *Post* a few days before the election, and then his resort to defamation, struck many as smarmy, and they grew more troubled as he kept sidestepping the charges. After his victory at the polls, he announced that he would no longer "make an issue" of the specific accusations and apologized if his behavior had caused "discomfort or embarrassment." A few days later, the Portland *Oregonian,* the state's largest newspaper, printed a front-page apology for not pursuing the story aggressively enough. By then, Packwood was irrevocably tainted.

A coalition of women's groups in Oregon decided to push an ethics committee investigation on the Senate and to press charges with their own secretary of state, and many women determined to drive Packwood from office. Foremost among them was former state supreme court justice Betty Roberts, who said, "It's about abuse of power. The guy deceived us and it was not a fair election. We didn't have all the facts." And in a widely reprinted column, Suzanne Garment, author of *Scandal: The Culture of Mistrust in American Politics,* accused him of buying immunity from exposure by supporting women's issues.

The senator subsequently announced he had been "just plain

wrong" in making the unwanted advances and added, "I recognize now that my personal conduct has been at variance with [my] beliefs [in women's equality] — not because my convictions are not genuine, but because my conduct was not faithful to those convictions." But his remorse came too late for many women in Oregon, and since Packwood had no intention of resigning, the job of booting him out fell to them.

They had a distinct advantage: highly effective, aggressive coalitions had been built over the past decade to defeat state referenda on issues around abortion and homosexual rights, and the structures were there to be reactivated. Therefore, they could act quickly, and since they'd fought these battles every two years, they knew how to persevere. Their working coalition then connected with women's organizations in Washington, D.C., most notably the National Organization for Women, to forge a coherent strategy and engage lawyers to argue before the appropriate Senate committees.

Their determination prompted more women to accuse Packwood of sexual harassment, so that within six months of the election, the total exceeded two dozen, about half of them willing to use their names. The ethics committee subsequently convinced the Senate to demand that he turn over his personal diaries. So even if Packwood held on to office, his effectiveness as a senator was clearly blunted, and his embarrassments seemed likely to warn others to be at least more circumspect.[3]

A friend brought Eliza Edwards to a dinner party of mine, and I became an admirer when she walked in in high-laced boots and a broad-brimmed felt hat with an enormous feather like Cyrano de Bergerac's. A willowy, mischievous African-American in her fifties, she was born and brought up in the South in a family of high achievers. As a spirited fund-raiser, she has come to know the power-tripping Washington from the inside. Eliza has a ribald laugh that is infectious, so when she came to my house again to tell her story, it took us a while to settle down. But when we did, I had occasion once more to note how astute she is.

I probably have fewer problems with sexual harassment than some women because I grew up with brothers, so I know how to joust and spar verbally and to give almost as good as I get. I've always refused to be overcome with embarrassment or to blush. So if you've got the nerve to be objectionable, I'm likely to go toe-to-toe with you.

In my first job, I worked for an important civil rights group when a nationally known leader met me. I was in my twenties, and he said, "Well, who's this cute little thing? What do you do?" I was an all-purpose program assistant, and I said, "Whatever the director asks me to do." He said, "Well, why aren't you pregnant?" We were in a room full of people. Disgusting man! So I said, "Could it be that I'm on the pill?" and tossed my hair and walked away. I was so appalled I didn't think fast enough to say something really cutting, but I wasn't going to be left there with my mouth open and turning purple. He pursued me a while until he finally gave up and said to somebody, "Don't think you'll get anywhere with this snow princess." Which was great! I was glad for that reputation.

Once Marion Barry came into my office when he was just getting started in Washington. I saw the look on his face, and I knew what he was about to launch into. So I said, "Don't do that! Whatever it is you were about to say, don't say it!" I know a wolf when I see one, and God knows, they're everywhere. *Now, I paid for that:* I'm not one of the people he's fond of. When I told his second wife that he'd never propositioned me, she said, "You're in a very exclusive club." I don't ever have to worry about that from him.

In those days, you didn't like that sort of thing, but you accepted it as the way men were. You learn very early that celebrity doesn't have anything to do with a person's character. I hear such reverence sometimes for a real jerk. It's difficult for people who are not in Washington or other power centers to understand the degree to which those sexual power plays go on. *Congresspeople are accustomed to getting what they want. There are enough people who say yes, and saying yes is sometimes the way to the top. So it's difficult for me to be judgmental.*

I worked once for a group over which a Senate subcommittee had oversight authority, and a senator I'd met found out I was there and asked me to lunch in the Senate dining room. I thought, "Oh boy, I don't think this is about work." We always know. So we had a lunch where I danced around all the little innuendoes. He wasn't going to be direct. (We were, after all, in the Senate dining room.) When I left, I thought, "This is going to be a problem." But then I got another job, so it didn't have to be.

It makes me so uncomfortable even to recall times those guys hit on me. It's such an act of disrespect, and you always wonder, "What makes him think he can treat me that way?" *You take it personally because it's a very personal kind of act — even when you know it doesn't have anything to do with you. You can't even feel flattered by something like that. One body to those guys is just about as good as another.*

I've always maintained that I've suffered more from sexism than from racism. You're subjected to racism from white people. You're subjected to sexism from black people *and* white people. I've never found that black men are any less abusive than white men.

I now talk very directly about things. I work with a wonderful young supervisor who doesn't have a sexist bone in his body. Let me take that back. He works very hard to eliminate anything that might be offensive. But there's a photographer who comes in now and then, and when the two of them get together, their male energies are synergized. And since this guy seems attracted to me, sometimes he gets into this banter. Recently I said, "You are not harassing me at this moment. But you're getting so close to the line that I think I should tell you now, in case you step over it." And he said, "Oh wow, the last thing I want to do is offend you." He backed off and the conversation changed.

Once I worked in a presidential campaign for a man I didn't like very much. He'd come into my office and lean over my desk and look down my blouse and leer. I'd be very cool — not unpleasant, but cool. So I was always made to feel I was not a part of the team, even though I always met my goals. I had the feeling I wasn't malleable enough. I went into his office one day when the finance chairman was there, and as I walked past him, he patted me on the behind. *Now, I needed that job, and I knew that socking him was not going to work. So I pretended to stumble and brought my very high heel down on the instep of his foot — just as hard as I could.* Then I said, "Oh, I'm so sorry I fell!" Well, he knew I hadn't just fallen and he could tell from the look in my eye that I wasn't sorry. Two weeks later I didn't have a job. The next cut they had to make, I was the first to go.

Dorena Bertussi was one of the first women on Capitol Hill to go public with accusations of sexual harassment against a member of Congress, Jim Bates of San Diego, California. Bates was called before the House Committee on Standards of Official Conduct, which found Bertussi's complaints to be valid. Bates was reprimanded and told to write a formal apology, and eventually he lost his seat. Bertussi's experience was so hard and ugly, however, that she is acutely suspicious of the press, and she asked me to meet her at a nearby sidewalk café so that she could take some time to decide whether to trust me. After she finally let down her guard, we ended up spending a good part of a gusty Sunday afternoon together.

I was in my mid-thirties, and I'd done a lot of different things with my life. I've been in the police department, I've been a nurse, I've worked with ex-offenders and gangs in East Los Angeles. I'd moved to San Diego when I graduated from college. It's a beautiful town, but I found myself alienated. So I went back to school and got a paralegal certificate, and then I had a kind of mini-middle-age crisis. I said to myself, "I'm not happy here, I'm really stagnant." I wanted to go to Washington because I was always so political. (Local politics — the sewers and the trains — has never appealed to me.) So I wrote Congressman Jim Bates a letter. I said, "I've just graduated as a paralegal, and I'm looking to change some things in my life. Would you have an opening in Washington?" I'd never been to the East Coast, and I didn't have a clue what I was getting into. But I got a call, and he opened his congressional office on a Sunday to interview me.

I'd checked Bates out at a town meeting and didn't really like the feeling I got — but then again, I didn't have anything to go by. He was defensive and got mad very easily when he was challenged. But he appeared to be very liberal; he was against contra aid and seemed to be for women's issues. At the interview he seemed to be smiling too much, and I became uneasy; I didn't know whether it was his personality or the arrogance of power. He said, "I want you to meet with my chief of staff, but don't tell him I've offered you the job. We'll keep that between us." Well, did I or did I not have the job? I had a house and a dog. I had to start making some serious choices. He said, "Just go with the process and don't worry."

Then he said that when I got to Washington I'd hear this rumor about him. The person I was replacing had claimed that he'd touched her fanny and she'd quit. He wanted to let me know that that wasn't the case: she'd brushed up against him, he didn't touch her, it was just a brush, she blew things all out of proportion, she's got problems. . . . I'd had lots of experiences with sexual harassment in the police department. Then, as a nurse, there are the doctors; residents are really famous harassers. I felt uncomfortable, but I stored the feeling.

I interviewed with his chief of staff, and that went well. Then Bates called and asked me to come in. He said I'd start working in the district office; I'd find out what goes on there for about two or three weeks, and then he'd fly me out to Washington. I signed papers that evening and started working for the guy.

So I came to Washington, and going to work that Monday was very exciting: here was a dream come true. I was working across the street from the Capitol, and going down the hall, I'd see people I'd seen on television. I'd always liked American history — George Washington and all — and I was going nuts. It was the ultimate: so much history, so much that was vibrant, so many cultures. I'd died and gone to Heaven.

But the other women in the office treated me very odd. They were young, and for most of them, this was their first job. (Bates had told me that one reason he'd hired me was that he was having problems in the office with kids talking and gossiping and things getting out of control, and he needed someone mature in there. I was ten or fifteen years older.) You know how we had cliques in high school? You didn't cross the lines, you didn't go into the cheerleading section if you were a bookworm? It reminded me of those days. I got the impression that I'd walked into a cheerleading meeting. (I found out later that they thought I was sleeping with him.)

I was a legislative assistant and started out focusing on health issues since I'd been a nurse, and then I worked on transportation and environmental issues. When I went into my first reception, I was so proud! But the people I met at receptions would laugh right in my face when I told them I worked for Bates. They'd say he was a joke. It got to the point where I'd just put my own name on my name tag — I wouldn't put "Congressman Bates."

Once I went back to the office after a reception to change from my high heels into my tennis shoes. Bates came in — he'd just got back from the airport. I was in the back room talking on the phone to my real estate agent about an offer on my house, and I had a sock in my hand. He got really close to me, just a few inches away, and he looked at my breasts and said, "They look really good!" I hit him in the face with my sock and said, "Stop it!" He backed off, but he was laughing. I told my real estate agent, "I just hit a congressman in the face with my sock. Maybe we shouldn't accept that offer. I may be coming home." But then he was fine — he never mentioned it again — so I accepted the offer.

I saw him as more and more erratic. In our staff meetings, he'd pick one staff member and then target them. He was very vicious and he enjoyed it; he had a smirk on his face. A lotta times you'd go into the bathroom, and there'd be a girl in there crying because he'd said something "unkind." When I walked into the office from the hallway, the only way I could cope was to make a joke out of it. Instead of the "twilight zone" I was entering the "Bates zone." Walking past those doors was like stepping into a whole other reality. But for the first six months, I couldn't leave. My house was sold. I had no family, no political connections, no experience on the Hill. I was one hundred percent trapped and just surviving.

That six-month period was very difficult. I lost a lot of respect for myself for taking it and seeing other women take it. I was trying to bond with 'em, but they wanted to please this man so much! He loved to play people off against each other, and he was good at it. So when you'd meet someone in the bathroom who was crying, and talk for a while until things were okay, it would get back that you'd said these things about him. It was the most bizarre working experience in my life. In Congress you become sorta like a family— very centered on helping the congressman succeed. So there are a lot of mind-games going on. So many people were beaten down in their self-images. It was not reality, but people started treating it as though it was reality.

He'd call me into his office and close the door. And instead of staying behind his desk, he'd come over to the couch and get really close. He'd get this real stupid grin. There's a term "ogling," and that's what he'd do. I'd be in there talking about legislation, and he'd want to know if I was doing okay.

"Yeah, I'm doing fine."

"You're doing a real good job here. . . ."

"Thank you, Congressman."

"But are you being physically taken care of?"

"I'm fine."

"Well, I'm kinda concerned about your overall health."

He kept repeating that sort of thing and he'd ask if I was seeing anybody. I kept saying, "I'm fine."

He wasn't attracted to me. I have a very good dating life, and I know when people can't live without me, and that was not what he was experiencing. He was using sexual behavior to make me uncomfortable. He didn't come after me like he did a lot of other women. It had to do with power and authority, and making us feel uncomfortable and watching us squirm.

Most of the other women had such low self-esteem. They were very young, and they took it. One woman figured out that he was nicer when she wore tight sweaters; when she didn't, he was more erratic. They were so broken that when the women got together, one of 'em would end up going off independently and telling Bates what the others said.

It escalated, and that scared me. I'd talked to my immediate supervisor and said, "Is this normal?" He said, "Yeah. He's been told before to stop it. He does it to everybody." Shortly after that, at a hearing, I met the woman I'd replaced and she told me the story. She'd left in disgust after three months, and she told me about other people who'd left. That confirmed everything.

The incidents started to increase. We'd be talking about legislation, and he'd come over close and say I looked like the type of woman who liked to have it done rough to her, the type who'd date men with hair growing out of their collars. I don't think I've ever felt so disgusted. I knew if I said anything he'd fire me because there's absolutely no protection for Hill employees. I had to get another job, but I had career goals — I didn't want to look for a job in a gas station — and I knew that once I got off the Hill it would be very difficult to get back. Thousands of people want a Hill job.

A constituent came in who was interested in one of the issues I was working on, and we were going over to the committee. While we were standing waiting for an elevator, this guy was saying how beautiful Washington is, and again Bates came in really close, looked directly at my breasts, and said, "Yes, they're really pretty, aren't they?" The constituent laughed. It was a nervous type of laughter. When we got back from the committee, I went into Bates's office and said, "Don't you ever do that to me again!"

"What?"

"Say what you said earlier about my breasts."

"I didn't say that. You misunderstood."

"I did not misunderstand. Don't you *ever* do that to me again." And then he said something like "Okay, I'm sorry. I was just joking."

Then I had to pick him up at National Airport. He was in my car and said, "What's so-and-so doing?" Again he was pitting one staffer against another, and out of the blue, he said, "You know, sometimes I just want to grab her and push her against the wall, and hit her repeatedly until blood trickles from her mouth." In the next breath, he said, "If I came to your apartment, what would be the first thing I'd see? Would it be your bed?" I could've made him get out of the car, but then I didn't need to bother going back to the office. This was three months into my job.

One of the last things happened when I was sitting at my desk with my legs crossed. He came over, grabbed ahold of my leg, so he's standing in front of me holding my leg in between his legs and bending down. He started to fondle my hand on my desk and came in really close with his face. He had a real stupid, goofy grin and started swaying back and forth on my leg like he was a dog. There were staffers in the office. I recoiled. And he walked away laughing. He came back about half an hour later with the same stupid grin, and he said, "Never put your leg between a congressman's. It doesn't look good!" And walked away laughing.

That was it. I said, "Jay, you tell him to stop it *right now.*" Jay did, and for the next two or three weeks, Bates wouldn't even talk to me. I thought for sure I was gonna be fired. Things were happening with this trauma care bill I needed to coordinate with him, but he wouldn't listen. He was hurting his own cause. But a few weeks later, he mellowed out and started talking to me again.

I remember thinking when I was going for an interview with another congressman's legislative director, "What am I gonna say when this guy asks me why I want to leave?" But he looked me straight in the eye and said, "You know, Rod is a very happily married man." And I said, "Good!" So I didn't need to tell him why I wanted to leave.

Patsy, another woman in the office, was married, and her husband got so disgusted with Bates grabbing her fanny that he called the ethics committee and said, "What do I do? He's touching my wife and I want him to stop." The person in the ethics office said, "What's the congressman's name?" He said, "I don't want to tell you that. I just need to know." But the ethics guy wouldn't give him any information unless he said certain things that he wasn't willing to divulge because he thought Patsy would be hurt.

I gave Bates two weeks' notice. But on the Wednesday before the Friday I was to leave, he kept calling people into his office one by one. Three came back and said, "He told me not to talk to you anymore because you're a troublemaker." At that time I wasn't even thinking seriously about going to the ethics committee. All I wanted was to get outta there and save my neck and my self-respect, so I walked out two days early.

Seven months later, a reporter from *Roll Call* [a daily newspaper that goes to every congressional office] came in and said she'd heard the stories and wanted to do an article. Would I be willing to talk? We met for lunch and she assured me it would be totally anonymous. I went to the congressman I worked for then and said, "I want to participate in this story. Are you going to fire me?" He said, "No. I'm not going to support you. But I won't terminate you. You're doing a good job." It took her about a month to convince me, and when the story came out in *Roll Call,* of course, I could be identified by what I said. He knew what he'd done, and he could still hurt me politically. Here's someone who talks to the press, so she can't be trusted any more.

I didn't actually sit down and plot out the scenario, but I *did* consider everything. I'd get to one stage and say, I've come this far, I can't back down now. I'd never been on TV, and whenever I told my story, I was assaulted by one stereotype after another:

"What did you do to deserve it?"

"Did you lead him on?"

"Did you want to date him?"

I said, "This has nothing to do with sex, it's about power."

It made me *much* more aware of my strengths and weaknesses — and what I had to change — so it was a very positive growing experience.

Bates used my name on a talk show, and then it was all out in the open.

I wasn't as secure as I'd thought, but I got stronger as I kept going. And in those first months, it was as though I was running for Congress against him. He kept escalating his denials and attacked all of us. He kept saying, "Why didn't you file a complaint? Why didn't you go to the ethics committee if this was so important? Why now?" So I said, "Okay, I'll complain."

I crossed a barrier when I filed my complaint. I got an attorney pro bono, but the ethics committee was no help. I called in and said, "Well, what do I do?" And they said, "We can't really tell you that."

"Excuse me?"

"Well, we have a book."

"Okay."

"Well, come get it."

It was like going down to the principal's office in grammar school. So I'm reading this book, but I don't know what some of the language means. I'm not a legal scholar, and the laws are confusing. My attorney was familiar with constitutional and civil rights law, of course, but not the laws pertaining to the House. I didn't notarize my complaint, and Bates told a reporter they were going to throw it out. He should never have seen the complaint — that's against committee rules — but it was leaked. When the decision came that they were going to investigate Bates, I found out about it first from a reporter.

I was working under a time problem: Congress was going to recess, and I didn't want 'em to recess without having this in hand. At first, it looked like another woman was going to file, too, but she didn't file that day. Then she said, "I'll go with you," so she put hers in the same format as mine and we got 'em notarized and found a member of Congress to carry them to the ethics committee. It took 'em months to take it up. Bates won the election and continued to say, "These women have problems," at the same time women in San Diego were saying, "He chased me around the desk, he did this and that, I wouldn't work for him any more. . . ."

I was beyond shaky, I was really scared because I was messing with a bunch of dysfunctional people. But I had this overwhelming feeling that if I didn't do something, or if something wasn't done, he was going to seriously hurt someone. That was my driving force. Both males and females came up and said they were glad I was doing this. A guy on one of the committees said, "You know, my boss is treating us nicer — he's afraid of the press." Our using the press as the main vehicle scared everybody an awful lot.

During the Hill/Thomas hearings I received a lot of press calls because I was the only one who had went through the process. The worst thing for me emotionally was having women *not* come forward and *not* support her. No congresswoman had called me and said, "Good show!" That hurt. But at that time, it wasn't politically fashionable. With Anita Hill, it became fashionable not to stand for sexual harassment.

Women *have* to come forward. They can't continue to pretend this doesn't happen. If you do, you're part of the problem. You're an enabler: you're making it possible for that person to continue. If we don't work together, there's nothing we can do about it.

Donna Britt, now a columnist for the *Washington Post* Metro section, was thirty-six in 1990, when the incident she recounts here happened. A journalist all her professional life, Britt is an African-American who went to Hampton Institute (now Hampton University) in Virginia. She interned at *Redbook* before working for the *Detroit Free Press* and *USA Today* and then coming to the *Post* as a feature writer.

The White House correspondents dinner is an annual bash in which journalists who cover the White House come together and have a big party. The president speaks off the record, and various news organizations invite the powerful Washington elite to sit at their tables. This was the year of Desert Storm, so Brent Scowcroft was there and so was Colin Powell. Mayor Sharon Pratt Kelly was at our table, which was mainly taken by people who write for the *Post* Style section. I'd never been before. My boyfriend was then covering the White House, and I was really excited about going somewhere with him in his tux and me in a strapless dress. I love the glamour of getting dressed up. And that's been a key to what distressed me; we're taught that when you are dressed a certain way, and you're among certain kinds of people, everything's going to be aboveboard and jolly and elegant.

So I was standing, probably with a glass of wine in my hand, speaking with Clark White, the Knight-Ridder bureau chief in Washington. It was during a break between speeches before the president came on. We were laughing— I'd re-introduced him to the woman who became his wife, and we were talking about her—and I was feeling very pretty and sexy and safe! Just then I felt myself being snatched off my feet. A strong arm was circling my thighs and pulling me backwards. (This person was seated and probably couldn't reach my waist.) I fell backwards and ended up sitting on the table. And I remember feeling immediately protective. After the moment of shock passed, I was so embarrassed, because I assumed that he would be embarrassed by having made me topple. And I was thinking this had to be someone I knew.

But suddenly I was staring into the face of someone I could not recall ever having seen. He was an older white man with white hair. So then I thought, "This is someone I've interviewed and don't remember." So I smiled. *Women are very protective of men — and of men's mistakes. We project onto them our own sensitivity and our own desire to please.* So there I was — still smiling and still shocked — and very aware that I was sitting on a table where everybody was looking at me sitting there in my strapless dress and dangling earrings. I'm wondering who this guy is, when he says something like, "What do we do now?" and looks around.

And then I realized that I *don't* know this guy and he doesn't know me. People told me later that he was probably drunk. This was a jocular affair with an open bar, and men outnumbered women, so there was a lotta testosterone in the air. I became sort of paralyzed. What do you do when things become inconceivable? You try to make them conceivable, and that takes a few seconds.

Clark pulled me off the table and away from this guy. And he said, "Donna, I'm terribly sorry that happened to you!" I said, "Who is that guy?" And he said, "That's the president's physician, Burton Lee." And then Clark outlined some embarrassing things he'd done that night. So Clark apologized profusely, and by this time I'm assuring him I'm okay.

I went back to my table, and the woman who was writing about the party for the Style section was there. I remembered that she'd written a piece about this man, and I said, "Is this the kind of thing he does?" She asked what had happened, and when I told her, she said she'd never heard of him doing anything like that. She wanted to write about it, and I said, "I have to think about that." And finally I said, "So long as it's not a big part of the story." Again, I was protecting him. Then, when the story appeared, *USA Today* called me, and I could see this becoming a big thing and didn't want him to be hurt. (I'd found out he was married, and I figured he'd gotten into his cups.) So I said it wasn't that big a deal and we should just move on. But when *USA Today* called him, he said he wouldn't know me if we were locked in a closet together. He said this girl was making a big deal out of nothing and he'd really been after a six-foot blonde — but she was taken! (Apparently the woman who called him had some sort of association with him, and when she asked him what happened, he didn't realize he was being quoted.)

I'd worked at *USA Today,* and they had an old picture of me on file. I may have said that he should apologize. But I picked up the paper and this is what I see. I'd never expected that he would not acknowledge what he did. I could've been somebody's secretary who was there as a treat — someone who had no access to a way of making this man acknowledge that this is wrong. But I felt like I had some obligation. This is the kind of thing that happens every day to women who have no recourse or access to any means of letting people know that it has happened.

I write about personal stuff all the time—even as a feature writer—so I thought it had happened to me for a reason. I didn't want to bury it, but at the same time, I didn't want to make a big deal out of it. What he said was patently hurtful and dismissive, and so I waited for something to happen. I waited for people to react, and I steeled myself for it. Here was a public figure, a guy entrusted with the president's care, and he'd made this incredible faux pas! What he'd done at the dinner had some innocence in it, but then when somebody called him, he dismissed it—and basically accused me of being vengeful for acknowledging that it had happened. For me, that was out of bounds.

So I expected there to be repercussions, but nothing happened! Several days later, a guy from Baltimore calculated that a thousand people had written about that woman sportswriter who was harassed in the New England Patriots' locker room. It had caused a big furor and the Patriots got a huge fine. But he said three people had written about the episode involving me, and this was the president's physician! And he wondered why this man was being allowed to get away with this. Frankly, I was, too. After the USA Today piece, I didn't think I had to do or say anything because he'd clearly shot himself in the foot, the mouth, and the hand. *But nobody was acknowledging it. And I had to wonder if it was simply because I'm black and he was a powerful white man. You always wonder when that's a part of your life.*

I couldn't figure it out, and I was consumed by the wrongness of it. And it made me examine my own culpability: *why did I instantly seek to protect him?* Why did even I dismiss the fact that a stranger had put his hands on me in such a forceful way that I lost my balance and my dignity? And in a public place. (If someone would do something like that in public, think what he might do in private!) I had to confront my own dismissiveness—as well as his and the media's. All this was swirling around in my head and heart, and I was feeling extremely vulnerable and hurt.

I generally believe that people don't mean any harm. (That's a bottom line for me.) And I think that matters. I don't think this man meant me any harm. I don't know that he thought about me at all. This was just somehow part of his good time, and he assumed because *he* looked at it this way, *I* would look at it this way.

But men need to understand that if you don't take other people's feelings

and rights and basic humanity into account, that's wrong. You're making assumptions you should never make. I'm a mom, and a woman, and a fairly sensitive
person. I want to protect people. I never, ever want to hurt people. By the
same token, I want the same kind of protection and consideration extended
to me. And that didn't happen here. The only reason color or gender matters
is that those things make it easier to deny other people's humanity, and that
dismissive impulse needs to be squashed. It finally made sense that I should
write a column excavating the emotions this brought up, and the tendency of
women *not* to confront the wrongness of these things. Who could deal with
that better than me — who was trying very hard *not* to deal with it and to
give somebody the benefit of the doubt who had not given me the benefit of
anything?

I got a tremendous response from women. The media and certain men
would like you to think that women are just lying in wait now, wanting to
expose and attack and entrap men into charges of sexual harassment. But I've
found that most women are involved in denying that these things happen, in
forgiving, in overlooking. Otherwise the world feels like a very dangerous place.

Washington continues to spawn problematic sexual encounters because
at bottom it is a city about power. And in the *Washington Post,* writer
Karen Lehrman cajoled her feminist sisters into acknowledging that
women on the Hill played their part in the game — that some still slept
their way to jobs and influence. "Women who treat their sexuality as a
bargaining chip hurt other women," she wrote with obvious under-
statement, "and the peculiar work environment of the Hill — where
subservience and loyalty are often more important than competence and
intelligence — should not be underestimated." Many feminists deplored
the article but were hard-pressed to refute her thesis.

Still, the men who were elected to Congress for the first time in
1992 were plainly watching themselves, anxious lest charges of sexual
harassment scuttle promising careers. Before the Hill/ Thomas hearings,
203 House and Senate offices had adopted the Capitol Hill Women's
Political Caucus's recommended policy on sexual harassment; by November 1993, the number had increased dramatically to 35 percent.

And the faces on the Hill were different now. In January 1993,
when they were sworn in, the twenty-four new female members doubled
the number of women in the House of Representatives, and Republican
Kay Bailey Hutchison's 1993 landslide victory in the race to be junior

senator from Texas raised the number of women in the U.S. Senate to seven. Although 11 and 7 percent respectively sound piddling, they represent a striking improvement.

Furthermore, women got important committee assignments. Carol Moseley Braun, the first African-American woman elected to the Senate, won a seat on the powerful Judiciary Committee, along with Dianne Feinstein from California, so institutional readjustments made it unlikely that the Hill/Thomas embarrassment would be repeated. Legislation was also pending that would lift the $300,000 cap on damages available to victims of sex discrimination and harassment under Title VII of the Civil Rights Act.

With its historic addition of two women members, one of the Senate Judiciary Committee's first acts in the 103rd Congress was to vote unanimously for the Violence Against Women Act. The legislation would stiffen penalties for federal sex offenses, provide half a billion dollars in grants to reduce attacks against women, and permit such victims to sue their attackers for damages. Congresswoman Patricia Schroeder introduced an identical bill on the House floor, and it was expected to pass within the year. After Janet Reno, the first woman to serve as U.S. attorney general, made her stunning debut, the federal government was obviously poised to take violence against women seriously for the first time in history.

Patty Murray, the new senator from Oregon, had run as a "mom in tennis shoes," making political capital of a term that had earlier served as a put-down for women, and she and Feinstein were named to the Senate Appropriations Committee, where some of President Bill Clinton's most ambitious legislation would be introduced. At the same time, a total of thirteen women would serve on the House Appropriations and the Energy and Commerce Committees, more than doubling the number of women who had served previously on those key bodies. With a prized seat on the Ways and Means Committee, Congresswoman Barbara Kennelly had advanced to deputy whip in the Democratic leadership of the House of Representatives. After a decade and a half, Pat Schroeder had worked up to second in rank on the Armed Services Committee. So women now had not only prominence on the Hill, but positions of more power.

As though to warn against premature optimism, however, in late February 1993, the *Washington Post* announced the results of a survey: one-third of the women who worked on Capitol Hill had been sexually harassed — one out of nine by a member of Congress. Even if we allow for a loose definition of sexual harassment, the numbers were startling. Furthermore, half the women interviewed said they were afraid to report the incident because they expected retaliation. "Women who complain, even privately, said they risk being labeled 'difficult' or 'whiners,'" according to the *Post:* "Some who protest publicly may find themselves ostracized by the lawmaker and co-workers" and even find themselves unemployable.

Three months later, the General Accounting Office confirmed the odds against whistle-blowing when they issued a report announcing that the House Office of Fair Employment Practices (OFEP) had almost no work to do. Established in 1988, it had received more than twelve hundred inquiries, but only sixteen complaints — nine of those informal. None had alleged sexual harassment, and congresswomen seemed exasperated. Schroeder underscored women's fear of retaliation, and Democratic members of the House and Senate began to talk about creating one OFEP to cover both bodies and enhance its efficacy.[4]

Still, the atmosphere was decidedly different. Not only were there many more high-profile women legislators, but key media jobs were increasingly filled by women who are far more likely than men were to take sexual harassment seriously. And they, too, were playing a role in permanently changing the rules. During President John F. Kennedy's reign, no newspaper ever suggested the kinds of games he and his confreres played with sexual power. Now a columnist for the *Washington Post* could actually say in print that men needed to take other people's feelings into account and insist that failing to do so was wrong. Only thirty years had passed, but the change was fundamental.

9

THE MILITARY

Any time you create an organization with a first- and second-class citizenry, the second-class citizens are going to be hit—and hit and hit.

—Retired Brigadier General Evelyn P. (Pat) Foote

Nowhere in American culture has sexual harassment been more blatant than in the armed services, where the Stealth bomber of the war on women has often taken the form of gay-baiting. Men would hit on women — "proposition" is too refined a term here — and as often as not, the women who turned them down were called "dykes." Since homosexuals were outlawed in the armed services, this accusation, if sustained, could mean that the women would be discharged. The possibilities for a reign of terror were very substantial indeed, and under many commanders that is precisely what happened.

In 1972, women made up less than 2 percent of the active-duty military personnel in the United States and less than 5 percent of the National Guard and Reserve, and those women served for the most part in "traditional" capacities — as secretaries, nurses, and so on. By 1990, over 10 percent of our active forces were female, along with more than 12 percent of the reserves. By 1991, 45 percent of our enlisted women served in "nontraditional" areas — up more than 30 percent in less than two decades — and 12.5 percent of our officers were female.

While the numbers of women in the armed services were building so dramatically, controversy swirled around two key questions: "Can women fight as effectively as men?" and "Can men fight as effectively if women are alongside them?" The overwhelming consensus of the military powers-that-be was that the answer to both questions was no, and so women were officially barred from combat roles. In late November 1989, the secretary of defense issued a policy statement with two key provisos: "Women will continue to be eligible to serve in all roles except those prohibited by the combat exclusion laws [and policies]. . . . No artificial barriers to career opportunity for women will be established or tolerated."[1]

Many women, however, argued that the use of gender to exclude them from combat was itself artificial, since modern weapons made raw physical strength increasingly irrelevant in a fight. And so the battle within the military about the role of women hinged on the nature of sexual difference, an issue that inspired a good deal of hysteria, both written and oral. Men in the armed services clung to a traditional definition of masculinity as though their lives depended on it, when in fact only their jobs were at risk.

For the combat exclusion laws kept the lid on women's career opportunities in the armed services, ensuring that women would continue to be denied the experience in combat and operational affairs on which promotion to the highest ranks ultimately rested. While there was one female officer in 1990 for every eight male officers, the slant toward traditional women's work still prevailed: 40 percent of the women officers on active duty and 56 percent in the reserves were nurses. In 1993, the U.S. Army had only three women generals. Along with the combat exclusion laws, sexual harassment had played a major role in preserving the traditional definition of women and keeping them in "their place."

I found myself enthralled by the furor that raged after women began to go into the armed services in the tens of thousands, in part because my father went to Texas A&M in the 1920s, and I grew up in a world suffused with the pride of an Aggie. I have a picture of him at twenty standing smartly at attention — his boots, spit-polished, reaching his knees. And I remember his tales of the tortures he endured to prove himself worthy of the corps — the most vivid being the one about the upperclassman who ordered him to bend over and hold his ankles and then smacked his rear with a paddle until his shorts were soaked with blood that trickled down his legs. This was hazing; he was in the military; only sissies whine; and my daddy was no sissy.

So not long after the Hill/Thomas hearings, when I read that a fact-finding panel had declared that pervasive harassment and discrimination plagued women members of the corps at Texas A&M, I was surprised only that anyone was surprised. There were seventy-five women among the 1,786-member elite corps, and I knew that if Daddy were alive, he'd tell those women to pack it. The army was its own world; Texas A&M was its own place; and for men like my father, women had no business there.

A&M had resisted change as fiercely as almost any institution in the country. In the mid-sixties, economics had forced it to open its doors to women, but the corps held out until 1974. Five years later, a woman named Melanie Zentgraff sued the corps for sex discrimination when the color guard denied her admission, and at graduation in 1980, the school's president, Jarvis Miller, refused to shake her hand. (In 1985, the suit was settled in her favor.) It takes a long time, as well as a lot of guts on one side and a change of heart and/or economics on the other, to shelve tradition.

So in the fall of 1991, as I sat in a College Station restaurant with Carolyn Muckley, the current leader of the women's assault against the Aggie sense of the fitness of things, I had visions of my father's ghost swooping down to skewer me for a traitor. As it happens, however, Muckley herself is an army brat whose own father had taught her to fight for a place in the ranks and has supported her battle. She was young enough to be my daughter, and so a crucial generation had passed and times were finally changing.

Being on these particular front lines is nevertheless tough and thankless. As Mimi Swartz put it in the *Texas Monthly*, women who can't live up to Aggie standards are viewed as wimps, while women who can and do are pegged as lesbians. Part Vietnamese, Muckley was telephoned by a corpsman who threatened to "rape your Viet Cong cunt till it bleeds"; she'd been kicked in the back near the kidneys and taunted as "a fucking Waggie." Proclaiming that right and wrong matter more than tradition, Muckley sent the administration a letter listing eleven instances of abuse at Texas A&M — assault and rape being among the charges — and gave the letter to the press. The faculty largely supported Muckley; most students and alumni stood with tradition; and the corps itself was split: some men quietly backed her, while some women hated her guts.[2]

Texas A&M turned out to be a microcosm of the military in an era of painful transition. About two months after I heard Muckley's story, retired navy commander Kay Krohne issued a study of sixty-one women officers in the U.S. Navy. Finding that close to two-thirds had been sexually harassed, she argued that this stunted the contributions women could make. More than half had not reported the incidents, largely because they feared reprisals and distrusted the system. "In a military environment," Krohne said, "you wear your rank on your sleeve. You're expected to follow the rules and never, ever say anything or do anything against your superiors."[3]

Then the Tailhook scandal hit the front pages of newspapers across the country. In the fall of 1991, at least twenty-six women — half of them officers — had been mauled as they were forced to run a gauntlet in a Las Vegas hotel during an annual convention of navy and marine pilots. Lieutenant Paula Coughlin testified to being passed down the third-floor hallway by men grabbing her breasts and buttocks and pulling at her pants and said she'd thought she was going to be gang-raped.

Coughlin, who was a navy brat, commented: "I've worked my ass off to be one of the guys, to be the best naval officer I can and prove that women can do whatever the job calls for. And I was treated like trash. I wasn't one of them." She had filed a complaint just days before Anita Hill confronted the Senate Judiciary Committee, but after fifteen hundred Tailhook men preserved an oath of silence, she finally went public — "putting a name and a face to this." Six months after the fact, and amid persistent rumors of a cover-up, more than a thousand promotions were held up and navy secretary H. Lawrence Garrett III was forced to resign.

J. Daniel Howard, who took Garrett's place, ordered a service-wide "stand-down" for a day-long training in sexual harassment, but it took the navy a while to "get it": two senior officers had to be subsequently relieved of their command after navy F-14 Tomcat pilots ridiculed Congresswoman Patricia Schroeder of the House Armed Services Committee in an annual review at Miramar Naval Air Station in San Diego. Acting secretary Howard admitted that although puerile acts had been "committed by a few," they had continued because "far too many" had excused them — including "all the leaders over the years who turned a blind or bemused eye to the crude, alcohol-inspired antics of a few idiots in our ranks."

But now the lid had blown and revelations were spewing out. Jacqueline Ortiz, a twenty-nine-year-old reservist, told a Senate panel that during the Persian Gulf War, she'd been forcibly sodomized by her sergeant in broad daylight. While two women captured by the Iraqis had been brutally raped, twenty-four, it turned out, reported being assaulted by their own colleagues, many of them officers. Traditionalists fell back on the plaintive cry that women had no business in the military. But those who believed that men had no business behaving that way counterattacked, with columnist Ellen Goodman leading the charge by calling it assault by "friendly fire."

Reports were widely distributed that more than one-third of all military women had been sexually harassed, and congressional panels heard testimony from several victims. (Ortiz told them she would "rather have been shot by a bullet . . . than deal with what I deal with daily.") Congresswoman Schroeder's office was overwhelmed with calls from victims of sexual assault and harassment, some of whom claimed, as Schroeder put it, that "the military affirmatively acted to harass the complainant and scuttle the complaint." A year after the fact, four women finally sued the Tailhook Association and the Las Vegas Hilton. The report on the navy's mishandling of the scandal ended two admirals' careers, and Tailhook officials apologized publicly to the women who'd been assaulted and promised to "correct those errors" that led to the incident.

But progress was very slow. A long article in the *Washington Post* catalogued ways the navy pitted women against each other, with one side complaining that the women on the other side were whiners who made them all look bad. Another showed how the military justice system was weighted against women.

The stories that follow describe the experiences of three women in the armed services, that repository of the "manly" virtues where the imbalance of power between men and women is particularly acute and where sexual harassment is therefore likely to be the most severe. None of these women is now in the army.

Evelyn P. (Pat) Foote is a crisp, no-nonsense woman who laughs wryly at the world and herself, though not necessarily in that order. A mature officer in the Women's Army Corps (WACs) when it was integrated into the regular army, she was naturally much harder to intimidate than an eighteen-year-old might be. (When Washington Redskins owner Jack Kent Cook allegedly grabbed Mayor Sharon Pratt Kelly by her rear end, Foote said, "I'd have snapped his wrist and recorded his screams!") Veteran reporter Sarah McClendon told me to look up Pat Foote, and the novelty of having a brigadier general in my living room was exceeded only by the charm of her company.

Repeatedly over the years, Foote has been what she calls the ONOW — the one and only woman. She went to the Army War College in Carlisle, Pennsylvania, as the first woman on the faculty and then to Europe as the first with a brigade command. She came back to the United States to be the first woman general in the Department of the Army/Inspector General Agency and has dedicated a healthy chunk of her early sixties to lobbying the Joint Chiefs to allow women into all combat units. Undaunted by their resistance, she comments in her melodious southern accent, "If they want to call me a strident, ineffective, shrill feminist, then I'm honored."

I came into the WACs in 1959 as a twenty-nine-year-old first lieutenant with seven and a half years' work experience in Washington, quite a bit of it supervisory. The WACs hung on by its toenails after World War II until people like General [George C.] Marshall and General [Dwight D.] Eisenhower got behind the impetus to retain a nucleus of women for active duty. We had an all-female training center and a mission like no other army mission. It was gender-specific: to sustain and perpetuate ourselves — in other words, to be a nucleus of trained women who, if we were to mobilize again, would be the training base for women coming in. This wonderful corps of ours had the best people, the best spirit, the most striking personal appearance and military courtesy of any corps of the army. We were tremendously proud to be a part of that. We were very tough on each other and on any woman who wanted to be a part of the corps — very demanding on standards of dress, appearance, conduct, the whole nine yards.

But we didn't have an army mission except to survive. We'd be detailed out and lent to other branches of the army for a two- or three-year period and then drawn back into the WACs to do women's work again — then, back out. Most men didn't even know there was a woman's army still and worked with very few women.

We have an integrated army now. Combat support, combat service support, all those branches that do everything to support the men who are combatants are the integrated part. The segregated part are the warriors, who have their own warrior mystique and ethic. They occupy the last tree house in the sky—and they do *not* want women in their tree house. This is why there's so much resistance to giving women the opportunity to see if they're capable of serving in the infantry.

The quality of the leadership at the top determines the man at the bottom. I've heard there were units in Desert Storm where the commander's idea of women was "Use 'em any way you can." And I mean use 'em in the worst possible way. But if the people at the top lay the law down and make sure their subordinates know their job's on the line if these things happen, then they don't happen!

With the end of the draft in 1973, we in the WACs knew they would come to women for their "manpower" because we were an untapped source. (The draft had provided all the cheap labor the army wanted from 1939 on.) So how do you get people in a volunteer mode? Among other things, you change the rules and regulations and the limits on how many women can serve on active duty. So in the seventies, we were bringing women into the army in great numbers and tearing down the barriers to most of the units and jobs to which women could be assigned. And we were throwing 'em into the whole cultural milieu of what the army had been for two hundred years, with no preparation of the base: no education of the men and no preparation of the women for what was coming. One man said it was like taking all the cultural furniture in the army and throwing it in the air. It was done by administrative fiat out of manpower necessity—not because of the women's movement.

When you're going from eleven thousand enlisted women and eight hundred officers [in 1972] to fifty thousand enlisted women and five thousand officers [in 1980], that's a monumental leap. We were also putting women in units where they'd never been permitted to serve before: we were training and utilizing them in military intelligence, in the quartermaster corps, transportation, you name it.

I'm convinced that dysfunctional policies are the heart and soul of sexual harassment in any organization, whether it's the armed forces or not. Unless you get the policies neutralized and create standards that are gender-neutral and *then* work the details out about whether men and women should be in a particular place together—unless you do that, you'll forever have the "us-and-them" mentality. When the leadership demeans women—badmouths them in front of subordinates—they create an environment that says sexual harassment is okay. So far, the worst Persian Gulf incidents reported were in reserve components, where they chose to look the other way and say, "Boys will be boys!"

The men, one on one with you in the army—your peers—will tell you how great the women are in their units; they'll say they could not get their work done without them. But when the old boys come together in the locker room, God forbid they should admit that the women in the armed forces are worth a damn. There are some wonderful exceptions: men who are not of the Neanderthal generation that still controls everything.

"Tailhook" is just the straw that broke the navy camel's back. The we-go-to-sea, we're-not-like-you, and we-don't-play-by-your-rules attitude has almost been pandemic in the navy. That's going to change. And the army, the air force, and the marines cannot sit back and say, "Natter, natter, natter" because they have their own incipient or real "Tailhooks" to deal with. The navy just relieved the commander of an oiler because he was bedded down with one of his own subordinates on shipboard. That same ship had a commander removed in '87 who'd talk about sex on the deck. He was derogatory and derisive about women—he'd joke about selling 'em off into white slavery—when maybe a third of his crew were female. That ship has a bad aura.

I had the wonderful experience of commanding an integrated basic training battalion at Fort McClellan, Alabama. I took a previously all-female battalion and brought the men in. It was reverse integration. I'd been integrated so many times, as had my fellow female battalion commander, that we knew everything *not* to do. First, you don't have a trumpet peal and bring in the press to make light of this poor bunch of terrified men who arrived thinking they were going to Fort Jackson. Second, you make sure the women don't go for retribution. They knew I'd fire their rears if they had any position of authority and started playing games. I said, "You're going to be very professional about it." We've learned from our own miserable experience what not to do. Women learn many of their incredible skills as commanders by watching men blow it.

We didn't get a woman general until 1970, and her position was tied to the position of director of the WACs. In 1992, we still have no more than four women generals, none above the rank of brigadier general. If you get to be a one-star general, you're supposed to be happy, and under the present rules, women will *never* have the operational experience required to be credentialed. The army has every opportunity now to be proactive, but Godzilla and crew up here [i.e., the Joint Chiefs], who are in a segregated mode, don't want to hear it. Well, they're going to have to. Any time you create an organization with a first- and second-class citizenry, the second-class citizens are going to be hit —and hit and hit.

A woman general said that when she was in Korea as a colonel, she was taken to task in her officer-performance evaluation because she didn't learn that when you are in the host country, you frequently defer to the will of the host. What he was referring to was that she wouldn't go to bed with the high-ranking Korean generals who kept trying to put a hit on her. And her boss put the hit on her in her evaluation report!

The worst sexual harassment I've ever had to deal with came when I was commanding an all-female unit at Fort Belvoir back in the sixties. I had many idealistic, patriotic, highly motivated, dedicated young women, who'd come out of WAC training to a military post where they were one in fifteen in the military population. Guys hit on them all the time. They could have serial dates every night if they wanted to. And if they refused to go to bed, the first thing the man would say is "What are you? A queer? A lesbian?" Many of these women didn't even know what that was.

And then people would put signs up in front of the company: "Home of the Queers." How do you give women defenses against this type of sexual harassment? We'd insulted the men, we'd refused to go to bed with them. Newspapers would have headlines: "Queers in the WACS." The women would wail, "How can they say that about us?" I'd say, "Because it helps sell newspapers."

At the Army Command and Staff College at Fort Leavenworth, Kansas, I was a student in Bravo Division, section 10, as their token woman. In that environment you need to be a little bit smarter than they are. I was also a little bit older, and I said to myself, The only way you survive this garbage is with humor. So when we had to introduce ourselves, I said, "Hi, I'm your token woman." We started there and worked up some good rapport.

I became the ex officio "couth control" officer. Some of the filthiest jokes you've ever heard were slung off the platform by the instructors, who'd get the men's attention by telling bawdy jokes. So I instituted a "crotch-mentality award of the week" that some instructor or student would get, based on how gross their behavior or comments had been. It got to be a hated moment in the week! They didn't want to be labeled.

I was there in the spring of '72, the year of the Burt Reynolds centerfold in *Cosmopolitan*. Two of us cornered every copy at the grocery store in downtown Leavenworth. These guys would come in with their *Playboys* and spread them out on their desks and ooh and aah to each other. The day we brought Burt Reynolds in, on a wonderful white rug, with very little guarding his crown jewels, these guys went crazy. One man said, "God, now I know how my wife must feel." And I said, "Well, we've made progress."

You'd get a few people who were so gross you'd take 'em out as fast as you could. But guys who were just doing what their conditioning had taught 'em — you could work with those guys. I've physically grabbed someone and then said, "I have your arm right now. If you do that again, I'll have something else!" They'll back off immediately. I've never had a man push himself after I say, "If you try that again, you'll regret it for the rest of your life."

I've used humor as a weapon. There are some who cannot. And there are times I can't, either. Sometimes you just have to go nose to nose and say, "Next time I'm preferring charges." In the seventies, I visited a unit where women were being physically mauled in ranks — I mean knocked down. The women told me, and I said, "Give me a statement." They said, "No, ma'am, we're just tellin' you." I said, "I cannot do a thing unless you give me some facts." They'd say, "If we give you a statement, we're dead." I was furious.

I had a woman whom I know was raped by a drill sergeant in a supply closet when I was a battalion commander. He was a twenty-two-year-old stud who loved to give out pictures of himself to the women in his unit. I'm sure he raped her. Would she give me a statement? No! She was terrified! I said, "If you give me a statement, we'll get rid of him." She said, "Then he'll come after me." Women have *got* to stand up and speak out. Of course in the seventies, women would say, "They'll say I'm a slut and I asked for it in the first place; I shouldn't have been there; my clothes goaded him into doing it . . . and they'll be checking my background, not his."

Until we get to the point where women, who are the majority population, are at those policy-making levels where you can truly influence policy, then we as a nation are going to continue to do dysfunctional things in the foreign and domestic arenas. Who in their right mind wants to go into combat? So what you do is have your best and brightest, male and female, at the top, who develop alternatives to making mincemeat out of each other. I'm so sick and tired of this warrior mentality in the world. It's brought us to the brink too many times. I'd never have stayed in the army all these years if I didn't think peace is the better solution.

Tanya Domi is a defense policy analyst, now in her late thirties, who tracks conventional arms sales. She came out of a middle-class, midwestern family, and at nineteen, in her sophomore year in college, enlisted in the army to get her education paid for. I met her at a noisy rally during the Democratic National Convention, and after she heard what I was up to, she said, "I've got something for you!" She certainly did. Among other things, her story shows that women as well as men can use gay-baiting as a weapon against other women.

When I was fourteen, I worked in Bobby Kennedy's presidential campaign in Indiana. I was a civil rights advocate and a feminist at sixteen. I went to a coed school with a stupid rule that didn't allow girls to be student body president. So I got 'em to change this rule. It was a year before I'd have been eligible, but nobody in the class ahead of me ran. So I ran and won — easily — four to one. I was a really good athlete; in '71, I was on the United States Pan American team in basketball, and I went to Indiana University to play on the women's basketball team. But Title IX had just passed and the benefits had not yet come through, so you drove to games — it was hand-to-mouth.

I was in-your-face. I was that kinda kid. My mother brought me up to think I could be anything I dreamed I could be. A friend says, "You're not a type A personality; you're a triple A." I've probably been an overachiever since I came out of the womb — always doing three jobs instead of one. And after my parents went through a real bad divorce, I decided to join the army.

All of a sudden I was in the barracks with thirty-nine other women, some from East St. Louis and Montgomery, Alabama, and I went through culture shock! A woman from East St. Louis was probably lucky to survive; it was up and out of the ghetto to join the army. I was saying to myself, As soon as I get out, I'm going back to school. I was probably one of the few college-educated women there. A lot of 'em were divorced; it was an opportunity to get back on their feet. A lot were older. And I did very well. I came out of basic training with an accelerated promotion.

The first incident occurred at Fort Devens in Massachusetts. At that time, in 1974, women still hadn't been integrated into regular army units: we were in Women's Army Corps (WAC) detachments. And people assumed that women who go places together, have lunch together, and hang out together are lesbians. That was the bottom line, and at nineteen, quite frankly, I didn't know what I was. I was just a nineteen-year-old kid living her life. But that spring I was very innocent and went with six other women to a gay bar in Boston. We were turned in by another woman in our unit, and I was investigated for eighteen months for being a lesbian.

I'm very outgoing and gregarious. I come from an Albanian family, and we touch and hug and kiss. I was accused of being a lesbian because of being affectionate, which women generally are with one another; it's the way we relate to one another. Maybe sixty women were dragged in, almost a fourth of the unit. My mail was opened, I was followed, it was incredible. So for the first time in my life, I felt backed into a corner. Everything you did was under suspicion; everybody was under suspicion; women were trying to commit suicide. They drove wedges between us — reaching out to other women was risky—and I developed a peptic ulcer. I began to read Ayn Rand books on the virtue of selfishness. You get these incredibly strong women characters in her books, and with their help, I was able to sustain myself. I've never experienced so much fear, and I lived under that for eighteen months.

Finally, I decided I was an American citizen. I knew the Constitution and knew I had rights. So I called a military counseling project in Boston, and they referred me to the American Civil Liberties Union, which eventually represented me. Fort Devens was an installation to train people in military intelligence, and you had to have a top-secret security clearance. Once you're under investigation, they pull it. At one point I was told that mine was going to be revoked permanently. I fought 'em and won. I had my security clearance reinstated.

But the army wasn't done with me yet. They were obligated to reassign me to a new job but wanted to teach me a lesson. So they reassigned me to a cooks' school. Now, to go into military intelligence, you have to be really smart, so they were clearly sending me a message. I decided I wasn't gonna accept that. I was a private first class, and believe it or not, I called my congressmen and then got on a plane to Washington. Father Drinan was my congressman. Ted Kennedy was my senator. Since I was from Indiana, I'd been in contact with Senator Birch Bayh's office. I'd already laid some groundwork with their offices, so they had open cases on me. And I hit Capitol Hill in a twenty-four-hour flurry. I told them what was going on, and their staffs talked to my attorney.

Fort Devens had had a ton of major media coverage. There had been publicity about other women in the unit. The *Boston Globe* had been there—and the *New York Times* and CBS. The story was breaking left and right. And the day after my trip to Washington, I had new orders reassigning me to a very technically demanding skill. I ended up being a petroleum/chemical analyst. I'd pull samples from aircraft to see if they were contaminated. I got about three months of training down in Savannah, Georgia, and then was assigned to a headquarters company for a quartermaster battalion, which performs logistics support. It was a highly demanding mission because we were assigned to the Eighty-second Airborne out of Fort Bragg. The Eighty-second goes all over the world. They're the first in, so you're always on alert.

At that time, women were always placed in headquarters companies, which were removed from the line units. They'd put women truck drivers in the platoon office as clerks. So here I come—triple A. My uniform was always pressed and starched; my boots were spit-shined; I looked good. And I loved it!

My supervisor was a staff sergeant who happened to be exceptionally disgusting. He'd come up behind me and put his arms around me. I was an E-4 and he was an E-6. I'd say, "Get away from me!" After you tell somebody that a few times, and they're in a position of authority, they can get real nasty.

I went to my boss, who was a female second lieutenant. But I began to see that he was doing the same thing to her and she wasn't doing anything about it. She was impotent and I was shocked. When I realized that she wasn't dealing with sex harassment as an officer, I was devastated. I went to her a coupla times, and then I realized. She'd say, "I understand, I'll look into it," but she didn't do anything and I lost all respect for her.

I'd just come out of the Women's Army Corps. I'd seen women being strong leaders and role models. They were good, and they could make things happen. When women were integrated, you lost the camaraderie and the advocacy. I used to call it the WAC Mafia; they looked out for women and protected them. But we had to give all that up to join the "real" army. After I got to Savannah, I longed to be back at the WAC center in Alabama and tried to get there as a drill instructor, but I was just too junior.

Young junior enlisted women are the most vulnerable people in the military. There aren't that many women noncommissioned officers to look out for you, and it takes the men NCOs a long time to catch on to how you take care of women troops. At that time, they didn't get it, so if I had a problem, they'd send me to the most senior woman in the company.

In 1975, the battalion was under investigation for discrimination against women. All the women were what we called "underutilized," and it was a totally ineffective assignment of personnel. (They weren't pulling only black men out to be clerks, or only men with blue eyes.) And if you didn't share in the equal burden of the unit, you were not considered as important.

The inspector general's office came down with a team to talk with all the women. Enlisted people are real candid: they don't try to put a political spin on things. So I told the guys, and they said, "Why don't you write it down on paper?" So I did. Stupid! The battalion commander was eventually relieved of his command. But just before he was relieved, my first sergeant came and said, "You're going over to the battalion commander. You're disloyal. I can't believe what you did." Of course, I didn't know what he was talking about. He grabbed my arm and marched me into the office.

The battalion commander began by saying, "I understand you have problems, Specialist Domi." I said, "Sir, I was asked to tell what I thought." He said, "I just want you to know whenever you have any problems, you need to come see me! And because you're one of our most senior women, we're gonna send you to the hundred and tenth quartermaster company because they need your leadership down there." Well, it was a hellhole; it was punishment. I said, "Yes, sir." So I ended up sweeping floors for eighteen to twenty months.

At that time, the women from all these different units in an installation lived in one barracks. So you didn't live with your fellow soldiers — which also marginalized women, for better or for worse. They always had fences around our barracks to keep the idiots out, but these guys would come in over the fence when it got dark. You might wake up with a guy on top of you. Under civilian laws it would be considered sexual assault. I ended up being the barracks sergeant because I was the highest-ranking woman. I'd established a rapport with the MPs, and I'd pick up the line and say, "Here they come again." So one night they were being really cute and climbed in the windows, but I orchestrated open rebellion — got all my baseball bats and handed 'em out. I bloodied a lotta hands that night and called the police afterwards. We beat the hell out of them. It was no way to live. . . .

Michelle Benecke is a slender, dark-haired woman in her early thirties who spent six years in the army as an officer. Subsequently she went to Harvard Law School, and for the past three years, she's been trying to change the way the military operates by agitating from the outside. The mutual friend who'd insisted that I talk to Michelle called one day to say that she was in Washington, and I managed to catch her just as she was leaving.

I'm an army brat — the oldest in my family — and I've always been aware that boys are treated better than girls in our society. (I was the first girl to be kicked out of the Alexandria, Virginia, Little League.) In the sixth grade, I was organizing other girls to crash PTA meetings to demand a softball coach and uniforms.

I went to the University of Virginia on an ROTC scholarship — more out of economic necessity than to follow in my dad's footsteps. I wanted to play Division One softball, so I went there instead of to Wellesley. Neither of my parents had gone to college, and when I was in high school, we'd been overseas. I was a working-class kid and didn't know what the Ivy League was.

Taking the scholarship was the only way I was going to school without having to work full-time, and the idea of being in the military didn't sound odd to me. We'd moved around a lot, and there was nothing I ever wanted to do that my parents barred me from doing because I was a girl. I was a tomboy: I played army out in the woods with the guys, I went fishing for crayfish, and did everything an active kid would do. I also had my share of Barbie dolls and Easy-Bake ovens and ironing boards.

At the University of Virginia, I found out pretty quickly that most things I wanted to do in the army I wouldn't be permitted to do. If it hadn't been for the combat exclusions, I'd have signed up for the infantry or for tanks, which are the most prestigious fields. (I came in gung ho, I was "Jane Wayne," I wanted to be a part of the core function of the military.) I ended up asking for air defense artillery because that was the closest I could get as a woman to the fighting branches, and they did allow me to be a platoon leader in command of combat soldiers.

The credibility of women officers is always in question in a way that men's credibility is not. There's some degree of testing that always happens. The soldiers will try to push the line with any new officer to find out what that officer's standards are and what they expect from their soldiers. For women officers, or for women leaders, that process is more intense. As a result, I pushed myself to be even more gung ho and do everything I could to prove myself according to the military's measures.

I went to airborne school when I was still a cadet — which qualifies you to be a combat parachutist. It's a very rigorous, intense, three-week training course to teach people how to do combat parachute jumps from military aircraft. Later, I went to air assault school, which teaches you how to rappel out of helicopters, do forced road marches, lay out landing zones, and hook up equipment to various types of helicopters so the equipment can be transported across the battlefield. I wanted to complete both schools because I was really into it — but also because very few women wear both badges. With them, I'd have a measure of credibility I'd need to be an effective leader. I came in to the army as a second lieutenant and left six years later as a captain who'd just finished her battery command.

Right from the beginning, I was in an environment where anything feminine is very much marginalized and even denigrated. Men are presumed to belong by virtue of being men. In order to belong, women have to meet an idealized male standard. My peers and I, and the women I commanded, tried very hard to belong. My branch of the military was divided into gun systems and missile systems. Women are allowed to serve in the missile but not in the gun systems. The guys in the gun systems were constantly trying to prove that women couldn't do the guns. So women officers — and enlisted women as well — have to deal with a whole set of issues that men simply don't have to deal with.

Women who can perform a nontraditional job as well as a man apparently pose a tremendous threat to that man's definition of masculinity. So the questioning starts immediately. Does she wear high heels or flat shoes? Does she wear makeup or not? Has she slept with anybody we know? Since there's an absolute obsession with whether a woman's straight, you see a hyperfemininity among military women. I never wore flat shoes with my uniform; I always wore heels. When I wore my dress uniform, I always wore makeup and made sure I had a man on my arm. The problem is that it's a direct contrast with what the military values, which are "masculine" traits. Walking that constantly shifting line is very tricky. If you look too "feminine," you're not going to be taken seriously.

Paula Coughlin [who sparked the Tailhook investigation] identified this well when she said, "I thought of myself as belonging to this group of navy aviators. I didn't perceive danger. . . ." What harassment did to her, and what it did to me and other women in the military, was to provide a message that we didn't belong, no matter how well we did. That's very devastating. Many women I know had commanders who were pressuring them for sexual favors. I didn't have that experience. But since I was one of very few women in the branch, many guys hit on me. And if you'd turn down a guy's sexual advances, you'd be called a lesbian. The rumor would then fly around the post. If I was sitting in the officers' club, talking with a few other women officers, invariably men would walk by our table and make a comment to the effect that we were conspiring.

I was in one unit where a male commander felt strongly that women didn't belong, and he allowed harassment to flourish. If you have a leader who doesn't take a strong stand against it, it's just like racial discrimination — it'll thrive. The harassment then ranged anywhere from verbal comments to rape. There was cornering, where a man would corner a woman and try to extort sexual favors.

The impact on a young officer who's gung ho and finds out that every effort is being made by the commander to root her and other women out of the unit is just devastating. Women try to deal with it by doing an absolutely stellar job, but it's extraordinarily frustrating when you learn it's not going to matter. There's nothing you can do to deflect or stop the harassment, and nothing's gonna keep you there if the commander doesn't want you.

Some men have taken advantage of this situation by extorting sexual favors from women. In Kaiserslautern, in Germany, there's a large army and air force military installation where men actually organized themselves into a group called Dyke-busters. (It was 1984, the year that *Ghostbusters* was popular.) They made up T-shirts with the word "dykes" across them and the international symbol for no—the red circle with the red slash through it. And they found out the bars or lounges where military women congregated after duty. They'd walk in, all of 'em wearing these T-shirts, go over to the jukebox and put on the theme to *Ghostbusters*. And then they'd proposition the military women in the room. They reported those who didn't agree to the military investigative services as dykes.

I saw in my female peers that this environment leads to very low self-esteem. Some of the most high-ranking military women I know have the lowest self-esteem because they've gone through an entire system that every day, through a variety of actions, denigrates women. The personal toll is so high. The lesbian-baiting and the fear of being perceived as disloyal keeps women from getting together in groups—from talking to one another and sharing their experiences. Anytime you're not seen as a team player, you're considered the enemy.

So you have to deal with that stress and fear every day—alone. For a woman leader in a nontraditional job field who already leads life under scrutiny—who lives pretty much in a goldfish bowl—it means living under terror. And women of color can just hang it up. I found myself less and less able to turn on the light switch, to try to carve out some personal space to be me, to retain my identity, to have a healthy place to be. I recognized how destructive an environment that denigrates women is to women, and I suspect many of us suffer from post-traumatic stress syndrome.

It was extremely difficult for me to leave the army, because I loved soldiering. Now I'm working hard from outside to influence it to change: I'm trying to create a safe space for women who are left in that environment.

Military women are sexually harassed because men whose egos are threatened by their competence need to control them. Nowhere are the psychic roots of harassment laid so bare as in an institution built on the traditional definition of masculinity. Nowhere is the sheer brutality of sexual harassment more apparent — or the staggering waste. And nowhere is the connection clearer between sex and power: to diminish or control a woman's sexuality is to diminish and control the woman.

In the uproar that met President Bill Clinton's announcement that he intended to lift the ban on gays in the military, few commentators remarked on the role gay-baiting had played in keeping women in jobs unworthy of their skills or even in driving them from the armed services altogether. For the most part, they seemed to worry about men, which of course came as no surprise to women. They panicked at the thought that *men* might be sexually harassed, which had at least the virtue of revealing, albeit indirectly, that they knew how damaging sexual harassment could be.

Women who had been harassed found an unlikely champion in Barry Goldwater, former chairman of the Senate Armed Services Committee, who wrote an op-ed piece regretting the military's waste of "a half billion dollars over the past decade chasing down gays and running them out of the armed services." Calling the gay ban "just plain un-American," he insisted that it was time to "get on with more important business."

While Goldwater struck a welcome note of sanity, the current chair of the Senate Armed Services Committee, Sam Nunn, used his formidable political capital to support the opposing side, and the legal wrangling that followed the infamous Tailhook convention showed that individual cases of harassment would remain hard to prosecute. Lieutenant Paula Coughlin identified marine captain Gregory Bonam as the "most brazen of her molesters," but at a preliminary hearing to determine whether he should be courtmartialed, Bonam flatly denied her charges. They disagreed dramatically on several key points, including the color of his shirt, and on that point at least, the corroborating evidence was on Bonam's side. As the *New York Times* would put it, memories had been clouded with alcohol and then with time, and "because of fear and loyalty and differing assessments of what represents sexual misconduct, most potential witnesses have stayed silent."

Still, in the spring of 1993, the air force announced that women would be allowed to fly planes in combat. Only months later, Sheila Widnall was named secretary of the air force, and the barriers to women's full participation in the armed services appeared to be on the verge of free fall. Images were even reconsidered and directives issued that the voluptuous women painted on fighter planes in World War II to "raise the boys' spirits" would become a casualty of history; from now on, the emblems were to be sex-neutral.

A new administration seemed more inclined to take ideas like retired brigadier general Pat Foote's seriously, experimenting with ways to integrate women more efficiently in the interests of a stronger military and insisting that commanders take the lead in outlawing sexual harassment. To the extent that it can defuse the hysteria of a powerful and well-organized opposition, the reconstituted national leadership seemed likely to take Foote's practical suggestions and others like them to heart. Perhaps more important, the daughters and granddaughters of proud military men had claimed their right to serve their country as their fathers did, so that the military will be a very different institution by the end of the twentieth century.

10

THE HOME

I'm gonna talk until somebody listens to me!
— Gina Pascale, battered wife

Most of us grew up with the maxim "A man's home is his castle," and many of us were in for a terrible shock. For nowhere has the presumption that the generic "men" includes women been more profoundly misleading: a man's castle may well be a dungeon for the woman and children who live there, and if the children are female, the danger escalates.

While domestic violence can be psychological rather than physical, more than 11 percent of women have been literally battered by their mates, and child abuse has burgeoned into an epidemic. The significance of domestic violence was underscored by Janet Reno, the first woman ever to be nominated U.S. attorney general, who told the Senate Judiciary Committee in her opening statement: "Until we focus on violence in the family, we'll continue to have violence in the streets." In fact, sexual harassment is merely an extension of the abuse women suffer in their traditional workplaces. And while most now join the paid workforce because they need the money, multitudes come as refugees from the institution of marriage.[1]

Most women simply won't put up with what their mothers did from men, who in turn are less likely to offer the security their own fathers did, and so women's position in this country, over the past fifty years, has changed more dramatically than in any five centuries before us. The middle-class women of my generation, who are now in our fifties, were the last to grow up assuming that we'd give our jobs as wives the pride of place and discover our highest selves in marriage.

While we were in our twenties, however, a birth control pill was developed that gave women a more certain command over their own reproduction. Then, in 1973, the Supreme Court handed down its decision in *Roe v. Wade* guaranteeing the right to legal abortion. In tandem, these two developments helped to demystify sex, and gradually we've realized that sexual ignorance had often made traditional marriage a trap that baffled, instead of releasing and channeling women's erotic energies.

These same developments also "liberated" men who, as Barbara Ehrenreich puts it, fled from commitment. "There is no guarantee," she writes, "that a man's emotional dependency on his wife will last as long as her financial dependency on him." And finally, the economy changed so drastically that most women now *have* to work outside their home — even when they have small children — to maintain the level of security they've come to take for granted.[2]

These technological, political, legal, and economic changes in turn have freed us to acknowledge traditional marriage as a problematic institution — a fact our ancestors may not even have had the luxury of recognizing. Men of our generation grew up expecting to have their way, as men had for millennia, while we had learned from our mothers, as they had from theirs ad infinitum, that men take precedence.

Many of us discovered, however, that we couldn't live with the sexual double standard that earlier generations of women had taken for granted. Women with many more options than their mothers were shocked to see that very little had changed in the century since John Stuart Mill had written, "The generality of the male sex cannot yet tolerate the idea of living with an equal." We found out that if, as Carolyn Heilbrun says, "Power is the ability to take one's place in whatever discourse is essential to action and the right to have one's part matter," a husband could flatly refuse to grant it, and many of us couldn't live with men who ignored and dismissed us.[3]

Ours has been a deeply conflicted generation. Many of us stayed in dismal marriages — in part, because we were raised on the ethic of obligation and believed in living with the consequences of choices freely made. But the novelist Larry McMurtry, who has created so many feisty, appealing women, admits that young women today are contemptuous of his female characters for putting up with dreary or difficult husbands. We called it loyalty; they call us suckers.

The ideas connected with women's roles as wives and mothers, however, were our received ideas, and they were powerful precisely because we didn't question them. They were simply part of our cultural furniture — to be dusted off perhaps, and peered at curiously from time to time, but for the most part to be taken for granted. But as the cultural revolt of the 1960s gave way to a movement that would profoundly affect the way American women saw themselves, the horizons to which we thought it natural and proper to aspire gradually began to lift. New surveys show that our ideas have changed: wives are far less satisfied than their husbands or their children, and half of all marriages now end in divorce.

Of the four stories that follow, two come from middle-class and two from working-class women; two of them are white and two are African-American. None knew much about sex before she married or began living with her mate. Three were married for more than a decade, though each suspected early on that she'd made a mistake in what the writer Elizabeth Janeway has pegged by far the most important choice in a woman's life. All had children, who made leaving immeasurably harder. Invariably, they called on every virtue — patience, tolerance, compassion, forgiveness — to make their lives and marriages work. Finally they broke the rules, and ultimately they rewrote a story that had traditionally closed with the words "and they lived happily ever after."

The Capitol Hill Women's Political Caucus has defined sexual harassment in the workplace as "a form of exploitation and intimidation which is economically enforced by virtue of the professional relationship." These women's comparable experiences in their homes came from their economic, social, and psychological dependence on a personal relationship. In 1869, John Stuart Mill had tactfully described the peculiar vulnerability of wives. The husband, he said, "can claim from [his wife] and enforce the lowest degradation of a human being, that of being made the instrument of an animal function contrary to her inclination." At the same time, he speculated that if justice governed the relationship between men and women, "all the selfish propensities, the self-worship, the unjust self-preference, which exist among mankind" would be rooted out.[4] More than a century later, his hopes for egalitarian marriage seemed like the beckoning, shimmery surface far ahead on a highway that retreats into the distance as fast as you stretch to reach it.

Gina Pascale is a fifty-year-old domestic-abuse counselor who was brought up in an Italian Catholic, working-class neighborhood in eastern Massachusetts. While spending a fine summer week at Wellfleet, on Cape Cod, I called a nearby women's center to ask if anyone there had a story to tell, and two days later I was sitting with Gina in an old Victorian house long since converted into warrens of offices. She has an operatic temperament, as well as the bosom and gestures to go with it, and if she had the voice, she'd have made a splendid Tosca. Although she has told her story many times by now, she still weeps.

I moved to a suburb of a medium-sized town when I was eight years old and grew up there, and it was like moving from a city to the country. It wasn't like it is today. You lived with your parents until you got married. I grew up in a strict, authoritarian household. My father was loud and he swore. He had his own chair; you couldn't talk at meals; you couldn't have a glass of water till the meal was done. My parents didn't get along, and I was the scapegoat. I'd argue and speak when I wasn't supposed to at the dinner table.

My father would have affairs, and my mother was this passive person who took it; that's what you did. But when I was sixteen, she blamed me for the affairs. She said, "You're having sex with your father." Which was totally untrue. She said, "Take your clothes off, and let me see if you're still a virgin." She was going to take me to the doctor! I said, "What you should be doing is asking your husband if he's attracted to me." Because I hated him. I was always afraid to be alone in a room with him. I'd back off and stand in a corner. I ran to my aunt's and told her my mother was accusing me of having sex with my father. She said, "Oh well, just be quiet and stay here." Then my father came and picked me up. He said, "Your mother's a little wacko. Get in the truck." And I did, because I didn't have any other place to go. After that, my mother would keep giving me these looks.

I graduated from high school into hairdressing school. I expected to get this part of my life over in six months so I could get married. That was the goal women had in those days. It was the only goal — not education. My brother had said, "Why don't you go to business school?" And I said, "That'll take two years. Hairdressing school will take six months." I expected to work, but it was secondary to being married.

I was happy-go-lucky and got married when I was twenty-one. I used to work in a hairdressing shop, and this guy worked across the street in the cemetery. He was a grave digger. He was handsome, he was a leader, he stood out. And I thought, "If I marry him, I won't have to work: he'll take care of me." I bet my friend that within a year, I'd date him. He used to go to the restaurant, and I'd go over there, too. But I wouldn't talk to him. That's what you did. You weren't assertive or aggressive. I'd speak to everybody in there but him, and that would pique his interest in me. I played hard-to-get the whole time and won the bet: I married him three months after we started dating. He was very sweet and kind and gentle, and he was accepted by my father because he was Italian. (He'd been afraid I'd marry an Irish boy who'd drink and wouldn't support me.)

There was definitely a sexual attraction for me. In this day and age, I'd probably have slept with him and not married him. I'd had one sexual experience before and lost my virginity. But it was more out of rebellion: I was trying to get outta my skin. I was being assertive and independent, but I didn't know what that was.

The only vacation I'd had as a single person, away from my parents, was in California. It looked like heaven to me. I went with my cousin and stayed at my cousin's. But I had this freedom that I'd never experienced. And it was so exhilarating I wanted to stay. So I called my father and said, "I like it here: it's good and it's fun, and this place is beautiful. The sun shines every day." And he said, "Get home or I'll come get you." I was scared, and I went back home. But I had that vision. I told my fiancé about it, and he said, "Why not?" So when I got married, we ventured on to California.

The abuse started within the first week because I didn't want to get pregnant. My brother had had a son at nineteen, at twenty he had another one, at twenty-one he had another one. I saw him struggling, and I made up my mind that I wasn't going to have kids right away. So I was very strict with my husband: I didn't know much about it, but I made him use a safe [a condom]. When he came, he used to say, "This is a dead baby. You did this!" And he'd throw the used condom in the basket. He'd say, "You're killing babies. You should be ashamed of yourself!" That's the way my honeymoon went.

I was Catholic, too, but I didn't think contraception was wrong. Now I was in a no-win situation. I was married to this person who thinks it's wrong and is controlling. But I didn't know those words then: I was twenty-one. I felt crappy, and I wanted to get away from him. So I called my father and said, "I want to come home." He said, "Well, you can." But marriage was so tied in to a woman's identity that I began to think, There's something wrong with me because I can't keep this together. My father had told me for twenty-one years that there was something wrong with me. Now my husband was saying there was something wrong with me. *So they must be right.* I kept thinking maybe I could make it right. So I said, Let me try it one more time. Let me try it *his* way. Let's not use a safe. I didn't know about diaphragms. I didn't have any sex education. I didn't know about going to a clinic so I'd have a *choice.* I hadn't been to a gynecologist.

My husband took over control of me. He thought that was the way he was supposed to be as a man. I fit into the stereotypical role as a woman — except that I wasn't passive like my mother. I was borderline hostile; I'd stick up for my rights. But if the dinner wasn't ready exactly on time, I was in trouble. If the spaghetti sauce didn't have meat balls and sausages and pork roast in it, I was in trouble. He'd say, "I'm throwing this in the sink."

For fourteen years, he never kissed me. I used to say, "Why don't you kiss me? Not like a mother kisses a daughter, but like a kiss — for a coupla minutes." And he wouldn't. He said, "If you kiss, you don't feel it down there." I said to myself he must be right, but it didn't feel like anything. I felt I was laying there and I didn't participate.

He'd say, "You're really stupid. You're a cunt. You're a fucking whore, I see you looking at men. You'd better come home when I tell you to." I never went out with other men. He just made this up. It made me sad, but I knew I was fighting for survival. I'd say, "Don't say those things, you fucking asshole, I'm not like that." He would swear, and then I started swearing.

At first, I'd fight back. I was four feet eleven and three-quarters and a hundred and twenty pounds. He was five feet eight and two hundred pounds. After three months of fighting, I stopped. I didn't like myself. I didn't like the feeling of getting physical with him. I said to myself, "He can do whatever he wants, but I'm not gonna fight like this. I'll fight with my mouth." But the feeling was always that I was in combat or in prison. I'd say, "I can't go out. Why should you?" And I'd hold the door. He was going out with some woman to cheat on me, and I'd say, "I don't like this. It's not right." And he'd say, "This is what men do." I didn't know how to say, "This makes me sad." I just knew how to fight.

I saved my money up, and after three months, I said, "I'm going home." He said, "Good!" Then, when I was at home, he'd call me up and say, "Mary Jane's over here and I'm having a ball!" It was uncomfortable at home, so after two or three weeks, I went back. It was my father's house or my husband's house. I said, This time I'm gonna work my ass off and make sure dinner's on the table on time. When I got back to California, there was come all over the bed. And he said, "See, this is what happens when you're not a good wife." I was the bad girl. At this time, I'd say I shut down all my emotions — to survive — like a prisoner of war. He could push me anywhere, and I was on rote. *Who says I didn't want to leave? But I had nowhere to go.*

Then we moved back to Boston. It was a total shock. He said, "We're going to move, and you're not working." We drove across the country and moved into his mother's house. She'd vacuum our room at five o'clock in the morning, and after two months, I went out and got my own apartment. I told him, "You can come, or you can stay. But I'm not living here with your mother anymore."

He'd go out with his friends, and I'd lie on the floor crying. In front of other people, I felt safe because he wouldn't show that side of himself. He'd be the ideal, charming, loving, caring person. I'd be the blabbermouth — talk, talk, talk — I'd stand up for my rights. They'd say, "He's a good guy, that's the way it is, maybe you should just keep quiet." His mother would say, "Why don't you keep quiet? Then he won't have to hit you." I'd say, "God gave me a mouth, and I'm going to use it."

He'd tell me about going out with these other women, and I'd have to sit there and listen. He made me sit for hours while he told me explicitly about his sex life. He'd say if I was a better sex partner, or if I didn't stink so bad, he wouldn't have to go out and cheat on me. He'd say, "Iron these pants so I can go out with Mary." He was very clear. At that point, I'd probably say, "I love you. Let me try again." But I'd also say, "I'm getting outta here some day! I don't know how, I don't know when. But I'm getting outta this mess some day — getting the fuck outta here!"

After five years I got pregnant. It was our happiest time. He was proud that he'd gotten me pregnant. My child was premature and sickly, and then my husband got jealous of the child. He said, "You don't pay attention to me." I kept thinking he'd mature. Two years later I got pregnant again: he'd forced himself on me. I felt like I was being raped, but I didn't have the words. How can a man rape his wife? I didn't enjoy any part of it. I wanted to puke. But it was just something I did before I went to sleep. It was survival.

The second time I got pregnant, he didn't like it. I don't know if he mentioned abortion, but it felt like that. I wouldn't do that, so he just took off. I called the police and gave 'em his picture. I said, "Bring him back and put him in jail for what he's done to me." My mother came and spoon-fed me and said,

"You gotta eat for the baby." He called me and said, "I'm coming home." I was so happy; I thought it would be over. The police arrested him, and he begged me to get him out. So I did: I signed a paper.

You have to be the strongest at the time that people perceive you at the weakest. You've gotta be able to get up and fix a bottle when somebody's just pushed you against the wall or choked you. That takes incredible strength. I realize in retrospect how strong I was then, because if you're not strong, you're not gonna survive.

My husband handcuffed my youngest son to the bed and left him there all day. So I said, "You'll never do that again." He was then a correctional officer, and he'd come home and tell me about how he'd broken this guy's toes. He'd go to jail and beat 'em up and then come home and beat me up.

He had guns in the house, and he'd shoot birds through the window. One time he shot this duck, and he sat there plucking the duck. As he's doing this, he's saying, "If you're thinking of leaving, you'll never make it without me. I'll kill your mother and your father and your brother. . . ." I didn't care about dying, but I didn't want him to kill my family.

I started thinking, "I'll kill him." But then I'd say, "No, then my kids wouldn't have a mother." I got a master's degree — I got a doctorate — in how to survive. Finally I went to the courthouse and got an abuse-prevention order. A woman came up to me and said, "Are you here for abuse prevention?" And I thought, "My God, do they stamp it on your forehead?" She said, "I'm from a woman's center, and I'm here to advocate for you."

Everybody I've loved who's a man has turned his back on me. I used to say, "What's wrong with me?" Today I'm forty-nine years old, and it's still hard. I'll take responsibility for all the things I've said and done: I take inventory of myself. But I'm not going to accept responsibility for what they've done.

Alice Baldwin is an African-American sculptor who has a gift for friendship and a fondness for bad puns. Her antic spirit went into hiding, however, when she thought about her story. We sat facing each other on my window seat, watching the late afternoon shadows fall on the Library of Congress across the way as she told it haltingly.

I got married when I was twenty-four and very young. I'd never lived on my own or been independent. I'd felt very attached to my father, who died when I was a teenager. His death left me without a father figure even though my

mother remarried. I had no respect for my stepfather, who was very material-
istic and didn't care anything about art or music or cultural things. He was also
a lawyer, but not one I could respect. And since my mother married him soon
after my father died, I felt she was very disloyal.

Even after college, my stepfather and my mother wouldn't let me get my
own apartment and my own job. When they reluctantly agreed that I could go
to graduate school, I applied to a school in Boston, where they insisted that I
live in an institution. That was very depressing. So here I was, stuck in this awful
place — very lonely and isolated — and Jim came along. He seemed like a nice
kind of guy. He was interested in the arts, and I thought, Hey, this might work. . . .
I was a virgin, and I'd never had a real relationship with a man. And he reminded
me of my father in ways that turned out not to be real. So we got married. I
knew on our honeymoon that I'd made a mistake.

I'd dated in high school and college but was never really in love with
anybody. And I got married because I didn't realize I could go out and get a
job and be independent and live my own life. I married this guy I didn't really
love. (Of course, I see that only in retrospect.) I didn't know sex was supposed
to be wonderful, and it wasn't. I tolerated it — I could do it — but I didn't enjoy
it, and I'd have preferred *not* to.

About a year after I was married, and before I had children, I was terribly
unhappy. And in the course of going to galleries, I met a man named Stephen
who was also a sculptor, and we'd meet and talk. After a while I realized that
I was attracted to him and I was married, and the two didn't go too well together.
So I blurted out one day that I didn't want to have an affair with him. He seemed
angry and insulted, and that was the end of our friendship. I'd had to put up this
barrier, but I think this was my awakening to my attraction to other men.

I began studying at graduate school, where I had a professor I really liked.
He was much older, and I thought of him as a sort of father figure although
we had no relationship outside the classroom. He was black and highly respected as an artist, and I trusted him. One day I walked into his office —
nobody else was around — and he grabbed me and kissed me. I pushed him
away, but I didn't think this was an awful thing. I knew I was attractive and got
positive reactions from men. But no one had ever made an inappropriate pass
before, and I thought this was what men do. From then on, I tried to keep my
distance. One day when he asked me to go to his home to see a painting, I
went and he did the same thing. It was limited to that: he didn't try to touch
any other part of my body, he just hugged me and kissed me on the mouth.

I always rejected these passes — and others like them — in a way that wouldn't make him angry; I kinda joked about it and laughed. I never really asserted myself in the way I would now. I was still a little girl. I never told Jim because I thought he'd think it was my fault. In fact, I didn't tell anybody.

Instead of getting out of my marriage, which was so empty, I started having kids. By the time I'd had the second, it was awful. From the beginning, Jim would come home late from work, and he'd have been drinking. He had people he went out with that didn't include me. He'd have office parties, and I'd ask if I could go, and he'd say no, it's just for the staff. At some point he started staying out all night. I'd call the police and the hospitals and his friends, but his friends were covering for him. One morning, when my younger child was just an infant, I found a love letter a woman had written him that he'd left on the bureau. When he came home, I said, "I found this letter. . ." and he told me I'd like her if I got to know her! I'd never been in therapy and didn't know how to handle my emotions, so my emotional state was very bad. I thought I deserved it. (I was a bad person or I was not worth being loved.) He didn't love me — that was quite clear — though he said he did.

When we moved to Washington, we lived opposite another couple who had one child. One night they invited us for dinner, and the wife was in the kitchen. Jim went into the kitchen, and they were in there together for a long time. I was sitting at the table talking to her husband when I looked up and saw a reflection in the glass over a painting hanging opposite the kitchen door of the two of them kissing. I pointed it out to the other man, and we didn't say anything. After that night, I spoke to Jim about it, and he said he was going to keep on having an affair with her. So I had an affair with her husband. I felt bad about it because I felt we were forced to and our children were all around. He'd come to my apartment on Sunday mornings, and Jim would go to his, and we'd each do the *New York Times* crossword puzzle. I don't know what the kids knew: they've never talked to me about it. But after we got going, it got to be a lot of fun.

Then Jim decided he was going to stop having an affair with her and told me I had to stop, too. And I told him no, even though this was not somebody I really cared about. I was just beginning to be able to stand up for myself — maybe in very inappropriate ways — and Jim was very angry. It was a very, very dangerous game.

Finally I just left. When Jim was away on a trip, I packed up everything and moved out. I called a friend of his and said, "Tell Jim I've left," and he did. I moved into a townhouse and painted on the inside of my bedroom door a poem of Emily Dickinson's: "The soul selects her own society, / Then shuts the door: / On her divine majority / Obtrude no more." I told this guy I had to show him something and sent him to look at the door, and it was the last day we ever spent any time together.

Diana Middleton, a southerner and a historian, is married happily to her second husband, who is also an intellectual and an academic. She had spent the day at the Library of Congress when she came over to recall how blithely she became a politician's wife. The story makes her clench her fists in the telling, though her first marriage ended more than fifteen years ago.

In my own family, my father was a really nice guy whom everybody liked. He was the spoiled youngest son of a well-to-do, upper-middle-class family — a Scott-Fitzgerald type. He had his little roadster, he'd had his nose broken in a car accident, he had a good time. My mother was from a working-class family. Her father died when she was fourteen, and she dropped out of high school. She was very pretty and probably smart, though it's hard to know because she was so neurotic. She read a lot but fantasized about her reading in an unlearned way, and she didn't do much work. I remember clothes in an ironing basket for years. You'd look down in the bottom and find something everybody had outgrown: a size two T-shirt when the youngest person was eight.

My mother seemed to get drunk on one glass of sherry. My earliest memories are of my parents having a little sherry before dinner and my mother getting drunk. Her speech got slurred, and if we made it to the dinner table intact, it was a good evening. She never got a grip. She felt inferior to my father's friends, who were the local country club set. The women among them had at least attended college. She was very insecure, and so she criticized them constantly and drank too much. My mother's mother was paralyzed from 1942 onwards — she'd had a stroke — and she stayed in bed till '63, taken care of by my mother's sister. So I had crazy females in my family, except for my aunt Helen, who lived in New York City and, when I was a senior in high school, said, "I'll send Diana to college." My mother and two of her sisters were certifiable; the three witches in *Macbeth* had nothing on them.

My greatest fear was that I was going to be like them. And I was convinced that my father put up with too much from my mother: he'd sit there and read while she ranted and raved and threw things. So I knew I wanted a man who wouldn't put up with any shit. I was a "good woman," and I would be supportive of a good man! (I was already a pretty good cook since my mother hadn't done it and I was the oldest of four kids.)

I had a high school boyfriend, but I always thought I was smarter than he was. I went to college and dated a while, and then I met this guy, Tony, who was a veteran a couple of years older than I. He was very charming, very good-looking, *very* attractive to women. He was brash, he seemed to come into a room and fill it up and then he'd want to flirt. We were both political science majors, and we met in our professor's office. We'd both made A's on our finals and had come to pick up our papers. A couple of weeks later, he asked me out. On our first date, he told me he was going to be governor of our state. And if he couldn't find the right woman, then he wasn't going to get married at all. My first thought was, Why is he telling me all this? My second was, Well, I probably could do that. So I began dating my first husband in my freshman year in college. Within six weeks, we went right into the fifties thing of going steady. Then I could transfer all my own desires to be important to him and be a good, supportive wife — unlike my mother.

I'd found somebody who didn't put up with anything. Of course, that meant he wasn't gonna pay any attention to me, either, but I hadn't figured that one out yet. On some level, I didn't know how to express feelings and didn't know that real emotional intimacy could exist between a man and a woman. I saw myself in terms of roles and in terms of the books I'd read.

Tony bragged a lot about all the women he'd been with in high school and during his three years in the army. I'd had one previous sexual experience with my high school boyfriend, and I told him that. This was around 1958, and he said, "Well, you're a nymphomaniac, but at least you're honest."

In 1959, I went to Cape Cod to work in a summer resort. But my job didn't work out, and so he said, "Let's get married." And I said, "Sure, why not?" I regretted it even before I did it. When we went to get the marriage license, something didn't please him, and he hit me, whack! — just like that [with the back of his hand]. I thought, I've got to call this marriage off, but I couldn't. At twenty, I couldn't admit I'd been about to make such a mistake! He was extremely short-tempered, and he'd blow up and throw things a lot. So for the first couple of months, even though he was always gone doing politics, I'd come home and be afraid to go upstairs. I was afraid there was somebody up there who wanted to kill me.

I thought he didn't care much about me, even though he liked it that I was smart. I'd modeled myself on my father's family, so he had a sense that I was in a class above him and knew how to do things right. I seemed to be a good political wife. He had no notion of any kind of intimacy between husband

and wife, so he felt he was doing his job just to come home. And it was up to me to cook, and so on. [In *Writing a Woman's Life*, Carolyn Heilbrun notes this problem: "Intimacy has been beyond most men, certainly beyond those men whose profound effect, usually unfortunate, has been registered in the public sphere. They have bonded with men, known sexuality with women, but been incapable of what a modern psychologist has called 'a highly loving, sexually free, and emotionally intimate relationship.'"]5

I was just overwhelmed — and deeply depressed. I didn't go to anybody for help, and I didn't try to sort it out with him. I was close to my college roommates, but I couldn't go to them. You just didn't do that then. We had such an idealized sense of the kinds of wives we were going to be. There was also a lot of shame then about divorce. Plus, he was always sorry after he'd blown up and broken something, or said something really ugly, or hit me — which happened maybe four or five times a year. He was always abjectly sorry. He'd say he really loved me, he'd never do it again, that sort of thing. And I always thought, Okay, let's start over. *I'd believe in his remorse.* I was such a complete fifties person; it took me eight or ten years to figure out that this was never going to change.

It was pretty terrifying when he'd start throwing things, although I'd watched my mother do this. A lotta glass and crockery got broken. Twice he punched his hand through a door. Once he punched his hand through a wall and had to plaster it over. A couple of times I called my father, whose basic advice was, "If you're not happy, get out of it." But I couldn't.

I got pregnant after five months, and for years after that, I was alone with my child. Tony was out doing politics, and if he noticed me, it was to criticize. He had a genius for grabbing you by your shorthairs and hanging on. So I was very much under. All I could do was take care of my baby and do the academic stuff. I taught junior high school for two years and then got a fellowship to go back and get a master's degree. I loved that year: I had something that was just mine. I liked the people and the work.

Dorothy was scared of her father. Once she ran in and jumped on him when he wasn't expecting it, and he jammed his hand through a wooden chest. Scared her to death. She got the message that she had to be superspecial. He'd brag on how smart she was, but he didn't want to be around her. *I couldn't prevent his ignoring her and I regret that more than I regret anything that happened to me. It took me so long to get strong for my kids.* For such a long time, I couldn't even put into words what was going on. I hadn't grown up with an emotional language, and I didn't have one in my marriage. This was a political household, and it felt like if you didn't have your case ready for the Supreme Court, don't open your mouth. To say "I feel" was to be laughed out of the room.

After about six years, I began to fight back: when he'd push me, I'd push him back. Or I'd throw things. I wanted him to see what it was like. But it didn't work, and I believe that the real abuse was emotional. The real pain was the constant denunciation of me. And there was nothing wrong with me! I was attractive, I was working full-time, I was often going to graduate school, I was bringing up two children. (Kitty was adopted in 1966.) But if you'd ask Tony, I did nothing right. I felt shame.

When we moved to the state capital, I had a choice of getting a job at this white private school in town or the black state college outside town. I took the job at the black college, and I think that was really the turning point; it was such a yeasty time for me, whereas Tony stayed the same. I was immediately immersed in real left politics, and though I didn't change my lifestyle, it was a real high for me. I got into things like equal housing and went to churches that held marches and meetings. Tony didn't do any of that, and he didn't like my friends. But we didn't see each other anyway. (Once in a while, we'd have a dinner party.)

In the summer of '68, all these women were on my front stoop when we learned that Bobby Kennedy had been shot, and Tony yelled, "Come in here and fix my breakfast," embarrassing me in front of my neighborhood friends. He was going up to Stafford a lot, and I found out later that he had a woman up there. Then we moved to another city, and I lost my identity; I spent a year in hell and almost committed suicide. I'd lost the life I'd made for myself, and now I was in this dinky little apartment with two kids, no job, and a crazy husband.

I'd had an affair that kinda liberated me and made me know the marriage was over. My lover was your basic I'm-gonna-write-the-great-American-novel-by-the-time-I'm-thirty type. He really liked the ladies a lot, but when he was with you, he was really *with* you. It started me thinking about getting out, but the marriage dragged on for another year and a half. Tony was having a walking nervous breakdown. I didn't care about that other woman. I just wanted him out of my hair, and the more he focused on her, the less he'd focus on me. Finally, while he was taking a shower, I got up the courage to put both girls in the car and left. I went to my sister-in-law's and then to my father's. I slept in my blue jeans for three weeks for fear Tony'd find out where I was and beat the door down.

By now, I knew I'd fight back, but he was stronger than I was. I remember bruises on my hip, and he hit me in front of the children. But the emotional abuse was the worst because he'd say, "Get your fat, potatoey self back into the kitchen." When I left, I just felt so liberated, so wonderful to be free of this miserable person. He contested the divorce; he thought I belonged to him. My father had to help me get me a lawyer, because everybody in the state was afraid of taking this case because they thought Tony would pull out all the stops. One of my old friends called and said, "I want to testify that Tony and I had an affair." And I said, "Oh, that's really sweet of you, but you don't have to lie for me." And she said, "It's not a lie." When he walked into the courtroom and saw two women with whom he'd had affairs sitting with me, he turned white. I had my divorce: he wanted nothing on the court record that would hurt him politically. I'd been married for twelve years.

The political stuff of the sixties did a lot for me, even before the women's movement. And it was extremely helpful to me when people started writing and talking about their lives. I always looked for answers in writing, but there hadn't been that kind of writing before. So now I thought, There are some other ways of putting a life together.

Meshall Thomas is a stocky, handsome African-American woman in her late thirties who works in Washington, D.C., as an advocate for battered women and children. A close mutual friend introduced us, and I sat in her plain office, with its rusting metal file cabinets and an old rotary fan, and listened to a story of terror and triumph in almost equal measure.

My mother was married twice — I'm an only child and so is she — and I'd been with my stepfather since I was two. He's an alcoholic, and my mother was the dominant figure in our home; if there was any battering, she did it. If he got drunk, she'd get angry and argumentative — and on occasion, she hit him. If I couldn't see it, I could hear it. One time she shot him — he was hospitalized, but he was okay; one time she stabbed him; and almost every weekend there was something going on between them. He'd get drunk, and I think I was scared that she was gonna kill him. So I wanted outta that house. One way to do that is you get pregnant and get married. I must have thought, I'll move away and live happily ever after. . . .

I thought it was abnormal for my mother to be dominant, since with my friends and their families, the man was the boss. So I thought it was normal for your boyfriend to keep you in line, so to speak, and when I was fifteen, I got into a relationship with a young man who was about two years older and very aggressive. Anything he wanted to do, we did. It was his way or no way at all: if we went to a movie, it had to be a movie he wanted to see. He started ordering me around, and when we'd play games — pushing and shoving — every time it would turn into a fight. He'd push me too hard, I'd push him back, and then he'd push me harder.

For about three months during the eighth grade, he convinced me to play hooky from school. Every morning my mother would give me money for lunch, and it was just about the cost of bus fare. I'd leave home for school, or so my mother thought, and go over to his house. Every morning his mother would let me in, and I'd spend the day there. Finally the school authorities called and said, "How sick is she? We haven't seen her in three months. When's she coming back to school?" Then my mother came over with the police and made a lot of threats about what she was gonna do to this guy. Nothing happened, except that I ended up going home.

She tried to separate us, but I'd tie sheets together and climb out the back window even though I was scared to death of my mother. I've always loved her — she has a grand character — and I knew she loved me. But I was also afraid she'd hurt me, looking at what she'd done to my stepfather. Then she sent me to my grandmother's in Richmond, Virginia, to go to school. But I'd catch the Greyhound back to Washington and see him, or he'd come there. This went on for a while, back and forth, back and forth.

I remember the first time my boyfriend hit me: he slapped me because he said I couldn't give him a straight answer. The slap itself hurt. But the look in his eyes said, "I'm letting you know what's gonna happen if you do this again." He convinced me that he was gonna hurt me if I didn't do what he said and that he wasn't afraid of my mother. He also got me feeling that he loved me and this was his way of showing me he cared — by keeping me in line and making sure I turned out to be a good woman. He became more controlling: he'd threaten my life if I said I wanted to see other people. I couldn't go out with certain girlfriends. I couldn't go out at all unless I told him where I was going. I got pregnant when I was sixteen, and after I had the first child, I felt like a piece of property.

My grandmother wanted us to get married. She was a Baptist, and she said, "We don't have illegitimate children in this family! I don't tolerate it!" I was in love with this man, and I thought abortion was wrong. And so we had the blood tests and applied for a license. But the weekend we were supposed to get married, he beat me up. All along, my mother had said, "She's too young to get married. This boy's hit her before, and if she marries him, he's gonna beat the crap out of her." So when he beat me up just before we were gonna get married, my mother said no to the marriage. In fact she said, "He's gonna end up killing you. . . ."

One day, she phoned his mother's house, and his mother said, "They've gone to the movie," which was a lie because we'd gone to the hospital. He'd beaten me up, and this big ring he wore caused me to need stitches in my head. My mother came over anyway and knocked on the door just as I happened to be coming up from the basement with this gauze bandage around my head, and she saw me and flipped out.

She got her gun and came charging through that house. His mother, father, sisters, and brothers all ran upstairs and got in the closet. She went downstairs after him, and my feeling was, "She's gonna kill him." But my daughter was just walking, and he grabbed her and ran up the steps. Mama told him, "Put the baby down. I'm gonna kill you. This is my only child, and I'm not gonna have her go through this kinda stuff with you." And she told me, "Meshall, get outta my way. I'd rather see you dead than going through this kind of abuse." I said, "Mama, please put the gun down." She kept saying, "Get back. . . ." They had this wooden bar down in the basement, and I hid behind it. He backed up the steps with my daughter, and when he got to the top, he just flew out the front door and left the child standing there. Mama was so angry — and she'd been holding her finger on the trigger so long — that the gun went off, straight through her hand, between her thumb and first finger. That calmed her down, but she made us go home with her.

Whatever bad things my mother said about my boyfriend, I'd throw tantrums and figure out how to get out of the house to go see him. Finally, I started staying at his mother's house. My mother had done everything she could do, and I was sure if she saw the bruises. . . .

It seemed like any trouble my boyfriend got into, his mother'd support him — no matter what it was. Once she came down to the basement after she'd heard us fussin' and said to him, "Don't do this!" But mainly she was there to get him outta whatever it was. Once he hit me hard enough to knock me out, and she came flying down the steps. He was cryin', and I played dead. And his mother said, "Look what you did! What are we gonna do now?" I was scared to death they were gonna do something to get rid of the body. But his sister's boyfriend came over and pried open my eyes, and he told her I was okay, I was just out. And he said, "You oughta be ashamed. You could've killed her!" I'd just crawl in the bed afterwards and go to sleep and hope he'd leave me alone.

My mother kept saying, "Meshall, he's gonna end up killin' you," and I'd begun to believe he *was* gonna kill me. As best as I can tell, I thought, I don't know why he's doin' this. Apparently he's got a problem, or I'm doin' something wrong. Didn't know what it was. And I kept thinking to myself, I've got to fix this problem. . . . *I took on responsibility for his beating me up.*

When I decided to go stay with my baby's father, my mother kept my daughter and threatened to have me put away as a teenager out of control. I just felt it was normal for him to slap me around; he wanted me to be his woman. But I was a *young* woman, so after a while, I got tired of not being able to go out to parties or the theater. Once I was determined to go to this concert, and while he was watching TV, I said, "I'm gonna put out this trash." I took my clothes, dumped the trash, and kept going. My girlfriend lived two doors down, so I changed at her place, and we went to the concert. When I came back, I was afraid to put the key in the door. I looked in, and he'd broken every mirror and smashed up the stereo. I was afraid to go further, but as I backed out, he caught me. I broke free and ran to my girlfriend's house, and he came after me. He told her if she didn't put me out of her apartment, he was gonna set fire to it.

Each time he assaulted me, it'd become more intense. I swear to God; it'd be worse. One time I went with a girlfriend to a party, and he found out where it was and walked right in. There were people dancing and sitting around the wall. I was sitting there with my female friends, and he came up and sat down beside me and said, "Come on, let's go." I was trying to get some power, some balance, and I said, "Look, I don't wanna leave. I'm havin' fun." He said, "Are you going now? Or am I gonna have to embarrass you in front of your friends?" I didn't move, and he just reached up real sneakily and gave me an undercut to my jaw. I thought to myself, If I get out that door, nobody's gonna help me. But if I start screaming, are they gonna laugh? Are they gonna call the police? Is somebody gonna stop him from beating me up? I got up and went with him because I didn't trust what other people would do. If I left with him, he was gonna beat me up, but it wouldn't be as bad as if I made what was happening public.

My girlfriend two doors down knew something was wrong, but she didn't know he was as dangerous as he was. After a while, I stopped associating with folks because I didn't want 'em to see the bruises and the scars. Toward the end, I even stopped calling my mother's house. I couldn't explain the abuse any more, and when I saw my mother, it was like she was taking inventory: "Meshall, where'd that mark on your eye come from? . . ."

When he was beating me, I'd think, I've gotta get outta here. I don't know when he's gonna kill me. A coupla times I ran to the back door, and he'd always catch me. Once he hit me in the back with the pick end of an African bush pick. Often he'd beat me and then go to sleep, or he'd beat me and force sex on me. Somehow he had me thinking I could never make it out before he'd catch me.

In the latter part of the sixties, first of the seventies, the police didn't provide any protection. It was a risk phoning 'em, because after they left, you'd get a more severe beating than the first time. And I didn't want my mother to know I'd failed. I didn't want her to know I'd fallen in love with a maniac. Once I stole away and called the police — had to whisper into the phone. And when they came, they asked me, in his presence, "Did you call the police? Didn't you say he was beating you?" I was terrified and didn't know what to say, so they got frustrated and left. I knew if they didn't take him into custody, I'd be at his mercy, and before they could hit the outside steps, he was on me again. So my faith in the system was rock-bottom. I was sure my mother would kill him if she knew the truth, and I didn't want her to go to jail. It wasn't her fault he was beating me up. . . .

I had two children with this person, and I still thought I loved him. But toward the end, I thought he was crazy and wasn't gonna get any better. *It took years for me to realize he was the one who had the problem. Till then, I was sure I was doing something wrong: maybe I wasn't showing him enough attention; maybe if I had dinner on time, or had it hot when he came through the door. . . .*

The last incident was when I'd saved about fifteen hundred dollars working at Woodward and Lothrop. I wanted to buy some new living room furniture, and instead of banking the money, I'd hidden it in a drawer. He came home one day and went through my things and found the money, and he said, "Well, I'm taking this. I need to pay some tickets, and my car insurance is due." I said, "I worked hard for that money. You're not taking it!" He grabbed me and I grabbed the money. I was stuffing it every place in my clothes I could stuff it in. And he was trying to take it from me. Then he grabbed my foot and started turnin' it counterclockwise. I was on the floor and he was twistin' it. My mother happened to be coming past my window; she heard me screamin' and came to the door. She partly broke the door down, and he got out the back. She said, "Meshall, get up!" I said, "Mama, I can't get up." She said, "Get up right now!" I think mostly she was angry that I'd allowed him to do this. But I couldn't walk, so she called the hospital.

When I came home, I put all his stuff in a cab and sent it to his mother's. This was 1971, and by then they'd passed a statute to authorize civil protection orders. So my mother went down with me, and we filed for one and had it served on him ordering him to come into court. Even then I wasn't real hopeful, but I'd got to the point where I told him, "If you're gonna kill me, just go ahead. I can't take it no more. I'm through."

I ended up getting married to a marine I went to school with. My son was two years old when we started living together. At the time, I wasn't in love with him and he knew the history between me and the father of my kids. He was very gentle and supportive and nice to my children. We got married the third year after living together, but the whole time I had contact with the kids' father. The day I got married, he called and said, "We can work this out. Just don't marry this guy. . . ."

I went to law school to become a paralegal. I'd always wanted do something with the law, because I felt there should've been other things that the law, society, and the government could've done to protect me against this person who had total control over my life. In '79, I started volunteering with a nonprofit organization that had just opened a shelter for battered women. I ended up with a job on staff, and things happened that opened my eyes. It was a group of feminist women, and some were lesbians — a whole different world — and they made me realize so many ways women are discriminated against. *After I learned more about battered women and domestic violence, I understood a lotta things about my own experience, and about my mother and father. It changed my whole life. I even stopped hating the kids' father. This job helped me gain strength, get my own self-esteem back, and realize I was a person.*

In 1976, I founded an organization that looks at what the city's doing to respond to the needs of battered women. We monitor the police and lobby to get abusers automatically arrested. I do training with the metropolitan police department twice a month and share my own personal experience to help them understand why battered women stay. I manage the emergency domestic relations project and act as an advocate for battered women in court. I negotiate consensual civil protection orders between the abuser and the victim, so I can help the person leave the courtroom with the relief she's seeking, whether it's a vacate order or a question of temporary custody and visitation rights. Mostly I talk to a lotta women — we've had more than twenty-five thousand come through this program. And we deal mainly with simple questions like, What do I do next? Where should I go next?

Once you experience domestic violence and know how hard it is to leave a situation, you understand how much pressure there is on a victim. On top of the violence, there are society's pressures and the family's pressures, not to mention the emotional trauma. I can never forget that. I can forgive, but I can't ever forget.

In *Fierce Attachments*, Vivian Gornick puts her tempestuous attempts at whole relations with men in a context startling for a woman of our generation: "I never doubted the desk — not the satisfactory resolution of love — was the potential lifesaver." For most of us, that faith was a heresy. We seemed born — and certainly we were bred — to believe that marriage was the core that gave our lives their meaning and resonance. But the women whose stories appear in this chapter ultimately *did* find work that gave them a new sense of who they are and should be.

Few things can poison the soul more entirely than being sexually available to an abusive man. And so, for abused wives, the initial challenge is to transform themselves from victims into survivors, which ordinarily means leaving the marriage. No doubt some men *do* change, but broken promises are far more common. This means finding a lawyer, a job to pay the bills, and for younger women, decent child-care arrangements. Statistics show that divorce is far more damaging, in a practical sense, to women than to men, and the process of shifting the blame from the victims to the perpetrators can be hard both on women in pain and on our friends.

Immediate practical necessities aside, a victim changes into a survivor by learning to see herself and her world differently, and for so basic an evolution, most of us need help. Friends, of course, are an invaluable part of the process — as Gina Pascale said, "I'm gonna keep talking until somebody listens to me!" — and at least as important is a good therapist, who can be a damaged woman's guide to a coherent, self-respecting life. (A revitalized women's movement should work to make psychotherapy more readily available.) Women who've been abused are commonly fragmented, demoralized, and frightened, and the process of change is so arduous that a therapist is more likely than a friend to help a woman see both how she bought into a relationship that may be destroying her and how she can summon the resources to buy out. A support group of women with similar experiences can be sustaining.

But a new era in the relations between women and men will begin only after the vast majority of decent people — male and female — stop condoning the abuse. For the most part, the hapless woman has been victimized — not because she is weak or bad and deserves it — but because men with too much power have abused it. The key questions, again, should no longer be, What did she do to deserve it? and, Why did she stay? but, Why did he do it? Why did those around him stand there and watch him do it — and in some instances help him do it? and, What can we do to change all that?

Changing "all that" involves coming to terms not only with the economics, but with the psychodynamics of a system that keeps women down. The concept of "forgiveness," for instance, has played a central role, along with cultural imperatives that mitigate male abuse by telling women that anger is ugly, silence is golden, and healthy people put it all behind them. *All this is dangerous nonsense.* Too often we are dealing, after all, with guys who'll cut off your arms and take credit when you've learned to type with your toes.

When "I am sorry" is a profound movement of the soul — when a man throws himself, figuratively speaking, at the foot of the cross — and when he then offers reparations in keeping with the injury, his remorse may well evoke an emotion we could fairly call forgiveness. But this is not what "I'm sorry" typically means.

More often, "I'm sorry" means "Get off my back!" — a dismissive gesture uncomplicated by remorse or amends. If the injured doesn't respond cheerfully, she is commonly labeled with a variety of terms that victimize her once again. "Bitter" is one and "whiny" is another. Each of us can rehearse the litany, and we need to expose those self-serving terms for what they are.

Quite naturally, a society designed by men muffles its blame of those who abuse women, and, as Dr. Judith Herman puts it, "The more powerful the perpetrator, the greater is his prerogative to name and define reality, and the more completely his arguments prevail." In a tight-lipped culture, for instance, that often dreads anger more than a social disease, well-meaning friends will beg a woman to put her anger and indignation behind her. But her challenge is to channel the anger — not to repress it. She needs to learn how to use her outrage to begin changing her world, and they need to learn how to help her do it.

11

UNDERSTANDING HOW WE GOT HERE

Who will believe thee, Isabel?
My unsoiled name, th' austereness of my life,
My vouch against you, and my place i' th' state,
Will so your accusation overweigh,
That you shall stifle in your own report,
And smell of calumny. . . .
Say what you can, my false o'erweighs your true.
　　　　　　　　—Angelo in *Measure for Measure*

This book began as a collection of women's stories and a call to action. Although the subject is sexual harassment and abuse, the women all across the country who confided in me over the course of a year, and who gave so abundantly of their time and experience, turned out to be remarkably resilient. Their stories, more often than not, are monuments to the human spirit.

At the same time, these are hard and troubling stories that have forced me to cast about for ways to understand them. And this quest for understanding has taken me on a great adventure — into the past, into poetry and song, into autobiography and novels — into likely places and unlikely ones as well. Mythical people stride brazenly across these pages, along with men and women from Hammond, Indiana, and Marfa, Texas. What started as a book about sexual harassment in the United States of America must end by taking on the Western tradition. For I have gone where the spirit beckons and have pursued its beguiling eccentricities until this book *of* stories has to become a book *about* stories and what they mean.

In the preceding pages, a wide spectrum of women have described their encounters with men who would maim, commandeer, and finally control their erotic power. A man does not bite a woman's ass if he wants her to live fully and control her own sexuality, much less enjoy it. Nor does he lick her ear or clap his hands with glee and say, "Oh good! We've got another member of the itty bitty titty club." And certainly he doesn't have sexual intercourse with his own daughter.

How, in the end, do we explain the fact that a Stanford University dean condoned a sustained and outrageous display of sexual harassment at the risk of losing the world's only tenured full professor of neurosurgery who was a woman? How can we account for the fact that the University of Iowa argued in court that a woman's repeated sexual humiliation by a handful of faculty members was "just the way it goes"? "Your Honor, this isn't sexual harassment," the university's lawyer insisted. "This is the way of the world." If our universities reason this way, what must we expect from people and institutions who don't claim clear thinking as their raison d'être?

In order to come to terms with stories like these, I've found that we need first to understand the role that women's sexuality has played in their lives, and then to think about these stories against the backdrop of familiar ones that have shaped us. Imagine, for instance, the influence of the tale of Peter Rabbit, who has a grand adventure in Farmer McGregor's garden while his sisters, Flopsy, Mopsy, and Cottontail, like good bunnies, cower at home. The author in this case, by the way, was a woman, Beatrix Potter, and stories like this one are embedded in our culture, implicitly teaching boys to live a certain way and girls to live another.

Even something as intimate and personal as sex is mediated by a cultural context. We grow up hearing stories — or more often silences — about what sex means for women, and these stories and silences descend from the experiences of women even before history began to be written. Ultimately, they derive from hard reality.

Until very recently, women's sexuality often worked against them, and even now, changes have come only in the most privileged parts of the world. Between the ages of fourteen and fifty, women perennially ran the risk of dying in childbirth, and those who survived it were as likely as not to have more children than the available resources could readily accommodate. For millennia, too, women have been taken as booty in wars and sexually violated as a matter of policy, and the end of this century promised no relief: from 1991 well into 1993, thousands of Yugoslavian women and girls in refugee camps were systematically raped and humiliated as a way of destroying hearths that belonged to an enemy.

The fruits of their wombs, in turn, have often been a source of agony for women. From the ramparts of a mythical Troy to the antebellum American South and the jungles of Vietnam, children have been snatched away and sold into slavery or murdered by the enemy. So if life for most people has been nasty, brutish, and short, for women down through the millennia, the agent of destruction has typically been male and survival has often been at odds with sexuality, so that ironically, the repression of eros has been a key to life itself.

Under sexual threat, then, for all but the last few moments, relatively speaking, of historical time, women for the most part could not allow either their erotic energy or their minds and spirits to play freely, much less with the urgency and singlemindedness it takes to create enduring works of art or lead nations. While men have seized the chance to quest and gambol and range freely — to sail the wine-dark seas to Troy and set out across the Atlantic Ocean in the Santa Maria — women have more often had to live bent over, closed off, and sealed away.

The male sex, furthermore, has arrogated to itself the power of definition, along with the authority to write the rules and the right to enforce them. For reasons about which historians and psychologists will always speculate, they have denied women virtually any control over their own lives or the lives of their children. Treating them as property, they've kept them poor and dependent, thereby ensuring their silence. And with incomparable chutzpah, they've expected women to like it. As Carolyn Heilbrun puts it in *Writing a Woman's Life,* "Above all other prohibitions, what has been forbidden to women is anger, together with the open admission of the desire for power and control over one's life."[1]

These rules that men have written for women have centered on their sexuality; chastity has been enjoined on them before marriage and fidelity to their husbands afterward on peril of disgrace and sometimes even death. In addition to the literal threats to which their sexuality opens them, then — on top of death in childbirth and exhaustion from too frequent childbearing and too many children; on top of rape, incest, and the many forms of sexual coercion — women have been stunted by a sexual morality that stuffed them into boxes far too small for their energies, talents, and imagination. A woman was either the white rose or the red, a virgin or a whore, a lady or a scarlet woman. Sexual harassment, in fact, is only the most recent of the stratagems that men have used to keep women "in their place." (Although I'm focusing here on Western culture, I should note that attitudes to women in Arab countries, or in India and Africa, for instance, are arguably even more destructive.)

In *A Room of One's Own,* Virginia Woolf imagined that Shakespeare had an equally talented sister, who gave in like him to her lust for adventure but soon, impregnated and abandoned, lay buried near the Elephant and Castle, dead by her own hand. The rules of the game were not designed with the world's Judith Shakespeares in mind. And with all the heavy artillery in the hands of the other sex, a woman unwilling to risk her fate bought into the systems that smothered her, and under the unrelenting pressure of hard realities, *propriety became a great crippler of women.*[2]

Men have therefore constituted the intimate, often beloved, but implacable enemy. This, of course, is not the way that men would have us understand it. They've persuaded women to see them as protectors, and in fact, women caught in their wars amongst and between each other have often had to choose sides. Finally, in order to survive and not go mad, women have had to make an uneasy truce with eros.

The subjugation of women was accomplished long before history came to be recorded — long before King Agamemnon sacrificed his daughter Iphigenia in return for favorable winds to Troy and, ten years later, raped the prophet Cassandra and carried her and many Trojan widows to Greece as spoils of war. Those of us living today are indisputably shaped by descent from violent societies in which women had virtually no authority and no say, and by processes whose antiquity has beguiled us into mistaking them for natural. Sorting out what is good, real, and necessary from what has merely seemed so to the men who've commanded the heights of political power and cultural authority is thus extremely difficult.

Definitions shaped entirely by men have left us with a skewed sense of reality and even of right and wrong. Power has so often been passed off as justice, foolishness (even rank stupidity) as tragedy, and arrogance as greatness, that the tangle can seem impenetrable and the strands that make it up impossible to separate. Women have lived for so long in societies that men have made that they must work very hard indeed to distinguish what is truly authentic to them from what they've been taught is authentic because it pleases men that they should imagine it so.

Some men, to be sure, have refused to take advantage of the power society has given them, and in 1869, one man — John Stuart Mill, widely revered as the patron saint of rationality — published as impassioned an argument for women's equality as any that women have written. Influenced from its inception by Harriet Taylor, who would become his wife, and called *The Subjection of Women,* it was cited triumphantly by British suffragettes in their protracted struggle for the vote. "The sufferings, immoralities, evils of all sorts, produced in innumerable cases by the subjection of individual women to individual men, are far too terrible to be overlooked," Mill wrote. "And it is perfectly obvious that the abuse of the power cannot be very much checked while the power remains."[3]

Mill's authority, however, has been undermined by men who think differently. Sigmund Freud, for instance, while translating *The Subjection of Women* into German, argued that "all reforming action in law and education would break down in front of the fact that, long before the age at which a man can earn a position in society, Nature has determined woman's destiny through beauty, charm, and sweetness." The position of women, Freud expected, would always be what it was at present: "in youth an adored darling and in mature years a loved wife." A man whose intellectual courage and insight transformed our understanding of human nature, Freud could sink into puerile sentimentality on the subject of women. And his influence — and the influence of those like him — has so far prevailed. As late as the 1950s, women were expected to like being put on pedestals, although there is nothing you can do on one and the only view of other people is down — an angle of vision that is disastrous, spiritually and ethically speaking.[4]

I do not believe that women are by nature the more virtuous sex, for everyone is heir to the wide range of human sins and foibles. In part to placate men and achieve some measure of control over their own lives, women have lied and cheated; they have prostituted themselves and even their daughters and undercut each other. Furthermore, men, too, are crippled by growing up in societies twisted by the exercise of undue male power. (The notion that they are crippled *equally* seems to me sentimental, although perhaps only God can be the judge of that.)

But, as John Stuart Mill knew, Lord Acton's celebrated maxim "Power tends to corrupt, and absolute power tends to corrupt absolutely" applies even more forcefully to the power of men over women than it does to the handful of men who hold power in the state. And if we think about it along with its corollary — powerlessness tends to corrupt, and absolute powerlessness tends to corrupt absolutely — we can better appreciate the depths of our dilemma.

Giving up on the idea that men are women's friendly, disinterested protectors and imagining them as potential antagonists instead is a hard and unpleasant task for a woman who likes men. (I have been publicly — and accurately — described as a flirt.) As Woolf put it in *A Room of One's Own,* "One has a profound, if irrational, instinct in favour of the theory that the union of man and woman makes for the greatest satisfaction, the most complete happiness." Since people who are cornered are likely to strike out, it may even be dangerous to speak of men as the enemy, and in the face of an impressive male arsenal of weapons, women do well to be wary. But accounting for the stories in this book requires seeing them in the context of our traditional stories — which, in turn means taking on the Fathers, whose point of view they commonly express.[5]

For it is through stories that we learn how to live. As Heilbrun says, "We can only retell and live by the stories we have read or heard. We live our lives through texts." Accordingly, we need to look at the stories we grew up with to see what ideas about women are encoded in them; to understand how they assumed a good woman would behave and what they taught us about truth and faithfulness; in short, to know the peaks and boundaries of the moral and emotional worlds we as women inherited as citizens of Western culture.[6]

Let us begin in the 1890s, when Elizabeth Cady Stanton, who was nearing the end of a long life dedicated to taking on the establishments of her time, testified to the importance of traditional stories by publishing *The Woman's Bible*. With about thirty colleagues, she had set out to rescue the eternal truths of scripture from the misogyny of Saint Paul and the morass of chauvinism into which centuries of male commentary had plunged it. For almost two thousand years the Bible had taught men and women how to live, and for Stanton, the message was dangerously wrongheaded.

In typically unsparing, if somewhat breathless prose, Stanton summarized the Biblical position on women: "The Bible teaches that woman brought sin and death into the world, that she precipitated the fall of the race, that she was arraigned before the judgment seat of Heaven, tried, condemned and sentenced. Marriage for her was to be a condition of bondage, maternity a period of suffering and anguish, and in silence and subjection, she was to play the role of a dependent on man's bounty for all her material wants, and for all the information she might desire on the vital questions of the hour, she was commanded to ask her husband at home."[7]

Stanton and her colleagues made it clear that the men who had written the Bible were by no means pristine vessels for divine inspiration; they were *men* and therefore decidedly self-interested. But while dedicating themselves to exposing the Bible's overall bias, Stanton and her coworkers strained to locate passages that might lend themselves to a more generous view of women. Among other things, for instance, they pointed out that there are *two* Biblical versions of creation, and according to the passage less frequently quoted, man and woman were created at the same moment in God's image. But she had once more proved to be a visionary and *way* ahead of her audience, politically speaking.

The Woman's Bible was a sensation, going through seven printings in six months. For her temerity in taking on the Fathers, Stanton was rebuffed by an organization she had founded, and *The Woman's Bible* was repudiated by a vote of 53 to 41 at the annual convention of the National American Woman Suffrage Association. (The controversy, they thought, would hurt their cause, though religious piety may have played some part in the vote.)

The problem *The Woman's Bible* was designed to address of course persisted, and in order to deal with their subordination more effectively, women needed to understand both how men had gotten permission to hold them in contempt and treat them unspeakably — and how women had gotten the idea that they had to accept these things. A century after Stanton scandalized her peers, the Hill/Thomas hearings and the stories I heard from women all over the country presented me with *exactly* her problem. And like Stanton, I looked to stories for answers. For her fundamental insight was correct: stories convey ideas that powerfully influence the way we behave, and many traditional ones insidiously diminish women.

To be sure, our stories come from a wide variety of sources. Some, for instance, are songs, and country music, the blues, gospel all have their own distinctive ways of seeing the world. Each of these, however, speaks to a special audience, when what we need in order to understand a major social phenomenon are stories more nearly at the intellectual and literary core of Western culture.

And so, leaving the Bible to Stanton, I turned to the greatest storyteller in English — to William Shakespeare, whose talent for capturing reality in words has made him, for almost four hundred years, our preeminent teacher. Virginia Woolf has called his mind androgynous, and of all the writers in the great Western tradition, he is among the least likely to strike us as harboring some personal, subconscious grievance against the opposite sex. His feisty, argumentative women — Rosalind and Portia spring to mind — are among the most appealing in literature; his victims — Juliet and Desdemona — the most affecting; and his temptresses — Cleopatra and Lady Macbeth — the most nearly irresistible.

Still, his plays are filled with women who are put in "their place," and as we begin to understand the male bias with which *even he* saw the world, and taught us to see it, we open everything in the Western tradition to question. By learning to take on Big Daddy, we free ourselves to write and live our own scripts.

In *The Taming of the Shrew,* for instance, we can see writ large the assumptions about woman's place that still have power in our world, just as they did in Shakespeare's. The action begins when Kate, the daughter of the wealthy Baptista Minola, meets Petruchio, an impoverished nobleman who decides to mend his fortunes by marrying her. A story that promises love, it will also be a tale of conquest, for Kate's keen wit and sharp temper have so terrorized the men of Padua that her sister's suitor says that only a devil would take her on.

Doomed by her independent spirit to solitude despite her prospects for a handsome dowry, the high-spirited Kate is stuck in her father's house until Petruchio comes from Verona and resolves to "board her though she chide as loud / As thunder when the clouds in autumn crack." He boards and she thunders through several scenes until Petruchio announces that her father has agreed on the dowry: "will you, nill you, I will marry you. /. . . For I am he am born to tame you, Kate." A horrified Kate appeals to her father to save her from "one half lunatic, / A madcap ruffian and a swearing Jack," but with Baptista declaring, "'Tis a match," she is sentenced to the altar.

So begins Petruchio's campaign to break Kate's spirit. Over the next few days he humiliates her by arriving hours late for their wedding and slugging the priest; wears her out by forcing her to wade through mud on their way to his homestead in Verona; terrifies her by throwing tantrums and beating up his household staff; weakens her by tossing out their food as ill-cooked; and exhausts her by keeping her from going to sleep. (In an aside, he explains that he has "politicly begun my reign" so she will "know her keeper's call.")

Even a tough woman like Kate at last grows desperate: "I am no child, no babe. / Your betters have endured me say my mind, / And if you cannot, best you stop your ears. / My tongue will tell the anger of my heart, / Or else my heart, concealing it, will break. . . ." But the claims of her self-respect don't faze him, and he goes on blithely forcing her to do as he says.

Then, on their way to her sister's wedding, Kate and Petruchio have a crucial exchange. When he calls the sun the moon, she corrects him, but he makes it clear: "It shall be moon or star or what I list, / Or ere I journey to your father's house." *Finally, she decides to play his game: "be it moon or sun or what you please. / And if you please to call it a rush-candle, / Henceforth I vow it shall be so for me."*

The test comes at the wedding feast, when Petruchio bets that his wife will prove more obedient than two other recent brides — and wins the bet! Stunned by this unwonted change in Kate, an onlooker marvels, "I wonder what it bodes," to which Petruchio answers, "Marry, peace it bodes, and love, and quiet life, / An awful rule and right supremacy." Kate then gives a long speech on the virtues of groveling to one's husband which ends as follows:

> I am ashamed that women are so simple
> To offer war where they should kneel for peace,

Or seek for rule, supremacy, and sway,
When they are bound to serve, love, and obey.

Finally, she underscores her capitulation by telling other wives to "place your hands below your husband's foot, / In token of which duty, if he please, / My hand is ready, may it do him ease." Petruchio's sally, "Why, there's a wench! Come on and kiss me, Kate," signifies that order is restored and happiness to come.

Our laughter depends, of course, upon our not taking Petruchio's boorishness seriously or his high-handed violence to heart. It depends as well on our refusing to take Kate's initial self-respect as seriously as she takes it, or as seriously as we'd be apt to take it were we in her place. It requires us *not* to hear her cries of pain and to ignore the suffocation of her will and good sense as matters of a moment that will pass. That is to say, he is being awful and she is being hurt for the sake of a larger goal that will benefit them equally.

Petruchio's rationale might be offered by *any* man who harassed *any* woman whose story is included in this book. And that is *not* the way these women see it.

Women ready to take on the Fathers are not likely to laugh at the sight of a woman abandoned, as Kate is, to the whims of a violent, self-satisfied boor. (The old rationale, "I'm doing this for your own good," no longer has compelling power.) Nor are they likely to find it funny when nobody comes to Kate's defense or when it dawns on her that she can count on nothing to protect her but her flair for lying. (In *Othello,* Shakespeare takes the same dynamic between a man and woman and plays it in the tragic mode, and if you look at the events of *Othello* through the eyes of Desdemona — if you reject the governing male point of view — the sense of tragedy is likely to metamorphose into horror. *Even lying doesn't help her, and she meets death at her husband's hands.*)

The story of *The Taming of the Shrew,* then, shows how the technique of manipulating, or lying for the sake of self-interest, has been *prescribed* for women, albeit at the price of allowing men to live in a world of make-believe. Kate ultimately embraces the strategy enjoined on her sex for most of recorded history, and the play invites us to believe that domestic happiness is impossible unless a wife lies to her husband and flatters him shamelessly.

In this way, women have been taught to suspend or obscure their own moral judgment whenever it is at odds with the men's who matter in their lives. In Henrik Ibsen's *A Doll's House,* when Torvald Helmer says to his wife, "No man would sacrifice his honour for the one he loves," Nora replies, "It is a thing hundreds of thousands of women have done." What is true of wives is even truer of daughters, and ironically, after laying their good sense on the altar of getting-along, they remain at the mercy of men whose fatuousness they've encouraged.

In short, the rules men have written to govern the relations between the sexes have given them permission to have their way, no matter what the cost to the women around them. In a culture, then, where lying is considered a sin or at best dishonorable, a contrary ethic has been mandated for women: they've been *expected* to lie to or on behalf of the men on whom they depend — to call the sun the moon if they say it is the moon. And the penalties for refusing have ranged from loss of sustenance to disgrace, dishonor, and death.

All this silence and duplicity, however, gets men and women both in trouble. Most people prefer not to think of themselves as liars, any more than they like knowing that flattery is mere tomfoolery, and so they tend to fall for the deception and lose touch with reality. Partly for this reason, Republican members of the Senate Judiciary Committee could speak as though innocent of facts that women in their twenties take for granted: as President Shirley Kenny of Queens College puts it, that women "struggle to acquire survival techniques for the jungles of male professional culture."

A great deal is at stake here. Men who are prepared to hear only what they want to hear are not very reliable guides, protectors, or even companions, and the women who lie to them to secure their love and/or their patronage end up being at best confused. Observing that "the personal profit of women bears but too close a relation to their power to win and hold the other sex," Charlotte Perkins Gilman worried about the fact that "woman's economic profit comes through the power of sex attraction." At bottom, she realized, there was no organic difference between wives and prostitutes. "When we see the same economic relation made permanent, established by law, sanctioned and sanctified by religion, covered with flowers and incense and all accumulated sentiment, we think it innocent, lovely, and right. The transient trade we think evil. The bargain for life we think good. But the biological effect remains the same." That is to say, if the "good" woman is to be defined by her skill at pleasing a man, she is virtually indistinguishable from the whore, who at least doesn't put on moral airs.[8]

Almost ten years after *The Taming of the Shrew,* Shakespeare wrote *Measure for Measure,* the classic story about sexual harassment, which anticipates Hill/Thomas by almost four centuries. It begins in Vienna, where the Duke turns over the reins of state to Angelo, a high-minded deputy, and vanishes. Unbeknownst to anyone, however, the Duke disguises himself as a friar and stays to spy.

Angelo turns out to be not only strict, but rigid — one Lucio complains that his "blood / Is very snow-broth" and he pees icicles — and he condemns Claudio to death for getting his fiancée, Juliet, with child. Claudio's sister, Isabella, however, who has entered a convent as a novice, agrees to sue for her brother's life. Angelo is smitten with Isabella, and as so often happens when natural instincts have been repressed, he turns into his antithesis. He tells her Claudio may live if she, "to redeem him, / Give up your body to such sweet uncleanness / As she that he hath stained."

Isabella retorts, "I had rather give my body than my soul," although in the eyes of her Church, the two are inextricable. "Better it were a brother died at once," she says accordingly, "Than that a sister, by redeeming him / Should die forever."

When Angelo makes it clear that he means what he says, Isabella cries out as many women have done, before and after her:

> I will proclaim thee, Angelo; look for 't;
> Sign me a present pardon for my brother,
> Or with an outstretched throat I'll tell the world aloud
> What man thou art.

And Angelo answers as many men have done, before and after him: "Who will believe thee, Isabel? . . . Say what you can, my false o'erweighs your true."

Isabella assumes that Claudio has "such a mind of honor" that he'd give up his life twenty times over "Before his sister should her body stoop / To such abhorred pollution." But Claudio finds her priorities less than compelling. After an initial burst of outrage and show of bravado, he begins to waver: "Death," he wails, "is a fearful thing," and he begs his sister to save his life. Isabella slices to the point:

> Wilt thou be made a man out of my vice?
> Is't not a kind of incest, to take life
> From thine own sister's shame?

At this moment of irreconcilable conflict, the Duke steps forward in the guise of the friar and tells Isabella he has a scheme to rescue everyone, virtue and life withal intact.

He persuades one Mariana, who'd been engaged to Angelo some five years earlier, to take Isabella's place in the tryst. Many twists and turns later, when Isabella confronts Angelo with his shameful coercion, Mariana confirms her story:

> This is the hand which, with a vowed contract,
> Was fast belocked in thine; this is the body
> That took away the match from Isabel.

Angelo tries to weasel out, but when the Duke reveals himself to have been the friar, he admits defeat and, upon the Duke's decree that he must marry Mariana, begs for death. Condemning him instead to love his wife, the Duke ends the play by asking for Isabella's hand:

> I have a motion much imports your good,
> Whereto if you'll a willing ear incline,
> What's mine is yours, and what is yours is mine.

As to whether Isabella would like to marry the Duke, Shakespeare falls silent.

By raising major questions about a woman's sexuality and its connection to her power in the world — and then by evading them — *Measure for Measure* tells, for my purposes, a peculiarly important story. In the first place, chastity either equals virtue, or it doesn't. The Church and patriarchal society say one thing, and common sense says another. Isabella speaks for the former, while Claudio speaks for the latter, and it seems hard that Isabella should come off like a prig when she takes the stand her culture and her Church insist that she take. Claudio is right, surely, in believing that a loved one's death weighs heavier in the scale than what a later age would call a roll in the hay, but Isabella is also right in feeling that rape, which Angelo proposes, is very terrible.

Since *Measure for Measure* is a comedy, Shakespeare can't have Isabella raped, but unlike the senators who presided over the Hill/Thomas hearings, he assumes that people with power abuse it, and he knows that the ruler of Vienna is likely to get what he wants. So a series of flukes takes the place of answers. A man with greater power becomes the unseen witness to another man's abuse so that he can stop it. A willing woman is substituted for one who is unwilling. Claudio's life and Isabella's dignity are both preserved, and so we don't have to decide, finally, how important a woman's rights are, or what chastity is worth, much less weigh the claims of earth against those of heaven.

But the inherent absurdity of the rules that men have written for women — among other things, the idea that chastity and virtue are synonymous — leaves us with a set of problems so troubling that even Shakespeare can't resolve them happily. Left to her own devices, Isabella was poised to deny her sexuality for the sake of God — a sacrifice that a man with Shakespeare's appetite for life was bound to think a waste. So three men, one after the other, put in their claims to Isabella's sexuality: first Angelo, then Claudio, and finally the Duke.

None of Isabella's options is particularly appealing. At least to the modern sensibility, chastity is nay-saying; rape, an outrage; being forced to sacrifice her integrity for Claudio, unfair; and giving herself to the Duke — well, we reconcile ourselves to that option as the best of the alternatives because we know that's the way life worked. Although Shakespeare has portrayed the Duke as an ineffective ruler, a voyeur, and a spy (although a sweet enough guy in his way), he will get Isabella because dukes *do* get their way. Power wins in the end — perhaps that was Shakespeare's point — but we don't feel right about it.

In *Measure for Measure,* then, as so often in life, even the best men silence and trivialize women. Even the most strong-minded, articulate women learn that to survive they have to shut up and play a man's game. A woman who has taken her sexuality seriously finds out that it goes to the highest bidder.

But understanding the way the rules have been written can be the first step in changing them. For in the end, it turns out that not even Shakespeare's genius was universal, as we were brought up believing. Like most people in his time — and well into ours — who wrote the poems and plays that have given us such a skewed notion of what it means to be human, he was a *man*. When we see how the assumptions that undergird these plays, along with the entire Western tradition, serve the putative interests of men at the expense of women, we can declare our independence.

Once we've done that, we can see that the labels we've been given don't always fit the people or situations for which they were designed. Female critics who now read Shakespeare's plays irreverently, for instance, find all manner of disturbing things there — among them the fact that in the name of defending virtue, his male characters are prone to irrational fits of anxiety in relation to women. Shirley Nelson Garner, for one, has found a pattern in four key plays in which men grow insanely jealous of their "appallingly" virtuous mates, conspire against them, destroy or think they've destroyed them — after which they repent. The hero "kills her, then loves her afterward," Garner writes, and sure enough, "the woman forgives him."[9]

Othello is the most famous of these plays, and there, as in the others, the hero finds another man with whom he plots a woman's destruction. The ultimate in male bonding, the men indulge in "voyeuristic and degraded fantasies in which they imagine [women] in bestial sexual acts." If that doesn't describe the Hill/Thomas hearings, you have to allow for the fact that by the fall of 1991, Shakespeare had been dead for almost four hundred years.[10]

Much the same thing happens in *Much Ado About Nothing,* and in Kenneth Branagh's sumptuous film, audiences gasp when Claudio slaps Hero at the altar, denounces her for infidelity, and cancels their wedding. After this shock, which is presented so realistically, neither Branagh's engaging Benedick, Emma Thompson's sprightly Beatrice, nor a dazzling cast of supporting actors can blind us to the play's preposterous denouement: Hero forgives Claudio and marries him anyway. But a Hero who blinks at such cruelty and gives herself to a headstrong fool, albeit a charming one in other respects, is not the woman to win modern hearts.

Sometimes Shakespeare's male characters learn from their mistakes, but invariably the women forgive them. This pattern would seem to Shirley Garner a product of male fantasy, since such forgiveness, as she puts it, is "possible only for a woman who is a saint or martyr or who has a perilously divided self." With its heavy prohibitions against female anger, however, Western culture has forced "good" women to become either saints or martyrs — or to cultivate a "perilously divided self."[11]

The problem of the "good" woman as she's been traditionally described is glaringly obvious in these plays. Critics have indulged in a great deal of handwringing over the difficulty of portraying goodness in fiction, but the problem lies mainly in the definition. When "good" denotes a woman whose primary virtues are that she does *not* indulge in sex, or at least sex with anyone other than her husband, and does *not* get angry when she's treated shabbily, we're likely to end up with a ninny. This is precisely what happens in the case of Hero, as it does with Mariana in *Measure for Measure.*

Offered as a model of female constancy, Mariana not only tricks a man into sleeping with her, but her faithfulness to a cad, a liar, and a potential rapist is revolting — not to mention her eagerness to marry a man who prefers to die rather than to be her husband. Though Mariana is plainly besotted, not even a sap deserves a fate so grim as to be yoked for life to a man like Angelo. If this is what it means to be good, it is no wonder that so few women try for it. Unwavering loyalty to a man, however, no matter how offensive or deluded he may be, is blessedly no longer the last word in female virtue.

To be sure, we can still find many of our own truths in Shakespeare's world, where heterosexual love is extremely precarious, which sounds right to me. As an editor of a collection of feminist essays on Shakespeare points out, for instance, in the tragedies "Good women are often powerless, and powerful women are always threatening and often, in fact, destructive." It is certainly true that good women are often powerless, but the vision of the Medusa that turns men to stone bears the sexual warp of its maker.[12]

Women, then, have now grown bold enough to look at Shakespeare's stories from a distinct set of experiences, informed by their gender. And perhaps the most intriguing and accessible instance of this new way of seeing is Jane Smiley's novel *A Thousand Acres,* a modern retelling of the King Lear story that won the Pulitzer Prize in 1991. Set on a flourishing Iowa farm in 1979, it tells of Larry Cook and his family, who've lived on the land for four generations, and the narrator is Larry's second daughter, Ginny. Her older sister, Rose, lives with her husband across the road, and on the way to the town of Cabot, barely in sight, live Harold Clark and his two sons. Ginny's youngest sister, Caroline, a lawyer in Des Moines, comes home now and again.

In the sixth chapter, the clues become unmistakable:

My father was easily offended, but normally he was easily mollified, too, if you spoke your prescribed part with a proper appearance of remorse. This was a ritual that hardly bothered me, I was so used to it. For all her remarks and eye rolling, Rose could perform her part, and after the fact, could even get our father to laugh about some things. Caroline, though, was . . . always looking for the rights and wrongs of every argument, trying to figure out who should apologize for what, who should go first, what the exact wording of an apology should be. . . .[13]

By now we understand that Smiley is *not* male, decidedly *not* intimidated by Shakespeare, and skeptical of traditional definitions of the good woman. Very soon we realize that when a strong-minded, modern woman does *Lear,* she is likely to end up with two very terrible old men. A woman who has been at the mercy of a narcissistic old man, or observed one at close quarters, is not likely to see Lear primarily as a grand figure towering above the heath or Gloucester as a faithful baron beset by unwonted cruelty.

In *A Thousand Acres,* women are no longer mere notations in the drama of a man's life, but complex moral agents in their own right. To the women in *King Lear,* Shakespeare allows no moral struggle or moments of spiritual discovery. For the women in Smiley's novel, life is precisely that: it is about coming to terms. "The focus of Smiley's narration," as the critic Madelon Sprengnether sees, "is not on errors committed (or repented) in the present, but on the gradual revelation of a corrupted past, including the fateful role of father-daughter incest in the evolution of family dynamics." Ginny has repressed the memory of her father's abuse, but Rose remembers and forces Ginny slowly to remember as well. And all along, they wrestle with the question of why it matters and what justice means.[14]

No timorous soul eager to put it all behind her and forget, Rose insists on remembering. "But he did fuck us and he did beat us," she howls at the recalcitrant Ginny:

And the thing is, he's respected. Others of them like him and look up to him. . . . However many of them have fucked their daughters or their stepdaughters or their nieces or not, the fact is that they all accept beating as a way of life. We have two choices when we think about that. Either they don't know the real him and we do, or else they do know the real him and the fact that he beat us and fucked us doesn't matter. Either they themselves are evil, or they're stupid. That's the thing that kills me. This person who beats and fucks his own daughters can go out into the community and get respect and power, and take it for granted that he deserves it.[15]

For millennia male sexual violence against women has been little more than a footnote to history, but at last these bills are falling due. Women are no longer content to accept the world that men have made for them or willing to assume automatically that men are friendly protectors. They are ready to rage against injustice: "We're going to be angry until we die," Rose declares. "It's the only hope." And after cataloguing the failures of her life, she insists:

So all I have is the knowledge that I saw! That I saw without being afraid and without turning away, and that I didn't forgive the unforgivable. Forgiveness is a reflex for when you can't stand what you know. I resisted that reflex. That's my sole, solitary, lonely accomplishment.[16]

Forgiveness as "a reflex for when you can't stand what you know" — *there is the sign of a woman who has freed herself from the ethical and psychological tyranny of patriarchal culture.* Poet Janice Mirikitani, president of the Glide Memorial Church Foundation in San Francisco, puts it even more succinctly: "Forgiveness is denial!" These women have refused to call the sun the moon and are prepared to take the consequences. Whether or not we like Rose, we recognize that she *is* authentic. And with authenticity, we can begin to construct a durable self.

12

THE HAZARDS OF COUNTING ON OTHER WOMEN

Silly women think that by turning against other women, they're going to be rewarded. They may be, and they may not be.
— Pauline Bart

The key to a healthier future lies with women who have learned to use the collective "we." The Zimbabwean women at the 1993 United Nations Conference on Human Rights in Vienna, Austria, made up a T-shirt with the logo "United we bargain. Divided we beg." They knew that if we allow men to splinter our focus and control our loyalty, we'll manage at best a holding action, and it really is that simple.

This is not to say that it will be easy. By all objective measures — money, rank, numbers in office, prestige — women are by far the weaker sex, and with the best will in the world, the accumulated power we can bring to bear at any one time is less than stunning. This means we have to work incessantly and choose our battles carefully. Most of all, we have to work *together,* and that's the crux of the problem, for women have traditionally imagined their well-being differently; until recently, for instance, women's stories were primarily about getting and keeping men. As the famous first line of Jane Austen's *Pride and Prejudice* would have it: "It is a truth universally acknowledged, that a single man in possession of a good fortune, must be in want of a wife."

It should come as no surprise, then, that women have looked on other women as rivals in the competition for scarce resources — whether for men, positions, or esteem — or that they've scapegoated those who try to do things differently. At a women's rights convention in the 1870s, for instance, Paulina Wright Davis used the sensational controversies that dogged reformer Fanny Wright to show how hard America could make it for women who fight for women's rights and justice for all, and she warned: "Women joined in the hue and cry against her, little thinking that men were building the gallows and making them the executioners. Women have crucified in all ages the redeemers of their own sex, and men mock them with the fact. It is time now that we trample beneath our feet this ignoble public sentiment which men have made for us; and if others are to be crucified before we can be redeemed, let men do the cruel, cowardly act; but let us learn to hedge womanhood round with generous, protecting care and love."[1]

Women have always counted on other women in birthing babies and raising them; they've taught children, built libraries, nursed the ill, and cradled the dying. Together, in short, they've nurtured families and created communities. But since women have lived in a society whose fundamental social unit is the family, where men held all the tangible power, most have naturally attached themselves to men. Not only have they fought other women for favor in the eyes of individual men — whether they be lover, husband, father, boss, or simply top rooster in the yard — but those who crave distinction and independence have commonly distanced themselves from other women. (Israeli Prime Minister David Ben-Gurion, for example, called Golda Meir, a good Milwaukee girl, the best man in his cabinet.)[2]

Hence the term "queen bee" or "female barracuda" for the special (or token) woman who makes it in a man's world — often by snickering at women who live by other values or think the rules in general should be different. Hence the women who learn to manipulate men to secure their own well-being. Hence the women who call the sun the moon to keep peace in the family.

The woman whose spirit curdles at the specter of playing to a man's weakness therefore lives at a disadvantage. Invariably, other women come onto the scene who have scruples that are less disabling, and rare is the man who welcomes the plain truth rather than the easier, more comforting account. He who prefers a woman who'll tell him what he wants to hear is likely to get what he asks for — especially if he is appealing, sexy, and powerful — so the manipulating woman is likely to win in the short term. By the time the consequences of acting on bad advice are clear, disaster has usually struck and it is too late.

To change this dynamic, women will have to learn *not* to undermine other women, but instead to "hedge womanhood round with generous, protecting care and love." Men have made that phenomenally difficult — especially when male sexual privilege is at stake.

In coming to terms with what happened to Anita Hill and grappling with sexual harassment, then, we need to look back at the long history of women in America who were ostracized when they tried to talk openly about sexual abuse and to stand up for women who were being victimized. From those who came before us, we can learn to recognize how women have colluded in a process that has short-circuited decency and progress so that we don't fall into the same trap again.

Truth-telling and compassion for slave women, for instance, was a dangerous business in nineteenth-century America, especially for white women, and even in the North. Men did *not* want to be held to account, and the imperatives to silence were enforced by every shred of power and authority at the disposal of patriarchal society: financial, social, psychological, and legal. Those who broke silence were the targets of ridicule and defamation seldom surpassed in the annals of American political vitriol, and women who spoke openly were often threatened with death.

The attacks, furthermore, were led by "gentlemen of property and standing" — preachers, editors, and even reformers — as well as by women like Catharine Beecher, Harriet Beecher Stowe's oldest sister, who played the role in the 1830s that women like Phyllis Schlafley have played in ours: to keep firm hold on their piece of the action, they took the position that the way men ran the world was just dandy.

So hard, in fact, was the subject of the sexual abuse of slave women to tackle, and so heavy were the cultural prohibitions against speaking out, that the two most famous descriptions of slavery by white women, *Uncle Tom's Cabin* and *Gone With the Wind,* do not mention it. (Of the former, the South Carolinian Mary Chesnut wrote, "Mrs. Stowe did not hit the sorest spot. She makes Legree a bachelor.")

Native-born white women, for the most part, were silenced, and it is not by accident that three of the most outspoken women were British, and so had not grown up in a society that took slavery for granted.[3]

In 1827, for instance, Fanny Wright, a Scotswoman turned American citizen, wrote that the races were mixing in the South — "viciously and degradingly, mingling hatred and fear with the ties of blood" — and the key question was "whether it shall take place in good taste and good feeling." Calling sexual passion "the strongest and noblest of the human passions," she attacked "ignorant laws, ignorant prejudices, ignorant codes of morals [that] condemn one portion of the female sex to vicious excess, another to as vicious restraint, and all to defenceless helplessness and slavery."

To talk openly about sexuality, however; to recognize the interconnections between slave women and free; and to acknowledge miscegenation was to scandalize a country where it was considered indecent even to use the word "corset" in public. Consequently, a Cincinnati newspaper referred to Fanny Wright's "treatise on the blending of the straight and the curly-haired races"; the editor of a New York newspaper ridiculed her as "a bold blasphemer and a voluptuous preacher of licentiousness"; and by the 1830s, when her meetings were stoned and the entire New York City police force had to be called out to protect her and her followers, she'd arguably become the most notorious woman in America. To be called a "Fanny Wrightist" was roughly equivalent to being called a communist in the 1950s, and a whole string of abolitionist women like Abby Kelley assured their audiences that they were *not* Fanny Wrightists. When truth-telling is so ill-rewarded, it is scarcely surprising that most people choose to know nothing whatever.[4]

The uproar that confronted the Englishwoman Harriet Martineau as she traveled around the United States in the mid-1830s might also have frightened anyone, which was no doubt the point. After lambasting southern morals that blinked at the sexual exploitation of slave women, she was threatened with lynching and, twenty years later, wrote of her last three months here, "I believe there was scarcely a morning . . . when it was not my first thought on waking whether I should be alive at night."[5]

About the same time, actress Fanny Kemble's ineradicable sympathy with slave women forced her to suffer excruciating personal loss. Married to the wealthy Pierce Butler before she saw the Georgia plantation on which his fortune depended, she quickly zeroed in on southern hypocrisy as regards sex between the races: it was "marriage (and not

concubinage) [that] was the horrible enormity which cannot be tolerated." The experience of actually living in Georgia — learning about
white women who flogged their husbands' black mistresses for spite,
and seeing the unspeakable conditions under which slave women were
forced to live — all this moved her to such despair that within a decade
she divorced her husband.

Compelled by law to give up custody of their two daughters,
Kemble kept silent publicly for many years on the subject of slavery so
as to avoid alienating them further. But in 1863, to discourage British
sympathy for the Confederacy, she published her *Journal of a Residence
on a Georgian Plantation,* which caused a sensation on both sides of
the Atlantic. In it, she eloquently described the disarray in which slavery
left the black family and excoriated southern planters whose "profligacy
and cruelty [are] the immediate result of their irresponsible power over
their dependents." At least one of her daughters never forgave her.[6]

But perhaps the most damaging testimony white women ever gave
against slavery came from two daughters of high privilege who grew
up in the city where the Civil War would begin. Sarah and Angelina
Grimke, who were born into a wealthy and distinguished slave-owning
family in Charleston, South Carolina, emigrated to the north out of
revulsion against slavery and became leading abolitionists. Angelina
insisted on facing reality: the "best blood" in Virginia — "even the
blood of a Jefferson" — ran in the veins of people held in bondage, and
the "posterity of our fathers are advertised in American papers as
runaway slaves." Sarah argued that "the moral purity of the white
woman is deeply contaminated" by standing by while "the virtue of her
enslaved sister [is] sacrificed without hesitancy or remorse."[7]

The Grimkes' clarity and outspokenness prompted Catharine
Beecher to write that they were an embarrassment to their sex. The
bishops of the Congregational Churches of Massachusetts, in turn,
issued a pastoral letter in which they worried about "the danger which
at present seems to threaten the female character with widespread and
permanent injury" because women "so far forget themselves as to itin-
erate in the character of public lecturers." The bishops were merely the
most prominent among those who believed the Grimkes dangerous to
society and isolated them from it.[8]

The sisters not only spoke up for black women and, like Fanny
Wright, made close friendships among them, but after the Civil War
they went so far as to violate a primary taboo: they made what amends
they could for their brother's abuse of a slave woman. In 1868, Angelina

found a reference in the *Anti-Slavery Standard* to a young black man named Grimke who was enrolled at Lincoln University in Oxford, Pennsylvania. She wrote asking about his family and was by no means surprised to discover that he was her brother Henry's son. "I will not dwell on the past," she replied to her nephew Archibald; "let that all go — it cannot be altered — our work is in the present. I am glad you have taken the name of Grimke — it was once, one of the noblest names of Carolina." She and Sarah subsequently invited Archibald and his brother, Francis, to stay in their home, gave money they could ill afford for yet another brother's education, and took pride in their very considerable accomplishments.[9]*

The price the Grimkes paid was as high as it gets: they gave up their home, their friends, and their family to speak the truth as they saw it. In return, they gained an authenticity that converted many people to their cause, especially when they pointed out the sexual humiliations of both black and white women under the slave system. Their welcome of men who were illegitimate and black condemned them to social ostracism, although they became heroines to later generations of feminists.

The sexual abuse of slave women was loathsome to many men, as well as to many women, but those who wrote the laws and controlled the press and pulpit dictated that considerations of property should be paramount. And power had its way. Those who objected became targets of ridicule; white women were driven to spiritual impotence and despair; and a deadly silence covered the most vicious crimes against women. Those whom the dictates of propriety persuaded to condemn their outspoken sisters were compelled to live secondary, derivative lives, and we are paying still.

More than a century and a half after her female ancestors had been left to the mercies of white men, Anita Hill broke through the silence that shrouded sexual harassment, and women rose up all over the country to support her. But long after the excitement of the hearings had died away, Hill remained the subject of sustained attack, and to carry on the

---

*For fifty years, Francis was pastor of the Fifteenth Street Presbyterian Church in Washington, D.C., and a trustee of Howard University. In 1919, Archibald, who was Henry Cabot Lodge's alternate to the 1884 Republican national convention, was given the NAACP's Spingarn medal for highest achievement by an African-American. Sarah, in fact, confessed that they were far more distinguished than their white cousins, including Angelina and Theodore Weld's children.

fight that she began, women clearly had a tough piece of work ahead. In the interests of the collective "we," they would have to stop making excuses for men and looking the other way when they behaved badly. In the jargon of the moment, they'd have to give up being male-identified.

Luckily, this shift in loyalties wouldn't require leaving men sexually, since few women will opt for so dire a solution. But since it would mean repudiating old notions of "woman's place," it will be easier for younger women to make the transition gracefully. For we mustn't underestimate the fact that we're talking about a potentially frightening shift, or fail to acknowledge how hard women can be, accordingly, on other women. It was from our own mothers that many of us first learned to distrust other women — those who agreed to call the sun the moon at their husbands' whim having made a devil's pact as far as their children were concerned — and so the anxieties at work here are quite fundamental.

Then, on top of our ancient and well-documented distrust of the mother, the terror of an unpredictable world in which women are so vulnerable may well promote fantasy. Women want to believe they can handle anything, and so they deny the immense practical disadvantage from which they operate and heap contempt on those whose coping mechanisms prove inadequate to the task of overcoming them. I'll call this phenomenon the Wonder Woman syndrome.

Wonder Woman is heavily represented in the audiences of television talk shows like Jenny Jones's and Oprah Winfrey's out of Chicago, and in their responses we can gauge how readily women find fault with other women — how profoundly they resist using the collective "we" and throwing their support to other women. After the Hill/Thomas hearings, one commentator after another worried that the balance of sexual power had shifted, leaving men at the mercy of malicious women who might toss sexual harassment charges about irresponsibly. For the most part, their anxiety has turned out to be premature, however, and women as well as men go on trivializing other women's claims.

Within a year of the hearings, for instance, when Jones and Winfrey each devoted an hour to sexual harassment stories, the audience was decidedly hostile to the women telling them. They would jump for the microphones to attack a woman who had just described her struggle to keep her job or home and maintain her self-respect. They needed to believe they'd have handled the scumbags better and won, and they could be merciless.[10]

Ironically, Jenny Jones began her show by saying that the worst thing about sexual harassment was that most women were afraid to report it. "These women aren't [afraid]," Jones said, pointing proudly to her three guests: "They'll tell the kinds of horror stories that are going to turn your stomach and, more important, to motivate other victims to take a stand." She invited a love-in, and the attacks obviously took her by surprise.

First came Bernadette Smith, who claimed that she'd been forced to sleep with her boss over a period of seven years. Perhaps the audience was put off when Smith admitted that for the first month she'd consented to sex; perhaps they turned against her because she looked like a bush-league Mae West, with delicate, china-doll features, big eyes lined with kohl, and masses of blonde, wavy hair. Whatever the reason, they reacted as though to a tart.

From the floor called a woman who strutted like a stevedore: "Honey, if you're a good secretary, you're in demand! They'll take you any place. Good secretaries run corporations!" Another stood up for Smith: "Why should *she* have to quit her job? Why should *she* be the one who has to leave?" But the audience was with the woman who screeched: "*Just get out of the situation!*"

"I put off going to a supervisor for seven years," Smith said in self-defense, "because there were no policies in place to protect me." Catcalls answered her. One woman yelled, "Don't you have *any* self-respect?" Another shouted, "You shouldn't be having sex with your boss in the first place!" A handful actually hissed, and then came the heavy artillery: "She compromised herself! She didn't leave because the money was good and she liked the corporation. *Isn't that prostitution — working for money?* You can get a job anywhere! But you chose not to because the money was good, and this was part of the job." The logic and economics may have been confused, but the contempt was clear.

Startled by the vitriol, Jones came not only to Smith's defense, but to her own: "This is not supposed to be a trial. I didn't bring you on here just to be attacked." After Christine Stapp, her second guest, gave a tearful account of being sexually hounded at a factory and was received almost as skeptically, Jones made her own confession: "I used to work as a stand-up comic with this headliner. I'd like very much to use his name, but I was told there'd probably be a lawsuit if I did. But he's well known; he's done movies; he's headlined everywhere. I was his opening act, and he told me to come get him in the room and then we'd go to the show. I knocked on the door, and [when he opened it,] he had a towel wrapped around him. He said, 'Come in, I'll get dressed,' and so I went in. He closed the door and threw me on the bed!"

At this point, Jones began to cry, and then she struggled for a few seconds before she could continue. "He sat on my chest and took off his towel. And I stayed in the room. I waited for him to get dressed, and finally I made a joke about it. I kept working with him because it was hard to get work as a comic and I was just starting out. So I worked with him again."

This story from so impeccable a source, along with Jones's gesture of solidarity with her guests, sobered the audience for a while, but then the boasting and denial started again. "When I take a tour through the plant and somebody smacks me on the rear, I'm gonna stop it *right there* so that the next ten guys don't do it!" After a woman suggested that Stapp's husband should have worked over the guys who were tormenting her, he stood up to say that "beating the crap out of anybody is not my idea of how you deal with it."

Stapp insisted that she'd tried everything. "I got in their faces and said, 'Cut it out!' and *they loved it*. They got off on it!" On top of that, she cried indignantly, the women on her jury had said, "We don't believe you!" and so she'd lost her sexual harassment suit. By now, Stapp was somewhat hysterical, as well she might be, and both she and her husband, who admitted suddenly that they were getting a divorce, ended up in tears. She cried pitifully, "He was just like all of you!" and he admitted: "I listened to her but I didn't hear. I didn't understand." It was gruesome.

The emotional rollercoaster ran its course until, near the end of the show, a woman summed it up: "Americans are raised thinking money is everything, but money is not worth risking your self-esteem over. *Get out of the situation!*" They *had* to believe there was somewhere else to go, so that like Huck Finn, you could always light out for the territories.

Stapp fought back. "So we leave, and they get somebody else to pick on!" Finally she hit on an analogy that worked: "Why didn't the black people quit when somebody called them a name? Because you *have* to stand up for the people to come behind you!" This struck a chord, especially with the African-Americans in the audience, and Jones closed the show by warning, "There's a heavy, heavy price to pay if we don't all support each other."

*   *   *

Oprah Winfrey's show on sexual harassment featured eight women from the Fairfield North Apartments in northern California — a Housing and Urban Development complex for low-income women raising children alone. The superintendent had terrorized his tenants for years until twenty-two women filed suit against the landlord and won a judgment of $1.6 million. (Molly McElrath tells their story in chapter 14.)

After each woman took her turn at telling a piece of the narrative, Oprah's audience pounced. With feigned sympathy, the first to take the microphone began by saying that she, too, lived alone with her son. But when a maintenance man who'd come to fix the electrical jack by her bed said, "I sure would like to wire your jack, and we've got the bed right here to do it!" she got rid of him on the spot. "I just politely told him, 'You know, you better be careful! Do you have any idea how easy it is to die accidentally while working with electricity?'" At this, the audience burst into manic laughter. Goaded by their applause, she pointed her finger at a hapless woman onstage and shrilled: "What was it that stopped you from taking matters into your own hands? If somebody had put his hand on my chest, he wouldn't have had a hand! The man's gotta sleep. He's gotta eat. He's gotta turn his back. And if I'm backed into a corner, I'm gonna fight. And I'm coming out hard!"

When the eight women collectively insisted, "We went through what we did for our children," very few people were buying. Though all eight had at one time or other been homeless, the women in the audience kept calling, "Why didn't you leave?" or "Why'd you wait so long?" When one woman onstage said plaintively, "I'd just come from a battered women's shelter; I didn't want any more confrontations," the audience's eyes seemed to glaze over.

One after another stood up to grandstand: "I sympathize with each of you all's situations. But there is no way in hell that I'd have let that man touch me or get my mail. They make Louisville bats. They got knives and box-cutters they sell at the hardware stores. You let him manipulate you! He wouldn't have come into my apartment. If he'd come in when I was in my nightie, he wouldn't have left with what he thought he was coming for!" (She probably meant "what he came with," but nobody noticed.) Amidst riotous cheers, the speaker plopped down and then jumped back up to add: "I love the legal system and all that, but *sometimes you gotta get right down to it* and nip it in the bud.

Because all the legality in the world ain't gonna work." The bravado was breathtaking.

Finally the Fairfield North Apartments women started fighting back. "I've got an example to set for my sons," one said proudly: "I don't want my children to see me stooping to his level. I want my sons to grow up knowing I have respect for myself." Molly McElrath joined the battle: "We organized to get him fired! We won a lawsuit! Now we have a nonprofit organization that'll teach women how to be safe in their own homes. And if you want to get off on all that, *shame on you!* I don't understand the hostility." From the audience, their lawyer stood up to say: "I understand the audience's frustration, but if any one of [the twenty-two women] had taken a gun to him, *she'd* be in jail. Now *he's* in jail!"

It was the best they could do with a bad business. Like Jenny Jones's audience, Oprah Winfrey's had given us a clue to how defensive women could be, and how ready they were to savage other women to show off their own toughness. Organizing either group would take genius, luck, and perhaps even mindless tenacity.

The stories that follow illustrate a range of negative responses that women have made to a girl or woman in need. Although the women who told them had not been left wholly defenseless by their defection, if you want the good news, for the most part, you'll have to skip to the next chapter.

Rosa Sanchez is a twenty-year-old Latina who lives in southern California and has been on her own since she was seventeen. She arrived with a screech of brakes at the home where I was staying in Santa Monica, trotted across the lawn, and bounded up the stairs. Her story echoes many that other women told me about being let down by their mothers. Luckily, Rosa found a gifted female therapist who helped her make her way through the pain and bad memories to the ebullient state in which I found her.

My mother's an alcoholic — and probably has been since I was born. That's very common in the Chicano community, and it's worse, I think, in the women than it is in the men. My father left when I was five. And by the time I was sixteen, my last brother had moved out of the house, so it was just me and my mother, living in a single in Hollywood.

I asked one of my teachers if there was anyplace I could take my mother to, and I got her into a rehab center in Long Beach. She was fine for a few months, but then she started drinking again and got really sick with hepatitis. She'd be diagnosed as terminally ill, and then she'd improve, but then she'd start drinking again.

I founded the first Chicano organization at my high school, but I was spread so thin and I was alone a lot when she was in the hospital. That's when I stopped going to school.

One night my brother came home. (He's three years older than me.) I was asleep, and he wanted me to get up. He was very rough with me, and I said I wasn't going to wake up because I wasn't going to school. He said if I didn't wake up, he was gonna call the police on me. So I said, "I'll call 'em myself." *So I did:* I called the police and said, "My brother wants to report that I'm being truant and not going to school." I went through with the whole thing — even told 'em where I lived. And when I hung up, my brother said, "They're coming for you." And I said, "Oh, bullshit!"

Sure enough, I was into my shower and my mom knocked on the door and said, "Rosa, the police are here for you." I said, "Oh my God!" My mom couldn't even look at me. My brother had always been the man of the house. I just started crying, but I didn't want to cry in front of them. I told the police what was going on, and they finally said, "We'll leave you here with your mom and your brother, but your mom looks really sick. You need to get her to the hospital." She had jaundice.

That whole year, she was in and out of the hospital. They'd admit her, but then she'd leave. And no matter what I did for her, it wasn't good enough. My brother didn't help, but she always wanted him there. It was horrible. So I was always resentful. I'd really took care of my mom since I was twelve. All my life, I think, I'd felt betrayed by her. Men were always her number one priority. My dad, her husbands, her sons — and then her bottle, above everything else.

When I turned seventeen, my brother was staying with us in our single for two or three weeks before he went into the army. We got on each other's nerves, and one day we had a confrontation. He beat the shit out of me, and nobody came to help me — the neighbors didn't wanta get involved. My girlfriend was there when it started, and she said, "Just leave!" And I said, "Why the fuck should I have to leave? He's the one who needs to go cool off!" I wasn't gonna budge, even though Tomaso was really strong. So she ends up leaving. He's hitting me, and when I try to call the cops, he rips the phone outta the wall and ends up taking off.

Before we were disconnected, 911 got the call, and they sent some officers over. When they got there, I was all hurt and beat up. And they said, "Who did this to you? Was it your father? Your uncle? Your brother?" I was crying, and I said, "Yeah, my brother did it." They said, "Where's your brother at?" I just said, "Forget it. I don't even wanta talk about it." They said, "You can press charges, you're entitled." But at that point, I could never go against him or Mom. I'd protect them before I'd protect myself. My mom came back a couple of hours later, drunk, and I didn't even attempt to deal with all the built-up resentment of three hundred and sixty-five days a year for seventeen years. I just took off, and that night I didn't go home. My mom knew why he'd beat me up, but she didn't do anything to him. So I tried to forget about it.

After Tomaso left to go to the army, she started yelling at me one night, and I thought, This is it. She's never gonna stop drinking. I don't want to live my life this way any more. And I just went crazy: I started breaking the windows, throwing crap everywhere. I wanted to fucking strangle her. I got all my things together and said, "I'm never coming back!" And I walked out. My girlfriend had been staying with me, and so we both went to live with her weird mom, who's another psycho. We put all our stuff in a shopping basket and walked about a mile to her house. And I never went back.

I was going to Adult Children of Alcoholics and accidentally went to two incest meetings. The first time, I went, "Wow, these people have problems!" I'd never heard anything like that. The second time, I cried through the whole thing. And I thought, Too bad for them! Poor things that they went through all this. But near the end of the meeting, I raised my hand and said I remembered being at my aunt's house with my cousin and my brother Tomaso when I was four or five. I was naked and they were playing doctor with me. I cried and cried during that meeting. And I was, like, "Why am I sharing this? I shouldn't be talking about this." I didn't even know it mattered to me. I'd always had the memory, but until that night, I didn't know I had any feelings about it.

It wasn't innocent play because I was shitting bricks for fear of what would happen if my mom found out. My brother had undressed me, and he was sticking things in me. I was laying on my back and he had my knees drawn up, and he was sitting in between my legs and playing with my vagina. I was really embarrassed that I'd shared that — and I sat there crying because it hurt me so bad to remember.

Then I remembered another time when I was seven or eight, when Carlo, my next-door neighbor, molested me. I didn't even want to think about that, because that was so horrible to me! Even when it was happening, I was shitting bricks! I remembered that we were in his house, and he turned me around and stuck his hands down my pants and started playing with me. At first it felt good, and I stood there for a moment enjoying the feeling. And then I just took off outta his house and ran home. But because he was a family friend, he just walked right into my house and followed me into my bedroom. I was trying to hold the door shut, and he was going, "Rosa, I want to talk to you. . . ." And I said, "No, no, go away." Tomaso was going, "What's wrong, Rosa? Open the door." But then Carlo said, "I'm going off to buy ice cream. What kind do you want?" And I said, "Orange sherbet. . . ."

When my mom came home, I told her what had happened, and she yanked me into the bathroom and pulled down my pants and started opening me up. She was screaming and stuff. I said, "He didn't stick anything in me. He just touched me down there." She went and banged on his door and cussed him out: "How dare you touch my daughter?" Tomaso was saying, "Why didn't you tell me he did that? I'd have kicked his ass!" He was about nine then.

What my mom did would've been cool, except that she allowed Carlo back in the house and continued the friendship as if nothing had happened, and he kept on doing it. He did it to all the girls — he'd touch us and we'd run away when he came near. Carlo was an old man — like forty. When we were living in Hollywood, he'd come in and try to grab me, and one time I hit him over the head with a broom. My mother came in and said, "Don't treat him like that. He's an old man." And a neighbor said, "He's trying to grab her! What's she supposed to do?" And *my mom just laughed*.

When I moved outta my mom's, I spent a lotta time in the library, reading things about Chicano history and stuff. I was still totally depressed and cryin' myself to sleep. It was the hardest time of my life. Then I was raped when I was nineteen, and I was referred to a rape crisis place. They sent me into psychotherapy. I've been doin' that about a year, and I've come so fucking far it's inconceivable; I'm a million times different. I run into people on the street, and they're just amazed with me. I've still got a lotta anger at my family and a love/hate thing with my mother. But I don't despair any more. I feel like the world is in the palm of my hand and I have total control over my life.

Now I have the most wonderful, dependable, compassionate group of friends anybody could have. Initially I thought those kinds of people were nerds, but my psychologist gave me a lotta help. I'd tell her about somebody I'd met, and she'd say, "Nurture that friendship!" It's taken a lotta effort on my part too. I'm dating a guy now I'd have considered a nerd a few years ago. I have to keep working, putting in a lot of effort, to get straight what the match should be.

So now I'm happy and at peace with all the forces — all the things that make up life: happiness, sadness, confusion, being sure, being unsure. I've dealt with a lotta big decisions in the past few months and haven't put 'em off. I can handle anything that comes my way, I really can.

Bobbie Pearl is a Jewish lawyer in her early sixties who lives in Austin, Texas, and does arbitration. Divorced after decades of marriage, she took her grandmother's last name because she was the one person in her childhood who'd made Bobbie feel safe and loved. We had Sunday breakfast in a noisy neighborhood café where more than the usual number of children seemed to be spilling their orange juice simultaneously.

My parents were separated when I was two and divorced when I was ten. I was kidnapped back and forth between my mother and father, and then my mother gave me to my grandmother to raise until I was ten. I was totally protected when I was with my grandmother; she'd divorced my grandfather many years earlier because he was always fondling women. But when I was between ten and thirteen, and living with my mother, my grandfather would come to visit, maybe every six months or so. And he'd put his hands on my breasts and between my legs. I froze; I didn't move while he did it, I just endured it. And I didn't tell my mother because I didn't think she'd believe her father could be doing this, but it was horrible to me.

Finally, when I was about thirteen, my mother asked me to take some pillows up to where my grandfather was sleeping, and I just burst out and said, "If I go up there, I'll throw him down the stairs." And she said, "Bobbie, how could you say such a thing?" I told her what he'd been doing, and her response was, "Oh, he does that to you, too!" It had been done to her.

She told me that sometime in her thirties or forties, when she'd been in the hospital, flat on her back, he'd run his hands under her breasts "to see if she was sweating." So she didn't have any trouble believing that he was doing it to me. But when she told me this, her voice was neutral. (At this time, she was going back to school studying to become a therapist.)

When I was fifteen, I was fondled by a family friend who was getting divorced, and when I told my mother, she said, "Poor Walter, he's so lonely for his wife." The message I kept getting from her was that I was to be sexually available.

Women in offices have often played sexual games — sometimes for the fun of it, sometimes to gain a competitive advantage, and, not infrequently, for both. Idanelle Lansing sat with me on a giant red divan in a posh hotel remembering why she'd left a job that had been "the biggest thing in [her] life." After uprooting herself and moving to another state, she'd watched its high promise dull because of the way another woman played office politics. Clearly some women *do* get a modicum of power through sex.

When I watched the hearings, I felt angry. I believed Anita Hill, and I knew she was gonna be put on the rack and then let go like a minnow to flounder off and try to heal herself. I knew immediately that she was gonna get a public retribution and be hurt again, and I felt afraid for her. It worries me that I'm getting to be such a pessimist.

If women would work together—we're the majority—we could change it! But at almost every job I've had, the boss has picked out some cute little girl and screwed her until he was tired of her. Then she lost her job or was moved away. It rarely hurt him and it always hurt her.

I was working for a magazine run by one of the best chains in the country. The three editors were all male, and they were *all* having affairs with women on the staff—which limited *my* access. Several of us staff members were basically left in the cold because these guys couldn't control their sexual organs. The magazine was in turmoil; all this sexual business was going on and the people who wanted to put out the magazine weren't a team. *It split the women from each other.*

April was from Boston. Her father was a physicist; she was very polished and had gone to Harvard. She was very bright and *real* sophisticated. I was from Mound Bayou, Louisiana. My father was an oilfield worker and my mother was a secretary. I went to a city university and had struggled to make it. It was the biggest thing in my life that I'd been picked up by a slick magazine and was being paid for the first time according to my abilities.

I'd been hired by an editor who quit right after he hired me. A guy named Jonathan had helped me come in, but we had a little trouble relating because he was thirty-four and real athletic. By then I was forty-five and not interested in climbing any mountains. But we were getting along pretty well when the first guy quit.

April came to me and said, "We don't want another editor coming in here and messing around. We need to get Jonathan made editor, so you need to tell 'em in the main office that you're gonna quit if they don't make him editor." And I said, "April, I'll be glad to tell 'em I support him for editor, but I'm not gonna tell 'em I'd quit." She got mad, and later I found out they were having a hot romance. Another woman was also in trouble with April because she hadn't "supported" Jonathan.

The front office brought in another guy with a wonderful background to try to make the magazine a little kickier and sexier. (This was a finance magazine.) Immediately after Gus came in, April and Jonathan and Gus became a team. April was always in the in crowd when they discussed covers, stories, and whatever, because Jonathan brought her in. She'd get the cover stories, and she was good.

The affair tore up the magazine: instead of us working together, it turned us into factions. We didn't complain to the front office because we didn't want to sound like whiny malcontents. We tried ignoring it, but that didn't seem to work either. Once April started trying to tear me down, I felt I was always having to defend myself. Finally, after eighteen months, I just left and came back home, and the magazine folded three months after that.

I know I'm a writer—I got a letter from the president of the chain praising the last story I did—but one reason I'm not writing now is that this experience damaged my self-esteem so much. April made fun of me, and that bond between her and Jonathan made things impossible for the rest of us. Three other women who were writers or editorial coordinators were hurt by it because April always won the arguments.

Marie Wilson, executive director of the Ms. Foundation for Women, is in her early fifties, and in response to the Hill/Thomas hearings, she wrote an op-ed piece for the *New York Times* in which she referred to an episode that happened during her second week as an executive at "a major financial trade association serving primarily white men." A woman had been raped in the local parking garage, and while discussing the need for precautions, a vice-president had smiled and said, "Sexual harassment, I love it." Marie wrote: "I remember the chill I felt as everyone laughed. The remark was made in the presence of other male executives, surrounded by female support staff and me. I knew then the environment was going to be hostile. . . . I was right."

I sat in Marie's office on Fifth Avenue clicking the tape recorder on and off when calls would come in that were too important to hold. She was on the committee to choose a new police chief for New York City at a time when the force was in even more turmoil than usual, so that cut into our time. Then her secretary put her head in the door to say that Gloria was on the phone, and I doubt that many people ask

Gloria Steinem to wait. Marie, by the way, has a wide, easy grin, so the job where a guy had to ask her to smile more often was patently a killer for independent women. Like Idanelle, she watched other women get temporary power through their sexual liaisons with men — but knew they'd ultimately pay. At the same time, Marie's story shows how women *can* work to help other women.

I had five children in six years, and when I went back to work, the youngest was probably six. I worked part-time at a university, where I ran a program in the school of continuing education to put women into the workplace. That's where I first ran into the question of power relationships between women and men. I was dealing with how you got women reentering the workplace to have power — my work also included women in middle and top management — so I had to deal with the whole intersection of gender and power.

Because of my husband, I understood that I didn't have a whole lot of power at home. I'd been lobbying — first on abortion and then on child care — and also working half-time at the preschool because we had all these kids. One day I came home from the legislature, and the house was a mess and the kids were all over it. *My husband was there, but he wasn't really there.* So I said, "I thought we'd agreed to work to change things in this country, and I can't do it if I come back and have to make up for all the things that happened while I was away." And he said, "I'll contribute in the home in proportion to the money you bring in."

It was really a wonderful awakening for me, because I'd thought we had another arrangement. He'd been doing social-change work through the church. He didn't bring in a lot of money and I'd made a big contribution. I said, "Oh, you mean if I go out to lobby or do things they don't pay me for yet, you don't do anything." He said, "Yeah, I'm not somebody who can afford a volunteer wife." It was clarifying. So I started preparing to do things that would make some money and went to the workforce knowing that the rules were about money and power. I'd learned that in my very own home.

I went to work in a fledgling program. The universities in the late seventies were trying to attract women, but those women not only wanted to be educated, they wanted to go out and work. So I had a dean who said, "Any program you create that brings in money, I'll support." He let me experiment with almost anything. We were focused on issues that connected women to work, so we got the university involved in the community in a way it never had been.

This dean had a doctorate, but he wasn't the academic type. Early on, I was at a university event, and I felt a spitball come right down my cleavage. I didn't have a horrible response! That man gave me a lotta respect for the work I did: he gave me support and made sure I had the staff I needed. And frankly, his kind of sexual stuff didn't bother me. I knew where he was coming from: we both came out of working-class families.

When I first came to work, I came on a grant with a half-time salary. I immediately began to create programs, and we ended up with the largest division of women's programs in the country. After I'd been there a while, I said, "I can't keep working full-time for part-time wages. This contradicts what we're saying about how women should be treated in the workplace." He said, "Don't tell people!" but I said, "Change it!" He was willing to be enlightened, and I got a full-time salary. So if he threw a piece of wadded-up whatever down my cleavage, I didn't let it become a major thing.

I moved on to a bankers' association because I needed a job with an appropriate salary. I was a feminist, and the whole tenor of that place was different from the university. There women had power through their relation-ships with men in management. What was happening is similar, I think, to what goes on in Congress. Associations do political work, and the atmosphere is a lot like what happens when you're a lobbyist. (When I was a lobbyist at the legislature, I'd find a hand on my knee before I got out my opening line.) At the association, there was a lot of flirting that went on; women in support-staff positions have power through their boss. We know that, and so we learn the names of people in secondary positions so that we'll know how to get to their bosses.

The women in this association worked hard but also looked pretty, and there was sexual teasing going on all the time. The bankers expected women to look pretty, and sound good, and smile. They even had a board member tell me I'd get along better if I smiled more. *The dean's expectation had been that I'd produce. The bankers' expectation was that producing had to do with how I looked and with showing myself to be a nice girl.* Women with lesser power there had liaisons from time to time. It was such a part of the accepted thing that I'm almost certain that a woman who worked for me was having an affair with the man I reported to. And I felt like she was also sabotaging me.

The man who ran the organization was brilliant and understood power as well as anybody I've ever known. I learned a lot from him, and I tried to warn him. I went in and said, "I think you'd be upset if you knew some things that are happening in your company." I think he liked and respected me, and I think he really knew some of what was happening but didn't want to know. I don't think he'd have sanctioned it, but a lot of people didn't think it was so serious.

There were women who were a little frightened of me because they wanted things to stay the same. They got power through men, and until we have more power, women will keep colluding with powerful men. When a woman got in a bind — when the affair ended, or she got to a hard place — she'd come to me. But until that point, I think they'd seen me as a troublemaker because I was shaking up things. There were some really hard times there — some times when I was truly mortified — but I believe people also learn from hard times.

When I left, I felt like I was in a good place. I had respect for a lot of the women and men there, and I think they had respect for me. But it wasn't easy. That association was a microcosm of the changing world we live in. The men weren't malevolent, but the ground rules had shifted on 'em, and I was coming in and saying, "Let's fast-forward this process. . . ."

Pauline Bart, a Jewish intellectual in her early sixties, is a sociologist whose book *Stopping Rape: Successful Survival Strategies* marked a new stage in feminist understanding. Most of her adult life has been focused on analyzing the plight of women and figuring out how to help them. This interest can be hazardous in an academic setting, since universities are by no means leaders in the fight for women's equity, and other women on campus have not always been helpful. In the fall of 1992, with two years to go before she was due to retire from the University of Illinois, Bart was barred from offering courses in the college of liberal letters, arts, and sciences by its dean.

In the preceding spring semester, Bart had been teaching an undergraduate class, Gender and Society, when she got into a dispute with a male African-American student, Donald Dixon, who subsequently accused her of sexism and racism. Dixon had argued in class that a female student defending Mike Tyson's rape conviction — a student who had herself been raped — was "ego-tripping." He also accused her of not knowing the difference between sex and rape. Women in the class had complained to Bart that they were silenced by Dixon's hostile comments, and she had said in class that she wouldn't allow male speech to silence and invalidate women's experiences.

When Dixon came to Bart's office and asked if she'd been referring to him, Bart suggested that he transfer. He stayed in her class, however, and so a number of women stopped coming. Filing a complaint with the university's affirmative-action office, Dixon claimed that Bart had pressured him to drop the course and said he fit the profile of a black male rapist. Bart countered by saying that Dixon was hostile and disruptive, and made remarks that trivialized rape — a position she couldn't tolerate in her class — but she insisted that she'd simply said Dixon believed in the myth that women want to be raped.

The associate chancellor for public affairs claimed that "our investigators found that men were not being allowed the same sort of classroom talking rights as women." Bart retorted that what she studies — violence against women — "is something people don't like to talk about. It deals with the harm men do to women, and it's not symmetrical — there are not as many female rapists as male rapists. Men find this very threatening, so I would not let male speech silence women."

Bart, whose appointment is in the department of psychiatry, could not be fired by the dean of the liberal arts college, but he had the power to cancel her courses, which he did. His decision sparked a controversy in Chicago that spread throughout the state and then the country. The head of the women's studies department didn't support her, but she manages to be philosophical about it. We sat over lunch in a quiet, real-folks restaurant on the second floor of a slightly seedy hotel not far from Lake Michigan, and Bart began our interview by saying she always gets in trouble.

Part of it is stylistic. I grew up in New York and then I lived in California. I dress West Coast, I think East Coast, and I live in the Midwest. I grew up during the Holocaust in a very political Jewish family. And as I get older, I get more concerned about how something like the Holocaust could happen. One thing that made it possible was that people kept quiet; they didn't want to make waves.

Any analysis of women's condition that doesn't use the concept of misogyny is not worth killing a tree for. Sometimes I try to keep quiet, but the next day I say whatever it is because it's gnawed at me. People say, "You're so courageous," but I don't see it as courageous. I don't think I have the psychological freedom not to. They try to kill the messenger because if they believe the message, they have to rethink so many things. Violence against women is endemic, and it's epidemic. Half the women in my undergraduate class had been raped, and 28 percent had been sexually abused as children. Almost all of them have been sexually harassed, and it's done by "normal" men — that's the thing people really resist understanding. My definition of a misdemeanor is a felony committed by a man the woman knows.

The only reason I'm not out on the street after what the university did to me is that the very powerful new chair of the psychiatry department, who's from the Bronx, is protecting me. (He says he's been around women like me all his life.) *I understand why I get no support from the women under the dean of letters and sciences's jurisdiction. These are tough economic times and tough academic times. Universities are part of the society, and women's studies is a particularly vulnerable field, so now they're trying to call themselves gender studies.* Ten years ago the issue was whether or not we should let men into class. Now the issue is how we make them feel welcome and comfortable. How are we going to do that if we're talking about violence against women?

The first time a university treated me badly — it was twenty-five years ago — I went into a profound depression. But then I decided they were the Cossacks. [Nobody expects anything good of the Cossacks, especially if they're Jewish.] My current situation is exacerbated by Chicago, which is a totally corrupt city: principles here are considered womanish and stupid. The only people who supported me for a while were the radical nuns, and I'm not Catholic. They were willing to act on principle, and nobody else was.

It's true that I'm not adjusted! If I were adjusted to the system, I'd be a "good German." Catharine MacKinnon [the radical feminist legal scholar who led the campaign to ban pornography in various cities] has had an enormous intellectual influence over me. Only the pornographers have free speech — leading to women's having unprotected lives. *My speech is not protected, for my speech may lead to censorship.* When you deal with violence against women, you walk around in a state of perpetual outrage and depression. As MacKinnon puts it, women are systematically punished and randomly rewarded. Silly women think that by turning against other women, they're going to be rewarded. They may be, and they may not be.

In earlier years when they were making things hard for me at the University of Illinois, I'd get these visiting professorships. I'd do anything to get out of Chicago. And that's why I have all this support now, because I've taught all over. I have E mail, and I've hooked into support networks — mainly women's studies networks — and I'd have died without them. I put out what happens, and then people I never knew respond.

So I'm a troublemaker! May I make a lot more of it!

Women who believe that what happens to other women is not their business run the risk of discovering that they're badly mistaken. Like the wives of slaveowners who abused black women, those who remain silent when another woman is harassed or exploited are acquiescing in a process likely to narrow their own options. When a woman thinks that while the guys are hitting on somebody else, she can use their preoccupation as a cover to dart to safety, she is likely to find they eventually tire of their quarry and turn their attention to her. So nothing will more nearly guarantee that things will stay the same than the splintering of women into factions.

Realistically speaking, a woman's freedom depends on her ability to make her own way. As Marie Wilson puts it, "Until we have more power, women will keep colluding with powerful men." When affairs or marriages end and women get to "a hard place," they are likely to look for help to other women. But until that point, many will see a feminist like Marie as a troublemaker because she is working for *fundamental* change.

An independent spirit is easier to cultivate if a woman is independent in fact, and most women remain financially precarious. They make, on average, seventy-two cents to a man's dollar, although black women average only sixty-two cents for every dollar earned by white men. Women are more likely to work at minimum-wage jobs, and those raising children alone have less than a third the amount of money available that a married couple has if the wife is in the paid work force.[11]

Fundamental change therefore means fighting battles on many fronts at once. Women need more money in order to support themselves and their children, and so they have to get access to better-paying jobs and networks that will sustain them. This in turn requires a new child care policy and legislation like that addressing family medical leave that serves women better. Female politicians are more likely to give these things priority, and so the more women in office, the greater the chance that good laws can pass.

Lest this wish list seem daunting, we can observe, over the past two decades, a synergy at work: with each success, the pace of change escalates and hope becomes less chimerical. Beginning in the early 1970s, women began to make a revolution, and therein lies the tale that follows.

13

THE MAKINGS OF A CULTURAL REVOLUTION

Being a nice, good girl got Anita Hill what all "hice girls" usually get:
nothing — but further abuse.

— Gloria T. Hull

In a cultural revolution — the civil rights movement of the 1960s is our
clearest example — first you have to tell hard truths to an audience that
bitterly resists the new message. Then you have to get angry enough to
act. And finally you have to organize effectively to pressure the powers-
that-be into changing laws and institutions to accommodate a new sense
of justice and an enlarged constituency. In the past thirty years, women
have done all this over and over again, with ever-increasing numbers
involved, so that Hill/Thomas would play a key role in extending a
process of fundamental change long since begun.

As writer Nellie Y. McKay said of the men on the Senate Judiciary
Committee, "They were forced to listen, but they did not hear." Pockets
of women across the nation *did* hear, however, and so "Hill's case
against Clarence Thomas [is] not closed, but wide open." The reaction
to the hearings was at once personal and political, and as the nation's

emotions fell to something more nearly like normal, it became clear that Thomas's victory would be pyrrhic.[1]

The level of anger that Hill had sparked was a measure of what serious issues her testimony raised and how deeply threatening women are who violate the injunction to silence. Having warned people against killing the messenger, she was spat on in the airport on her journey home and subsequently got death threats that may or may not have been serious. In Texas, a man yelled in the direction of the TV set when Hill held her first press conference, "You dumb bitch! You bastards opened the door for all the women!" and, the next day, killed twenty-three people as revenge on "those mostly white tremendously female vipers" who had "wronged" him.[2]

But this time, women in large numbers would not be intimidated, and the hearings fell at the most fertile moment for women, politically and culturally speaking, in American history. Those who sat aghast as they watched Hill treated shamefully had organizations they could call and women candidates they could run against men who had voted for Thomas. "If the polls showed that only a third of the nation believed Hill's accusations," historian Christine Stansell would write, "that one-third was nonetheless mobilized, partisan, angry, and utterly solid in their support." After three decades of speaking out and building institutions that could work for them, women across the spectrum of class and color were galvanized.[3]

Once more, outrage turned into the blood and sinews of organizing. The National Women's Political Caucus took out a full-page advertisement in the *New York Times* with a drawing of women in the Senate Judiciary seats and a caption that read "What if?" The number of women applying for caucus training sessions doubled in response, while more than $85,000 and over thirteen hundred letters poured into its Washington office. Within a month, applications for membership to the National Organization for Women tripled. Money flowed into the Women's Campaign Fund at double the rate it had come in earlier.[4]

African-American law professor Margaret A. Burnham summarized our lesson: "*What this nomination process taught is that black progress and progress for women are inextricably linked in contemporary American politics, and that each group suffers when it fails to grasp the dimensions of the other's struggle.*" Any arbitrary limitation on rights spreads easily from one group to the other. White men who believed that it was all right to limit black people's access were reasonably likely to find it in their hearts to limit white women's access as well — and vice versa. The hearings had simply reminded us of a crucial dynamic: all through American history, the political progress of women had been intertwined with the fate of African-Americans.[5]

One key stage in the collective response was a new round of truth-telling that could lead in turn to a more sophisticated level of understanding; as more and more women broke their silences, for instance, they came to see that experiences they'd assumed were peculiar to them were in fact quite common. And when people discover that they're not alone, they can make common cause, confront their problems together, and take responsibility for changing them.

African-American intellectuals took stock and admitted to sex and class differences amongst them. The journal *The Black Scholar* put out a special edition on the hearings with a preponderance of essays sympathetic to Hill. In it, Professor Gloria T. Hull shrewdly observed the double binds that the history of African-American women had imposed upon them. To negate familiar assumptions that black women are promiscuous, for instance, Hill had had to be prim and proper. But compelled "to subdue her emotions and behavior and deaden her affect," she lost some power. "Unlike those early women crusaders, she could not then rise to the kind of outraged righteousness which gave force to their personalities and platforms."[6]

Still, the African-American community was primed to hear the new round of revelations that the Hill/Thomas hearings inspired precisely because prominent women among them had been writing about sexual violence within families for at least twenty years. The director of Spelman College's Women's Research and Resource Center, Beverly Guy-Sheftal, recalled the uproar that greeted Alice Walker's *The Color Purple* in 1982, for instance, and then Stephen Spielberg's film adaptation of it. On the first page of Walker's book, the heroine, Celie, is raped by the man she takes to be her father. He tells her, "You better not never tell nobody but God. It'd kill your mammy," and then proceeds to father her two children. (Twenty minutes into the film, an African-American man some five rows behind me shouted out so the entire theater could hear, *"I don't like this movie!"*) Guy-Sheftal identified the male anger this portrayal sparked as the beginning of a "decade-old family battle" between men and women, and noted "a perceptible but unspeakable misogynist strain in African-American thinking."[7]

As early as 1971, however, two women who are now literary leaders in the African-American community had published first books that were only marginally less inflammatory than *The Color Purple*. In her autobiographical *I Know Why the Caged Bird Sings*, Maya Angelou described being raped by her mother's lover — whom her uncles then murdered. In Toni Morrison's *The Bluest Eye*, the central figure, Pecola Breedlove, was raped by her own father.

But younger women had taken the brunt of men's anger. Like Walker, Ntozake Shange had also become a target after the Broadway debut of her play *For Colored Girls Who Have Considered Suicide / When the Rainbow Is Enuf*. And in 1979, when Michelle Wallace published *Black Macho and the Myth of the Superwoman*, the three had become an unholy trinity in the eyes of many black men. However fiercely criticized, though, their work had evidently made an impression.

For now a good many male African-Americans who wrote about the hearings saw fit to take the women's side. Calling the workplace "the traditional bulwark of penis power," writer Calvin Hernton, for example, whose earlier work could hardly be labeled feminist, charged that sexism is pervasive: "Lawyers, doctors, professors, preachers, judges, politicians, business men, as well as construction workers and garbage men, black and white, yellow and brown, share the attitude and the behavior that men are primary and righteous, and women are secondary and profane." "Let's face it," Hernton wrote: "Very few if any black folk, let alone white folk, doubt that Clarence Thomas did what Anita says he did. . . . Women feared that all women who took her side would be punished. . . . *Women are blackmaled* [sic] *into silence for fear of being attacked as 'sluts,' 'whores' and 'nymphos.'*"[8]

The essays in the book on Hill/Thomas that Toni Morrison edited took Hill's credibility as a given. Referring to what happened to her as "uncomfortably close to a gang rape," novelist Michael Thelwell acknowledged that of the people he talked to, "only one black woman did not believe in the literal and unvarnished truthfulness of Professor Hill's account." Philosopher Cornel West chastised the black leadership's "failure of nerve" in refusing to say publicly that the nomination was "an act of cynical tokenism" or to attack "the ugly authoritarian practices in black America that range from sexual harassment to indescribable violence against women."[9]

Kimberle Crenshaw raised the important question, "To what

authority can women who have been consistently represented as sexually available appeal?" — calling attention to "women's own participation in this conspiracy of silence [that] has legitimated sexism within our community." Historian Paula Giddings pointed out that many African-American teenagers who have babies and later regret it have been shaped by the "tremendous amount of sexual abuse" within their own families, "sometimes traced through two, three, or more generations." No one could speak more plainly.[10]

If the African-American community had dramatically stepped up its pace in a long-standing internal debate over the realities of women's lives, the same was true among other groups, and the ground here was equally fertile. Since the mid-twentieth century, the convention that had dominated the novel for over two hundred years — "and they lived happily ever after" — had begun to fray, and over the past two decades, it had shredded altogether. No longer was "the decent drapery of life" drawn over the lives of women and children.

Like African-Americans, white and Asian women novelists had begun to violate the old proprieties by writing about sexual abuse. The prolific Joyce Carol Oates was bringing to the surface themes of violence against girls and women that had been implicit in her earlier work. A promising new writer, Amy Tan, detailed the sufferings of Chinese women at the hands of men. Ancient prohibitions against admitting to incest began to crumble. Carolyn Chute, in *The Beans of Egypt, Maine*, Mary Gaitskill, in *Two Girls, Fat and Thin*, and Dorothy Allison, in *Bastard out of Carolina*, treated incest fictionally, while Sylvia Fraser and Betsy Petersen wrote autobiographically.[11]

For intellectual background, we needed and had gotten work of a more general nature. In 1971, for instance, Elizabeth Janeway's *Man's World, Woman's Place* had analyzed the tenacity of power configurations between men and women that had long since outlived their usefulness. "If there's nothing more powerful than an idea whose time has come," Janeway had written by way of openers, "there is nothing more ubiquitously pervasive than an idea whose time won't go. The division of the world by sexes, challenged a century and more ago by the militants of the first wave of Feminism, still endures and, what's more, still prevails, in spite of new attacks upon it."[12] The new attacks continued.

After 1972, when it was founded, *Ms.* Magazine quickly became the repository of good reporting, outrage, humor, and hope, as a series of writers who at last had a monthly forum reevaluated women's position in American society. All through the seventies, poet Adrienne Rich published incisive prose dissecting women's experiences under patriarchy, and her books joined others like Betty Friedan's *The Feminine Mystique* and Kate Millett's *Sexual Politics* in questioning ideas of male dominance that women had taken for granted because they had been in the air we breathed — ideas that owed their overwhelming power precisely to their ancient immunity from criticism. *For more than twenty years, the atmosphere had been filled with the sounds of silence breaking.*[13]

Since the 1960s, when the modern American women's movement began springing to life, scholars and journalists had also been exploring the subject of sexual violence against women. In 1975, for example, Susan Brownmiller's *Against Our Will: Men, Women and Rape* argued that rape should be seen primarily as an act of violence. Later writers like sociologist Pauline Bart, psychotherapist Judith Lewis Herman, and legal theorist Catharine MacKinnon were more likely to underscore its sexual dimensions. (Responding subsequently to the William Kennedy Smith rape trial, MacKinnon wrote of rape as sex discrimination.)[14]

So by the time Hill/Thomas erupted, the subject of sexual violence against women had been discussed repeatedly and at length in the feminist community. Legal scholars following Catharine MacKinnon's lead, furthermore, had carried on a campaign to ban pornography. Though the campaign had failed, it had nonetheless engaged many academic women in political organizing, and their savvy and skills might now be available for less divisive causes.

For by now, the political earth had been plowed and planted for almost three decades. Beginning in 1962 with John F. Kennedy's Commission on the Status of Women, a committed network in the nation's capital that included a handful of men worked to change laws and regulations that held women back. As one of the most indefatigable among them, Catherine East, would put it thirty years later, most "didn't expect to benefit personally; in fact, most ran the risk of damaging their careers or reputations if their activities became widely known. And some *did* damage their careers." Still, a series of presidential advisory commissions and task forces followed hard on the first, and while commissions on the status of women proliferated in the states, Republicans and Democrats in the Women's Bureau, the Labor

Department, and all through the federal bureaucracy came together to identify problems and figure out how to solve them.

An African-American lawyer, Pauli Murray, who would become an Episcopal priest, coauthored a seminal law review article, "Jane Crow and the Law," and Congresswoman Martha Griffiths from Michigan inserted sex into the language of Title VII of the Civil Rights Act of 1964 prohibiting discrimination in employment. (Many male representatives treated Griffith's addition as a joke.) Almost half a century after it was first introduced, the Equal Rights Amendment passed the Congress and went to the states for a ratification that did not come. But a lawyer for the American Civil Liberties Union, Ruth Bader Ginsburg, succeeded in making lasting change by winning four of the five cases she argued before the Supreme Court extending women's legal rights — a triumph for which she was rewarded in 1993, when she became the second woman in history to become a Supreme Court Justice.

The United Nations declared 1975 the International Year of the Woman, and in 1977, a path-breaking National Women's Conference in Houston, Texas, produced an agenda for women's full participation in society that remains visionary almost two decades later.

Community activists had meanwhile responded to a need that grew ever more apparent by setting up rape crisis hot lines and battered women's shelters in virtually every American city. Most often they discovered that more women needed their help than they had the money and/or professional resources to satisfy. By 1993, there were over fifteen hundred shelters throughout the country, and two-thirds of their residents were children. A stunning 87 percent of Americans had come to see that "the beating of women by their husbands or boyfriends is a serious problem facing many families," while across the spectrum of race, ethnicity, and class, they understood that "violence is not just a physical assault but also an attack on women's dignity and freedom."[15]

Abortion had played a critical role — both as an issue and as an organizing tool — since it had to do with the control of women's bodies. After the Supreme Court's 1973 decision in *Roe v. Wade,* giving American women the right to legal abortion, many had come to take that right for granted. But when a far more conservative Court handed down the Webster decision in July 1989, granting states the right to restrict access to abortion, women who had never given a thought to politics jammed the phone lines and flooded the mailboxes of women's organizations, and a constituency was mobilized that abortion-rights activists called "a sleeping giant." All the major national women's organizations took the stand that they would not support a candidate unless he or she was officially prochoice, and politicians who had previously wavered or downplayed the issue — among them Democrats Bill Clinton and Al Gore — now discovered that the better part of wisdom was to be solidly prochoice.

Furthermore, it appeared that women themselves might finally be gaining real political power. Women candidates exasperated by male politicians' indifference to their issues had begun to run for office and win. Sarah Weddington, who argued *Roe v. Wade* before the U.S. Supreme Court, went back to Texas, gathered a group of tough-minded women to run her campaign (among them an Austin housewife named Ann Richards), and won a seat in the state legislature. Weddington's example was followed by women all over the country.

Until 1960, women for the most part had done the political drudgery: they stuffed the envelopes, painted the yard signs, and made the phone calls. Only three decades later, women occupied 17 percent of the seats in state legislatures and were Democratic candidates for governor in two of the three most important races in the country. In 1990, Ann Richards was running for governor of Texas and Dianne Feinstein for governor of California. Along with Florida, those were the key states in that election year because, on the basis of the 1990 census, they would get three and seven new congressional seats, respectively.

Richards and Feinstein were mainstream women taking much the same positions Fanny Wright had been turned into a pariah for taking a century and a half earlier. Neither was braver, smarter, more principled, or more dedicated than she, and neither was nearly so well educated. *Apart from technological and economic change, however, two crucial things had happened to make it possible for women to take those stands and not only survive, but thrive politically. One was that we had gradually extended the promise in Thomas Jefferson's Declaration of Independence to include African-Americans and women of all colors. The other was that women had organized politically to a degree unprecedented since they won the vote in 1920.*

The question those two gubernatorial races posed was, Can women candidates attract the money necessary to run a winning campaign for a major political office? And the answer, finally, was yes. The Democratic women's political action committee, EMILY's List, gave

Richards well over $400,000, and after the election she said repeatedly that she could not have won without it. (EMILY stands for "Early Money Is Like Yeast: it makes the dough rise.")[16]

Richards's victory gave heart to women all over the country. Since she'd clearly won because women had worked so hard to help her, she'd benefitted from two decades of organizing. During that time, the National Women's Political Caucus and the National Organization for Women had been founded, along with the Women's Campaign Fund and the National Abortion Rights Action League. Most of these had state affiliates, some of them almost as strong as the national organizations — California and Texas being prime examples. The Hollywood Women's Political Committee had regularly raised millions for progressive candidates. So, when Hill/Thomas shattered so many remaining silences, politicians were primed to see that the women's vote might make or break their candidacies.

In the fall of 1991, even before the fateful hearings, the caucus, along with the Women's Campaign Fund and EMILY's List, had commissioned a poll to discover what voters thought about women candidates. It had revealed that "when all other factors are equal, both parties are more competitive when they nominate women": that is to say, the party that nominated a woman was more likely to win! Voters saw women as populist outsiders less beholden to special interests and more focused on the domestic problems they took ever more seriously.

Then the hearings blew off the political roof. During the 1990 electoral cycle, EMILY's List had spent $1 million. In the 1992 cycle, its resources topped $6 million, making it one of the most powerful political action committees in the country. By midnight, November 3, when the cycle ended, women had come several steps further in their quest for equality. Senator Brock Adams of Washington had been forced out of the race because eight women publicly accused him of harassing them, and the seat he vacated was won by Patty Murray, a self-described "mom in tennis shoes." Carol Moseley Braun of Illinois, the African-American Cook County registrar who ran against Senator Alan Dixon in the Democratic primary because he'd voted to confirm Clarence Thomas, had become the first black woman ever to be elected to the United States Senate. Arlen Specter, the Republican point man who had attacked Anita Hill so savagely, was very nearly defeated by Lynn Yeakel, a political unknown.

Learning the lessons from her losing 1990 gubernatorial race and thereby running first and foremost as a woman, Dianne Feinstein was elected by a sizeable majority to finish out Governor Pete Wilson's term as a U.S. senator. And during the last week of the campaign, Feinstein used her formidable resources to help Barbara Boxer defeat a last-minute surge from her Republican challenger to win the six-year Senate seat from California. *The state that sets the tone for the American future had elected two women to represent it in the United States Senate.*

Twenty-nine more women were elected to the U.S. House of Representatives, bringing the total there to 48 out of 452. Another 2 percent were added in state legislatures across the country, for an average of 20.2 percent, and countless numbers were elected to state and local offices.

Most dramatic of all, women made up 54 percent of the electorate nationwide; they voted for the prochoice candidate for president by a margin of 6 percent, and Democrat Bill Clinton defeated an incumbent antichoice president with 43 percent of the vote compared to George Bush's 38 percent. (Independent Ross Perot, who was also prochoice, got 19 percent of the vote.) "Women came of age in politics on November 3, 1992," announced Ellen Malcolm, the president of EMILY's List. "Women candidates won big races, women voters propelled Bill Clinton into the White House, and women became serious financial players." For their unprecedented political success, the Hill/Thomas hearings had provided the galvanizing spark. (EMILY's List went from 3,500 members in 1990 to 24,000 in 1992, while the Women's Campaign Fund and the National Women's Political Caucus more than doubled their membership. The Caucus spent ten times more money in the 1992 electoral cycle [$500,000] than it had two years earlier, and the Women's Campaign Fund went from $500,000 to $1.2 million. EMILY tripled the number of women candidates they supported, while the Fund more than doubled theirs. The Caucus went from 865 candidates to 1,133 in the two-year period.)[17]

Silence, then, was broken and action followed. The hearings prompted lead articles on sexual harassment in every periodical of note in the country, and virtually every female columnist, along with many men, has written at least once since then on the subject. Along with William Kennedy Smith's and heavyweight champion Mike Tyson's trials for rape, the hearings focused unprecedented attention on the subject of women's vulnerability to men. And women at all levels of society, from plumbers to navy pilots, initiated lawsuits against their employers.

In its first issue after the hearings, the *Washington Lawyer* noted that law firms specializing in employment law had been overwhelmed with calls from employers who wanted to implement or update their sexual harassment policies. Plaintiffs' lawyers and public interest groups were fielding many more inquiries from women as to the channels available for bringing charges. The Women's Legal Defense Fund, the National Women's Law Center, the Washington Lawyers Committee for Civil Rights Under Law, and comparable organizations in other cities were hiring temporary staff to handle an explosion of interest. In 1992, the EEOC and the Fair Employment Practices Agency received 10,513 sexual harassment complaints — up from 6,871 in fiscal 1991, an increase of more than 50 percent.[18]

The 1991 Civil Rights Act, which allows women to collect damages up to $300,000 for sex discrimination, finally passed Congress and was signed by a president who had vetoed similar legislation and, until the Hill/Thomas hearings, had threatened to veto this as well. And corporate America took note: with its passage, companies began to institute seminars and hire lawyers to educate their workforce and thereby diminish the chance that they would have to pay out.

Since men like prizefighter Mike Tyson began going to prison for acting on contemptuous attitudes to women that rich, prominent men had gotten by with for millennia, it seemed as though public opinion might have permanently shifted. But acts of sexual violence against women were occurring with stunning frequency, and no one knew whether women were simply more likely to report them, or whether the numbers were actually increasing. According to Department of Justice victimization studies, for instance, one woman in twelve will be raped or threatened with rape during her lifetime, while the National Institute of Mental Health found that one in twelve college men actually *admitted* that he'd raped or tried to rape a woman. In states like Texas and California, where women are politically conspicuous, the figures are much higher, suggesting that men's anxiety increases to toxic levels as women advance in their quest for equality.

Domestic violence was now taken seriously by police departments that had been inclined to dismiss it little more than a decade earlier. In 1985, the National Family Violence Survey estimated that more than 11 percent of all women had been hurt in one way or another by their mates and reported that a woman in the United States is battered every fifteen seconds. Eight years later, a House subcommittee on health and the environment heard that between two and four million women are battered annually by their partners — 95 percent of them men — resulting in more serious injuries to women than muggings, car crashes, and rapes combined.[19]

Worst of all, children were being hurt, and the evidence is overwhelming that abused children will become abusers in turn. The second National Incidence and Prevalence of Child Abuse and Neglect study discovered that the number of children who'd been sexually abused by family members was *two and a half times higher* in 1986 than in 1980. Using the most stringent definition of sexual abuse, and *excluding* neighbors, friends, or strangers, they arrived at a total of nearly 120,000 children. (At least 82 percent of the perpetrators proved to be male.) The majority of these sexually abused children, furthermore, were *not* among those reported to Child Protective Services.[20]

Whether the burgeoning women's organizations and the growing legions of female politicians can effectively address the heightened violence against women and children remains an open question. It is clear, however, that the issues have been exhaustively discussed in virtually every forum there is; that the necessary machinery is in place; that a political constituency is there to be mobilized; and that the stakes are very high indeed.

I'm cautiously optimistic for a variety of reasons — especially since women have gained an eminence in key institutions that had earlier excluded them and you can *see* them there. Barbara Walters and Marlene Sanders have been joined by women like Diane Sawyer, Connie Chung, Charlayne Hunter-Gault, Lesley Stahl, Carole Simpson, Judy Woodruff, and Cokie Roberts as news commentators on the major networks and public television. Tough-minded syndicated columnists like Ellen Goodman and Anna Quindlen make no apologies for writing about the events of the day from a woman's perspective or consistently taking feminist positions. The percentage of women who get front-page bylines on major newspapers is rising, albeit slowly, and so are the numbers of women in newsrooms across the country. Women like Nannerl Keohane, Ann Reynolds, and Shirley Strum Kenny are college and university presidents and chancellors, and women have organized within every profession to support each other and push for greater access to top positions and more tangible power. Finally, traditional women's magazines like *Vogue* and *Vanity Fair* have begun publishing serious political articles and putting their imprimatur on a more substantial and complex femininity.

As his first key appoinment to the U.S. Supreme Court, President Bill Clinton chose Ruth Bader Ginsburg, who had won four of the five cases she had argued before the Court in the 1970s to extend the legal rights of women. In the fall of 1993, while hearing arguments in *Harris v. Forklift Systems,* only the second sexual harassment case to come before the Court, Justice Ginsburg asked if sexual harassment could not be defined simply as conduct that on the basis of an employee's sex makes it more difficult for one person than another to perform the job. Although legal experts had speculated that *Harris* would be decided on narrow grounds, the Court chose instead to stand on a "broad rule of workplace equality." Speaking for a unanimous Court only three weeks after hearing arguments, Justice Sandra Day O'Connor wrote an opinion that made sexual harassment easier to prove, while rejecting lower court decisons that required plaintiffs to demonstrate "severe psychological injury."

For three decades, then, a commitment to truth-telling, a heightened consciousness, a series of legal decisions extending women's equality, an expanding infrastructure of institutions, and a burgeoning political involvement all have worked together, the parts feeding into each other and stimulating the whole, to bring us to a new stage in a cultural revolution. These same elements are at work today, at heightened levels of effectiveness and intensity. And though the momentum will wax and wane, there is no going back.

14

WOMEN WHO GROUND THEIR LIVES IN HELPING OTHER WOMEN

I have a support system that never says, "We can't do it!"
— Gail Abarbanel

The belief that kills the spirit is the belief that we're stuck — that we cannot change our world — and it is mistaken. Real change is hard to make and often painful, but in the past thirty years, the women's movement has proved that we *can* make it and we *will*. In the context of that ongoing revolution, women who suffer sexual harassment and abuse can struggle, with Dr. Margaret Jensvold, to "see [their experience] in a bigger historical perspective" and work through it psychologically to a place like hers. "As awful as this has been, I'm really able to participate in effecting some positive change. When you've been harassed, discriminated against, and fired, and you're in federal court, why not tell the truth?" Why not, indeed?

For the silence of the victims and the shame that binds them to secrecy protects those who inflict the injuries at the same time it shores up a system that leaves abuse unpunished. This failure of justice and resolution then undermines the survivors further by making the offense seem inconsequential. But the women who account for the four stories that follow have all transformed abuse by gaining an insight into the attitudes and institutional structures that fostered it and then by devoting themselves to reshaping them. All of them acted in a historical moment alive with promise for women, and their courage came in part from the very cultural air they breathed.

The person most responsible for breaking silence, repudiating shame, and leading the way to a new stage in the battle for decency and equality in the United States is Anita Hill, a woman of breathtaking courage in the face of hostility that would have withered a lesser person. Hill's experience, in which so many women saw their own reflected, may have begun in Washington, but it went on long afterward. And since what she *made* of what happened before the Senate Judiciary Committee became a critical part of the experience itself, her method can serve as a model for others.

Little more than a year after the hearings, Hill told a rapt Washington, D.C., audience how she gradually came to terms with those confusing days and retraced the steps by which she grasped their meaning. With Emma Coleman Jordan, a member of her legal team, she held a conference at the Georgetown Law Center, a few blocks from the Russell Building where it all started. They called it "Race, Gender, and Power in America" and filled a large auditorium with a predominantly female audience convinced that Hill had been telling the truth.

From the podium, Hill spoke of "the daze in which the hearings left me" and told how she eventually put them in perspective by "reading and rereading, learning and relearning, thinking and rethinking." Stepping back from her own trauma, she'd looked to literature and the past for analogues and to statistics for a context; she'd used the familiar tools of the academic trade to help her understand what had happened so that she could move beyond the pain and build on the experience. From her reading, she had "learned of the denial, not only of the pain of the experiences [of women in slavery], but of the experiences themselves," Hill said. "And worse yet, I learned of the denial of the right of African-American women to *complain* of the experiences. I learned of the silencing of women who dared not speak about the abuse they experienced — the beatings, the rapes, the forced breedings, and the further denial of the humanity of slave women as their children were swept from their arms and sold into slavery."

Casting the hearings into the context of that heritage, she could alleviate the personal sting by seeing herself in the long line of African-American women who'd been abused by white America and then, too often, by their own people. From Zora Neale Hurston's novel *Our Eyes Were Watching God,* for instance, she took a powerful image. As Janie Crawford is tried for murder, she looks at a crowd of "colored" people in the back of the courtroom and realizes they hate her: "a light slap from each of them would have beat her to death." Listening to polls that showed the African-American community solidly against her, Hill felt a kinship with Janie.

But the year that followed restored her self-confidence. Though trashed in conservative magazines like *The American Spectator,* Hill received an avalanche of letters and telegrams, most of them from admirers. (By mid-December, two months after the hearings, the number was close to twenty-five thousand.) The National Coalition of Black Women presented her with its coveted Ida B. Wells Award. *Glamour* magazine named her one of its ten Women of the Year. And she was lionized by huge gatherings from New York City to San Diego, where women leapt onto chairs and tables to applaud her.*

Within this supportive community, Hill gradually discovered that she could finally analyze the way a fact-finding hearing had been twisted into the trial of one black woman. And she could take comfort in the fact if the polls didn't immediately show that the public "got it," people had watched an intelligent, well-educated, competent African-American woman; stereotypes like the welfare queen had been shattered; and many would never be the same.

What the senators did not expect, Hill concluded, was that "their abuse of power in the hearings — indeed, the hearings themselves — would become a metaphor for the sexual and gender abuses suffered by women through the experiences of battering, rape, incest, and harassment as well." Nor did they expect that in response, women would insist on telling their own stories and going back to study their own history as narratives they needed to share with a large community of women.

*In Washington, on the other hand, Senator Alan Simpson, one of her most vitriolic critics, was hissed by three hundred luncheon guests at the International Women's Forum, described in the *Los Angeles Times* as a "prominent group of executives, scientists and political leaders known for strict decorum and cautious, nonpartisan politics." Some women not only applauded but pounded their tables when Simpson complained that he and his colleagues on the Judiciary Committee had been "portrayed as totally insensitive asses."

And who could have imagined that 1,603 African-American women would sign a full-page ad in the *New York Times* insisting on their right to define their own lives and to speak out on racism and sexism? For tracing the path by which she transcended her own anguish, Anita Hill received yet another standing ovation. (Reporters in both the *New York Times* and *U.S. News & World Report* sniffed at the academic cast of Hill's presentation, however, so it would be well to understand that no matter what you do, somebody won't like it.)

A month later, Hill was the honored guest at the twentieth anniversary celebration of the National Women's Law Center, where a now famous academic and the women's world of legal activism sealed their collaboration. Comparing Hill's testimony to Rosa Parks's refusal to move to the back of the bus, which sparked the civil rights movement of the 1960s, Professor Susan Dellar Ross credited her with singlehandedly making the whole country talk about sexual harassment — "what it was, how it felt, and what to do about it" — and listed some of the tangible consequences: the 1991 Civil Rights Act; the scramble of employers to settle harassment claims and train their employees to recognize and prevent it; the Supreme Court's unanimous decision allowing a high school student harassed by a teacher to sue her school for damages; and a reenergized women's movement that in 1992 elected unprecedented numbers of women to public office at every level of government. With her "centered strength," Hill had made "vivid and real," as Ross put it, "the cost of a one-color, one-gender leadership."

Hill had the last word. "In 1980, when I graduated from Yale Law School," she began, "the Center was five years into its work, but I had never heard of the Center and the Center had certainly never heard of me." Its work had nonetheless helped poor women like her get the education they needed and then secure the jobs for which they were finally qualified. "Now that our paths have crossed," she said, "I don't think we will ever be separated again. I would like to move forward with you into a new century of real and true equality." Concluding with a quote from African-American poet Langston Hughes, who wanted to "make America American again," Hill beamed down on more than a thousand cheering women who had enlisted in the fight, and the movement was rolling.

In 1985, at forty-three, Penny Harrington became the first female police chief of a major city in the country. She'd gone to Michigan State University in her hometown and, in 1964, had joined the Portland,

Oregon, police department, where she stayed for more than a quarter century. Now she works in the Los Angeles area training police officers to see the dynamics of sexual harassment and helping them understand how to overcome it.

By a fluke I met a policewoman when I was a senior in high school. They had a career day, and I went just to get out of school. I'd never heard of a policewoman, but I spent the day with her and was enthralled. Right there, I decided that was what I was going to do. Michigan State happened to have a police administration program, one of the few in the nation, so I went there. I got married to a fellow student before I graduated. One of our professors moved to Oregon to be undersheriff, and he said, "Come out!" So we did. We were under the impression that we were both going to be hired as deputy sheriffs. Well, they hired my husband and didn't hire me. (They said they couldn't have a man and wife in the same department.) At the time, I never asked why. It was the way things were.

So I joined the city police department. At that time, women had to have a college education when men only had to have a GED [General Equivalency Diploma]. You couldn't work in a uniformed patrol, and you couldn't promote or transfer anywhere. That was your job for life. We had eighteen women out of about seven hundred men, and we got paid less, even though we had college degrees and the men didn't. Policewomen could only deal with women and children, so I became an expert in child abuse and sex offenses. It was a big shock.

When I started in the police department, I wasn't even aware of child abuse. I'd had child psychology courses, but they were more about the growing cycles of children. The department hadn't hired women in a very long time, so the ones there were a lot older. And they were nervous about going into some of the neighborhoods and didn't like to deal with these kinds of issues. So another woman and I became partners and worked almost all the child abuse cases.

At that time, child abuse didn't go through the regular court system; it went through the juvenile or domestic court system. So they wouldn't bring criminal charges for child abuse! You might be able to get somebody arrested for murder, and you could go in and get the child removed and put in a foster family. But *actually to go against the abuser—you couldn't do it!* Who can testify if the victim is a two-year-old? They want a competent witness. We got that changed! And it was because of one particular case.

One Saturday, I received a call to go to a doctor's office. He told me a young couple had brought their baby in with a broken arm and collarbone. They'd told him the baby had had his arm through the crib slats, and it had turned and gotten broken. He said, "That's not true. This is a green-stick fracture. You'd almost have to take the child's arm and twist it in order to break it this way." So the doctor wanted me to come see the child and talk to the parents and figure out what we could do.

I got up there and the parents were young—the mother was about sixteen, the father about eighteen—and they weren't married. The child was seven months old—a beautiful little boy—and they were sticking to their story. At that time, you had to have probable cause that this was a criminal act in order to take the child. So I said to the doctor, "They're not gonna admit anything, so I need to rely on your testimony." I went over what he'd told me on the phone and said, "If you'll testify to that, I can take the child." And he wouldn't do it. He said, "I'll get sued." So I could only write it up and send it to the courts.

About a month later, I got a call from some neighbors who said they heard a baby screaming and thought it was being abused. I got there, and it was the same couple, who were living then with her grandmother. You could see bruises on the baby—and cigarette burns. The grandmother was screaming at the father, and it was obvious that I had enough to take the child. The mother was saying, "He hurt my baby, I want him outta here." So I took the child into protective custody but couldn't do much about the father. I went into juvenile court to get permanent custody of the child. I was really concerned and told the judge, "Even though the mother is mad at the father today, he'll be back." But the judge said, "We don't have enough proof, and I believe the mother is trying." So she gave the child back to the mother and told her the father was not allowed to come around. I was *not* happy with that decision.

In another month, I got a call on a Sunday. It was a different address, but again a neighbor said, "This baby has been screaming and screaming. . . ." So I went out there, and when I saw the two of them standing on the porch, I knew the baby was dead. I asked 'em what was going on, and the father took off running. The mother took me upstairs, and I saw the baby. The father had picked him up by his feet and swung him into the wall and hit his head and killed him. That just tore me up. I put out information on the radio to arrest the guy for murder and went out to the court and yelled at the judge. The father got convicted of manslaughter and had to spend a little time in jail—not very long.

It was then that I decided the system was really messed up and there had to be a better way, and I became a fanatic about learning everything I could about child abuse. It was in the early stages of public awareness, and people were just beginning to come out with articles and reports. As I got better and knew what to look for and how to prove it, I finally had a good case and went to the district attorney with it. He was a new DA, and I had pictures of the child. It was alive, but it had been terribly beaten. I took the photographs one by one and put 'em down in front of him. He had children of his own, and he looked at those pictures and said, "We can't ignore this." So we arrested the father for assault and won. He went to jail.

Then the DA put it out to his people — and we put it out through the police department — that anybody who beats a child, we're gonna take through the criminal process on assault charges. We got quite good at investigating those cases, but finally I had to get out: I couldn't take it any more. By this time, I had my own baby. And to see these babies who were either terribly physically abused, or emotionally and mentally abused — or just so neglected that they looked like concentration camp victims — I couldn't deal with it after a while. I'd go home at night and find my son asleep in his crib, and I'd pick him up and cry. I felt so powerless: there were so many children and not very many of us. And it took so long and so much to get 'em removed — it was horrible! So I said, "I need a rest." I'd worked with abused children for eight years. Thank God some people can stick with it.

Before I could be police chief, I had to change the laws — and it was this last incident that did it. I decided I wanted out of the child abuse unit — I needed to work with facts and figures, and paper and pencil, for a little while and get away from people — but they wouldn't let me out. So I had to challenge the laws that kept women closeted in that little division and finally forced 'em to transfer me to a planning unit. I forced changes in the promotional system. Then I had to fight toe-to-toe with the men to be accepted on their level — all the way up the police department. And finally, after twenty-three years of struggle, I was made chief.

For a year and a half, I lived with the press. They never left; local, national, international — Germany . . . Paris. I never had to call my parents because they could read the paper and find out what I was doing. I put in a no-smoking policy, and it made headline news across the country. It was fun, but you had no privacy and it was a time-drainer. But I wouldn't have changed it for the world, and I'm proud of what I was able to do.

When I started in the police department, the men kinda ignored us women. In fact, they liked us because we'd take dirty kids off their hands. But *once we broke the barriers and got women out in patrols and in various parts of the police department, the men became very threatened and reacted in a very hostile way.*

When I finally went into a precinct in uniform, most men were fine, but several felt there was no way they were gonna take orders from a woman — a woman didn't belong in uniform. So I'd come to work in the morning and there'd be used condoms in my desk drawer. Or pictures of some really obnoxious pornography, with my name written over the woman's head and a criminal's name written on the man's. It was kinda constant — remarks, touching. . . .

I'd just throw the stuff out. I didn't want 'em to see they were gettin' to me in any way, but they were. It came at you at such a gut level because it was violence! You knew somebody out there hated you — for no reason other than that you were a woman. It's hard not to take it personally when the condom's in *your* drawer.

For years, I'd been filing sex discrimination complaints to get the rules changed and take promotion exams, so I was the focal point of the men's anger. At the beginning I'd try to reason with 'em when they said, "Women can't be detectives," or "Women can't be sergeants." But finally, I saw that no amount of reasoning was gonna change anything. It was fundamentally irrational.

By this time I was divorced, so I was a single parent raising my son. My sister joined the department about five years after I did, so we were emotional supports for each other and living together at the time. And I had a really good woman friend who had a son the same age as mine, so when the department was retaliating by changing my days off, calling me on holidays, putting me on weird shifts, she'd take care of my son. We called her his other mother. If I hadn't had her and my sister, I couldn't have done what I did.

I don't necessarily recommend my approach. But any time anybody said anything sexist to me, I was in their face. If you called me a girl, I was right in your face saying, "Don't call me a girl!" Or if you asked me for coffee, I was liable to say go fuck yourself, pour your own coffee. My language became as rough as theirs. (There's shock value in those words coming out of a woman's mouth: it stunned 'em.) They got so they wouldn't say those things to me any more. They'd say 'em to other women, but they left me alone. So I took this confrontational position all the way through.

A good percentage of the department supported what I did, because changing the rules — getting 'em in writing and getting 'em published — made it fair for everybody. I've had many men come to me and say, "If it weren't for you, I wouldn't have been hired, because I wasn't five ten or whatever." So I had a lotta support. But there was a core group of diehards who weren't gonna support a woman in any capacity.

By the time I got to be a lieutenant, I thought we had it pretty much in hand. Gross behavior wasn't tolerated and we'd made some massive strides.

But one day I walked in and found the captain of the precinct with the secretary backed up against the filing cabinet. He had his hands on her, and I went over and pulled him off. She was crying, and I told him to go home. When he left, I tried to find out what she wanted to do. And she didn't want to do anything! So I called the chief, told him what I'd seen, and asked him to do something. He assigned one of the deputy chiefs to investigate. The captain who'd done this was leaving for a two-week vacation, so we had a little breathing space. The secretary told 'em she was afraid of him and afraid for her job. They told me they were gonna take some action against him, and I was pretty satisfied that things were gonna be taken care of.

Then he came in to get his check. I happened to be in the precinct when he walked in, and I was startled. He went to his office and called me back there to ask for an update because I was acting commander while he was gone. And while we were standing there talking, out of the blue he grabbed my hand and shoved it across his crotch. I was so shocked! There was no lead-up to this — *I was telling him who was sick and what crimes were going on. I was so astonished that all I did was react: I pulled my hand away and punched him and knocked him down. It happened so fast!* I heard a noise and turned around and saw two of my officers standing there laughing. I helped him up and told him to get outta there and not come back until he'd talked to the deputy chief. Then I called the chief and told him what had happened. He laughed and said, "I've gotcha now!" — hitting my commanding officer and all that — but he was really shocked. None of us had expected the guy to come back.

So they called him into the office and were gonna fire him. But he said it wasn't true, I was making up these charges because I was trying to run everything. He was just trying to keep me in my place! Then they chewed *me* out for unprofessional conduct in not being able to get along with this man and transferred *me* out of the precinct! So even when you think you've raised consciousness to a level where those things aren't gonna happen, they still do. They believe the man and put their heads in the sand.

Then a new mayor came in and put me in charge. Shortly after I became chief, some women came to me about a sergeant who was harassing 'em in the roll call. At that time we had teletypes, and information would come in from agencies across the United States about people they thought were gonna be in Oregon — wanted people, that kinda thing. And you'd read these out at roll call so everyone would know. Sometimes bizarre things came over the teletype, and one day the man they were looking for had a tattoo on his penis! So they read that out at roll call. There were a coupla women officers there, and the sergeant started in on 'em with sexual remarks, like, "If we find this guy, we'll call you gals over to check him out and see." Or "Do you want me to draw a picture of what it looks like?" That kinda thing—harassment in front of the entire roll call. The women would complain to their lieutenant, and he'd say, "Aw, that's just the way he is." Like, can't you take a little ribbing?

So one night this woman stopped a van. The guy was a suspect, and she got permission to search it. When she opened the back, it was loaded with pornographic books, sex toys, and lingerie. He probably had some kinda store he was working out of. This same sergeant had driven by to cover the call, so he gets in the van and starts picking up the sex toys and making remarks about 'em, saying why don't they go to a motel room and test this stuff out? And holding the lingerie up in front of her. People on the sidewalk were listening to this. That was the final straw for her.

She got the other women together and they filed a complaint against him, and it came to me for discipline. He'd lied during the investigation, and we'd been able to prove it. And when I took over as chief, I'd said there were three things I wouldn't tolerate: lying, excessive force, and disrespect. So lying was a firing offense, and they knew the chances were he'd get fired. So the women called me and said, "We want to withdraw the complaint!" I said, "Why? I'm gonna fire him." And they said, "Our life will be a living hell if we get him fired. These men are gonna retaliate on us. Please don't do it." I was really upset that they were putting me in this position. I said, "We *have* to take a stand! We *cannot* allow this to happen." *And they said—this really got me—'Chief, you just can't imagine what it would be like!' I'm the one who'd opened the door for all of 'em to be there, and they're telling me I can't understand.* So I didn't fire him, but he got some pretty severe discipline, like a thirty-day suspension, and I said next time, he was out the door. But any time a male was disciplined for sex harassment, there *was* retaliation. Any time a woman complained, she'd pay.

Everybody wants to be part of the group and do a good job. Some women have tried to be like the men to gain acceptance, so they put down the other women. They go out drinking with the boys. They adopt the male way of policing: they're rude, crude, and tattooed. The men think it's funny if they can get the women fighting among each other. But these women find out down the road a piece that those men are the first ones who're gonna throw 'em to the wolves. It's only the other women who'll help them and be their support. It takes a while for 'em to get it.

The men'll welcome some of them with open arms. If they think there's a gal who's got it on the ball—she's real strong, she jogs, she plays pool, she's one of the boys—they'll sorta bring her in. She'll think she's all the way in, but she's not. Then they'll put her up to things. Or they'll say things about the other women and she won't dare say anything because then she'd lose her position with them. It's a vicious thing that happens.

We have to stand up for each other. I fought awfully hard for a lotta years and paid a tremendous price to make changes and open the doors to let other women in. And then I mentored them, I stood up for them and fought their battles. And *when I see 'em giving away what I paid so dearly for by not confronting men when they do these things, by going along to get along—it makes me angry. They don't know how bad it was, but it'll get that bad again if they don't keep fighting. We need to walk 'em through history.*

Born and raised in California, Molly McElrath just turned thirty, and her experience with sexual harassment in housing has been going on since she was twenty-four. I met her in Catherine Hanson's home in Vacaville, where they've set up their offices for WRATH, Women Refusing to Accept Tenant Harassment. They are blondes who complement each other. Molly is at once voluptuous and innocent-looking; Cathy is rail-thin, sharp-edged, and shrewd.

In 1989, they led a group of fifteen women in a lawsuit against the owner of Fairfield North Apartments and won better than $1.6 million in settlement. With a $10,000 donation from their attorneys, along with several grants, they then set up WRATH. Their work involves them in doing group interventions, explaining their civil rights to tenants, discussing the dynamics of group organizing, helping tenant groups find attorneys, and supporting the process as it evolves. Both have given up careers to focus on it, and Molly predicts that by 1994, claims of sexual harassment in housing will be front-page news across the country. I asked Molly to tell their story — the choice was arbitrary — but Cathy now and again threw in a clarifying word.

More than seventy-five newspaper and magazine articles have been written about them and WRATH, and along with six other former tenants, they appeared on the Oprah Winfrey show. As I described above, several women in the audience were hostile, and when Winfrey came to shake hands afterward, Cathy folded her arms and said, "I didn't fly two thousand miles for this shit." Molly cried. Then they argued that Winfrey hadn't prepared well for the show. Before the encounter with sexual harassment that she recounts here, Molly describes herself as essentially passive, so this experience has not only changed her professional focus, it has also changed her character.

I have two sets of parents—my mother and father were divorced when I was five—so I have a mix of southern and northern California attitudes because I've gone back and forth between them. At twenty-four, I was considered passive, naive, and trusting. I was a people-pleaser because of the dynamics in my family structure. My dad was an alcoholic for many years, and when you grow up in that kind of home, you tend to try to keep everybody happy. My parents confided their problems in me, and from the time I was young, I felt a responsibility to fix their problems and make them feel better. By the time I was an adult, I was kind to people I probably shouldn't have been kind to. If someone asked me to do something, I always said yes. I didn't want to disappoint anybody.

I got pregnant when I was seventeen and was supposed to give up my daughter for adoption. (My parents told me that's what I should do.) But about two weeks before I gave birth, I realized I couldn't do it and had to call the adoptive parents I'd chosen and tell them it wasn't going to happen. I finished high school eight months pregnant, and about two months after she was born, my father put me on a train and sent me north. He said I had to get out of the San Fernando Valley. My daughter's father was interfering in my life a lot and was real abusive. If I was going to have any chance, I had to get away from him.

Mom helped me get an apartment. I had a coupla roommates, but that didn't work out. One moved in the middle of the night without paying her rent; another had such bad personal problems that they interfered. I was on AFDC [Aid for Dependent Children], and nobody in my family had ever been dependent on any kind of system.

Then I got to be friends with Cathy Hanson. She'd been homeless and desperate: she had two kids and nowhere to go. So she'd called Fairfield North Apartments to see if they had any vacancies. It was a HUD [Housing and Urban Development] complex—that means 20 percent of the units were subsidized. And the woman manager took her in. Cathy didn't have to go through a waiting process, which she should've had to do. She got an apartment and started college, and I'd go there to visit her. I saw her really change: she was more stable and really excited about college. When I went to her apartment, she'd have her typewriter out and she'd be getting A's on her papers. And I thought that was neat. I'd sit there and say, "Gosh, you're so lucky! You've got a two-bedroom apartment in a nice neighborhood."

I was going to beauty college, but I was about to get tossed out on the street, so I was facing homelessness. My mom's husband got very upset when she suggested that I stay with them for a coupla weeks. So I rented a house with another woman, who moved abruptly. Everybody else I interviewed was a nut, and the house flooded. So I filled out an application for the Fairfield North Apartments, and the same manager Cathy got in under gave me an apartment. (She liked me, and since my mom came with me, she liked the idea that I had support.) I only had to wait a month, so I really lucked out.

Since Cathy lived downstairs, we became even better friends. After six months, we got new apartment managers who were really good to the low-income tenants: they got us new carpeting, treated us with respect, and took a lotta personal interest in us and our successes. If we felt we'd be a week late on rent, they were supportive as long as we eventually paid it.

Six months later, Jim Skinner and his wife took their places. We didn't have any notice they'd be taking over. He just knocked on our doors with a piece of paper telling about his background and saying he'd had years of management experience. He said he wanted this apartment complex to have a family atmosphere and wanted to do a really good job. He was about thirty-five — overweight, short, round-faced, with a military haircut — and he had a southern accent. He seemed full of energy, but that first day when he knocked on my door, he never looked me in the eye.

I didn't have any problems with him for a while, but one day I was sitting with a girl at the pool who pointed to somebody across the way and said, "She's sleeping with Jim." I said, "You're kidding! Why would she do something like that?" And she said, "She's getting her rent free." I kept hearing stories like that. I didn't think he was actually coercing women, but I began to notice that whenever I left — even if it was at five-thirty in the morning — he was walking around patrolling the complex. If I came home at two A.M., he'd be there, coming out of someone's apartment.

About this time, Cathy and I formed a support group, and we were trying to get our bylaws incorporated so we could have a nonprofit organization called SPARCS [Single Parents Action Resource Committee and Supporters]. I'd started going to college, and for awhile I worked full-time as a hairdresser. But my boss fired me because I was studying between appointments. So Cathy and I were both in college, and we thought it was amazing that all the women we knew who were on welfare were *not* in college, when you can get a Pell grant to help you get educated and get off welfare. (It's easy to get on and hard to get off.) You can also get Lifeline, which is a telephone company supplement for low-income people. We found out that the SEOC [Salano County Economic Opportunity Council] provided for child care. And we started helping women fill out the forms for Pell grants.

Cathy's a very strong, articulate, frightfully intelligent person. I'm six years younger and I learned a lot from her. She protected me from the evils of the world; if I couldn't do something, she'd do it for me. So even though I was learning a lot watching her be assertive, she was very protective of me and I was too dependent: I needed her to do things for me as much as she needed to do them, and that's how it was for a long time. It was like having my mom live next door. She'd tell me not to be passive, and then she'd say, "In the meantime, I'm gonna beat up the guy who just broke your heart." Her boyfriend did the same thing.

We were starting to get suspicious of Jim Skinner. We'd be walking along, and a woman would open the door and drag us into her apartment. She'd lock the door, drag us into her bedroom, close all the curtains, and make us sit on the floor beside her bed. And then she'd start crying and telling us what Jim was doing to her. We'd say, "We knew he was a jerk, but is he this much of a jerk? Guess he is." Cathy tried to avoid him, and I was always nice to him. Neither way worked.

One day we came home from school, and for some reason I didn't have my keys. So I went to him and said, "Will you let us into my apartment?" When he was letting me in, I saw a note taped to the door and said, "What's this?" And he said, "It's a love letter from your secret admirer. Do you know who that is?" I said, "No." And he said, "It's me." My first thought was that he was just being goofy, but Cathy started warning me about him.

We were beginning to get mail for our organization, and we used Cathy's mailbox as our address. Almost every day we'd get something exciting — a letter of encouragement or an agency reaching out to us. But the mailbox is right next to Jim's office, and one day he came out and said, "Do you guys belong to Parents without Partners?" We were so excited we started telling him about SPARCS. Then he got upset and said that under no circumstances could we operate this organization out of our home; it was an illegal business, and he told us to disband. We later realized that he was threatened because we were helping women, we had contacts within the community, and women were starting to confide in us.

I had finally qualified with the SEOC to get my child care paid for so I could go to college. It meant $250 more a month, so that was really terrific. They sent me a registered letter to inform me, but he wrote on it "Tenant no longer lives here" and sent it back. I found out a month later when I got a phone call asking for my new address. I said, "I haven't moved." *They told me what he'd written on the envelope, and then I knew he was after me.* I'd baked the Skinners cookies at Christmas. Like other women, I'd befriended his wife, thinking that would help. I'd conversed with him and consoled him. I'd given him my queen-sized bed for his in-laws to use, hoping to avoid harassment that way.

I knew Jim referred to me as "the blonde with the big tits," and I thought he was making fun of me because I'd been made fun of in high school about it. (Like somebody who has a big nose is sensitive about that.) Once I was at the pool, and he said, "Why don't you put on that yellow bikini you had on the other day?" You feel belittled and degraded, and I felt responsible for opening up that conversation by wearing that bikini once.

When tenants began to come up and say, "Are you sleeping with Jim?" that was very threatening, since I knew what was happening to other women and I knew darn well that's exactly what he'd say. I'd say, "Where did you hear this?" and a couple said they'd heard it from the maintenance workers. One day I went to pay my rent, and he said, "Shut the door." And then he said, "Did you hear that we're having an affair?" I couldn't believe that came out of his mouth. I said, "Exactly what are you talking about?" He said, "We're having an affair!" I know that sounds weird.

He was really trying to get me to have a sex talk with him, but I didn't understand that yet, so I said, "When are we having this affair?" And he said, "When I take my garbage out. People ask me why I take my garbage out on your side of the building, rather than my side." I said, "What does your wife think about all this?" And he said, "I don't want my wife to find out, and she's starting to get suspicious." He was talking as if we really were having an affair. That was so confusing, and I couldn't figure out how to approach him and say, "Stop this. . . ."

I did ask Jim, laughing, "You don't really think we're having an affair, do you?" And he said, "It's not me; it's your blonde friend, Cathy." He'd tell me she was low-life and I was better than her, and he told some tenants that Cathy's business was actually a prostitution ring. (He'd refer to the women who went to the monthly tenants' support group meetings as her "girls.") He also accused her of being an alcoholic. Since I came from an alcoholic background, that was threatening, and sometimes she seemed to be suffering from a hangover. I'd go to her apartment, and she'd be sitting in bed moaning and groaning, and then she'd run to the bathroom. I'd leave feeling really distressed, and he'd see me leaving and say, "She's no good."

Cathy turned out to have diverticulitis, which is an intestinal disease and rare for somebody so young, and she was having attacks five or six times a week. It's related to stress, and she'd be in the bathroom for seven hours or so and have the kinds of pains you'd normally associate with appendicitis. Often she'd pass out. But the disease had been misdiagnosed, and neither one of us knew what was going on.

So Jim told me if I continued the friendship, he'd evict me, and he did things on the sly to make me feel more vulnerable. He got Child Protective Services to contact me and say they heard I was leaving my daughter alone. They could take her away, and so that was another weapon he could use against me. I couldn't tell Cathy the truth about why I was cutting off from her. So Cathy and I didn't talk to each other for two years. It was devastating.

But I was very happy there. My daughter had her own bedroom, it's in an upper-class neighborhood, and the alternative was some apartments that by now have been demolished because they were so disgusting. So I really wanted to hold on to what I had.

There was another woman, Annette, who's just like Cathy, and Jim succeeded in separating us too. He said, "I want you to write a letter to me, saying that Annette is a terrible mother. I want you to say her eight-year-old son hit your daughter." I said, "I can't do that." And he said, "If you don't, I'll evict you." Those words were too hard for me to hear. He grabbed me by the arm and dragged me onto the balcony of his office. And he pointed to my apartment — you could see right into it from there. He said, "I have a log of your male visitors' comings and goings, and that's against HUD policy." I didn't know whether it was or wasn't, but it didn't matter. *If he wanted to evict me, he didn't have to give "just cause."* So for seven days straight, he hassled me into writing that letter.

Much later, Annette invited tenants to come to a meeting in her apartment to talk about problems we were having, and two Legal Aid attorneys were gonna be there. I was on my way to the meeting, and Jim was hiding behind the bushes and jumped out and said, "I know where you're going. I'm gonna evict every woman who goes." But I was feeling more and more that I was disappointing my friends, and I had to find my way out of this — a rock to climb up on. So I went to the meeting, and every time there was a knock on the door, people would push each other outta the way to get into the kitchen or the bathroom. People even hid behind the curtains. That's when I raised my hand and told Annette what I'd done. I was really crying. Annette's really a great person, and she took it fine.

But the Legal Aid attorneys eventually dropped the case altogether. They didn't even understand what sexual harassment was and didn't understand it was a form of sex discrimination. They failed us miserably, and that made Jim feel great. He *did* evict some women for going to the meeting, and then I *really* started to panic. *It wasn't that we were so naive, like it said in the press. Skinner had real leverage, and he got tenants to spy on other tenants and lie about them. People say, "Why didn't you just move?" But you have to have money to do that, and you have to get references from the last place you've lived in order to be admitted somewhere else. By then, Cathy and I had both lived there for years, and Jim was gonna ruin our credit and give us bad references.*

Cathy had written a letter to notify the owner that his manager was acting in this way, and she thought he'd be worried about being liable. Eleven tenants were brave enough to sign it, but the owner never talked to 'em. The response said that maybe we'd resisted Jim's management style and were faithful to the previous manager. Annette had written more than a hundred letters to HUD, but they turned around and investigated *her* and sent the paperwork to the management company, which let Jim Skinner know. So he said Annette did drugs and was trying to cheat HUD. For six months she thinks HUD's investigating him, when they're investigating her!

So we'd really been trying! We'd tried tenants' meetings; we'd written the owner; we'd gotten in touch with the agencies; we'd gotten in touch with the National Organization for Women in Sacramento, and they said they usually chose one or two political issues a year, and this year, sexual harassment wasn't one of them. (This was right before the Anita Hill business.) I called Congressman Vic Fazio's office, and they said it wasn't a congressional matter. I called a sexual harassment clinic and asked for a list of attorneys. Six weeks later, they called back and asked if I still needed the list. Several attorneys we contacted said we were too high-risk—we were low-income, and they couldn't see how sexual harassment could apply to housing.

Then Cathy and Annette moved out, and with the two thorns in his side gone, for a whole year things got worse: he started actually molesting and trying to rape women. He was asking women to pose in their lingerie, and a coupla women gave in to his sexual demands. Finally, it got so bad I decided that if I didn't do something, nothing was ever gonna happen. So I started talking to tenants and hearing *even worse* stories. One night a woman woke up, and he was standing there with his pants down. Her mother reported it to a state agency, and they sent an investigator, who let Skinner intimidate tenants into not talking. The mother kept pushing and went to HUD and found the attorney we ended up getting. Now we had an investigator, Paul Smith, who was on the case and on the ball.

Finally Cathy and I started talking to each other. I saw her at a local tavern with her husband—she'd moved out about ten months earlier—and I wrote on a cocktail napkin, "Please talk to me. I'm so sorry!" and the bartender took it down to her and made a big deal about presenting it. Cathy couldn't handle it on the spot, but her husband came up and said, "You know, she really loves you, and she's been real hurt." He was thrilled.

So we finally got together. I went over to her house and told her everything that had happened, and it made perfect sense to her. I did the same for Annette. Then the three of us could operate together, and a month later, HUD got re-involved. I finally insisted to the Child Protective Services that they *had* to tell me who'd reported me. They said that was privileged information, but *I said, "You don't understand. I've been reported for welfare fraud, I've been reported to HUD, now I've been reported to Child Protective Services—all of this for things I'm not doing! I'm a really good mother, and everybody around me is complaining about unfounded reports. What is going on?"* Then she said, "Wait a minute. You live at the Fairfield North Apartments?" I said, "Yes," and she said, "It never occurred to me. We're getting calls from one person about people in that complex. . . ." She wasn't supposed to be telling me this, but I was crying so hard.

I moved out of the complex—I was getting married—but I was determined to do something about this. Paul Smith called and asked me to go back to give women his phone number. I didn't want to do it—I was so nervous—but Cathy said, "Here's a clipboard. If you take this, anybody'll talk to you." And it worked! Some women shut the door on me, but others pulled me in and closed all the curtains and started talking. Jim was taking one woman's food stamps in partial payment for the rent, which is illegal. Then I told the new assistant manager what he was saying about her, and it made her so mad she ran over and called the owner.

For two and a half years, we hadn't been able to get through to the owner! So here Janie's on the phone with Betty Lou, their representative, and I grabbed the phone and said, "Betty, I want to talk to the owner." She said, "I'm sorry, but he's not in town." So I said, "I want to forewarn you"—I'm making this up as I go—"that we've been painting signs, and tomorrow morning, we'll have pickets outside the apartment complex. We're beginning a rent strike, and we also have three interviews set up with the media." (It wasn't a total lie; one reporter was interviewing me as the commencement speaker, and I told her what had been happening and she said they might want to report on it.)

I got caught up in the moment, actually, and Janie was standing there getting so excited. Betty said to stay where I was. Within five minutes the owner called me. (He's the guy who'd been outta town!) And he was really freaking out. Saying he was an honorable businessman, hadn't heard about all this, blah, blah, blah. *Finally he said, "I'll do all these thing if you'll promise not to sue me."* And we said to ourselves, 'Sue him!' We hadn't thought of that.

He wanted to meet with me and one woman who'd been sexually harassed by Jim. It was better than nothing. Just then Jim knocked on the door and said, "Step outside." So I did. He was there with his wife, and he said, "Are you making people sign petitions that I'm sexually harassing tenants?" *I meant to say no, I really did. But I said, "Yes!"*

He turned red and his eyes bugged out. And he tried to grab my clipboard with all the notes that said, "He tried to grab my breast," or "He did thus and so to me," and we had a tug-of-war. He grabbed my arm and said, "I'm gonna have you arrested." And I said, "For what?" He said, "For trespassing. You don't live here anymore." I didn't know whether I really could be; the police had been called a million times and always took his side. His wife just stood there. She thought everybody'd turned against her, and she'd say, "He ain't no pervert." So *he ran off to have a heart attack, and I went in and called Cathy.* She said, "Stay right there." I called Paul at HUD, and he wrote a complaint for me over the phone about Jim's manhandling me. And he told me I *did* have a right to be there. So that made me feel a lot better.

Then I decide it's time the welfare department knew about this food stamp stuff he'd been doing. So I call them, and it's my lucky day. Usually the fraud investigator's out working in the field, but this guy, Jim Boyer, gets on the phone and all this stuff comes outta me in about two minutes.

"Where'd you say this was happening?"

"Fairfield North Apartments."

"We've been investigating Jim Skinner for welfare fraud for over a year now, but we were about to close the case because we didn't have enough evidence."

I told him we were about to have a meeting with the owners, and he said, "I want to be there." I felt like I was on "Mission Impossible." He said he'd get there an hour early, and we should pretend he was somebody local.

Mind you, I'm getting married in three days now. Cathy's going to be my maid of honor after our not talking for two years; we're making flowers for the wedding; I was finishing up with finals, graduating from college, getting ready to give the commencement speech — and here I am, spending two weeks knocking on doors getting signatures on a petition. This became an obsession for all of us.

So here's the meeting! I don't know how the word got out. All of a sudden there are fifteen women and two men at the door. Boyer, the guy from the welfare department, comes in; Paul Smith's there. They look exactly like they're supposed to, briefcases and all. Mark Chim, the owner, walks in, expecting to find two tenants, and here are seventeen, not counting us. You shoulda seen his face! So I introduce myself and shake his hand. I'm trying to be nice 'cause I figure Cathy won't be. But we have to create an atmosphere so he'll incriminate himself!

He sits down, and right off, Cathy asks if he's aware of the letter dated June whatever, with all the sexual harassment complaints, and when he says no, she hands him a copy so he can review it. He thinks Cathy's the attorney, and so then *they* start interrogating *him!* He gets so flustered, because there's so much hostility, that he starts contradicting himself. Cathy's furiously taking notes.

Chim's scared to death — he has strict liability — so he wants us to talk about sex harassment, and we don't know whether we want to yet, because we don't trust him. We're talkin' about being spied on, and all that stuff, and say, "If you want to see our evidence, you can talk to our attorneys." (Which we did not have.) And then Jim Boyer stands up and says, "Mr. Chim, I think you have enough to fire this man without making them talk about the sex harassment." But there was a woman who'd come to the meeting as a spy for Skinner, and even she stands up and tells about how she'd come from a battered women's shelter, and when she gave him cash for the first month's rent, he reached over and put his hands between her legs and said, "I'll take anything you've got!" — in front of her eight-year-old daughter.

Chim turns bright red. Then he says, "How many women here have been sexually harassed?" Nobody really knew. And one by one, about three-fourths of the hands in the room go up. Chim fired Skinner. But he gave him three months' severance pay and a letter of recommendation. So we sued Chim and won $1.6 million!

Initially fifteen of us filed a civil suit, and then Cathy and I found eight other people who'd been subjected to Skinner's threats, and the Department of Justice represented them. Outside those twenty-three women, we know of twenty others we couldn't locate because they'd moved. The case was mediated by the judge and settled out of court. We wanted to get the litigation part over with and get on to the public-awareness part because we thought this was probably happening everywhere — which we're finding to be true. There's a case in Chicago, with fifteen women. There's one in Ohio, with ten women. The NAACP Legal Defense Fund had a case in Wisconsin with twenty-five women. *When sexual harassment connects with housing, it seems to happen to a large number of women. In offices, three or four might be hit on by one guy. In housing, you're talking about one perpetrator and maybe twenty-five women.*

Our case showed that it's winnable. And it established monetary amounts, even though ours were relatively low: adults got from fourteen thousand to sixty thousand dollars, children got two thousand to six thousand. (All thirty-six children were included as plaintiffs because they witnessed their moms being sexually harassed and discriminated against.) Ours were still higher than any previous awards for sex harassment.

In the spring of 1992, the government released a survey estimating that more than 680,000 women had been raped in 1990 — a figure five times higher than the number of sexual assaults actually reported for that year by the Justice Department. (Fewer than one-fourth were raped by strangers.) Since the estimate did not include children or adolescents, the survey speculated that this figure accounted for less than half the rapes in the United States. It went on to estimate, further, that 12.1 million American women have been forcibly raped at least once, over 60 percent of them as minors; almost 30 percent before they were eleven years old; and just over 30 percent between the ages of eleven and seventeen.[1]

Gail Abarbanel, director of the Rape Treatment Center in Santa Monica, California, has never been raped herself, but in helping women who have, she's created an organization so effective that her facilities should be replicated throughout the country. Abarbanel started the Rape Treatment Center in 1974 to provide all the services victims need — medical, legal, and psychological — in one place. Offering twenty-four-hour assistance, the center evolved in response to particular experiences and shows what commitment, passion, and camaraderie can do when linked firmly together.

By now, almost fifteen thousand victims and their families have gotten free, expert care from the center, which has been nationally recognized and is beginning to have worldwide influence. The center has widely disseminated statistics like the following:

A rape is reported once every six minutes, and this figure may represent only 10 percent of the actual rapes.

In half of all reported rapes, the victim, the offender, or both, are teenagers.

Four out of five teenage rape victims are assaulted by someone they know.

In 1984, after the McMartin preschool case of alleged child abuse made front-page headlines across the nation, and a television movie on incest, *Something About Amelia,* was aired, the Rape Treatment Center was flooded with requests to treat child victims. (In 1989, 114,000 cases were reported in Los Angeles County alone.) And so Abarbanel established Stuart House, which treats sexually abused children in a unique one-stop center where they can be given medical attention and psychiatric help, and can be interviewed by police and prosecutors. A landmark article about incest in *Lear's* magazine featured Stuart House as a model program for the nation. As Abarbanel puts it, "We wanted to do something to change the system and come up with a better program for children. There are two issues — justice and healing. That's what Stuart House is about."[2]

In an interview with the *Los Angeles Times,* Abarbanel was asked what she personally brought to the Rape Treatment Center, and she said, "A strong sense of justice, I think, and maybe an ability to take what we learn from victims and translate it into social action and programs and reforms that have created an environment in which victims receive better treatment." Gail Abarbanel has made a difference in many lives and taught others how to help her do it.

I got involved by chance in 1974, eighteen years ago. I have a master's degree in social work, and I was Santa Monica Hospital's first social worker. It's a private community hospital that really has a heart, so I got requests from everybody to do everything—cancer patients, cardiac patients, pediatric patients. And one day I was called to the emergency room to see a woman who had attempted suicide. She inspired the creation of the Rape Treatment Center.

She had gone for a walk on the beach on a Sunday afternoon, and a stranger raped her very brutally. Nobody talked about rape that early in the seventies, and she felt a deep sense of shame and fear. She was afraid of the way her family might react, and so she told no one. A week later, she slashed her wrists. When I saw her—and then discovered that she'd been raped—I was profoundly affected by the experience. *In trying to find a way out, she expressed the heart of the rape problem in this country: silence and secrecy. Society blames the victim, although the first step in the healing process is talking about it.*

I was so moved by her experience that I decided to see any rape victims who came to this hospital, so I went to the emergency room and offered my services. But if the rape happened in the middle of the night and I wasn't there, and then I tried to reach the victim at a later time, after she'd gone home, it wasn't as effective. So we decided to begin a twenty-four-hour service for rape victims.

Ours was one of the first hospitals in the country to provide a full range of services. At that time, there were a lot of complaints about hospital responses to victims and the way they were treated by the police. (Too often, people were callous.) Some women's groups advised victims not to report their rapes to the police. They were well motivated, in that they wanted to protect women from being re-victimized, but I felt that this would not solve the problem. Instead, we began to provide training to police departments and hospitals to increase their understanding of rape trauma and help them learn to respond more sensitively.

Every major achievement we've had at the Rape Treatment Center has come out of our work with an individual woman. From the beginning, we not only provided services for victims but tried to change attitudes, systems, laws, and policies that kept them silent. We saw all those things as part of our mission. The Rape Treatment Center has always been structured differently from rape crisis centers because it is hospital-based; we've always had professional staff, rather than volunteers, doing treatment; and we've always advocated for long-term, in-depth treatment for victims because we've seen the trauma they suffer and their favorable response to treatment. Over time, we've changed our thinking, recognizing that crisis services are not enough for recovery.

We are a voice for victims because they're a part of everything we do. That's what makes this work so rewarding and inspiring. People always say to me, "How do you do this work? Isn't it hard and depressing?" *But dealing with victims isn't hard. It's the confrontation with the system that's hard and can be depressing. When you work with victims, you see their incredible strength and courage. They're remarkable women who really touch your life.*

We had a case involving a college student in library science who was taking a public bus from her job, which was in downtown Los Angeles, back to the campus. She was the last passenger left on the bus, and when she went to get off, the driver said, "There's only one way you're getting off this bus." She tried to escape by getting to the lever and opening the door, but he had control of the locking mechanism. She begged and pleaded and reasoned with him to let her off the bus. He came and grabbed her. It was a hot day in a stuffy bus, and she went into shock. She absolutely froze! So he took her to the back of the bus and raped her.

As in most states, our rape laws defined rape as intercourse accomplished against the will of the person: she resists, but her resistance is overcome by force and violence; or she is prevented from resisting by the threat of great and immediate bodily harm. So what happened on the bus didn't qualify as rape, because of her "nonresistance," and the district attorney rejected the case.

Crimes like robbery and assault — and even the other sexual-assault crimes that men can be victims of, like sodomy or forced oral copulation — had no victim-resistance requirement. So this was a very discriminatory law because it meant that women were expected to behave differently from other crime victims. And the law focused more on the behavior of the victim than the conduct of the assailant. No matter what he did on that bus, if she didn't resist — according to their definition of resistance — it wasn't going to be considered rape.

So we decided to change the law! And we used this case to educate the public and the legislature about resistance. We went to Mel Levine, our assemblyman, who later became our congressman. We got a great editorial in the *Los Angeles Times*. And the bill ended up passing without a single dissenting vote.

After several years, the hospital could not support any further development for the Rape Treatment Center, because it had grown so much and they just didn't have the resources. I was upset and frustrated, but it forced me to go out into the community to get support. And without that support, I don't think I would have been able to change the law or do many of the other things the Rape Treatment Center has done.

In 1977, Norman Lear was making an episode of "All in the Family" dealing with rape, and they called and asked if I would be a consultant. Norman said to me, "If you could talk to forty million people about rape, what would you say?" That was his challenge! So I worked with them on that episode, which turned into a one-hour special instead of a half-hour show. And it was a real milestone in public consciousness about rape because it got a huge amount of publicity. It was a comedy show, and Edith Bunker was a beloved character. A lot of producers would *not* have let a person in that role become a rape victim or the victim of attempted rape, and they had to deal with a serious subject like this in the context of comedy. But the way they handled it was brilliant.

When they did the show, they also funded a huge national outreach program. We wrote a study guide and program notes on what the show demonstrated about rape, and we sent them to every agency we could find in the whole country—anybody dealing with rape—to get a lot of publicity focused on the issue when the show aired. So it was like a national event. They had a screening in Congress and in various communities.

Several women in Lear's company came forward while they were making the show and disclosed their own rape experiences, and they also said, "If you ever need help. . . ." So I eventually went to them, and they helped me build the first support system for the Rape Treatment Center. Some of them continue to be involved.

It showed us a whole new way to use our experiences and reach the public on a level and in a way we'd never imagined. What a contribution and a gift to be able to take this information and incorporate it in a television show that reaches so many millions of people! So we've continued to provide consultation for television shows that have been done on rape—"Cagney and Lacey," "Hill Street Blues," and "LA Law."

We had a case that inspired us to work to establish a human relations award in the police department. The woman was a young Latina who came from an overprotective family and had never stayed away from home before. She went to stay at a girlfriend's house for the first time and was abducted in a robbery attempt at a store. She was taken somewhere and sexually assaulted by multiple assailants — and then abandoned in a deserted part of the city. She had been separated from her friend, so she went for help and the police were called. She was taken to a hospital in another part of the city, where a doctor advised her that the best thing to do was go home and try to forget about what happened. She took that advice to heart. And when her parents found out what had happened, they were very ashamed, and they also put pressure on her to keep it secret. So she didn't tell anyone, and she got sick. Actually, she was hospitalized several times but never told anyone about the rape. She was becoming increasingly depressed and unable to eat: she had a lot of trouble swallowing.

The detective who was investigating the case was a wonderful man who saw that she was becoming very frail and depressed and withdrawn. And he persuaded her to come to the Rape Treatment Center on the day it turned out she had planned to kill herself. Policemen always get recognized for heroic acts and catching criminals. But we wanted to recognize him for what we believe is one of the most important parts of police work. It was so moving to tell this story and honor him at a public event. And finally, I convinced the chief of police to establish a human relations award to recognize this kind of behavior in police officers so that it has as much significance as catching criminals. (After all, the police spend much more of their time with victims.) I'm really proud of that.

About four years ago, we started seeing a dramatic increase in the number of women coming here who were college students. I think a majority of rapes in this country happen now on college campuses. We had one case of a woman whose dream was to come out to California and go to the university. She came from a wonderful, close-knit, supportive family, and she met a guy who was her boyfriend in college. He was an athlete, and she went to a party with a couple of his friends who were also athletes. They went out to get some beer, and one of the guys said he wanted to stop at his apartment to pick something up. So they did. There, one raped her while the other watched. When she went to the university administrators, they said, "You can pursue this if you want to, but you might be sued for libel." They intimidated her into silence, but fortunately, somebody referred her here for treatment.

We had another student who was living away from home, for the first time, in a dormitory. Her parents had come to visit her for a holiday weekend and dropped her off. She went to sleep and then was awakened in the middle of the night by a stranger who'd walked into the dormitory when the doors had been left open. She was sexually assaulted and physically attacked very savagely. (She tried valiantly to fight this guy off.) When he fled, the police were immediately called and she was taken to the hospital.

The wonderful thing about this story is really the other students, who formed her support system. There were sirens and ambulances, the dorm was roped off, there was a lot of attention focused on what had happened. And she insisted on coming home. She didn't want to stay at the hospital overnight, and she was concerned about how the other students would be feeling. She was someone who always had trouble speaking in front of class, but she came home with a swollen face and black-and-blue eyes and asked to have a meeting *right then* in the dormitory, where she told her story! She didn't want there to be any rumors that weren't true. Afterwards, the students stood in a line, and every one of them gave her a hug.

No one from the university ever contacted her after the rape — *ever* — to see how she was or to see if she needed any help. She had severe post-traumatic stress symptoms: she couldn't sleep; she had fears about her personal safety; she had nightmares. And her friends formed this incredible support system: they slept on her floor; they walked her to class; *they really made it possible for her to stay in school. It was a triumph of friendship!*

Those experiences made us realize that the colleges were totally unprepared. They didn't know how to handle these cases. Victims weren't getting any help; they had no rights or protections. When the rapist was another student, he was rarely, if ever, subject to a disciplinary hearing, let alone expelled from school. So we wrote a book called *Sexual Assault on Campus: What Colleges Can Do.* We incorporated many of these cases and stories and developed a ten-point plan which included recommendations about how to combat the violence and provide more support for victims. It's been used all over the country, and a lot of people say it's their bible.

We also kept hearing from these young women that nobody ever talked about rape at school, so in 1990, we decided to make a film we could export all over the country. It's called *Campus Rape,* narrated by Susan Dey and Corbin Bernsen of "LA Law," and it incorporates the stories of four victims who are college-age students. We've distributed six thousand copies and it's used in every state in the country and on the vast majority of college campuses.

This is doing something about the problem. We've been able to have a big impact on public and private attitudes, and on public institutions. A lot of people who work here have a part in everything we do. Aileen Adams, our legal counsel, cowrote the book and worked on the rape legislation with me.

Every time I've gone to my board—whether it's for building Stuart House for children, or making a campus rape film, or changing the law—they've always supported me. And the Rape Treatment Center wouldn't have become what it is without the support of a hospital that sees part of its role as much broader than the way most hospitals define their mission. *Nobody ever does this alone.*

Each of these women transformed a private trauma by shaping it, ultimately, into a constructive action. To do that, each had to root out the "silence and secrecy" Gail Abarbanel identifies at "the heart of the rape problem in this country" — as it is at the heart of virtually every other abuse that has its roots in sexuality. Each found that she was not alone and reached out to others. And each has created models to emulate.

After making accusations of sexual harassment that shocked the nation, Anita Hill learned to place herself in the historical context of African-American women whose personhood had been denied, and then to connect with women organized on the front lines to fight legal battles for women. Molly McElrath and Cathy Hanson worked through a tangled personal relationship to make common cause and then joined with others who'd been harassed to win a landmark settlement for women. Penny Harrington turned a "woman's" job on the Portland police force into a fight for justice — first for abused children and then for women's equal treatment on the job. Gail Abarbanel took particular rapes and turned them into a series of concrete actions — laws, books, television performances, awards — that changed the way our society deals with rape victims. By way of their example, other women may find the tenacity, strength, canniness, and wisdom to engage their own life-enhancing struggles for dignity and equality.

15

A NEW DAY

I have nothing to offer you but your pride in being a woman, all your dreams you've ever had for your daughters and nieces and grand-daughters, your future, and the certain knowledge that at the end of your days you will be able to look back and say that once in your life, you gave everything you had for justice.

— Jill Ruckelshaus

Bearing witness may be only the initial stage in a long process, but truth-telling is easier now than it was even a generation ago. As his inaugural poet, for instance, President Bill Clinton chose an African-American woman who was raped as a child, lived for a time in abandoned cars, worked as a barroom singer, raised an illegitimate son, and has written candidly about her life for two decades. If symbols really matter, Maya Angelou's appearance at the West Front of the United States Capitol on January 20, 1993, marked an end to the era when women could be shamed into silence.

The issue was no longer whether Angelou fit into a preconceived mold prescribed for women but whether she spoke with authenticity, and the answer, unmistakably, was yes. In her inaugural poem, she spoke directly to our need to confront the past: "History, despite its wrenching pain, / Cannot be unlived, but if faced / With courage, need not be lived again." Reminded of the last time a poet had spoken at an inauguration — it was John F. Kennedy's, thirty-two years earlier — many saw Angelou with Robert Frost's shadow behind her. An austere, laconic, white-haired New England farmer-poet had been superseded by a dark-skinned, street-savvy, blues-singing woman, and the country would never be the same.

It might, however, inch along, and that depends on us. To the extent that women learn to use the collective "we" and organize to win *real* power, the pace of change will quicken. This power is something quite different from the influence women have so famously been supposed to exercise over men. As retired brigadier general Pat Foote puts it, "I have a heck of a lot of referrent power. People come to me because they respect the fact that I'm an uppity old woman. They know I speak from the heart, and I do it because I think it's right. But if I had policy-making power. . . ."

Our ultimate goals, then, are real power and an equal say with men in all the business of public and professional life. Meanwhile, as ideas that sanction inequality between the sexes fall into disrepute, men and women in leadership positions can cut sexual harassment drastically. "If the people at the top lay the law down," Foote says, "and they make sure their subordinates know their job's on the line if these things happen, *then they don't happen!*" Lawsuits and disciplinary action against harassers will eventually alter the way men behave, and manuals like *Step Forward* and *Sexual Harassment: Research and Resources* will prove invaluable to every organization where men and women work together. For as Meredith Curry puts it, "The hearings allowed us to use words in a whole new way. The laws and regulations have helped a great deal. We have the language and process for it. It alerts senior people to it, and it's made young people aware in ways they weren't."[1]

Investment banker Jewelle Bickford, the chief executive officer of Bickford and Partners, explains how this can work on a daily basis:

I'm a woman-owned business, and I work with men all the time. Things I would not have made an issue of before — because I thought they were too trivial or impediments to getting ahead — now I see as points of honor. There are eight of us — two men and six women — and we have a synergistic relationship with a company that shares office space with us. A very, very attractive woman works there, and up until a month ago she was not married. Almost every male who came into this office noticed how attractive she is — some of them very politely and legitimately. It used to be something I just took in stride.

But one day I walked into the office and found the former head of an insurance company that's a client of ours massaging her neck. He said she had a migraine headache. And I had a conference with her, saying this was totally inappropriate behavior under all circumstances; she didn't have to sit there and let her shoulders be massaged. I said if she needed any help in rebuffing these advances, she should please let me know. Otherwise I expected that behavior never to be repeated in this office.

And I had a talk with him. He was sheepish and embarrassed. I did not use humor, nor was I a little old maid. I said I'd appreciate it if that did not take place again. He told me I'd lost my sense of humor and become overly sensitive. I agreed that I'd become sensitized since Anita Hill but I was not overly sensitive. I made no big deal, but I was not going to let it pass. Ten years ago, I would have ignored it.

More fundamental change will come far less easily. Institutions resist it — that is their nature — because they shore up people who, by virtue of having power already, have readier access to the law, people who not only know how to find astute lawyers but are more likely to have the financial resources to sustain a protracted suit. Since the law presumes that each party deserves a vigorous defense, and each lawyer takes the equivalent of the Hippocratic Oath to defend a client to the best of his or her ability, the already powerful start out way ahead. Under such a system, the struggle is so costly in time, energy, and money that even those who win will often later feel they've lost.

In the landmark case of *Meritor Savings Bank v. Vinson* in 1986, for instance, Patricia Barry successfully argued for the plaintiff before the U.S. Supreme Court. Mechelle Vinson, a Washington, D.C., bank employee, claimed that her supervisor fondled her in front of other employees; that he followed her into the ladies' room, where he exposed himself; and that on several occasions he raped her. Both the supervisor and the bank denied her claims, but the court sided with Vinson, establishing the principle that sexual harassment violated a person's civil rights.

Two years later, Patricia Barry, the winning lawyer in that suit, made it clear that the Vinson experience had been the exception rather than the rule. Filing for bankruptcy, she announced that she was giving up civil-rights work, and reflecting on her years of challenging the system, a discouraged Barry observed, "Most judges perceive themselves as identifying with the man — no matter how horrible he is — and it becomes the woman versus the man." In 1986, the New York State Task Force on Women in the Courts reported that "women uniquely, disproportionately and with unacceptable frequency must endure a climate of condescension, indifference and hostility." Five years later, a similar task force in Connecticut found that "women are treated differently from men in the justice system and, because of it, many suffer from unfairness, embarrassment, emotional pain, professional deprivation, and economic hardship." Women of color are likely to be even more thoroughly victimized than white women.[2]

This bias persists because most judges are male. In mid-1990, for instance, only 7 percent of some 750 sitting judges with life tenure in ninety-four federal trial courts were women. (Almost two-thirds of those courts had *no* women judges with tenure.)

To be sure, women lawyers and judges will not necessarily treat their own sex more fairly. As Patricia Barry discovered to her cost, "making it" may well be at odds with working for women. In fact, male defendants often hire women lawyers, especially if they are accused of crimes against women, because this can confuse a jury. To get ahead in their chosen profession, many women feel compelled to prove their toughness by being hard on their own sex, and finally, men command the resources to pay the larger fees.

For that matter, even the American taxpayer seems to take the perpetrator's side by footing substantial bills to defend men accused of sexual harassment at government institutions like the National Institutes of Health. (We taxpayers are financing the case against Dr. Margaret Jensvold, for instance, which is to say that Dr. Jensvold herself is helping to bankroll the other side.) Since 1987, the government has spent more than $1.6 million to address close to one thousand informal complaints at NIH, and about $3 million more on formal allegations that are usually about harassment. These figures don't include the money paid to settle cases out of court, much less the immense sums lost to women in careers that have been damaged and even destroyed.[3]

We can see how the institutional bias in favor of men actually works by looking at what happened to a Colorado woman, Melissa Roberts-Henry, after she engaged Dr. Jason Richter as her psychiatrist. Following eleven months of therapy, they had an affair that lasted a year and a half, and during that period, she became progressively distraught, immobilized, and ultimately suicidal. Finally she confided in her husband, who confronted Richter and told him that what he had done was both unethical and illegal. (Richter agreed, though he showed no apparent remorse. In his notes, he had written that a physical relationship between them would be "harmful" to her — a category he downgraded under questioning to "high risk.") Roberts-Henry then put herself in the hands of a female psychiatrist, Dr. Martha Gay, and sued Richter for sexual malpractice. Gay had done forensic evaluations of victims and offenders in more than four hundred cases, and Melissa was the twelfth who had had a sexual relationship with her therapist.[4]

During the trial, Dr. Cynthia Rose, past president of the Colorado Psychiatric Society, pointed out that sex with a patient is a violation of a doctor's Hippocratic Oath. Studies have shown, nevertheless, that approximately 7 percent of psychiatrists indulge in it, and two-thirds of all psychiatrists know at least one colleague who has been or is involved with a patient. For obvious reasons, female psychiatrists commonly treat women who've been sexually exploited by male psychiatrists, and the trial made it clear that there is a male/female split within the profession.

Richter was insured through the American Psychiatric Association, and his defense lawyer was Paul Cooper, who had successfully defended *Playboy* magazine in a sensational defamation suit brought by a former Miss Wyoming. Since then, he had enjoyed a flourishing practice by defending doctors charged with sexually abusing their patients. A lawyer committed to "zealous defense," during the Richter trial Cooper showcased a young, blonde female colleague, Kay Rice, who argued the defense case to the jury. (Rice told an interviewer that women needed to reject the role of victim, as though Roberts-Henry had deliberately chosen it and persisted because she was having the time of her life.)

The legal maneuvering took two years. Then, as the trial date approached, the defense actually put Roberts-Henry under surveillance. Being tailed and treated like a criminal reduced her, as no doubt it was intended to do, to a quivering mass of anxiety. Dr. Gay even considered the possibility that Melissa was becoming psychotic and worried more than once about whether her patient would be *alive* for the next scheduled session. When asked why Roberts-Henry should be under surveillance at all, Cooper wondered disingenuously why she didn't simply drop a case that was causing her such pain!

The trial lasted three weeks, and in her three days on the stand,

Roberts-Henry was subjected to brutally degrading cross-examination. The video camera captured a woman who not only could barely speak but looked like a concentration camp victim. The defense strategy was to cast her as a wanton woman: her sexual history was exhaustively looked into and openly discussed; confidences she had entrusted to her psychiatrist were paraded before the jury; and salacious letters she had written her lover were used to discredit her. ("I was trying to be what Jason wanted," she explained on the stand — to give him "something I'd never given anybody else.")

Richter, on the other hand, could be asked only one question about his sex life: had he previously had sex with a patient? (As Roberts-Henry's lawyer pointed out, the prosecution had no sure way of finding out whether he was telling the truth.)

The next line of defense was to discredit Dr. Martha Gay, accusing her of *causing* Melissa's post-traumatic stress disorder rather than simply *diagnosing* it. No proof was offered that Dr. Gay was giving her patient anything less than the best care, and three other experts on sexual abuse who examined Melissa agreed with Gay's diagnosis — as did Richter's own psychiatric expert. Nonetheless, the defense continued to charge Gay with manipulating Roberts-Henry for her own purposes. On top of that, they tried to undermine Gay by floating an unspecified rumor as to *her* sexual history.

Finally, the defense accused Melissa Roberts-Henry of victimizing her psychiatrist: his wife had tried to commit suicide and he was feeling rejected!

The jury was not persuaded by this nonsense, finding Richter 82 percent guilty and awarding Roberts-Henry $218,000 — a sum that might or might not cover the medical expenses she was likely to incur in the process of recovery. But Richter came out of his ordeal with very little damage. Using its resources in support of an acknowledged offender, the American Psychiatric Association had spent $100,000 defending him. The Colorado Medical Examiners Board neither revoked his license nor placed restrictions on his right to practice. Four hospitals renewed his privileges, and other doctors continued to refer patients to him.

Dr. Martha Gay was another matter altogether. Through the APA, she, too, had bought malpractice insurance and even had the same insurance agent as Richter. When the abuses against her escalated, however, she discovered that this agent had actually *authorized* the attacks. While defending herself, she ran up $30,000 in legal fees, which the APA subsequently refused to reimburse. At the same time, her referrals dropped off dramatically and she was forced to resign as vice-chair of the Colorado Psychiatric Society's ethics committee. So savage and successful was the strategy against her that she decided to close her Denver practice and move. (She then tried to get *ten* different psychiatrists to take Roberts-Henry as a patient, but they all refused. Doctors whose calling was to help the wounded had been scared witless by the unprincipled nature of the defense.)

After a stormy meeting, the American Psychiatric Association declared itself satisfied: it would make no changes in the defense strategy authorized for future offenders. Nor would psychiatrists who chose to treat patients whom male psychiatrists had exploited sexually be offered any further protection by APA insurance than Gay had gotten — which was nothing. In response to the Richter defense and the APA's endorsement of it, Dr. Nanette Gartrell of San Francisco resigned from the organization. Since 1982, Dr. Gartrell had led the effort to document psychiatric sexual abuse and served as chairperson of the APA committee on women.

At the same time that institutions are by definition the bulwarks of the status quo, many will find it simply easier to stand by the man. In *Trauma and Recovery: The aftermath of violence — from domestic abuse to political terror,* Dr. Judith Lewis Herman writes: "All the perpetrator asks is that the bystander do nothing. He appeals to the universal desire to see, hear, and speak no evil. The victim, on the contrary, asks the bystander to share the burden of pain." Nobody likes pain, and victims aren't fun. Furthermore, those of us who have been raised to laugh so as not to cry may find it hard to switch modes, especially since men are likely to ridicule us if we try. ("Can't you take a joke?" is perhaps the handiest put-down in the male repertoire.) And the downside of our otherwise admirable stoicism is that after a while, it becomes harder to recognize what there is to cry about.[5]

In 1990, for instance, a guy who didn't know the difference between a violent crime and a joke was almost elected governor of Texas. Clayton Williams, the Republican nominee, commented on a spate of bad weather delaying a roundup by saying, "It's like rape; if it's inevitable, just relax and enjoy it." A woman who was by no means atypical told an ABC television reporter that, good grief, she'd grown up in

Texas; boys will be boys, and that was just Claytie. Many more women, however, did not find him funny and came together in unprecedented numbers to elect Ann Richards. (Five days after his "joke," a man raped a woman in Austin, Texas, and told her to relax and enjoy it like Claytie Williams had said. Just before the election, he was sentenced to fifty years in prison.)

The truth is that men are losing control of a potent weapon: the power to define what is funny. And so when a note of panic creeps into men's exchanges with women, it may be because they suspect, deep down, that the last laugh will be on them.

Women who don't laugh at the old jokes and pratfalls any more can expect to be called humorless, hysterical, shrill, strident — fill in the blanks — *but they are finding each other to be both a solace and a political weapon.* Dr. Margaret Jensvold, for instance, has witnessed a change in a period as brief as five years:

We have women leaders in psychiatry now. When I was at NIMH, I'd get calls repeatedly saying that one after another, they were being turned down for chairmanships. Each time that happened, this wave of discouragement would go out around the United States. In those early years, I felt a kinship with a network that I knew was there and aspired to become a part of. . . . Now there's some sense of our fighting this battle together. In the past few years, there's been a series of women's health research scandals — the Dalkon Shield, the discovery that most government-funded scientific research is targeted at men, silicone breast implants — and there have been women speaking out about sex harassment. To me, these two things are clearly related.

That network has been galvanized to support Dr. Jensvold in her suit against the National Institute of Mental Health and to remove "self-defeating personality disorder" from the list of officially recognized mental illnesses.

Women, to be sure, will have to take the initiative. As Dr. Frances Conley puts it:

There's a horrendous chasm of misunderstanding between men and women. What men will consider fun or flirtatious, women may find demeaning or degrading. Women need to develop the communications skills to transmit that message without building a huge wall of hostility. Men tend immediately to back off. So in the next five to ten years, women are going to find themselves in a difficult dilemma when they try to bridge this gap.

This means learning to put up with some hostility, although women have been taught traditionally to duck or to dispel it. Conley's experience has taught her how to deal with controversy and how *not* to mind when people get angry:

Women are taught to conduct ourselves so that everybody will love us. Life's a popularity contest, and we want to be the pom-pom girls. But I've been giving a lot of talks since my story broke in the press, and some groups are very put off about what I have to say. And that's fine: I love it now. I enjoy the dialogue. In mixed audiences, the women are nodding their heads while the men are shaking theirs. After my talk, I've heard couples, when they're leaving, just going at each other, while a bunch of people are saying to me, "Lady, you're just wrong. . . ."

Like most women who stand up for themselves or other women, Conley has been accused of male-bashing, though she is very careful "to emphasize the fact that this is a societal thing we're all born into and the men of today are not responsible for its presence. They *are* responsible for its perpetuation. But what many men hear is, 'She doesn't like me! . . .'"

In the face of indifference and even hostility, then, the woman who has been harassed or abused — and who refuses to call the sun the moon — must find a group that supports her, along with a constructive way to channel her pain and outrage. The group she finds will *never* apologize for abuses of power. They will *never* advise her to swallow her anger, nor will they trivialize the damage that has been done her. They will *never* advise forgiveness in the absence of remorse or counsel her to "put it all behind" her — for that energy should be invested in the future, in doing something to change the conditions that demean and undermine women.

The constructive channel a woman finds may be as simple as a heightened empathy for people who've been treated unfairly, and especially for women. This is likely to evolve into a fierce commitment to justice. The women who told me the stories that make up this book, for instance, contributed to *Bearing Witness* as a way of reaching out to other women. And they were determined to call attention to injustices we can rectify when enough of us decide that injustice is a bad thing.

Nothing could be simpler, in fact, than finding tangible ways to channel our indignation and build a saner future. There are battered women's shelters to fund, along with rape crisis centers and places like Stuart House in Santa Monica for children who have been abused.

There are burgeoning numbers of women to elect to office; women's health initiatives to sponsor and lobby for; professional networks to build and nurture. And there are promising young women who need help and counsel in getting an education commensurate with their talents and ambition.

The general cultural indifference to injustices against women has begun to fray, and it will gradually disintegrate as women gain more tangible status because there is a direct link between women's power in the world and the dignity and respect with which they are treated. The money we have to spend in our own self-interest, the degree to which we are represented in positions of authority and influence, the cohesiveness of our organizations, the measurable effect of our vote — all these things decide how far we can vitiate dismissive phrases like "Boys will be boys." For as women grow richer and our organizations become more effective, we shall enter into a time when our progeny will collectively wonder at that era — as quaint to them as Edith Wharton's New York is to us — when grown men were excused for behaving like children.

As former legislative aide Dorena Bertussi observed of the Hill/Thomas hearings, by the fall of 1991 it had become fashionable to disapprove of sexual harassment. It will move from the fashionable to the commonplace as women continue to win court cases and handsome financial settlements, and women like Betty Roberts keep organizing to force prominent politicians like Senator Bob Packwood to step down when compelling charges of harassment have been lodged against them. As always, however, the price of victory is perpetual vigilance.

For all these individual battles are waged in the context of a larger struggle, and there is a constant dialectic at work between the parts and the whole. Women who are now poorer, weaker, and so, more nearly trapped, will grow stronger as their actual conditions improve and they no longer operate at such a great practical disadvantage. When they have more options, they will grow stronger psychologically, evolving more readily from victim to survivor.

Silence has played a crucial role in muffling the dialectic of that struggle. Until very recently, as Judith Herman puts it, "To speak about experiences in sexual or domestic life was to invite public humiliation, ridicule, and disbelief. Women were silenced by fear and shame, and the silence of women gave license [in turn] to every form of sexual and domestic exploitation."[6]

But now women journalists have taken the lead in exposing abuses that women suffer. In 1988, for instance, *Working Woman* magazine did a survey of sexual harassment in the Fortune 500 companies, and using the language that business understands best, they summarized their findings: "The problem costs a typical Fortune 500 company $6.7 million a year in absenteeism, employee turnover, low morale and low productivity."[7]

Four years later, Rhonda Cook of the *Atlanta Constitution* exposed a pattern of systematic sexual harassment and abuse over a thirteen-year period at the Georgia Women's Correctional Institute in Milledgeville, Georgia, and the following year, Sheila McVicar reported the scandal on ABC national television news. For the Washington, D.C., affiliate of CBS television news, Andrea Austin did a three-part series called "Harassment 101," focusing on the schools. (Austin claimed that 70 percent of the nation's high school students had been sexually harassed, often by men who grabbed them physically, and she showed how this damaged their ability to study.) And the American Association of University Women released the troubling results of their survey of sexual harassment in the schools.[8]

Newspapers like the *Dallas Morning News,* for decades one of the most conservative papers in Texas, did a long series on violence against women throughout the world and subtitled it "A Question of Human Rights." In an opening article, Anne Reifenberg reported from the United Nations: "Human-rights organizations, which view systematic discrimination based on race or religion as persecution, are only now beginning to wrap some gender-based violence in the same ugly package. Only now are they beginning to consider the implications of the fact that women are regularly sexually or physically injured or killed because they are women."[9]

New York investment banker Jewelle Bickford realized that there are a number of concrete steps women can take in their own self-interest: "With Anita Hill I saw that sexual harassment is endemic to the system. We don't ask for it. I also saw there are some ways we can be *proactive* to prevent it. We can help ourselves, and I've started. I want to support other women when they're going through something — but not wrongfully. I've started thinking very carefully about candidates. I organized New York to help Lynn Yeakel [who ran against Republican senator Arlen Specter of Pennsylvania and very nearly won]. We have to *not* play along."

We also have to keep *thinking,* and reinterpretations will be constantly necessary because men have naturally cast the evidence in terms the least unflattering to them. Women who have been sexually abused as children, for instance, are overwhelmingly likely to be abused again, and commonly they are said to invite it. The truth is that the original abuse is crippling: their self-protective antennae are damaged, and they do not fully recognize danger. *Most victims do not invite or enjoy their victimization, but their blood is in the water, and the sharks will feast.*

Because of the exalted rhetoric that celebrates them, women invariably fancy themselves freer and more secure than they are, and, as Herman puts it, "traditional socialization virtually ensures that women will be poorly prepared for danger, surprised by attack, and ill-equipped to protect themselves." The qualities we as women have been taught to honor and cultivate — tenderness, compassion, patience, tolerance, forgiveness — all these work against us in abusive situations. Nevertheless, they remain the fundamental qualities of decent human beings, and the challenge for an abused woman is to reconnect with a real world in which they count. For this we need colleagues committed to the proposition that *there are no excuses for men who abuse women* as well as friends who will bear witness with us — friends who believe that abuse is unjust and that justice matters.

Mourning plays a large role in the healing process, and so does patience. But perhaps the most important thing is hope — hope that we can shape a world that is more nearly just. As Jill Ruckelshaus told a convention of the National Women's Political Caucus fifteen years ago, "We are in for a very, very long haul. I am asking everything you have to give. We will never give up. You will lose your youth, your sleep, your arches, your strength, your patience, your sense of humor, and occasionally the understanding and support of the people that you love very much. In return, I have nothing to offer you but your pride in being a woman, all your dreams you've ever had for your daughters and nieces and granddaughters, your future, and the certain knowledge that at the end of your days you will be able to look back and say that once in your life, you gave everything you had for justice."

This future in which we invest is one in which women control their own sexuality and men share power rather than impose it. It is a future that matters profoundly for our sons' sakes as well as for our daughters'.

And so we reach out and touch. We laugh. We love again. And all the while, we organize.

NOTES AND SOURCES

Chapter 1

1. *New York Times,* November 1, 1992.

2. Dorene Ludwig, *But It Was Just a Joke . . .! Theater Scenes and Monologues for Eliminating Sexual Harassment* (Los Angeles: UCLA Institute of Industrial Relations, 1991).

3. *Sexual Harassment: Research and Resources* (New York: National Council for Research on Women, 1992), pp. vii, 7. See also Susan L. Webb, *Step Forward: Sexual Harassment in the Workplace — What You Need to Know!* (New York: MasterMedia, 1991). Both volumes summarize the history of sexual harassment legislation and outline the pertinent research. They include valuable statistics, descriptions, definitions, bibliographies, guidelines, and lists of both organizations and individuals who are experts in the field of sexual harassment.

4. Carolyn G. Heilbrun, *Writing a Woman's Life* (New York: Ballantine Books, 1988), pp. 43–45.

5. Quoted in Gayle Pemberton, "A Sentimental Journey: James Baldwin and the Thomas-Hill Hearings," in *Race-ing Justice, En-gendering Power: Essays on Anita Hill, Clarence Thomas, and the Construction of Social Reality,* ed. Toni Morrison (New York: Pantheon, 1992), p. 176.

6. More recent books that would redress this injustice by dealing with black women's experience in this country include Adele Logan Alexander's *Ambiguous Lives: Free Women of Color in Rural Georgia, 1789–1879* (Fayetteville: University of Arkansas Press, 1991); Barbara Hilkert Andolsen's *"Daughters of Jefferson, Daughters of Bootblacks": Racism and American Feminism* (Macon, Ga.: Mercer University Press, 1986); Angela Davis's *Women, Race, and Class* (New York: Ran-

dom House, 1981); Elizabeth Fox-Genovese's *Within the Plantation Household: Black and White Women of the Old South* (Chapel Hill: University of North Carolina Press, 1988); Paula Giddings's *When and Where I Enter: The Impact of Black Women on Race and Sex in America* (New York: Bantam, 1984); bell hooks's *Ain't I a Woman: black women and feminism* (Boston: South End Press, 1981); Jacqueline Jones's *Labor of Love, Labor of Sorrow: Black Women, Work, and the Family, from Slavery to the Present* (New York: Random House, 1986); Gerda Lerner's *Black Women in White America* (New York: Vintage, 1973); Susan Tucker's *Telling Memories Among Southern Women: Domestic Workers and Their Employers in the Segregated South* (New York: Schocken Books, 1988); and Deborah Gray White's, *Ar'n't I a Woman? Female Slaves in the Plantation South* (New York: W. W. Norton, 1985).

7. Adele Logan Alexander, "'She's no lady; she's a nigger': The Demeaning Legacies and Images of African-American Women." Dr. Alexander's speech was the keynote address at the 1992 Georgetown University Law Center conference, "Race, Gender and Power in America," and will be included in a collection of essays to be published by Oxford University Press in 1994.

8. Joel Williamson, *New People: Miscegenation and Mulattoes in the United States* (New York: New York University Press, 1984), p. 59.

9. Robert Penn Warren, *All the King's Men* (New York, Modern Library, 1953), pp. 179–181.

10. Harriet A. Jacobs, *Incidents in the Life of a Slave Girl: Written by Herself* (Cambridge: Harvard University Press, 1987), pp. 27–28 and 51. Originally published in 1861 under the pseudonym Linda Brent, Jacobs's narrative was edited for modern publication by Jean Fagan Yellin.

11. *Mary Chesnut's Civil War*, ed. C. Vann Woodward (New York: Oxford University Press, 1981), p. 29. Mary Boykin Chesnut lived at the vital center of Southern society; her husband was a wealthy South Carolina planter who served as one of Jefferson Davis's closest aides. And she was just as clear as Englishwomen like Fanny Wright and Harriet Martineau about the way the sexual abuse of slaves maimed white women. As her most recent editor, C. Vann Woodward, writes, "Her bitterest indictment was what slavery did to the wives, children, and families of the masters, as well as to the masters themselves. Like the slaves, women were all subject to the absolute authority of the patriarchal system. The feature that most offended her was the sexual abuse of slave women . . . [but] what outraged her beyond endurance was the hypocrisy of the stern puritanical code these libertarian patriarchs imposed on their womenfolk and children." (p. li). In 1861, Mrs. Chesnut castigated "this hated institution," this "*monstrous* system," this "curse" of slavery, and when she wrote of "the mulattoes one sees in every family," this was not a theoretical issue. Her own father-in-law had children by slave women, and his licentiousness had corrupted Mulberry, the sumptuous plantation where she lived. "*Rachel* and her brood," she had confided to her diary, "make this place a horrid nightmare to me — I believe in nothing, with this before me." (p. 72).

12. As early as the 1940s, Lillian Smith, a courageous southern white woman, began to write insistently and repeatedly about the tragic consequences of the sexual exploitation at the heart of slavery. Her books include *Killers of the Dream* (New York: W. W. Norton, 1949), a brilliant analysis of southern culture and those who would speak for it, and *Strange Fruit* (1944), a novel about lynching and the doomed love between a white man and a black woman. *How Am I to Be Heard?: Letters of Lillian Smith*, edited by Margaret Rose Gladney, was published by the University of North Carolina Press in 1993. In the spring of 1989, more than twenty years after Smith's death, Clemson University in South Carolina sponsored another look at the topics she had explored by hosting a conference on the effect of slavery on private life in the South. In her introduction to the book of essays that grew out of that conference, historian Carol Bleser wrote that "the legacy of slavery continued to play havoc with the institution of marriage and family life in the South long after the Civil War had been fought and slavery had ended, keeping that region and its people psychically isolated and socially regressive until well into the twentieth century. . . . [Slavery was] the poison affecting Southern family life, doing damage to the institution of marriage and wrecking the private lives of men and women, especially the men, for generations." Those who can pursue these topics in greater detail will want to read the book Bleser edited, *In Joy and in Sorrow: Women, Family, and Marriage in the Victorian South 1830–1900* (Oxford University Press, 1991). The essays most pertinent to my own subject here are Catherine Clinton's "Southern Dishonor" and Peter Bardaglio's "'An Outrage upon Nature': Incest and the Law in the Nineteenth-Century South."

13. hooks, p. 37.

14. Alexander, "'She's no lady; she's a nigger': The Demeaning Legacies and Images of African-American Women."

15. See Diane Miller Sommerville, "Sexual Anxiety and the Rape Myth: The Intersection of Race, Gender, and Class in the Antebellum South," presented in 1993 at the Ninth Berkshire Conference on the History of Women; and Martha Hodes, "Sex Across the Color Line: White Women and Black Men in the Nineteenth-Century American South," especially chapter 6 (unpublished Ph.D. dissertation, 1991). For a historical account of the role lynching played in the social control of blacks by whites, and of women by men, see Jacquelyn Dowd Hall's superb *Revolt Against Chivalry: Jessie Daniel Ames and the Women's Campaign Against Lynching* (New York: Columbia University Press, 1979).

16. Clinton, "Southern Dishonor," in *In Joy and in Sorrow*, p. 58; Alice Walker's "Advancing Luna — and Ida B. Wells," in *You Can't Keep a Good Woman Down* (New York: Harcourt Brace Jovanovich, 1980), pp. 91–92.

17. Gerda Lerner, *The Creation of Patriarchy* (New York: Oxford University Press, 1986).

18. Unless otherwise specified, the quotes of statements made during and about the Hill/Thomas hearings are taken from the *Washington Post*, the *New York Times*, and Ofra Bikel's "Frontline" program on the Public Broadcasting System

(October 13, 1992). For a detailed analysis of the hearings and the politics that shaped them, two books are key: Senator Paul Simon's *Advice and Consent: Clarence Thomas, Robert Bork and the Intriguing History of the Supreme Court's Nomination Battles* (Washington, D.C.: National Press Books, 1992) and Timothy M. Phelps and Helen Winternitz's *Capitol Games: Clarence Thomas, Anita Hill, and the Story of a Supreme Court Nomination* (New York: Hyperion, 1992). Jane Mayer and Jill Abramson are writing a third book analyzing the hearings. Tentatively titled *Strange Justice*, it will be published in 1994 by Houghton Mifflin. For the African-American community's response, two other books are required reading: *Race-ing Justice, En-gendering Power: Essays on Anita Hill, Clarence Thomas, and the Construction of Social Reality*; and *Court of Appeal: The Black Community Speaks Out on the Racial and Sexual Politics of Thomas v. Hill*, ed. Robert Chrisman and Robert L. Allen (New York: Ballantine Books, 1992). Ofra Bikel's "Frontline" program is excellent. In *The Real Anita Hill* (New York: The Free Press, 1993), David Brock takes a position diametrically opposed to the one that dominates the books and film cited above. A putative exposé of Hill that evolved from an intemperate article in the *American Spectator*, within three months of publication, 160,000 copies of the book were in print; among other things, its wide circulation is a testimony to the potent need many had at once to discredit Hill and to diminish the importance of sexual harassment. In "The Surreal Anita Hill," *The New Yorker* (May 24, 1993), Jane Mayer and Jill Abramson ably critique Brock's arguments and demolish his claims to objectivity.

19. See "Thurmond and the Girl from Edgeville; Old Stories Have Reemerged About the Senator and his Longtime Ties with a Black Woman," *Washington Post*, August 4, 1992. The story told of the decades-old rumor that Thurmond had fathered a daughter by a young black woman who worked as a maid in his parents' home.

20. Quoted in Gayle Pemberton, "A Sentimental Journey: James Baldwin and the Thomas-Hill Hearings," in *Race-ing Justice, En-gendering Power*, p. 180.

21. See the trenchant, respectful exchanges between Orlando Patterson and Rhonda Datcher in *Reconstruction* (vol. 1, no. 4, 1992), pp. 64–77. A model of engaged, astute criticism, they persuaded Patterson ultimately to rethink his position and even to change the nature of his scholarly work so as to focus on the relations between African-American men and women.

22. Virginia Woolf, *A Room of One's Own* (New York: Harcourt Brace Jovanovich, 1981), pp. 35–36.

Chapter 2

1. Cited in *Sexual Harassment: Research and Resources* (New York: National Council for Research on Women, 1992), p. 5.

2. Ludwig, *But It Was Just a Joke . . .!: Theater Scenes and Monologues for Eliminating Sexual Harassment.*

3. *Washington Post*, February 26, 1993.

Chapter 6

1. Maria's story was translated by Wenndy Hernandez, who listened to the audiotape with me as I sat at my computer and we worked the story out together.

Chapter 8

1. The caucus's definition comes from Catharine MacKinnon's *Sexual Harassment of Working Women: A Case Study of Sex Discrimination* (New Haven: Yale University Press, 1979).

2. Unless otherwise noted, the quotes are from the *Washington Post.*

3. Trip Gabriel, "The Trials of Bob Packwood," *The New York Times Magazine,* August 29, 1993.

4. *Roll Call,* May 31, 1993.

Chapter 9

1. See *Military Women in the Department of Defense* (Washington, D.C.: U.S. Department of Defense, 1990); "Population Representation in the Military Services: Fiscal Year 1991" (Office of the Assistant Secretary of Defense: October 1992), p. 60; and Major General Jeanne Holm (USAF Ret.), *Women in the Military: An Unfinished Revolution* (Novato, Calif.: Presidio Press, revised edition, 1992).

2. Mimi Swartz, "Love and Hate at Texas A&M," *Texas Monthly* (February 1992). Unless otherwise noted, all other quotes are from the *Washington Post* or the *New York Times.*

3. *Los Angeles Times,* February 10, 1992.

Chapter 10

1. *Washington Post*, April 20, 1993.

2. Barbara Ehrenreich, *The Hearts of Men* (New York: Anchor Press, 1983), p. 10.

3. Heilbrun, *Writing a Woman's Life,* p. 18.

4. John Stuart Mill, *The Subjection of Women* (Cambridge: The MIT Press, 1974), p. 32.

5. Heilbrun, p. 102. Speaking of feminists who led the sexual revolution, Barbara Ehrenreich, Elizabeth Hess, and Gloria Jacobs write in *Re-Making Love: The Feminization of Sex* (New York: Doubleday, 1986): "We did, as the critics so loudly complained, take some of the 'mystery' and 'magic' out of sex. This was perhaps coldhearted and unromantic of us, but we had come to understand that the 'mystery' was simply a form of obfuscation. . . . Draped in mystery and mythic themes, sex itself was an act of sublimation for women: not an immediate pleasure to be appropriated but a symbolic act to be undertaken for ulterior aims — motherhood, emotional and financial security, or simply vanity."

Chapter 11

1. Heilbrun, *Writing a Woman's Life,* p. 13. For a range of thoughtful essays on the nature and impact of sex on modern life see Kate Millett's *Sexual Politics* (New York: Doubleday, 1970); *Powers of Desire: The Politics of Sexuality,* ed. Ann Snitow, Christine Stansell, and Sharon Thompson (New York: Monthly Review Press, 1983); Ehrenreich, Hess, and Jacobs's *Re-Making Love: The Feminization of Sex;* and John D'Emilio and Estelle B. Freedman's *Intimate Matters: A History of Sexuality in America* (New York: Harper and Row, 1988).

2. In her provocative book *The Chalice and the Blade* (San Francisco: HarperCollins, 1988), Riane Eisler writes: "A woman who behaves as a sexually and economically free person is a threat to the entire social and economic fabric of a rigidly male-dominated society. . . . Laws regulating women's virginity were designed to protect what were essentially economic transactions between men." (p. 97). Eisler describes two fundamentally different forms of social organization, the partnership society and the dominator society. We live in the latter. Eisler may or may not be correct in imagining that our society was preceded historically by ones based on partnership, but I find her argument that our survival depends on our moving beyond the dominator into the partnership society quite persuasive.

3. Mill, *The Subjection of Women,* p. 79.

4. Cited in Mill, p. xxi.

5. Woolf, *A Room of One's Own,* p. 98.

6. Heilbrun, p. 37. The phenomenal success of Clarissa Pinkola Estés's *Women Who Run with the Wolves: Myths and Stories of the Wild Woman Archetype* (New York: Ballantine Books, 1992) suggests that women are beginning to spurn the bland image of the "good woman" that has worked to repress their spirit, energy, and talents.

7. Elizabeth Cady Stanton, *The Original Feminist Attack on the Bible (The*

Woman's Bible) (New York: Arno Press, 1974), p. 7. In Chapter 7 of *The Creation of Feminist Consciousness* (New York: Oxford University Press, 1993), Gerda Lerner discusses the long history of women's attempts to deal with the Bible's misogyny. Stanton was by no means the first or the last.

8. Charlotte Perkins Gilman, *Women and Economics: The economic factor between men and women as a factor in social evolution* (New York: Harper and Row, 1966), pp. 63–64.

9. Shirley Nelson Garner, "Male Bonding and the Myth of Women's Deception in Shakespeare's Plays," in *Shakespeare's Personality*, ed. Norman N. Holland and Sidney Homan, p. 136.

10. Ibid., p. 143.

11. Ibid., p. 145.

12. Madelon Sprengnether, "The Gendered Subject of Shakespearean Tragedy," in *Shakespearean Tragedy and Gender*, ed. Shirley Nelson Garner and Madelon Sprengnether (unpublished manuscript).

13. Jane Smiley, *A Thousand Acres* (New York: Knopf, 1991), p. 33.

14. Sprengnether.

15. Smiley, p. 302.

16. Ibid., pp. 355–356.

Chapter 12

1. Celia Morris, *Fanny Wright: Rebel in America* (Champaign: University of Illinois Press, 1992), p. 282.

2. For American women's role in creating communities, as well as a thoroughgoing account of women's organizing and its effects, see Anne Firor Scott's *Natural Allies: Women's Associations in American History* (Urbana: University of Illinois Press, 1992).

3. *Mary Chesnut's Civil War*, p. 168.

4. Discussed in Morris, *Fanny Wright*.

5. Harriet Martineau, *Society in America* (New Brunswick, N.J.: Transaction Books, 1981), edited and abridged by Seymour Martin Lipset.

6. Fanny Kemble, *Journal of a Residence on a Georgian Plantation in 1838–1839* (Savannah: Library of Georgia, 1992).

7. Gerda Lerner, *The Grimke Sisters from South Carolina: Pioneers for Woman's Rights and Abolition* (New York: Schocken Books, 1974).

8. Ibid., p. 189.

9. Ibid., p. 361.

10. Videotapes: Oprah Winfrey, March 28, 1992; Jenny Jones, September 18, 1992.

11. *The American Woman 1992–93: A Status Report,* ed. Paula Ries and Anne J. Stone (New York: W. W. Norton, 1992).

Chapter 13

1. Nellie Y. McKay, "Remembering Anita Hill and Clarence Thomas: What Really Happened When One Black Woman Spoke Out," in *Race-ing Justice, En-gendering Power: Essays on Anita Hill, Clarence Thomas, and the Construction of Social Reality,* pp. 288–289.

2. *Dallas Morning News,* November 24, 1991. For the worst mass murder in American history, see the *Washington Post,* October 17–19, 1991.

3. Christine Stansell, "White Feminists and Black Realities: The Politics of Authenticity," in *Race-ing Justice, En-gendering Power,* p. 264.

4. See my article "Waiting for Ms. President," *Harper's Bazaar* (July 1992).

5. Margaret A. Burnham, "The Supreme Court Appointment Process and the Politics of Race and Sex," in *Race-ing Justice, En-gendering Power,* p. 319. Catharine MacKinnon has also pointed out the special connection between African-American women and the civil rights struggle: "Most of the women who have brought forward claims that have advanced the laws of sexual harassment have been black. Because racism is often sexualized, black women have been particularly clear in identifying this behavior as a violation of their civil rights" (*People,* October 28, 1991). For an African-American woman's analysis of the way racism within the women's movement has undermined it, see bell hooks's *Ain't I a Woman: black women and feminism,* especially chapters four and five, "Racism and Feminism: The Issue of Accountability" and "Black Women and Feminism," pp. 119–196. The immediate political cost of class and race schisms within the women's community became obvious in mid-July 1993, when eleven of the forty-seven women in the House of Representatives voted against federal funding for abortions under Medicare, and in a stinging defeat for the women's movement, the Hyde Amendment was handily reinstated. At the same time, Senator Carol Moseley Braun of Illinois withdrew her support for the Freedom of Choice Act on the grounds that the legislation as written "discriminates against young and poor women." Congresswoman Maxine Waters of California called the schism "very serious": "It is the first time I've witnessed this division in the women's movement on this issue."

6. An expanded version of this issue of the *Black Scholar* was subsequently made into a book, *Court of Appeal: The Black Community Speaks Out on the Racial and Sexual Politics of Thomas v. Hill* (New York: Ballantine Books, 1992), ed. Robert Chrisman and Robert L. Allen. Gloria T. Hull, "Girls Will Be Girls, and Boys Will . . . Flex Their Muscles," p. 98.

7. Beverly Guy-Sheftal, "Breaking the Silence: A Black Feminist Response to the Thomas/Hill Hearings (for Audre Lorde)," in *Court of Appeal,* pp. 73–77.

8. Calvin Hernton, "Breaking Silences," in *Court of Appeal*, pp. 88–89.

9. Michael Thelwell, "False, Fleeting, Perjured Clarence: Yale's Brightest and Blackest Go to Washington," in *Race-ing Justice, En-gendering Power*, pp. 86–126; Cornel West, "Black Leadership and the Pitfalls of Racial Reasoning," in *Race-ing Justice, En-gendering Power*, pp. 390–401.

10. Kimberle Crenshaw, "Whose Story Is It, Anyway? Feminist and Antiracist Appropriations of Anita Hill," pp. 402–440, and Paula Giddings, "The Last Taboo," pp. 441–463, in *Race-ing Justice, En-gendering Power*.

11. See Joyce Carol Oates, *Marya: A Life* (New York: E. P. Dutton, 1986) and *You Must Remember This* (New York: E. P. Dutton, 1987); Amy Tan, *The Joy Luck Club* (New York: G. P. Putnam's Sons, 1989) and *The Kitchen God's Wife* (New York: G. P. Putnam's Sons, 1991); Sylvia Fraser, *My Father's House: A Memoir of Incest and of Healing* (New York: Harper and Row, 1989); Betsy Petersen, *Dancing with Daddy: A Childhood Lost and a Life Regained* (New York: Bantam, 1991).

12. Elizabeth Janeway, *Man's World, Woman's Place: A Study in Social Mythology* (New York: Dell, 1971).

13. Betty Friedan, *The Feminine Mystique* (New York: W. W. Norton, 1963); Adrienne Rich, *Of Woman Born: Motherhood as Experience and Institution* (New York: W. W. Norton, 1976) and *On Lies, Secrets, and Silence: Selected Prose 1966–1978* (New York: W. W. Norton, 1979); Kate Millett, *Sexual Politics: A Surprising Examination of Society's Most Arbitrary Folly* (New York: Doubleday, 1969).

14. Susan Brownmiller, *Against Our Will: Men, Women and Rape* (New York: Simon and Schuster, 1975); Pauline Bart, *Stopping Rape: Successful Survival Strategies* (New York: Pergamon Press, 1985); Judith Lewis Herman with Lisa Hirschman, *Father-Daughter Incest* (Cambridge: Harvard University Press, 1981) and *Trauma and Recovery: the aftermath of violence — from domestic abuse to political terror* (New York: Basic Books, 1992); Catharine A. MacKinnon: *Sexual Harassment of Working Women* (New Haven: Yale University Press, 1979), *Feminism Unmodified: Discourses on Life and Law* (Cambridge: Harvard University Press, 1987), and *Toward a Feminist Theory of the State* (Cambridge: Harvard University Press, 1989); Diana E. H. Russell, ed., *The Secret Trauma: Incest in the Lives of Girls and Women* (New York: Basic Books, 1986).

15. The poll was conducted for the San Francisco–based Family Violence Prevention Fund by EDK Associates of New York, with a grant from the Ford Foundation. Some of its findings were reported in the *Washington Post*, April 20, 1993.

16. See my *Storming the Statehouse: Running for Governor with Ann Richards and Dianne Feinstein* (New York: Scribners, 1992).

17. *Washington Post*, November 8, 1992.

18. *The Washington Lawyer*, November/December 1991. A poll done by Louis Harris and Associates for the American Association of University Women

Education Foundation on sexual harassment in the schools, grades eight through eleven, indicated that 76 percent of girls had gotten sexual comments or looks, 65 percent had been "touched, grabbed, or pinched in a sexual way," and a third, in consequence, had not wanted to go to school (*New York Times*, June 2, 1993).

19. *Washington Post*, April 20, 1993.

20. See Andrea J. Sedlak, "National Incidence and Prevalence of Child Abuse and Neglect: 1988," revised September 5, 1991 with the support of Westat, Inc. The original report was sponsored by the National Center on Child Abuse and Neglect, the Children's Bureau, the Administration for Children, Youth and Families, the Office of Human Development Services, and the U.S. Department of Health and Human Services.

Chapter 14

1. *New York Times*, April 24, 1992. Rape statistics are subject to fierce dispute. See Katie Roiphe, "Date Rape's Other Victim," the cover story in *The New York Times Magazine* on June 13, 1993, as well as the angry letters to the editor that it provoked. The cover itself carried the legend "Rape Hype Betrays Feminism." The excerpt came from *The Morning After* (Boston: Little, Brown, 1993). Ms. Roiphe has many virtues — among them a bracing skepticism of emotional and intellectual fads and a graceful prose style that has miraculously survived the deadening influence of academic literary criticism. However, her book is a personal essay and she is only twenty-five; both her parents are feminists, and her mother is a respected novelist; she and her sisters were raised to take feminism for granted; she went to an exclusive girls' school in Manhattan, and then to Harvard for a B.A. degree and on to Princeton for graduate work. Her experience is therefore quite unusual. She may well be on target as she skewers some of the absurdities of contemporary feminism in elite universities, but if so, this says far more about those universities and students than it does about American society in general or feminism throughout the country. The extraordinary media attention given her book seems to me a product of the phenomenon Susan Faludi so ably chronicled in *Backlash: The Undeclared War Against American Women* (New York: Crown, 1991).

2. In *God Bless the Child: A True Story of Child Abuse, Gambling, Southern Politics — and One Woman's Struggle Against the Odds* (New York: Atheneum, 1993), James Colbert writes brilliantly about Sue Hathorn's fight for a similar center in Jackson, Mississippi. The desperate plight of sexually abused children — and what it takes to help them — could not be more vividly and powerfully described than in Colbert's masterful book.

Chapter 15

Epigraph. Jill Ruckelshaus, in a speech to the 1977 biennial convention of the National Women's Political Caucus.

1. See note 3, chapter 1.

2. *Newsweek,* October 21, 1991. See also Judith Resnik, "Who Cares? The Burden of Thinking about Wrongs Done to Women," a paper presented at the conference "Race, Gender and Power in America," held at Georgetown University Law Center, October 16, 1992. Revised versions of the conference papers will be published in a volume by Oxford University Press in 1994.

3. "Sexual Harassment at NIH," WJLA-TV, the Washington, D.C., affiliate of ABC News (October 20–22, 1992).

4. "Frontline" program, "My Doctor, My Lover," videotape.

5. Judith Lewis Herman, *Trauma and Recovery,* p. 7.

6. Ibid., p. 18.

7. "Sexual Harassment in the Fortune 500," *Working Woman* (December 1988). See also their follow-up study, "Sexual Harassment: The Inside Story," *Working Woman* (June 1992).

8. *The Atlanta Constitution,* March 12, 1992, and intermittently until January 22, 1993. *New York Times,* June 2, 1993. See also Jane Gross, "Schools Are Newest Arena for Sex-Harassment Cases," *New York Times,* March 11, 1992, and "Suffering in Silence No More: Fighting Sexual Harassment," *New York Times,* July 13, 1992.

9. *Dallas Morning News,* March 7, 1993.

INDEX